THE
INDONESIAN
ECONOMY

BANK INDONESIA
BANK SENTRAL REPUBLIK INDONESIA

Bank Indonesia is the Central Bank of the Republic of Indonesia. Bank Indonesia has a single objective, namely to achieve and maintain the stability of rupiah value.

The **Institute of Southeast Asian Studies (ISEAS)** was established as an autonomous organization in 1968. It is a regional research centre dedicated to the study of socio-political, security and economic trends and developments in Southeast Asia and its wider geostrategic and economic environment. The Institute's research programmes are the Regional Economic Studies (RES, including ASEAN and APEC), Regional Strategic and Political Studies (RSPS), and Regional Social and Cultural Studies (RSCS).

ISEAS Publishing, an established academic press, has issued more than 2,000 books and journals. It is the largest scholarly publisher of research about Southeast Asia from within the region. ISEAS Publishing works with many other academic and trade publishers and distributors to disseminate important research and analyses from and about Southeast Asia to the rest of the world.

THE
INDONESIAN
ECONOMY

ENTERING A NEW ERA

EDITED BY

ARIS ANANTA · MULJANA SOEKARNI · SJAMSUL ARIFIN

BANK INDONESIA
BANK SENTRAL REPUBLIK INDONESIA

INSTITUTE OF SOUTHEAST ASIAN STUDIES
Singapore

First published in Singapore in 2011 by ISEAS Publishing
Institute of Southeast Asian Studies
30 Heng Mui Keng Terrace
Pasir Panjang
Singapore 119614

E-mail: publish@iseas.edu.sg
Website: <http://bookshop.iseas.edu.sg>

The responsibility for facts and opinions in this publication rests exclusively with the authors and their interpretations do not necessarily reflect the views or the policy of the publisher or its supporters.

ISEAS Library Cataloguing-in-Publication Data

The Indonesian economy : entering a new era / edited by Aris Ananta, Muljana Soekarni, Sjamsul Arifin.
1. Indonesia—Economic conditions—1997–
2. Indonesia—Economic policy.
I. Ananta, Aris, 1954–
II. Soekarni, Muljana.
III. Arifin, Sjamsul.
HC447 I44   2011

ISBN: 978-981-4311-65-6 (soft cover)
ISBN: 978-981-4311-66-3 (E-book PDF)

Cover photo: The two statues are the so-called "Tugu Selamat Datang" (Welcome Statues) erected in 1962, to welcome visitors to Jakarta. The seven-metre high statue, sketched by Henk Ngantung and constructed by Edhi Sunarso, depict a young man and woman greeting visitors with flowers.

Photo credit: Courtesy of Muljana Soekarni and Abdul Hamid.

Typeset by International Typesetters Pte Ltd
Printed in Singapore by Markono Print Media Pte Ltd

Contents

PART I   INTRODUCTION

PART II   MONETARY AND FISCAL POLICIES

List of Tables

List of Figures

MESSAGE from the Deputy Governor of Bank Indonesia

I am indeed delighted to provide a Message to this distinguished book, *The Indonesian Economy: Entering a New Era.*

This book, in my view, is issued at an appropriate moment against the backdrop of the global financial crisis of unprecedented scale since the Great Depression. I notice a number of significant changes in the global economy and financial environment that have significant bearing on emerging economies, including Indonesia, such as the unsynchronized global economic recovery in tandem with the closer link between macroeconomic and financial stability. Despite the recent turmoil, Indonesia, as part of the Asian region, has proved to be more resilient than earlier anticipated though not entirely unscathed from the global crisis. However, global challenges have not entirely abated. In fact, new risks have emerged as the Fed launched the quantitative easing two (QE2) which has heightened the volatility of capital flows.

My commendation on this book mainly rests on the wide range in topic, rigour in analyses, and novelty in policy recommendation, thanks to the collaborative work of authors from Bank Indonesia as well as other academicians and scholars who add exceptional value to this book. In terms of coverage of topic, while it focuses on macroeconomic and financial issues, mainly reflecting a central bank's purview, it does not lose sight of other areas shaping Indonesia's economic development. It also looks backward at the era beginning with the New Order government, as a reflection of the past successes and existing constraints, while also looking forward towards the future challenges. Other areas exhaustively addressed in this book include population dynamics, industrial relation, domestic regional trade, governance in both micro and macro levels, and the readiness of Indonesia in entering the new era of the ASEAN Economic Community 2015.

The rigour of the analyses is reflected in the various models the researchers employ to unravel empirical findings such as the computable general equilibrium (CGE) model in assessing the effectiveness of fiscal stimulus. Structural equation modeling (SEM) has also been applied to measure the impact of the quality of governance on economic growth and per capita GDP.

Given the changing global economic and financial environment as well as the structural changes in Indonesia's economy, this book attempts to seek a new development paradigm as the basis of policy recommendations to reinvigorate Indonesia's economy by laying the foundation for a more sustainable development. Seeking to explore beyond the conventional paradigm, instead of focusing on growth, it proposes three development objectives, namely: people-centered development, environmentally friendly development, and good governance. To this end, it calls for the support of a financial architecture which reduces speculative activities.

On behalf of Bank Indonesia, I wish to express my appreciation to ISEAS for giving the researchers at Bank Indonesia the opportunity to take part in the publication of this book. I am confident that readers will find this book an important reference for both policy studies and further scholarly researches.

Hopefully the valuable experience gained from such a mutually beneficial collaboration will be followed by other forthcoming topics which will be beneficial to all of us.

Dr Hartadi A. Sarwono
Deputy Governor
Bank Indonesia

Message from the Director of the Institute of Southeast Asian Studies

The Institute of Southeast Asian Studies (ISEAS) produces research and policy papers on social, political, and economic issues in the region. As part of its work, it interacts with scholars outside ISEAS, including those in regional institutions. This interaction widens and deepens the studies that ISEAS conducts. For a country study, it works with experts from the country concerned.

This book is the result of our collaboration with Bank Indonesia (BI), the Central Bank of Indonesia, which shared with us not only expertise but also the financing of the research.

This book is important because Indonesia is ASEAN's biggest country in terms of population and national income. It has become an attractive market and production base in ASEAN and, indeed, in the rest of the world. The 1997–98 Asian crisis and the recent 2008–09 global crisis have affected Indonesia in different ways. Indonesia today is different from Indonesia forty years ago or even ten years ago. Moreover, what Indonesia does can have significant social, political, and economic implications for the region and the rest of the world.

This book does not discuss all issues relating to the Indonesian economy but contributes to better insights into the direction in which the Indonesian economy is moving. Reflecting cross-border collaboration, it is a product of formal seminars, meetings and conferences conducted in both Singapore and Jakarta, in addition to many informal meetings held among the three editors in Singapore and Jakarta. Comments on the draft of the book came from ISEAS, BI and other institutions. The fact that some of the authors are involved in policy-making in Indonesia gives this book added importance as a contribution to research and policy-making.

I would like to thank Aris Ananta, an economist and Indonesianist at ISEAS, who coordinated the research and is one of the editors of the book. My appreciation also goes to Bapak Muljana Soekarni, who initiated this collaboration and is also one of the co-editors. I would also like to acknowledge the contributions of Bapak Sjamsul Arifin, who joined the team of editors.

Ambassador K. Kesavapany
Director
Institute of Southeast Asian Studies

Foreword

Very few observers in the international community fully appreciate the fundamental transformations that have occurred in Indonesia since the late 1990s, just as there has been a tendency to prematurely write off the country's prospects in the past. At the time of independence, there were doubts that the sprawling archipelago would hold together. Yet it has, decisively, unlike some other highly diverse nation states such as the former USSR, the former Yugoslavia, and Pakistan. By the mid-1960s, the standard development economics textbook of the time, by long-time Indonesia expert Benjamin Higgins, characterized the country as a "chronic dropout". Gunnar Myrdal, in his classic *Asian Drama*, observed that, "As things look at the beginning of 1966, there seems to be little prospect of rapid economic growth in Indonesia." History was not kind to either observation, as income per capita quadrupled in the next three decades through to the late 1990s. In the early 1990s, the World Bank classified it as one of the "miracle economies".

There were similarly gloomy prognostications in 1998: *Indonesia: From showcase to basket case* was one of the more sensational titles at that time. The economy seemed to be in free fall, the formal banking system had collapsed, the demise of the Soeharto regime had left a political and institutional vacuum, ugly ethnic violence was widespread, and even the nation's territorial integrity appeared to be under threat. Thirteen years later, Indonesia has been transformed. It is now the most vibrant democracy in Southeast Asia, with two rounds of peaceful, legitimizing nationwide elections at the central and regional levels. The economy has bounced back strongly to rates of growth not far short of those of the Soeharto era. It successfully navigated the global financial crisis, with just a very small decline in growth momentum. Growth returned to above 6.0 per cent in 2010. Commencing in 2001, there has been a bold, "big-bang" decentralization, which has transferred administrative authority and financial resources to the *kabupaten* (districts). The painful separation of East Timor proceeded smoothly, and the two countries enjoy a harmonious, productive relationship. Indonesia has also begun to look outwards again, to the great benefit of its immediate ASEAN neighbours. It is widely regarded as a leader of the moderate Moslem world, and it has also joined the pre-eminent international forum, the G20. Inventive authors are currently debating modifications to the "BRIC" acronym that accommodate Indonesia, and possibly other major developing economies in the G20 club.

The authors of this comprehensive and authoritative volume, a fruitful collaboration between researchers at Bank Indonesia and the Institute of Southeast Asian Studies, examine these and many other developments over the past decade. The timing is good. A decade after this great transformation, and well into the second SBY presidency, Indonesia's "new normal" and its development challenges are becoming a lot clearer.

Part I of the volume provides an overview of economic development during the Soeharto era, 1966–98. Part II consists of four chapters that focused on the various aspects of macroeconomic policy, consistent with the core mandate of Bank Indonesia, the country's central bank. Parts III and IV are broader in focus, raising *inter alia* whether, going forward, Indonesia needs a new development paradigm.

The authors are surely correct, harking back to the work of J.M. Keynes, that major global events of the type that occurred in 2008–09 call for a fundamental rethink of institutions and policies, especially in the current context with respect to financial market regulation and international financial architecture. More speculatively, the authors wonder whether ASEAN might adopt a common currency. I have the impression that, if such an initiative were ever adopted, it would most likely also involve the larger Northeast Asian economies. Presumably this would in turn entail anchoring the region to the monetary policy of the largest economy, namely China, as is the case with Germany in the EU. Whether the rest of East Asia is prepared to accept this reality remains to be seen. The current problems with the European Monetary Union also caution against such an approach without fully coordinated fiscal policy and deeply integrated markets. Thus a common currency seems more like a distant option than an immediate policy concern. But it is precisely the sort of issue that this forward-looking volume should examine.

Standing back from the volume, comparing the Soeharto and *Reformasi* eras, one is reminded of both the many continuities and the differences. This is a very wide subject, and the emphasis will vary among observers. To this author at least, the following stand out.

Among the continuities, first, there is a consensus in Indonesia on the desirability of growth. Members of parliament and the informed commentariat may disagree on a lot, but it seems clear now that administrations and political parties that do not deliver on this objective will be rejected by voters. Second, Indonesia stands out as a reasonably prudent macroeconomic manager. Since this objective is central to the mandate of Bank Indonesia, several contributors dissect this issue. A significant achievement in the wake of the Asian financial crisis has been central bank independence. Although life for successive governors has been extremely challenging, and Indonesia still struggles to contain inflation at a rate comparable to its neighbours and major trading partners, this major institutional reform, combined with the gradual adoption of inflation targetting and a floating exchange rate regime, must be counted as a major achievement.

Third, Indonesia remains a reasonably open economy. It did not close up in response to the Asian financial crisis, and in spite of the rough treatment it received from the IMF and donors. It might still be regarded as "precariously open" in some respects, given the widespread anti-globalization critiques in the domestic media. But the policy settings appear to be durable. No doubt having the best Minister for Trade in the Asia-Pacific region helps. As does the oft-heard quip that "with 17,000 islands, Indonesia was made by God for free trade"! A final continuity is that, as in many countries, and for similar reasons, Indonesia still struggles to achieve microeconomic reform. For the reformers, it ranks uncomfortably low on various international ranking exercises, such as Doing Business, Transparency International, Economic Freedom, and the Global Competitiveness Report. On reforms of regulations, the civil service, state enterprises, the judiciary, and corruption, the policy agenda remains a daunting one.

The differences between the two periods are also striking. Here, too, at least four stand out to this author. First, as described in detail in this volume, economic policy-making processes have been completely transformed. The days of Hadi Soesastro's "low politics", of the technocrats going directly to the president to persuade him of the case for reform, have gone forever. This is the notion, developed in Hadi Soesastro's classic 1989 article, "The Political Economy of Deregulation in Indonesia" in *Asian Review*, that Indonesia's successful 1980s reforms were based on a strategy adroitly developed and implemented by the technocrats that deliberately eschewed grand ideological debates in public, which in all likelihood they would have lost. Rather, they formulated a series of trade and investment reform packages, and sold them quietly and directly to the president as a pragmatic means of promoting economic recovery and employment growth in the wake of the threatening collapse in international energy prices in the early and mid-1980s.

The government now has to deal with many actors, some highly vocal. In the authors' understated words, parliament can be "difficult". The president of course does not directly command a majority in either house. The cabinet is a "rainbow" coalition. There is a vibrant civil society and an unshackled media. More than 500 sub-national governments, some very wealthy and independent-minded, have to be heard.

Second, although the political rules of the game are becoming clearer, the investment climate remains uncertain in some respects. The observation that "the only thing worse than organized corruption is disorganized corruption" appears to be apposite. It also explains why investment projects with long time horizons or uncertain yields are under-supplied. Real estate and shopping malls are more attractive than infrastructure and mining, even though the former is badly needed and more of the latter should be occurring in an era of unusually high commodity prices.

A third difference concerns the regulation of factor markets. Prior to the Asian financial crisis, Indonesia was a very light regulator of both its financial and labour markets. Both are now much more heavily regulated. In the case of the former, the tighter regulation is clearly desirable, even if much remains to be completed, including reform of the state-owned banks. The increased labour market regulation is more contentious. Obviously the greater protection of workers and the freedom to organize are major advances. But Indonesia's severance laws are among Asia's most restrictive, and they appear to be a central explanation for the jobless industrial growth that has been evident since 1999.

Finally, environmental issues now assume much greater significance in policy debates. This rise reflects the greater activism of NGO's, rising regional and international concerns, and the fact that the country's rapid deforestation places it among the world's major CO_2 emitters. Whether international cooperation will deliver much — poor countries like Indonesia should not be expected to shoulder the burden of providing international public goods — remains to be seen.

The authors of this volume canvass many of the most challenging contemporary development issues, and they are not afraid of advocacy in the cause of furthering the debate. Inevitably, readers will not necessarily agree with everything. For example, the authors maintain that Indonesia should be "less dependent on export promotion and financial liberalization". Should it? Clearly, small open economies like Singapore and Malaysia were badly affected by the contraction in global trade and investment in 2008–09, and it is therefore tempting to point to Indonesia's much smaller economic shock then as extolling the virtues of being less trade-dependent. Nevertheless, notwithstanding the very successful trade and investment reforms of the 1980s, Indonesia is arguably the least open among the six major ASEAN economies, and it has missed out on profitable opportunities for employment creation. Notable examples include the global production and buying chains, particularly centred on the electronics and automotive industries, where Indonesia is a surprisingly minor actor. In automotives, Thai industry policy has been more nimble, resulting in it becoming the major automotive producer in ASEAN, a goal to which Indonesia could have aspired, building on its large domestic market. Equally, the country's disastrous experience with premature financial liberalization of the 1980s, which was a precursor to the banking collapse in 1997–98, underscores the importance of high-quality financial regulation. Yet it is not obvious that Indonesia currently has the sort of financial sector it requires to support a modern, market economy.

As the authors emphasize, Indonesia's development strategies are continuously evolving. The Yudhoyono administrations have emphasized the importance of a "pro-growth, pro-poor, pro-employment" programme, as well as ambitious anti-corruption initiatives. There have been some notable successes in all four dimensions: growth is back, employment is growing again, poverty is declining, and there has been some progress in the fight against corruption. But it remains a "glass half-full, half-empty" story. Growth has not yet got back to Soeharto era rates, much less those of China and now India. Poverty appears to be declining more slowly, in that it has become less growth-elastic. (Perhaps because removing the last 10–15 per cent of hardcore poverty is more difficult.) Employment growth is still not fast enough to absorb both the new workforce entrants and the existing pool of unemployed. And for every "big fish" that is caught in the anti-corruption drive, others seem to slip through the net all too easily.

There is much to chew over in this stimulating volume, and I commend it to you the readers. *Selamat membaca*!

Hal Hill
H.W. Arndt Professor of Southeast Asian Economies
Australian National University

Preface

Indonesia and the world have changed rapidly, particularly in the first decade of the twenty-first century. The Asian financial crisis in 1997–98 has also dramatically changed the course of Indonesian development, switching Indonesia from an authoritarian era to a democratizing one. Economic issues can no longer be discussed in a social and political vacuum. This book is an attempt to see Indonesian economy in the changing era, to examine Indonesian economy beyond the conventional macroeconomic variables. It is also expected to trigger a new debate in the creation of a new development paradigm for Indonesia and the world.

This book is a result of a collaboration between the Institute of Southeast Asian Studies (ISEAS) in Singapore and the Centre for Central Banking Studies, Bank Indonesia (BI) in Indonesia. The draft has been discussed in three stages. In each stage it has its own discussants. The first draft was discussed in a closed door conference in ISEAS, Singapore, on 24 June 2009, followed by a public seminar on "Indonesia's Response to the Global Financial Crisis" with three speakers: Made Sukada (BI), Halim Alamsyah (BI), and Marleen Dieleman (National University of Singapore) on 25 June 2009. We would like to thank the following discussants in the conference: Evi Nurvidya Arifin (ISEAS), Richard Barichello (University of British Columbia), Aekapol Chongvilaivan (ISEAS), Rizal A. Djaafara (BI), Melanie S. Milo (ASEAN Secretariat, formerly with ISEAS), and Yohanes Eko Riyanto (Nanyang Technological University).

The second draft was examined in an internal meeting with the authors and staff of the Centre for Central Banking Studies (PPSK), BI, and some invited discussants in Jakarta on 3 and 4 September 2009. We owed the comments and questions on the drafts from Mas Achmad Daniri (National

Committee on Governance), Gunardi Endro (Bakrie University), Djoni Hartono (University of Indonesia), Maddaremmeng A. Panennungi (University of Indonesia), Agus Pramusinto (Gadjah Mada University), Asep Suryahadi (SMERU), and Bob Widyahartono (Trisakti University).

The third draft was presented in an open seminar by the PPSK in Jakarta on 17–18 February 2010. The discussants were Aviliani (Economic Observer), Faisal Basri (Economic Observer), Anton Gunawan (Danamon Bank), Berly Martawardaya (University of Indonesia), Friska Parulian (Economic Research Institute for ASEAN and East Asia), N. Haidy A. Pasay (University of Indonesia), Bernadette Robiani (Sriwijaya University), Sugiharso Safuan (University of Indonesia), Hermanto Siregar (Bogor Institute of Agriculture), Taufik (MarkPlus), Ninasapti Triaswati (University of Indonesia), and Kodrat Wibowo (Padjadjaran University).

Moreover, the draft was much enriched by the active participants of the closed-door conference, internal meeting, and open seminar. Likewise, we would like to thank Shima Hashemian (University of British Columbia) for her contributions to the substance and editing of the language of the draft. We also appreciate the committed support from the staff of the Publications Unit of ISEAS to make this publication possible.

Finally, without the dedicated contributions from the authors, this book would have never been published. We appreciate the support of ISEAS and Bank Indonesia for conducting this study and for their encouragement to the editors to finish the book.

Aris Ananta
Muljana Soekarni
Sjamsul Arifin

Contributors

Aris Ananta is Senior Research Fellow at the Institute of Southeast Asian Studies (ISEAS), Singapore.

Evi Nurvidya Arifin is Visiting Research Fellow at the Institute of Southeast Asian Studies (ISEAS), Singapore.

Sjamsul Arifin is Senior Advisor to the Board of Governors on International Relation, Bank Indonesia, Jakarta, Indonesia.

Silvia Mila Arlini is Research Scholar and Ph.D. candidate at the Department of Southeast Asian Studies, National University of Singapore.

Ascarya is Senior Researcher at Centre of Education and Central Banking Studies, Bank Indonesia, Jakarta, Indonesia.

Siti Astiyah is Chief Economist, Bureau of Monetary Operation, Directorate of Monetary Management, Bank Indonesia, Jakarta, Indonesia.

Aida S. Budiman is Deputy Director, Directorate of International Affairs, Bank Indonesia, currently an Alternate Executive Director in Southeast Asia Voting Group, International Monetary Fund, the United States.

Yati Kurniati is Senior Economist in Directorate of Economic Research and Monetary Policy, Bank Indonesia, Jakarta, Indonesia.

Salomo P. Matondang, Researcher at Centre of Education and Central Banking Studies, Bank Indonesia, Jakarta, Indonesia.

Haris Munandar is Senior Economist and Assistant to the Governor of Bank Indonesia, Jakarta, Indonesia. He also lectures at the Graduate School of Economics, University of Indonesia, Jakarta, Indonesia.

Yohanes Eko Riyanto is Associate Professor at Division of Economics, School of Humanities and Social Sciences, Nanyang Technological University, Singapore.

Suhaedi is Senior Advisor, Directorate of Banking Research and Regulation, Bank Indonesia, Jakarta, Indonesia.

Guruh Suryani Rokhimah is Researcher at Centre of Education and Central Banking Studies, Bank Indonesia, Jakarta, Indonesia.

Iskandar Simorangkir is Head of Economic Research Bureau, Bank Indonesia, Jakarta, Indonesia.

Ferry Syarifuddin is Senior Analyst at Centre for Central Banking Education and Studies, Bank Indonesia, Jakarta, Indonesia.

Muljana Soekarni is Director of Indonesian Banking Development Institute, Jakarta, Indonesia.

Indrasari Tjandraningsih is Labour Researcher at AKATIGA-Social Analysis Centre, Bandung, Indonesia.

Pungky Purnomo Wibowo is Head of Macro-prudential Surveillance and International Banking, Financial Stability Bureau, Directorate of Banking Research and Regulation, Bank Indonesia, Jakarta, Indonesia.

PART I
Introduction

1

Economic Challenges in a New Era

Aris Ananta, Muljana Soekarni, and Sjamsul Arifin

Indonesia today is a different Indonesia compared with when it first proclaimed its independence in 1945, when it started a new economic paradigm in 1966, and even when it began its democratic reforms in 1998. Today, Indonesia exists in a vastly different social, economic, and political environment.

Indonesia and the rest of the world have entered a new era of economic and other challenges. The new era in both the global and local contexts necessitates different approaches as economic policies are not made in a social and political vacuum. This book on the Indonesian economy has been prepared with this new era in mind. It aims to examine what has been happening in the current Indonesia in the new era. It focuses on the events during the reform period while also discussing the events since the beginning of the New Order. It presents as well some policy recommendations for the current Government of Indonesia in the context of a search for a new world development paradigm.

The book is expected to be very useful to both beginners and experts on the Indonesian economy. However, the book does not cover all the economic issues Indonesia faces in the new era. It focuses on three macro issues examined in three parts, in addition to the introduction. Part I starts with this chapter which introduces the book and provides a brief history of the Indonesian economy since the beginning of the New Order (1966–98). Part II, consisting of four chapters, covers the monetary and fiscal issues that are the core tools in macroeconomic policies that have been important sources of boom and bust in the economies. Recognizing the importance of Indonesia's large population with its rising income and aspiration, Part III, comprising three chapters, examines the domestic market. This focus on the domestic market is a recognition that Indonesia should be less dependent on export promotion and financial liberalization. Had Indonesia been very successful in its drive for export promotion and financial liberalization, the impact of the 2008–09 global crisis on the Indonesian economy would have been much greater. Part III indicates the need for a change of the development paradigm in Indonesia's economic development by providing more weight to the domestic economy.

The search for new development paradigms has also been going on all over the world. The main focus of Part IV, which comprises three chapters, is to discuss new world development paradigms further, but from an Indonesian perspective.

Paradigms develop after a period of time as issues and challenges change. J.M. Keynes revolutionized the ideas of economics in 1930s by introducing the important role of government when mainstream economics believed in the complete reliance on the market mechanism, with very minimum government intervention. Keynes used a combination of government intervention and market mechanism. Like Keynes, during the 1960s in Indonesia, Widjojo Nitisastro, who then became the main economic architect in the first half of the New Order era, introduced the role of the market, in contrast to the then mainstream policies which ignored economic analysis. Nitisastro also recommended a combination of market mechanism and government intervention strategies. Likewise, the most recent global crisis should also necessitate the emergence of new world development paradigms.

In the rest of this chapter, a brief history of the Indonesian economic policies is presented. It is then followed by an examination of the "new era" in detail, covering the new global era and the democratizing Indonesia. Then, some main findings of the book are summarized and, finally, a conclusion is made along with some recommendations for the Government of Indonesia, particularly on paradigms shifts and necessary statistical indicators.

BRIEF HISTORY OF INDONESIAN ECONOMIC POLICIES

As is elaborated by Soekarni and Syarifudin in Chapter 2, the New Order Era began when General Soeharto replaced Indonesia's first president, Sukarno. Starting in 1966, General Soeharto restored the inflow of western capital, brought back political stability with a strong role for the army, and led Indonesia into a period of economic expansion under his authoritarian New Order regime which lasted until 1998.

During the New Order, Indonesia completed six Five-Year Development Plans, known by the Indonesian acronym, Repelita. The first five Repelitas (from 1969/70 to 1993/94) form the so-called the First Twenty-Five Year Development Plan (PJP I — Pembangunan Jangka Panjang I). The sixth Repelita is the first Repelita in the Second Twenty-Five Year Development Plan. However, there was no more Repelita after 1998, when Soeharto was toppled.

Throughout the twenty-five year implementation of the PJP I, the development was carried out continuously in line with the "trilogy of development" — the maintenance of a harmonious balance among equity, economic growth, and national stability. The average economic growth rate in the PJP I was 6.8 per cent per annum. However, the high levels of economic growth had masked a number of structural weaknesses in Indonesia's economy. A weak legal system, non-tariff barriers, rent-seeking by state owned enterprises, domestic subsidies, barriers to domestic trade and export restrictions, all created economic distortions. Furthermore, the absence of good governance principles resulted in new problems such as an increase in foreign debts, weakening bank supervision, corruption, collusion, and nepotism (known in Indonesia as KKN—*korupsi, kolusi, dan nepotisme*). These were the factors that led Indonesia to the 1997–98 economic crisis.

The economic distress of the 1997–98 crisis led to serious political chaos, which forced President Soeharto to resign in disgrace after holding power for thirty-two years. His vice-president, Professor B.J. Habibie, took up the presidential post in June 1998. He lost this position after conducting the second democratic presidential election in 1999.[1] Abdurrahman Wahid, often known as Gus Dur, was then sworn as president for a five-year term in October 1999, with Megawati Soekarnoputri as the vice-president. At that time, Wahid was also the moderate head of the National Awakening Party (PKB).

The Wahid administration reversed some of Soeharto-era restrictions on free expressions. It released political prisoners, eliminated the feared security coordination body, and increased freedom of the press. However, his administration did not last long either. Ignoring Wahid's threats to dissolve the Parliament, the legislature impeached Wahid and replaced him with Vice-President Megawati Soekarnoputri on 26 July 2001.

The Megawati administration made significant progress in stabilizing Indonesia's economy during its first year in office. It rejuvenated Indonesia's economic reform programme and restored Indonesia's relationship with the International Monetary Fund (IMF). In 2004, it introduced the direct presidential election, conducted in two rounds. This was not the case in the early years, including the year 1999, when people voted for parties, which then chose the president and vice-president. With the new system of election, Megawati lost to Soesilo Bambang Yudhoyono, who then became the first Indonesian president directly elected by its people.

After taking office on 20 October 2004, Yudhoyono moved quickly to implement a "pro-growth, pro-poor, pro-employment" economic programme. In addition, he announced an ambitious anti-corruption plan in December 2004. At the second direct presidential election that took place in 2009, Yudhoyono was re-elected as president for the period 2009–14.

In the so-called National Medium-term Development Plan (RPJMN) 2010–14, the government delivered its paradigm for the next five years, called "Development for All", consisting of six strategies. The first strategy is inclusive development, which emphasizes justice, balance, and equity. The second strategy is Indonesian regional development, as one region is recognized to be different from another, such as the island of Java compared with the island of Sumatera. The third strategy is social and economic integration among regions in Indonesia. The fourth strategy is local development, which encourages each province and district to develop its own comparative advantage. The fifth strategy is growth with equity, based on pro-growth programmes to create employment (pro-jobs) and reduce poverty (pro-poor). And finally the sixth strategy concerns quality of life of the people, with an emphasis on health and education.

NEW GLOBAL ERA

The recent financial debacle that began with the collapse of the U.S. subprime mortgage market by the end of 2007 had a devastating impact on the global economy and, consequently, marked a global change which underscored the need for a new paradigm to manage the global economy. Historically, the world has witnessed three episodes of major capital-account crises: the early 1980s in Latin American countries, the late 1990s in a number of

Southeast Asian countries, and recently, 2008–09, in the industrial countries. All three crises prompted a sudden and massive reversal of capital flows and output loss, disrupting hard won gains in development. Of the three, the recent crisis appears to have affected the world on a more pervasive scale and with deeper severity, and is commonly referred to as the worst crisis since the Great Depression.

The recent crisis negatively impacted developing countries, resulting in falling external demand, deteriorating commodity prices, and limited access to external financing which led to a contraction in output, sharp currency depreciation, along with the collapse of the capital market. In general, the speed of recovery from any crisis depends on the strength of policy responses by the industrialized countries. Nevertheless, despite the common adverse impacts of the crisis, the severity conditions vary in each country, to a large extent depending on the countries' initial position, especially their exposure to external obligations, the global financial environment, and the availability of external assistance.

Like some of the other emerging markets, Indonesia has maintained open trade and foreign exchange regimes with financial sector integrated to the global market. On one hand, such openness and integration have benefited the economy in terms of respectable economic growth. On the other hand, it has made the economy susceptible to exogenous shocks. Learning from the 1997–98 crisis, Indonesia has sought to strengthen its economy by maintaining sound macroeconomic policies and enhancing the soundness of its financial system while maintaining adequate international reserves. Such an endeavour has contributed to the resilience of the economy against modest external shocks, but apparently not against an exogenous turbulence of the recent magnitude and which is in tandem with the looming global recession. In fact, virtually all countries around the world have been affected by its ramifications.

Interestingly, the global nature of the recent crisis has "united" many countries in the form of concerted efforts to recover from the crisis. A substantial amount of government expenditure (which has resulted in soaring budget deficits and rising public debts), popularly known as a "stimulus package", in tandem with quantitative easing,[2] has been used as a means to boost rapidly falling economies in almost all countries, to lessen the depth of economic contractions and to cut the duration to recovery.

However, real economic recovery takes a somewhat longer period of time. The slow recovery can be explained by at least two reasons. The first is that a financial crisis is significantly different from other kinds of crisis that tend to arise from a particular shock, such as oil shocks and natural disasters. The stylized recovery from a financial crisis is often impeded by the following factors: the negative feedback between asset prices, credit, and investment, sharp falls in household wealth in some economies, and the larger-than-usual declines in private consumption because of the need to rebuild household balance sheets. The second reason to slow recovery is that the recent recessions were highly synchronized, occurring simultaneously in almost all countries in the world, thus further dampening prospects for a normal recovery.

Towards the end of 2009, the world was finally able to breathe a sigh of relief from the difficult economic crisis. Some optimism had even emerged. Although the real sector and employment seemed to lag behind, the financial sector had returned to its huge profit-earning situation it enjoyed before the crisis. Accepting the "reality" of a regular cycle of boom and bust, some economists were already comfortable in predicting the return of a bright Asian economy.

Yet, the respite may only be a harbinger of longer, deeper, and wider financial and economic crises to come. Worse, these will be accompanied by social and political crises. Indeed, in December 2009 many countries realized the impact of the various government stimulus packages that had been used to counter recession. Some countries such as Vietnam and China have already felt the impact of inflation and are worried about their heating, bubbling economies. They are also concerned about government debt and cooling the economy. Some European countries, such as Greece, Spain, and Portugal, have faced soaring government deficits and rising public debts. The rapid ageing populations in those countries have further aggravated the heavy financial burden. Population ageing has also become an important issue in many Asian countries, including Indonesia.

Unless the world implements a fundamental change in its financial architecture and development paradigm, the pessimistic scenario may become a reality. Fortunately, as detailed by Ananta in Chapter 12, an increasing number of scholars and political elites have been working hard to introduce and implement a new development paradigm.

On 20 January 2010, China started changing its expansive lending policy and curbing the amount of lending by increasing the reserve requirement of large banks. On 21 January 2010, President Barack Obama of the United States overhauled the U.S. financial architecture, the largest reform on the U.S. financial architecture since the 1930s. This overhaul resulted in policies which did not allow deposit-taking banks to run propriety trading that is unrelated to their customers. The purpose of this overhaul was to reduce any fragile, risky behaviour on the part of the banks, and eliminate systemic risk in the financial system. At a wider scope, the overall growth-oriented model itself has even been heavily questioned by world elites such as President Nicolas Sarcozy of France. On 14 September 2009, Sarcozy recommended replacing GDP with some other indicators, such as income and wealth distribution, education, and health, to measure development.

On the political front, the aspiration of democracy seems to circulate worldwide at an increasingly rapid rate. China and Vietnam are already experiencing a rising demand for democracy. The very rapid high growth rate in China, coupled with the very low level of fertility, may have been the fuel for the rising demand for democracy. Changing to a democratic system may be costly and produce some temporary impact on the economy. Nevertheless, although this impact is only temporary, an economic crisis in China may have a worldwide impact.

At the same time, climate change, in particular, global warming, may seriously affect the welfare of many countries in the world, especially developing economies. The "failure" of the Copenhagen Conference (7–18 December 2009) to produce strong measures to avoid or slow down global warming, and cope with climate change, has heightened the pessimistic scenario whereby the earth we live in today will be very different twenty years from now, meaning, that the earth will not be friendly to human beings then.

The rapid digitization of the world will also drastically change the behaviour of people all over the globe. With the very fast pace of change in stages of digitization itself, people from different age cohorts may have different attitudes and behaviours. As a result, communication problems among people of various age cohorts may occur.

As economic issues do not exist in a political vacuum, we also have to view Indonesia against the backdrop of a changing balance of political and economic power in the world, with a possible shift of power from the United States to China and India. Brazil and Russia may also join these two countries in what is now called the emerging BRIC (Brazil, Russia, India, and China). Moreover, Indonesia and Turkey have been tipped to join this group soon as well.

DEMOCRATIZING INDONESIA

Within Indonesia itself many changes have also occurred. Indonesia has been making and implementing economic policies in a democratizing manner, different from the time Indonesia was under the authoritarian government of Soeharto. Democratic and direct elections, the independence of Bank Indonesia, regional autonomy, the emergence of labour unions, mass media's and civil societies' enhanced power, rising people and digital power, and an increasingly "difficult" parliament, are some features of the new era in Indonesia today.[3]

Although a democratic election of the president and heads of the lower administrative units were held in 1955, none was held during the New Order Period of 1966–98. Thus, 1999 marked the first democratic election of the president of Indonesia since the first one in 1955. In the 1999 election, the people democratically voted for the parties, then the representative of the parties selected the president. However, in the 2004 election, people not only continued to choose the political parties they wished to represent them in parliament, but they also directly voted for the president. Thus, political parties no longer decided the appointment of the president. After 2005, the people also voted directly for their choice of governor, mayor, and regents. As a result, there were many local elections taking place from 2005 to 2008 in Indonesia. By the time of the 2009 election, Indonesia had democratized so profoundly that the people were not only directly voting for the president, but were also directly voting for the individual members of the parliament as well, rather than just for the political parties.

As is discussed by Soekarni and Syarifuddin in Chapter 2, the year 1999 also marked the independence of Bank Indonesia (BI — Indonesian Central Bank) from the government of Indonesia. Prior to its independence, under Law BI no. 13/1968, Bank Indonesia assumed two functions. Its first function was to safeguard and maintain the stability of the rupiah. And its second function was to raise production, promote development, and create employment, thereby increasing the people's income. Under Law no. 23/1999, Bank Indonesia was to focus on maintaining the stability of the rupiah. In other words, with the 1968 law, Bank Indonesian functioned as an agent for Indonesia's development. With its independence since 1999, Bank Indonesia is no longer an agent for development. However, currently there is a debate on whether Bank Indonesia should again function as an agent for development.

In Law no. 23/1999, later changed in Law no. 3/2004, independence was given five meanings: institutional independence, goal independence, instrument independence, personal independence, and financial independence.

Institutional independence meant that although Bank Indonesia had to work within the existing laws of Indonesia, the government or other parties could not intervene in its implementation of its duties. This independence characterizes modern central banks such as the Federal Reserve of the United States, the European Central Bank, the Bank of Japan, the Bank of England, and the Bank of Canada.

To achieve and maintain the stability of the rupiah, Bank Indonesia was given goal independence, meaning, the freedom to determine its short-run target. However the target had to be made in consultation with the government. Bank Indonesia then had the freedom to choose policies to realize the target. The Federal Reserve of the United States and European Central Bank are examples of banks with higher degrees of goal independence — in that they have the freedom to set monetary targets.

The independence instrument gave Bank Indonesia the authority to determine its operational targets without any government intervention. Therefore, to implement monetary policies, Bank Indonesia would have the full authority to determine its interest rates without government and other organizations' intervention. As for the exchange rate, Indonesia implemented a floating exchange rate system. Moreover, Bank Indonesia would not be allowed to monetize fiscal deficits or give credit to the Government of Indonesia. Bank Indonesia's instrument independence is as high as that of the Federal Reserve and Bank of Japan, but not as high as that of the European Central Bank.

The personal independence meant that no other parties would be allowed to intervene in Bank Indonesia's duties and it gave Bank Indonesia the right to reject any sort of intervention by any organization. However, the members of its board of governors, who manage Bank Indonesia, would be selected with the approval of parliament. Thus, in terms of personal independence, Bank Indonesia may not be as independent as the Federal Reserve and the European Central Bank.

It is noteworthy that its personal independence does not automatically make Bank Indonesia a super body institution. It still needs the approval of parliament to decide its budget. The government needs the approval of parliament to appoint the governor, senior deputy governor, and all deputy governors of Bank Indonesia. At this juncture, it may be worth considering that the independence of Bank Indonesia should be enhanced by waiving the approval from parliament to select all deputy governors. The approval of parliament should only be needed for the appointment of the governor and senior deputy governor.

Its financial independence provides Central Bank with the freedom to decide and manage its own budget and wealth without parliament's approval. However, Bank Indonesia must make a report on the use of its operational budget, monetary policies, payment system, and its supervision of banking to parliament. Furthermore, Bank Indonesia must send its annual financial report to the BPK (Badan Pemeriksa Keuangan — State Audit Board). The evaluation of the BPK is then submitted to parliament. And finally, Bank Indonesia must make the report available to the public through the mass media.

To bring the government closer to its people as part of the democratization process, on 1 January 2001, Indonesia started to implement its regional autonomy programme, which provided districts with much larger power. This meant that many decisions could be made at local levels, without having to go to Jakarta. The provinces and districts could make their own development planning and optimize their own competitive advantages. As is described by Astiyah, Matondang, and Rokhimah in Chapter 9, regional autonomy also meant fiscal decentralization, where local governments have the authority to decide the use of money with the approval of local legislative bodies. Most sources of the local budget are still from the central government, but the central government does not intervene in the allocation of the budget.

Consequently, as is described by Arifin in Chapter 7, regional autonomy created the fragmentation of provinces and districts (regencies and municipalities). The number of provinces rose from 30 in 2001 to 33 in 2008; the number of regencies, from 268 to 387; and the number of municipalities, from 73 to 96. Some provinces and districts were even split into more than one province and district as a means to accelerate development.

Furthermore, regional autonomy also brought some negative impacts, such as the tendency of regional "protectionism" within Indonesia. The problem of availability of qualified human resources at the regional level, particularly at the district level, has resulted in problems in good planning and the implementation of development at the regional level.

The democratization process is also seen as an effort to reform industrial relations from a corporatist or regulatory model to the contractual model. The reform is supposed to reduce government intervention in labour relations. As is elaborated by Tjandraningsih in Chapter 8, during the reform period, new laws were made to liberalize trade unions, which significantly changed the face of trade unions in Indonesia. The number of trade unions rose quickly. As of 2008, there were three confederations, 90 federations, and 10,000 trade unions at the company level. On the other hand, the number of organized workers and members of trade unions dropped significantly as a consequence of legalized contract work and labour outsourcing.

Indonesia's democratization process has also been proceeding hand in hand with the rising role of civil society. Civil society functions not only as opposition groups as had done during the authoritarian governments of Sukarno and Soeharto, but it also helps fulfil areas that cannot be served well by the market. Civil society functions can be in the form of voluntary help and self-help networks, traditional and modern religious organizations, local representatives of international organizations, pressure groups and political lobbies, as well as combinations of all those groups. In a democratizing Indonesia, civil society can be expected to fill in the areas where the state and market fail (Kreager 2009).

One recent example is the case of Prita Mulyasari, a housewife who complained in her e-mail to friends about the poor treatment she received at a private hospital in Jakarta. By accident, her e-mail was widely circulated. The hospital then sued her for defamation. Subsequently, the district attorney punished and jailed her for defamation. The public was very angry with the decision. Their unhappiness was poured through Facebook and blogs. The relatively free mass media also got involved and helped bring out the "injustice" practised by the hospital and court. It became such an enormous issue that the case was brought to the district court. Consequently, with the overwhelming support from the public through the mass media, Facebook and blogs, the judge panel in the district court found her not guilty of defamation.

This is an illustration of the transformation of "people power". Whereas in 1998 a very large, noisy, and chaotic crowd went into the streets to topple President Soeharto, now a changed form of "people power" sees demonstrations made without a noisy and chaotic crowd in the street. This new kind of "people power" is now happening in a peaceful manner through the mass media, Facebook, and blogs and is expected to continue. Furthermore, any public policy, including economic policies, will be subjected to the monitoring of the people through "people power" using the mass media, Facebook, and blogs, or other digitized means.

Another consequence of democratization was its "noisy" politicking. The governments in the Reform era do not have as much power in making policies as it did during the authoritarian Soeharto period. During the reform period, government policies were subject to evaluation by parliament. A recent example is the famous Bank Century case at the end of 2009. The government's decision to bail out a failed small bank in November 2008, feared to have systemic risk amidst world financial uncertainty, had been heavily attacked by parliament from November 2009 to February 2010, about a year after the decision was made. Parliament did not agree that there had been systemic risk associated with the failure of Bank Century; it disagreed with the decision to bail out the bank. This was a political decision, made by voting among members of the parliament — the result was that the members of parliament who did not agree with the bailout outnumbered those who supported the bailout.

At last, with the success of the economy and increased democratization, as well its large number of population, Indonesia was invited to become a member of G-20 in 2009. Joining G-20, a powerful international institution that "regulates" the world economy, was very important for Indonesia as it now has the opportunity to speak to the world and contribute to world peace and prosperity.

MONETARY AND FISCAL POLICIES

Monetary and fiscal policies are often seen as closed partners in any economic policies. Fiscal policies are supposed to intervene in the market economy in order to help correct market failures. These policies are directed at the real sector which is related to the production of goods and services. At the same time, the economy needs money to lubricate the process of production. This is where monetary policy comes in.

Without money, we would not have what we have today. Money has three functions. Its first function is to serve as a means of making an efficient transaction. Its second function is to serve as a means to store wealth. And its third function is to serve as a precautionary motive. This precautionary motive, however, can become a speculative motive. Money itself can be a commodity — produced and traded. Nevertheless, money, which is supposed to facilitate the smooth functioning of the real sector, has its own life. Particularly in the last two decades, the financial sector has grown much faster than the real sector.

When there is too much money, the economy becomes overheated. On the other hand, when there is too little money, the economy becomes gloomy. Therefore, the function of monetary policy is to stabilize price or inflation, in order to have the "optimum" price or inflation rate so that the flow of money can facilitate, rather than become a hindrance, to the process of production. In addition, monetary policies may also be used as a direct instrument of development.

In Chapter 3, Ascarya discusses the historical dynamics of monetary policies in Indonesia, starting from the period of Sukarno, Indonesia's first president, where politics was the most pressing agenda; until the present one, including the most recent global financial crisis. Monetary policy received much more important attention during the period of Soeharto, the second president of Indonesia. The first monetary policy of Soeharto was designed to curb the rampant inflation that took place during the last years of the Sukarno period.

Indonesia's financial liberalization that started in 1983 ended in 1997 with the Asian financial crisis. Ascarya describes how the crisis resulted in the awareness that Bank Indonesia (BI) had often been contaminated by the political interests of the government. Therefore, one of the first things the government of the post-financial crisis did was to free Bank Indonesia from the government.

With the occurrence of the recent global crisis, and all other previous crises, it is critical to raise questions on the fundamental root of frequent and widespread financial crises. Speculative activity, for example, is seen as one of the most important causes of financial crises. Therefore, Ascarya argues that monetary policy should be able to minimize, if not eliminate, speculative activities. He also mentions that an Islamic monetary system can offer an alternative for reducing speculative activities, among other things, and hence, reduce the possibility of financial crises occurring.

He elaborates on the emergence of Islamic monetary policies in Indonesia and shows how Indonesia has been following a dual-monetary system since 1999. The Islamic financial system has been existing side by side with the conventional monetary system. In democratizing Indonesia, people are free to choose whether they want to join the conventional financial system, the Islamic financial system, or both.

The issue of the contribution of monetary policies to economic growth is examined in Chapter 4 by Suhaedi and Wibowo. In particular, they discuss how the Indonesian financial system should be developed to ensure the existence of an optimal balance between the stability of the financial sector and the economic growth in Indonesia. They argue that this issue becomes more important when financial instability is relatively high. To discuss the issue, they use the 1997–98 Asian crisis, which hit Indonesia severely, as their case study.

They find that the financial liberalization conducted before the crisis had resulted in an economic boom. However, the liberalization had also led to the severe crisis in 1997 because it had resulted in a vulnerable economy, where liquidity pouring into the Indonesian economy had been used mostly for unproductive and speculative projects. Furthermore, the lax banking system, the very high concentration of bank ownership, and weak corporate governance in the banking sector had aggravated the impact of financial liberalization on the crisis.

Learning from the 1997–98 crisis, they have three recommendations for creating a balance between financial stability and economic growth. First, bank capital should be raised, particularly Tier 1 capital, consisting of paid-up capital, or common stocks and disclosed reserves. Second, governance and performance in the bank sector should be strengthened. Third, the capacity of bank supervision should be enhanced, to make sure that all regulations are well complied with. In addition, BI should continue its compliance with *25 Basel Core Principles for Effective Banking Supervision*, published by the Basel Committee on Banking Supervision.

After discussing monetary policies and issues, this book examines the real sector which is supposed to be supported by the monetary sector. In the Indonesian economy, both monetary and fiscal policies have also played a very significant role. As is described by Arlini and Riyanto in Chapter 5, both policies were used at the beginning of the New Order era to bring down the high inflation rate and open Indonesia's economy to the world economy. This includes attracting foreign investors and promoting the oil and gas sectors as the most important source of revenue.

Unfortunately for Indonesia, its reliance on oil and gas for revenue had made its economy very vulnerable to shock in oil and gas world market. When world oil price went down drastically in the early 1980s, the country suffered greatly. Therefore, as is elaborated by Arlini and Riyanto, the government made a radical policy to move away from its heavy reliance on its oil and gas sectors and diversify its sources of government revenue. But the effort to raise revenue from taxation had not been successful. Therefore, to finance its rising expenditure, the government had to rely on foreign aid and borrowing.

The authors show that the Asian financial crisis then get Indonesia's finance sector into big trouble. Its short-run fiscal policy of stimulating domestic aggregate demand and raising subsidies had contributed to an escalation of foreign debt. The government then requested a moratorium and rescheduled the payment of its debts.

After the Asian crisis, Indonesia was able to function with a manageable budget deficit. This has often been cited as one of the reasons Indonesia survived relatively better than other countries during the recent global recession. In addition, its fiscal stimulus is cited as another important contribution to its avoiding a deeper crisis in Indonesia.

Nevertheless, we may wonder whether its stimulus package was really helping the Indonesian economy during the global crisis. Arlini and Riyanto mention many other factors, including the huge spending during the two general elections in 2009, which may also have contributed to the relatively better performance of the Indonesian economy in the same year.

The question is the effectiveness of rising government expenditure in arresting an economic downturn and in speeding up the process of recovery. For example, the International Monetary Fund (2009) concluded that a one percentage point increase in real government consumption expenditure during the recession is associated with a 16-percentage-point increase in the probability of exiting from a recession. With the rising role of public finance in adjusting aggregate demand, it is therefore important to understand fiscal policy cyclicality in Indonesia.

Chapter 6 applies a Computable General Equilibrium model to investigate the role of fiscal stimulus in maintaining the resilience of Indonesian economy. This chapter, written by Munandar and Simorangkir first reviews the recent financial crisis where many governments and central banks introduced a number of measures to deal with and solve liquidity problems. Many governments all over the world, including the United States, the United Kingdom, Germany, China, and India, have used fiscal stimuli to counter the downturn of their economies into recession by rapidly increasing government spending to lift and push aggregate demand. The package consists of increased spending for infrastructure development and cutting tax simultaneously. Indonesia is not an exception as it follows the G-20 consensus in applying fiscal stimulus.

Munandar and Simorangkir use the Indonesian 2005 Social Accounting Matrix to simulate the impact of fiscal stimulus on the Indonesian economy in 2009. Because not all the planned budget for the stimulus package has been realized, they do the simulation for both the planned and realized fiscal stimulus budget. The simulated results show what would have happened to the Indonesian economy if the economic interdependence during the recent global crisis were the same as that in 2005.

They conclude that the realized fiscal stimulus may have had a favourable and expected impact on the overall performance of the economy, though the resultant increase in the GDP was only 0.365 percentage point. In other words, without the stimulus package, the 2009 economy would have grown by 4.185 per cent, which is not much lower than the empirical 4.55 per cent. If the planned stimulus budget had completely been all realized, the economy would have grown by 4.673 per cent.

They also support the claim that the stimulus package is pro-poor and show that the urban poor would have benefited most from the fiscal stimulus as their consumption would have increased by 0.50 percentage points. Interestingly, both the rural poor and urban non-poor would have benefited equally from the stimulus package. Each of them increased their consumption by 0.37 percentage points. In other words, the stimulus package would have benefited urban poor households more than rural ones.

The relatively small impact on the GDP may be because of the absence of a countercyclical policy in Indonesia. Several factors may have adversely affected the Indonesian fiscal policy as a countercyclical tool. First, the existing tax structure has three weaknesses. The first weakness is that the narrow tax base does not provide sufficient fiscal space, with non-oil and gas tax revenue at about 11 per cent of GDP, which is low in comparison to other countries with similar income levels. The second weakness is that dependence on oil and gas taxation is still high at about one fourth of total revenue and characterized by high volatility. And the third weakness is that the small direct share of discretionary spending (less than one-third of total expenditure) reduces the space for direct expenditure intervention.

The second factor is the weak budget execution which remains high with 30–50 per cent of annual outlays disbursed in Q4 from 2002–08. Weak capacity to execute the budget also reduces the effectiveness of measures to support aggregate demand in the short term. Furthermore, limited diversification of debt instruments and the investor base reduce access to financing in bad times, when pro-cyclical risk premium tends to rise. Thin secondary market volumes for government securities put downward risks on the price of sovereign paper when risk appetite deteriorates in the financial markets.

The third factor is vulnerability to terms of trade shocks which constrains the budgets' response capacity in periods of economic stress. Exposure to terms of trade shocks remains high, reflecting the dependence of budget revenue on natural resources and non-energy exports. This results in declining output volatility.

The fourth factor is that budget size fiscal anchors matter. The small size of automatic stabilizers on the expenditure side of the budget — as most transfers are pro-cyclically linked to energy prices — reduces the scope for intervention to support private consumption. The limited use of medium-term budget frameworks to make fiscal developments consistent with long-term objectives, and the remaining weak links between current and development budget, are two additional factors of vulnerability.

Finally, as is surmised by Arlini and Riyanto, further studies are needed to draw clear conclusions on what has helped Indonesia achieve relatively high economic growth during the recent global crisis, and in particular, to what extent the stimulus package has contributed to the Indonesian economy in avoiding the fall into recession.

DOMESTIC MARKET

Indonesia has been seen by people outside Indonesia as a lucrative large market and strong production base. The existence of Indonesia's population and economy has contributed importantly to the attractiveness of ASEAN, a regional economic grouping consisting of Brunei Darussalam, Cambodia, Laos, Malaysia, Myanmar, Singapore, the Philippines, Thailand, and Vietnam. Indonesia has the largest population in ASEAN as it comprises about 40.0 per cent of ASEAN's total population. It also has the largest economy, measured both by GNI (Gross National Income) and PPP (Purchasing Power Parity) GNI. In 2007, it produced about one third of the total production in ASEAN.

The discussion on population dynamics becomes more important as Indonesia, with a 237-million population in 2010, has been democratized. Arifin in Chapter 7 examines some new faces in Indonesia's population, which has shifted from a female-surplus population to a male-surplus population and from a young to an old population. Its ethnic and religious landscape is also discussed.

In addition, it examines educational attainment across provinces. One interesting and sensitive finding results from an analysis of educational attainment in relation to religious affiliation. She shows that Indonesian Muslims are more likely to be less educated than Indonesian Christians, except in Aceh, North Maluku, East Kalimantan, East Nusa Tenggara, and Papua.

This discussion gives special attention to the regional population in Indonesia, where issues may differ between regions. Understanding this regional variation is very important as it is becoming more difficult to talk about "Indonesia" as one unified country because issues vary from one region to another. Therefore, this chapter starts with a relatively extensive introduction of the decentralization in Indonesia.

The importance of the population as a factor of production is further detailed by Tjandraningsih in Chapter 8, particularly the relationship between workers' and business' interests. An important feature of this chapter is the authors' effort to highlight the democratizing context of Indonesian industrial relations. Democracy can be "bad" or "good" for the economy, depending on which perspective we see it from. For example, an expansion of the number of trade unions can be seen as a nuisance or even trouble making for the business but it may be seen as an indication of rising public participation in economic development.

Tjandraningsih elaborates on the debate on industrial relations during the reform period between those who support a rigid labour market (often seen as very protective towards the workers) and those who prefer flexible labour market (often seen as very pro-capital). The flexible labour market was initiated by the International Monetary Fund (IMF) as one of the conditions the Indonesian Government had to abide by if it wanted the IMF package of aid and economic reform to save Indonesia from the economic crisis in 1997–98. The winner of the debate, as observed by Tjandraningsih, seems to have been those favouring the flexible labour market model. Thus, the government has been under pressure from the global economy to create a much better investment climate, at the expense of the welfare of the workers, particularly the low-skill workers.

The author warns that insufficient attention paid to workers welfare, particularly when compared with the employers and foreign employers, may result in social chaos as they may show their unhappiness towards the business. Only a government which works with a spirit of justice can help its workers raise their welfare.

The contribution and regional variation of "non-human" factors, particularly variables that are directly related to trade and economic development, is examined by Astiyah, Matondang, and Rokhimah in Chapter 9. They focus on regional domestic trade in an era of democratization and fiscal decentralization. In particular, they examine the interconnection among regions through trade. This study is very important as the results can be used to understand to what extent the economy of Indonesia, a very large country, has been integrated domestically. They use the Inter-Regional Input-Out (IRIO) model to explain the interdependence of regional trade in Indonesia. They also use the IRIO model to simulate what would have happened during the recent global crisis if the domestic trade relationship remained as it was in 2005.

They find that the gap between Western and Eastern Indonesia still continue to widen. However, the centre of regional trade interconnection has changed from East Java in 2000 to West Java in 2005. West Java has become a central or primary market for other provinces. The connection between provinces outside Java and those in Java, rather than with their adjacent provinces, was particularly stronger in 2005 than in 2000.

They argue that the existence of a regional economic interdependence through trade can be used as a means to increase regional and national competitiveness, though they also warn that a negative performance in one region will be quickly transferred to other regions.

From their simulation exercise they find that Banten would have been the province worst hit by the recent global crisis. Banten would have suffered from both the direct impact to its sectors in Banten, as well as an indirect impact through the impact of the crisis on sectors in its neighbour, Jakarta. Some provinces would not have been affected because they did not have a significant trade relationship with the provinces assumed to experience the direct impact of the global crisis.

IN SEARCH OF NEW DEVELOPMENT PARADIGMS

The discussion on the search for a new paradigm starts with examining the relationship between Indonesia and other countries, particularly with ASEAN countries. It deals with the question on the extent of economic integration, including the debate on what is meant by economic integration in general, and, in particular, what it means in ASEAN. The question is especially important as the ASEAN countries have committed to the creation of an ASEAN Economic Community (AEC) by 2015. One fundamental feature of the AEC, which has been agreed by all heads of members of ASEAN, is the creation of a region as a single lucrative market and strong production base. The region is guaranteed with a free flow of goods, free flow of services, free flow of investment, free flow of capital, and free flow of skilled labour. The free flow of low-skill labour is not part of the commitment in AEC because some heads of the countries feel that the free flow of low-skill labour will be harmful for their own domestic economy and politics.

A related, yet unsolved, question is on the currency to use in ASEAN. Should the economy use a single currency, and if so, which one? It is not easy to have a consensus on this question, as it also involves domestic economic and political issues in each country. Yet, unlike the issue of the free flow of low-skill workers, the one on monetary union has been raised on many occasions. It is also discussed by Kurniati and Budiman in Chapter 10.

They mention that ASEAN economies have undergone a dynamic trans-formation as a process to speed up its economic and financial integration with the global market. The volume of ASEAN trade and financial linkages, both within Southeast Asia and outside Southeast Asia, has risen very fast. Although the integration has benefited the region, it has also exposed Southeast Asian economies to the risk of external shocks.

One of the crucial aspects in coordinating economic policies in Southeast Asia and increasing the possibility of having a monetary union is information on business cycle synchronization. Kurniati and Budiman find encouraging results from the business cycle synchronization between Indonesia and ASEAN-4 (Indonesia, Malaysia, the Philippines, and Thailand), and bilaterally with Malaysia, Thailand, and the Philippines. To promote trade within Southeast Asia, Southeast Asian economies need to have product differentiation and different stages of production. Currently, the production structure within Southeast Asian economies, except for Singapore, is very similar. They also conclude that there is an important existing two-way causal relationship between trade and financial linkages among Indonesia, ASEAN-4, and Singapore.

However, Kurniati and Budiman also emphasize that Indonesia must be careful not to let its negative international exposure ruin the Indonesian economy, particularly with regard to the dominant flow of short-term capital, which is very easy to reverse. The Indonesian macroeconomic and financial stability must be given the highest priority and this can be the first line of defence against any international shock. Therefore, they recommend that the Government of Indonesia seriously prepare a blueprint and strategic plan to maximize the benefits and minimize the costs of the creation of AEC. The government should ensure that domestic players have equal opportunities to benefit from Indonesia's own lucrative market and strong production base. This blueprint should be part of the agenda of the national development plan.

Furthermore, Indonesia needs to remain cognizant of the new challenges, given the continual changes in its external environment, such as the coming into force of the China-ASEAN Free Trade Agreement (CAFTA) implementation. As is commonly known, China has been a powerhouse, especially in manufacturing. The "China Price" (Engardio 2007) has been the main factor behind its sustained robust expansion in exports, which has also contributed to its high economic growth over the extended period and its burgeoning international reserves. While there are certain areas in which Indonesia will gain from free trade with China, there is also widespread concern over the competitiveness of the Indonesian manufacturing sector. So far, the Indonesian manufacturing sector is considered to be able to provide more jobs than sectors such as agriculture and mining.

The recent global financial crisis also underscores the need to change "global governance", including an appropriate forum to discuss global economic issues and the international financial architecture. This need arises because the source of the recent crisis was in an advanced industrial country, and the growing importance of emerging markets in the integrated global economy. Given this changing global financial environment, the decision of G-20 leaders in Pittsburgh in September 2009 to officially replace the G-8 with the G-20 as the forum to discuss the global economy is considered to be a step in the right direction. In this regard, the inclusion of Indonesia as a member of the G-20 reflects the importance of Indonesia in the global economy.

The second topic discussed in the search for a new development paradigm is good governance. The World Bank (1992) defined good governance as the way power should be used to manage a country's economic and social resources in its development. Good governance is a process and the process itself can influence the quality of the outcome of development. Pramusinto (2006), for example, showed that in any democratic society, information transparency and public participation are important features of good governance. Therefore, in any discussion on governance, the process of producing the output should receive an important consideration when assessing economic development. Ananta (Chapter 12) suggests that good governance must be one of the objectives of development.

Soekarni and Arifin in Chapter 11 analyse activities on governance, particularly after the establishment of the National Committee on Corporate Governance Policy, because the lack of good governance was blamed as one of the determinants of the 1997–98 crisis in Indonesia. The importance of good governance was soon raised with its incorporation in the Letter of Intent signed by IMF and the Government of Indonesia in October 1997. Since then, Bank Indonesia has issued regulation concerning governance. The state minister of state-owned enterprise also produced decrees on governance for state-owned enterprises.

Soekarni and Arifin mention that Indonesia has moved in the transition of its governance, already passing the state of awareness of governance (1997–2006) to a new state of conformity (2007–16). During the state of awareness, Indonesia conducted socialization and communicated to all stakeholders of every organization the need to adopt principles of good governance. In the state of conformity, all stakeholders have understood these principles and have been willing to adopt and commit to applying them.

Soekarni and Arifin focus on both macro and micro issues of governance. The macro issues cover constitutional reforms and the overall role of the government. The micro issues consist of cases of state-owned enterprises and commercial firms (including banks) often defined as corporate governance. They also elaborate on the Indonesian Banking architecture, with a vision to producing a sound, strong, and efficient banking system. This architecture is expected to create a stable financial system in order to support national economic growth. They also show how Bank Indonesia has created the Information Credit Bureau to reduce asymmetric information and, therefore, eliminate unfairness to customers.

They also empirically examine the relationship between governance, economic growth, and per capita income. They find that good governance contributes more to a higher level of per capita income in developed countries. However, in developing countries such as Indonesia, good governance produces more support to higher economic growth than per capita income.

In the last chapter (Chapter 12), Ananta presents a global change of development paradigms. The aim of the last chapter is to trigger a modest contribution in the search for a short-term rescue plan for the recent crisis and a long-term new world development paradigm. A revolutionary interdisciplinary solution is needed to prevent the repetition of the crisis and to promise a more sustainable and peaceful development in both developing and developed countries.

The main message of Chapter 12 is that economic development should not put economic growth as the objective of development. Rather, economic growth is simply a means to achieve three equally important objectives of development: people-centred development, environmentally friendly development, and good governance.

Consequently monetary policies should not be growth oriented but should rather be made to help produce the three objectives of development stated above. Furthermore, the world financial architecture should be reformed to avoid dangerous risk taking behaviour that has been the root of all crises. Without eliminating fragile, speculative behaviour, the world will always suffer from boom and burst. The financial sector will always recover first, leaving the real sector behind to suffer. He also argues that political support is needed to implement this paradigm change. As time and space are limited he only discusses economic issues.

CONCLUDING REMARKS

The new era has brought with it some new issues and challenges. Because of this, we need a new development paradigm. As is discussed by Ananta (Chapter 12), Keynes revolutionized the teaching of economics during the Great Depression in the 1930s. Nitisastro radically changed the economic paradigm of the Indonesian Government during the 1960s. The recent largest crisis, which took place in 2008–09, has forced us to rethink our development paradigm. We need new world development paradigms to avoid the occurrence of wider, deeper, and longer economic crisis with large social and political implications.

We recommend three objectives of development: people-centred development, environmentally friendly development, and good governance. In this paradigm, economic growth is still important, but it is not an objective of development. It is only one of the many important means of development. In other words, we should not be too obsessed with achieving very high economic growth. Rather, we should be more concerned with the welfare of people, the rising quality of the environment, and good governance.

With this new development paradigm, monetary policies should also change from growth-oriented monetary policies to those oriented at achieving people-centred development, environmentally friendly development, and good governance. At the same time the financial architecture should also be transformed to eliminate or alleviate speculations in the economy. Therefore, *shariah* finance, which is far removed from speculative activities and activities that produce speculation, could be promoted. Economic activities may then become a little boring, but this would promise a more stable and sustainable financial architecture. Such a stable financial structure will help achieve the three objectives of development mentioned above.

When this book was being prepared in the middle of 2010, "recovery" was the word often mentioned in many countries as their economies started to grow. The more intriguing question perhaps is whether the poor remains poor, worse, or better off, after "the crisis is over". In other words, is the crisis really over for the Indonesian poor?

Here are some specific recommendations for the current Government of Indonesia, though it may also be applicable worldwide.

Monetary Sector

1. Reform the financial architecture to eliminate dangerous speculative behaviour.
2. Regulate inherently shadow banking and resulting credit creation.
3. Let the central bank concentrate on targeting asset price stability, rather than price inflation of consumer goods, to help manage credit creation and, therefore, avoid financial instability.
4. Let the banks return to their function as an intermediary of savings and investment, and promote *shariah* finance, which is not supposed to carry out speculative activities or create products with speculative motives.

5. Drop the paradigm of credit expansion-led growth.
6. Enhance the financial literacy of the general public as a means to empower customers of the financial sector.
7. Re-examine the function of Bank Indonesia, whether it should also function as an agent for development, or simply carry out one function — stabilize the monetary situation.

Real Sector

1. Move away from the growth-oriented model
2. Move away from the export-promoting growth model
3. Move away from the FDI-led growth model

The Statistics Indonesia (BPS) should provide the following additional statistics:

Every three months
– Statistics on poverty and income inequality
– Statistics on health status
– Statistics on population mobility
– Statistics on feeling secure

Every six months
– Statistics on quality of environment
– Statistics on renewable and non-renewable natural resources
– Statistics on natural and man-made disasters
– Statistics on emission of carbon dioxide, methane, and nitrous oxide
– Statistics on good governance

NOTES

1. More discussions on the democratic elections are referred to in a later section in this chapter.
2. The term quantitative easing refers to monetary policies used to stimulate the economy.
3. The parliament in the Reform era is very different from that in the New Order era. During the New Order era, parliament almost had no objections to whatever was suggested by the government. Now, proposals by the government can be rejected by parliament.

REFERENCES

Engardio, Pete. *Chindia: How China and India Are Revolutioning Global Business.* New York: The McGraw-Hill Companies, Inc., 2007.

International Monetary Fund. "Indonesia: Selected Issues". *IMF Country Report* no. 09/231, July 2009. <publications@imf.org>.

Kreager, Philip. "Ageing, Finance, and Civil Society: Notes for an Agenda". In *Older Persons in Southeast Asia: An Emerging Asset*, edited by Evi Nurvidya Arifin and Aris Ananta. Singapore: Institute of Southeast Asian Studies, 2009.

Pramusinto, Agus. "Building Good Governance in Indonesia: Cases of Local Government Efforts to Enhance Transparency". Paper presented at the EROPA Conference "Modernising the Civil Service Reform in Alignment with National Development Goals". Bandar Seri Begawan, Brunei Darussalam, 13–17 November 2006.

World Bank. *Governance and Development.* Washington, D.C.: World Bank, 1992.

2
Government Economic Policies since the Beginning of the New Order Era

Muljana Soekarni and Ferry Syarifuddin

CHAOTIC ECONOMIC DEVELOPMENT, 1945–66

When Sukarno and Hatta declared Indonesian independence in 1945, people cherished the hope that in the atmosphere of independence, development efforts could be initiated to raise their standard of living and bring progress for them. The abundance of natural resources and favourable climate and geography, together with a large labour force, would allow for a large potential for development in Indonesia.

In colonial times this potential was only developed in the interest of the colonizers through the concentration on agriculture, especially plantations, with most of the products sold abroad. As a result, the structure of the Indonesian economy became unbalanced because of too great an emphasis on the heavily export-oriented agriculture.

During the decades known as the Old Order era (1945–66), the economy was a servant to politics. Rational economic principles were unacknowledged and ignored. Furthermore, domestic and foreign resources were squandered. The direct result of these conditions was a drastic decline in the economy, accompanied by hyperinflation which reached more than 600 per cent in 1966. Shortages were felt in many sectors, such as food, textiles, and tools for production, spare parts, and raw materials. Moreover, the irrigation system, plantations, mines, factories, road networks, electricity, drinking water, railways, airports, harbours, and telecommunication facilities were neglected. During that period, food production did not keep pace with population growth. Export proceeds decreased significantly, while imports were paid for by ever increasing loans from abroad.

Consequently, as the economy declined, employment opportunities became fewer. The only ever expanding field of work was government service. The increasing number of civil servants pushed up routine expenditures. However, revenues available in real values were not proportional to the number of people employed, resulting in the declining real income of civil servants. As a result, the annual rate of economic growth during 1961–66 was very low (2.0 per cent) and slightly lower than the annual rate of population growth (2.1 per cent). Income per capita had become stagnant.

This chapter aims to provide a brief introduction to government economic policies after the Old Order era. The next section elaborates on government policies and performance during the New Order era (1966–98), which were a radical change from the previous Old Order era. The section is then followed by one on policies during the 1997–98 Asian financial crisis, which resulted in a total crisis in Indonesia. Next is a section on the democratizing era which started in 1998 and has been ongoing until the present time. It consists of three subsections: the independence of Bank Indonesia; slowly, yet continuously growing economies; and finally the global recession. Before closing with a concluding remark, this chapter presents some economic strategies for the years 2009 to 2014.

STABLE AND GROWING ECONOMIC DEVELOPMENT, 1966–98

The New Order (*Orde Baru*) era began when General Soeharto replaced Sukarno, Indonesia's first president. Starting in 1966, General Soeharto restored the inflow of western capital, brought back political stability, with a strong role for the army, and led Indonesia into a period of economic expansion under his authoritarian New Order regime which lasted until 1998. During this period, industrial output, including steel, aluminium, cement as well as products such as food, textiles, and cigarettes, quickly increased. From the 1970s onward, the increased oil price on the world market provided Indonesia with a massive income from oil and gas exports.

Wood exports shifted from logs to plywood, pulp, and paper, at the price of large stretches of environmentally valuable rainforest. Soeharto managed to apply part of these revenues to the development of technologically advanced manufacturing industry. Referring to this period, where there was such an unwavering economic growth, the World Bank Report of 1993 spoke of this period as the "East Asian Miracle", emphasizing the macroeconomic stability and the investments in human capital (World Bank 1993, p. vi).

Rapid and sustained economic growth under the New Order Era enabled Indonesia to move up from the ranking of "low income countries" to the "lower middle-income countries". Thus, by the mid-1990s its per capita income had risen from US$100 in 1970 to above US$1,000 in 1997. This achievement was a result of two conditions. The first was the high growth of the economy at an average annual rate of 7.0 per cent during the period 1965–97. The second was the rapidly slowing down of the population growth rate due to the family planning programme's success. By the 1990s, the annual increase in population was less than 2.0 per cent annually. The rapid growth of per capita GNP led to rising standards of living, reflected by the high average growth rate in private consumption, underpinned by the rapid and sustained expansion of gross domestic investment. In the 1970s, Indonesia heavily relied on primary exports, in particular oil and gas exports. After the oil boom ended in 1982, the Indonesian Government made a serious effort to promote manufactured exports. The resulting surge in manufactured exports, however, was short-lived, as manufactured export growth slowed down after 1993. Many observers attributed this change to strong international competition and the relatively low international competitiveness of Indonesia's manufacturing sector.

Another important aspect of the economic and financial policies of 1966 was the establishment of a balanced government budget. The 1967 budget was prepared with revenue and expenditure balance at Rp. 81 billion. However, it incurred a deficit of Rp. 2.7 billion, that is, a balance of actual payments (Rp. 87.6 billion) over actual receipts (Rp. 84.9 billion). A balanced budget policy was successfully implemented in 1968, such that actual total government receipts and payments were balanced at Rp. 185 billion. The economy grew by 5.0 per cent annually from 1966 to 1968 (Bank Negara Indonesia 1968).

It should be further mentioned that by government decree, the fiscal year was changed from January-December to April-March. The implementation of the 1969/70 Budget of Revenues and Expenditures was successful. In this fiscal year, the government economic policy was more direct and in tune with development efforts. The new monetary discipline and better implementation of the Budget of Revenues and Expenditures increased confidence in the government's efforts to improve the standard of living of the people through development activities. The outputs of various economic sectors increased impressively, the foreign trade sector progressed meaningfully, and the efforts to attract funds from the general public scored fairly impressive results. This state of affairs together created a favourable climate and became a prerequisite for achieving the targets in the Five-Year Development Plan of 1969.

Furthermore, during the New Order era, Indonesia went through six Five-Year Development Plans, known by the Indonesian acronym Repelita, which specified development objectives, policies, programmes and projects for each of the five-year periods, beginning on 1 April 1979. The plan was based on the Guidelines of State Policies, named "Garis-garis Besar Haluan Negara", which were adopted by the MPR (People's Consultative Assembly) in 1978.

The first Five-Year Development Plan (Repelita I), for the fiscal year of 1969/70 to 1973/74, emphasized rebuilding the economy through improving agriculture, irrigation, and transportation. It dealt with the urgent need for stabilization and the first stages of development. The development focused on agriculture, with its primary attention on food production. Priority was also given to the production of clothing and upgrading infrastructure. After having gone through a stagnant stage and suffering great setbacks for a number of years, the economy began to grow during Repelita I. In this period, the rate of economic growth was approximately 7.3 per cent annually. At the beginning of the New Order era, inflation had drastically declined to an average of 19.6 per cent annually, from more than 600 per cent.

Although the implementation of Repelita I showed favourable results, some problems, such as the even distribution of development output, had still not been resolved. These problems were the focus of Repelita II which followed.

The aim of Repelita II (1974/75–1978/79) was to increase the welfare of all the people and lay a solid foundation for the following stages of development. Being part of the chain of development stages, Repelita II formed the continual and improving sequel to Repelita I. It had the following specific targets: the availability of better quality food and clothing that would be within easy reach of the people; the availability of building materials and other required facilities; the expansion and improvement of infrastructure; more equitable distribution of welfare benefits; and the rise of employment opportunities.

In this period, the real GDP rose on an average of 7.5 per cent per annum and the inflation rate decreased to 17.6 per cent. The oil boom by the end of 1973 had resulted in high pressure on the domestic rate of inflation. Hence, the rate of inflation was 33.3 per cent, the highest ever during the second period and thereafter.

Repelita III (1979/80 to 1983/84) introduced "trilogy of development", comprising high economic growth, national stability, and equitable distribution. It continued to treat the issues in Repelita II as central problems of development, and set the order of priorities accordingly, such as increasing job opportunities, enhancing regional development, strengthening weak economic groups and cooperatives, increasing food production, improving education and health facilities, and other social matters. The Indonesian economy grew 6.1 per cent during Repelita III, with an inflation rate of 13.6 per cent.

The end of Repelita III indicated the first half of the Indonesia period under Soeharto. There were two contrasting groups of economic thought during this period. The first group believed that the Indonesian Government should play a big role in improving the people's welfare through various allocations of funds to rural development and social programmes involving education and health. The second group supported economic liberalization, requiring wide open capital flows and markets in order to be able to enhance rapid economic development (Triaswati 2005). By the end of Repelita V (1984/85–1988/89), the second group seemed to have won by convincing the government to deregulate the capital market through the 1987 package.

Repelita IV continued to emphasize self-sufficiency in rice production and industrial machinery. During that period, the GDP grew by 5.2 per cent and inflation was at 7.2 per cent on average. As Indonesian economy depended a lot on its export, including that of oil, the slower economic growth was partly attributed to the world recession of the early 1980s, as well as the sharp decline in the world oil price following the breakdown of OPEC arrangements. Other aspects which were also under attention in this period included high technology-based industries, sustainable development, the regional dimension, and social welfare.

Repelita V, from fiscal year 1989/90 to 1993/94, stressed rapid development, with an emphasis on the industrial and agricultural sectors. During the time of this Repelita, the economic growth was on average 6.9 per cent, while the inflation rate was 8.1 per cent. By the completion of Repelita V,

Indonesia had succeeded in completing the first Twenty-Five Year Long-term Development Plan (PJP I) of 1969/70 to 1993/94.

TABLE 2.1
GDP Growth and Inflation Rate

	Repelita I 1969/70– 1973/74	Repelita II 1974/75– 1978/79	Repelita III 1979/80– 1983/84	Repelita IV 1984/85– 1988/89	Repelita V 1989/90– 1993/94
GDP Growth	7.3%	7.5%	6.1%	5.2%	6.9%
Inflation Rate	19.6%	17.6%	13.6%	7.2%	8.1%

Source: Compiled from Badan Pusat Statistik, various years.

During the PJP I, Indonesia overcame various fundamental problems as it had enhanced the standard of living of the people and established a strong foundation for implementing the subsequent stages of development. Various basic policies, such as a balanced and dynamic budget principle, an open capital account system, along with prudent macroeconomic policies, made major contributions to the attainment of development objectives. Satisfactory economic growth and equitable development were attained in conjunction with economic stability (Department of Information no date). The average economic growth rate in the PJP I was 6.8 per cent per annum. The inflation rate, which was very high in the 1960s, declined to an average of 17.2 per cent per year in the 1970s, which further fell to an average of 9.7 per cent per year in the 1980s.

All economic sectors, including the industrial, agricultural, and services sectors made significant progress. The industrial sector grew at an average rate of approximately 12 per cent per year between 1969 and 1992. In the same period, the agricultural sector also made significant progress, as reflected in the achievement of self-sufficiency of rice since 1984. This success dramatically altered Indonesia's position from being the world's largest rice importing country in the 1970s, to a country capable of supplying its own rice consumption needs. The attempts to establish a strong economic base, characterized by a growing industrial sector and supported by a solid agricultural sector, had been realized.

High economic growth coincided with a more balanced economic structure. The share of industry in the national product continued to rise such that since 1991, the industrial sector's contribution to the national product has exceeded the share contributed by agriculture. Furthermore,

Indonesia's income dependence on oil has fallen since the early 1980s. In 1981, the contribution of oil and gas to national product dropped to only 13 per cent as a result of the healthy growth of non-oil sectors. The increased share of non-oil and non-gas exports in total exports, along with the larger proportion of domestic non-oil and gas revenues of the government, strengthened both the balance of payments and the government's budget.

The PJP I also witnessed a drastic decline in the number of people living below the official poverty line. Although 70 million people in Indonesia were identified as poor in 1970, by 1993 this number had dropped to 25.9 million people, or approximately 13.7 per cent of the entire population. From the above description of the achievements in development, it is evident that the PJP I succeeded in realizing the goal of enhancing people's welfare and laying down the foundation for subsequent stages of development.

Then came Repelita VI which also became the first stage of PJP II (1994/95–2018/19). This was a continuation of the enhancement and renovation of PJP I and became an important part of the whole national development process. In PJP II Indonesia would enter the take-off stage in its effort to become a developed, prosperous, self-reliant, and just nation. PJP II was also the second era of national awakening, during which development was to be increasingly reliant on Indonesia's own ability and resources. Moreover, the energy of the entire nation would be directed towards achieving a standard of living that would place Indonesia on an equal footing with developed nations (Ministry of Information 1996). Repelita VI began to encourage foreign investment while abandoning policies such as high tariff barriers, heavy regulation, and import substitution. The greatest success in attracting investment up until today has been in textiles, tourism, shoes, food processing, and timber products.

Another achievement of the New Order government was its success in combining rapid growth with a steady reduction in absolute poverty. The prevalence of absolute poverty gradually declined from 40 per cent of the population in 1976 to 11 per cent in 1996. Furthermore, the corresponding number of people living in poverty fell from around 54 million people in 1976 to 23 million people in 1996 (Badan Pusat Statistik 1999). On the other hand, the Gini ratio, which indicates the degree of income distribution, remained almost the same. However, the Gini ratio in Indonesia may have underestimated the degree of income inequality because of the difficulty in obtaining expenditure data from high-income groups. Also, rising global consumption aspirations within the local wage environment may make people frustrated and perhaps even feel injustice in enjoying the fruit of development. Because of this reason, many Indonesians perceived that economic growth, particularly that during the late New Order era, had actually widened inequality. This perception might have been strengthened by the rise of large conglomerates, many of which were owned and controlled by relatives and cronies of then President Soeharto, and by the opulent lifestyle of the rich elite.

As rising income inequality may reflect inequality in distribution of wealth or productive assets (Ahluwalia and Chenery 1974), Indonesia's rapid economic growth may indeed have led to greater relative inequality in asset concentration. This asset concentration could have included both physical assets (land, ownership of companies, banks, and other economic entities), and non-physical assets (human capital made possible by access to high quality education, including overseas tertiary education, by the privileged groups in society).

During the New Order era, Indonesia also made rapid progress in education, as was reflected in the increase in the ratio of primary school enrolment for both male and female students. In 1980, Indonesia's net primary enrolment ratios were already quite high as a result of the government's large investments in the expansion of primary education, particularly in the rural areas. This expansion was made possible by the oil boom windfall profit gained in the 1970s (Jones 1994). The goal of universal primary education had been largely achieved. This was, of course, assisted by the family planning programme's success as it slowed the growth of the primary school-age population down. The government also made good progress in expanding primary health care, as reflected by the steep decline in infant mortality rates over the period 1970–97, and the provision of safe water to the population.

In the area of food, the government was successful in maintaining stable food prices, particularly in Java, during the 1970s. Increased agricultural production during the 1970s and early 1980s was made possible by the government's commitment to developing rural infrastructure and implementing new production technologies in the food crop (particularly rice) sector. This then generated new employment opportunities in production, processing, and marketing. Moreover, rapid growth of the non-tradable sectors, including construction and trade, created new employment opportunities for the large number of unskilled workers (Booth 2000).

However, in the 1980s, poverty declined at a slower rate than during the immediate post-oil boom period of the 1970s. With greater priority given to large-scale capital-intensive manufacturing (including hi-tech projects, such as the aircraft industry), and large-scale modern services and physical infrastructure, economic policies following 1987 became arguably less pro-poor (Booth 2000).

In a nutshell, the Indonesian economy had experienced an unprecedented rapid and sustained growth during the New Order era. This growth transformed Indonesia from Southeast Asia's "chrome underperformer" in the early 1960s into a "high-performing Asian economy" (HPAE) in the early 1990s. During this period rapid industrial growth also transformed Indonesia from an agrarian economy into a "newly-industrializing economy" (NIE) along with Malaysia and Thailand (World Bank 1993).

TOTAL CRISIS, 1997–98

The rapid economic growth in the late 1980s was attributable to the implementation of wide-ranging deregulation measures. Nevertheless, many observers and academic economists during that time began to voice growing concern about various economic and social problems.

The corrosive effects of "KKN" (*korupsi, kolusi, nepotisme* — corruption, collusion, and nepotism) practices also eroded the legitimacy of the government. These problems had aggravated the perception of the widening gap between the "haves" and the poor, and between non-indigenous (mostly Sino-Indonesians) and indigenous Indonesians. This perception might have undermined the social cohesion required for political stability and national development.

Since the early 1990s many economists have also been expressing growing concern about the erosion of the government's financial discipline. This was due to the allocation of off-budget funds to finance the controversial and costly projects that were outside the control of the minister for finance. Consequently, abuses by the increasingly corrupt and oppressive New Order elites eroded its political legitimacy, as overt criticism led to ruthless suppression and violence, which ultimately led to its infamous downfall when the regime was unable to deal effectively with the Asian economic crisis. The legitimacy of Soeharto and the New Order fell with the onset of the Asian financial crisis in 1997 as the financial crisis led to massive protests, which forced Soeharto to step down. The steep depreciation of the rupiah which made domestic inflation very high, along with the downturn in the economy, ignited the people's revolt in asking Soeharto to give up his presidency. Thus the New Order era came to its inglorious end amidst the misery of a seriously damaged economy, which subsequently had to rely on large infusions of foreign and domestic loans to prevent an economic breakdown. The costs of this hugely enlarged foreign and domestic debt was to continue being a burden on the Indonesian economy for many years to come.

Only two months after the release of a World Bank report on Indonesia's brighter medium-term economic prospects, the economy in July 1997 suddenly changed for the worse. The financial shock that began with the high depreciation of Thailand's baht to the U.S. dollar contaminated Indonesia and some other East Asian countries (Hirawan 2007*b*). The Indonesian economy also came under pressure, causing the rupiah to depreciate rapidly as foreign and domestic investors scrambled to purchase U.S. dollars to reduce their exposure to Indonesia. Beginning in August 1997, Indonesia experienced a huge depreciation of its rupiah, which went from Rp. 2,300/USD to Rp. 15,000/USD by mid-1998. The stock market also suffered from this high pressure as was indicated by the decline of the Jakarta Composite Index (JSX) at the end of 1998, caused by massive capital outflow from Indonesia.

After three decades of a stable and growing economy, in 1997/98, the Indonesian economy stumbled into a crisis. The crisis began in the second half of 1997 with the depreciation of the exchange rate of its currency. This crisis developed rapidly, given the openness of the economy and its reliance on the external sector, and was further exacerbated by the existing structural weaknesses in its domestic economy. Inefficient economic management, poor corporate governance, and a fragile banking system also contributed to turning the exchange rate crisis into a deeper crisis by affecting private external debt and the banking system.

To prevent its further deterioration, the government initiated a variety of endeavours. However, these efforts were slow in showing any favourable outcomes due to the erosion of confidence in the government's management capability and the country's unfavourable economic prospects. Furthermore, the spread of various rumours in the area of politics, in tandem with the further deterioration of its economic performance, also hampered the process of economic recovery. As the crisis deepened, financial intermediation, particularly in the banking sector, was interrupted, impeding the flow of funds for financing investment and production. Accordingly, economic activity experienced a sharp contraction, which brought about a drop in gross domestic product (GDP) from 8.0 per cent in 1996 to 4.7 per cent in 1997, a hike in open unemployment from 4.9 per cent to 7.5 per cent, and a soaring inflation rate from 5.17 per cent in 1996/97 to 34.22 per cent in 1997/98, or about 82 per cent (year on year [y-o-y]). As a response to the uncontrolled inflation, Bank Indonesia (BI), Indonesia's Central Bank, increased interest rate (SBI rate). In mid-1997, the interest rate rose significantly to about 60 to 70 per cent. Consequently, the higher interest rate had lured people into investing their money in the bank's high-interest short-term fixed deposits (one to three months) rather than keeping their money in hand.

To prevent the economy from worsening, in late October 1997, the Indonesian Government asked the International Monetary Fund (IMF) for a standby arrangement to restore global market confidence. This was the second effort by the New Order government to turn to IMF for assistance to combat hyperinflation, the first one being at the beginning of the New Order era in 1966. However, IMFs involvement failed to restore market confidence because of political uncertainty regarding the government's ability to restore the economy, as well as doubts about the government's commitment to implement the economic reform programme faithfully. This made the rupiah continue to depreciate by 80 per cent in January 1998, and inflation to rise to 60 per cent, while the economy continued to contract,

When confidence in the banking system was eroded, the financial intermediary function of banks virtually came to a halt, resulting in a sharp fall in production and investment. To address the crisis, the government initiated a number of policy measures to restore stability, notably in the monetary and banking sectors, and to revive economic activities. However, given the complexity of the problems and constraints on the economic and political fronts, the measures failed at the implementation level to produce the expected outcome. Evidently, the effectiveness of macroeconomic policies was blunted in resolving the crisis in such an environment.

Absolute poverty, which had declined during the New Order era, began to rise again. Moreover, Indonesia was also hit by the severe El Nino drought which damaged rice harvests, and by falling oil prices, which reduced the government's oil and export revenues. The worsening economic crisis caused the economy to contract by almost 13.1 per cent in 1998, far worse than the 3.0 per cent economic contraction in 1963 (World Bank 1998). The economic distress led to serious political chaos, which forced President Soeharto to resign in disgrace in May 1998, after holding power for thirty-two years.

The process of stabilizing the Indonesian economy went quite well in 1999. A much more steady monetary situation, favourable domestic socio-political developments, and improved international economic conditions had paved the way for a return to earlier rupiah exchange rates and price stability, with stronger national economic activities. Developments for several monetary indicators, such as the rupiah exchange rates, inflation, and interest rates, had been encouraging.

Indonesia's economy started to recover in 1999, indicated by declining inflation and a stronger rupiah, which provided room for a phased reduction of interest rates. Significant progress was also recorded in the restructuring of banks and external debts, especially those of banks and the government. With positive hindsight, it can be seen that the stock market was bullish, signalling an initial return of investor confidence in Indonesia's economic prospects. However, the process of economic stabilization and recovery in Indonesia was, in fact, slower than that in other Asian countries in crisis.

After the crisis, conditions for the main sectors changed fundamentally. The World Bank (1999) mentioned that there had been structural changes as seen in the shift of production from agriculture to manufacturing and modern services; the relative decline of the agricultural labour force, and the growth of urban centres; the greater role of trade in the economy; the increasing role of the central government in the economy; and finally, the monetization of the economy as a result of stable economic management. However, the primary sector was definitely still needed to support Indonesia's economic growth, especially after the 1997/78 economic crisis.

DEMOCRATIZING ERA, 1999 ONWARD

Independence of Bank Indonesia

Looking at the magnitude and complexity of the problem in Indonesia's economy, the government saw that the strategy adopted to solve the crisis and reinvigorate the economy could no longer rely solely on macroeconomic policies, but had to include appropriate microeconomic policies. In addition, the strategy institutional reforms requires, including an adequate legal system. To this end, along with the pursuit of a policy balanced between a tight monetary and expansionary fiscal stance, the government also adopted appropriate microeconomic measures.

The microeconomic measures pursued by the government were focused on rehabilitating the banking system and the business sector, including resolving corporate debt overhang and regaining access to the international financial market. These measures had been complemented with steps to overcome institutional weaknesses, particularly in the legal system, such as improvements in a number of regulations and laws on the monetary, banking, and real sectors. One of the important laws made was the Central Bank Act 1999, which created the independency of Bank Indonesia.

The independency of Central Banks very often relates to the development, as well as the performance of this institution. It becomes very important when central banks have a very specific target, that is, achieving a low inflation rate. Actually, the issue of independence of the bank had been lingering for a long time, although there are still a lot of debates on the advantages and disadvantages of the independency of a central bank. Even, during the late eighteenth century and the beginning of the nineteenth century, the issue of "independence" had been an eminently political issue in England. As described in Cassis (2010), the Government of England decided to make the pound sterling non-convertible to gold in 1797. This had given the government much power and large profits from the money market. Since banking was a private institution, the decision to make pound sterling non-convertible to gold was seen as government intervention in the market mechanism. Therefore, in 1821, the pound sterling was returned to gold convertibility, making the government unable to influence the money market heavily.

According to the Central Bank Act no. 23/1999, the independence of Bank Indonesia includes goal independence, instrument independence, and personal independence. The main task of Bank Indonesia, as stipulated in the Act, is to achieve and maintain the stability of the rupiah's value. But, with goal independence, Bank Indonesia has the freedom to determine its short-run target.

With instrument independence, Bank Indonesia has the authority to determine its operational targets without any government intervention. Thus, to implement its monetary policy, Bank Indonesia has full authority in determining interest rates without intervention from the government and other organizations. Moreover, Bank Indonesia, unlike in previous times, is not allowed to finance the government.

With personal independence, based on the Act, other parties cannot force Bank Indonesia's course of actions because it has the right to reject any kind of intervention by any organization.

As a result of the Act no. 23/1999, the degree of independence of Bank Indonesia rose significantly to 0.87 (with 1 as the maximum on the scale), from a very low score of 0.45 when Bank Indonesia still followed Act no. 13/1968 (Sugiyono and Ascarya 2003). The degree of independence was measured in terms of its dependency, as an institution, on the government or other organizations, in setting its own budget and goals, and in the process of electing its board of governor members.

SLOWLY, YET CONTINUOUSLY GROWING ECONOMIES

In June 1999, the first democratic presidential election in forty-four years took place after Soeharto's vice president, Professor B.J. Habibie, assumed power. After years of restrictions on parties and campaigning, forty-five parties participated in the election. After the election, Abdurrahman Wahid, the moderate head of the National Awakening Party (PKB) was sworn in as president by People's Consultative Assembly (MPR) for a five-year term in October 1999, with Megawati Soekarnoputri elected as vice-president.

The Wahid administration reversed some of the Soeharto era's restrictions on free expressions, such as releasing political prisoners, eliminating the feared security coordination body, Bakorstranas, and increasing freedom of the press. In 1999, Indonesia's economic growth returned to a positive rate, albeit at only 0.3 per cent. This was a very significant improvement from the minus 13 per cent in the preceding year. Although Indonesia had generally pursued a free market approach to economic development, the government kept state control over enterprises in sectors such as oil plantations and some areas of technology. The role of state-owned enterprises increased during the first decades of the New Order, contributing 30 per cent of GDP by 1990, while remaining dominant players in banking, plantations, transportation, and some areas of manufacturing. The bankruptcy of nearly all of the major conglomerates and the subsequent bailout left the government officially owning major segments of the economy at the dawn of the twenty-first century. There were pressures from the IMF to sell assets and privatize the state-owned enterprises, but movement in this direction had been slow.

Wahid's policies were aimed at encouraging foreign direct investments and, in accordance with IMF agreements, taking steps to strengthen the weak banking and corporate sectors. However, President Wahid was distracted in pursuing these goals by such factors as the ongoing violence in certain regions, allegations of government corruption, difficulty in reforming the political role of the military, and "battles" with parliament.

Entering 2000, with the Wahid administration, Indonesia's macroeconomic indicators became better. Overall, during that year, Indonesia experienced a stronger and more balanced economic recovery. Gross domestic product (GDP) grew by 4.8 per cent. The bank recapitalization programme was completed, progress was achieved in resolving the government's foreign debt, and an agreement was reached between Bank Indonesia and the government on resolving the BLBI's (Bank Indonesia Liquidity Support) problem. Nonetheless, the continuation of several fundamental economic problems limited the speed of recovery. These problems mainly concerned the slow pace of corporate debt restructuring, the absence of a significant recovery of the bank intermediation function, and the lack of a significant fiscal stimulus that could promote economic recovery.

With the continuation of these economic structural problems and the increasing domestic uncertainty, the process of economic recovery during 2000 was accompanied by increased pressure on domestic price levels and exchange rate. During this period, the rupiah depreciated as its average exchange rate became Rp. 8,400 to the U.S. dollar. Furthermore, pressure on the exchange rate increased particularly after April 2000 due to political and security developments in the approach to the Annual Session of the People's Consultative Assembly held in August 2000, and also in response to the strengthening of the U.S. dollar relative to almost all other major world currencies. On the other hand, internal factors contributing to the depreciation arose from the still limited supply of foreign exchange in the market. The limited supply was due to three factors: a continued low level of private capital inflows and the fact that export revenue was not fully repatriated; continued private demand for foreign exchange, particularly to repay foreign debt; and negative market sentiments regarding domestic political and security disturbances.

Externally, the rising of world interest rates, the global strengthening of the U.S. dollar, and the regional exchange rate volatility, put pressure on the rupiah. The high volatility of the rupiah was also due to the increased offshore trading of the rupiah by non-resident market players, causing the rupiah to become increasingly internationalized. Because of the extremely limited supply of foreign exchange, the foreign exchange market was so thin that a small increase in demand would cause sharp changes in the exchange rate. Moreover, the market tended to be asymmetric, thus reacting excessively to negative news.

By 2001, the legislature, in response to popular protests, carried out impeachment proceedings against Wahid. Ignoring the president's threats to dissolve parliament, the legislature impeached Wahid and replaced him with Vice-president Megawati Soekarnoputri on 26 July 2001. The Megawati administration made significant progress in stabilizing Indonesia's economy during its first year in office. It rejuvenated Indonesia's economic reform programme and restored Indonesia's relationship with the IMF. Between September 2001 and April 2002, the Government of Indonesia pushed through several important economic reforms, including a reduction in fuel subsidies, and the selling of a majority stake in Bank Central Asia, Indonesia's largest formerly private bank.

Compared with 2000, the Indonesian economy did not perform too favourably in fiscal year 2001 and this was attributable to the persistently higher risks and uncertainties of this period. Furthermore, there were still remaining domestic problems associated with debt and corporate restructuring, and bank consolidation, in addition to the constraint in fiscal stimulus. These developments eroded business confidence, which hampered expansion in production and investment. GDP grew by only 3.3 per cent. This economic growth was not adequate to provide jobs for new entrants to the labour force, estimated to have increased by 2.5 per cent. Consequently, the unemployment rate in 2001 increased to 8.1 per cent, compared with 6.1 per cent in the previous year.

In the financial sector, the higher risks of this period led banks to extend a smaller amount of credit to support productive activity. The weak link between the real and financial sectors did not only result in financing constraints for investment and production, but also resulted in the build-up of excess liquidity in the banking system, which in turn exerted more pressure on the exchange rate and inflation. On average, the rupiah depreciated by 17.7 per cent relative to 2000, meaning, from Rp. 8,438 to Rp. 10,255 to the U.S. dollar. On the basis of these developments, the inflation rate accelerated to 12.55 per cent, well above the 9.35 per cent in 2000.

However in 2002, in line with improved macromonetary indicators such as the exchange rate, inflation and interest rates, the Indonesian economy continued to grow. Economic growth, mainly driven by consumption, was 3.7 per cent. The significant strengthening of the rupiah and weak aggregate demand helped put inflation on a downward trend in 2002, as reflected in both the CPI (consumer price index) and core inflation. CPI inflation in 2002 declined to 10.03 per cent. Inflationary pressures originated in, among other factors, the government policy on prices and incomes. These pushed prices up by 3.31 per cent, compared with 3.83 per cent in 2001. In addition, inflationary pressure also originated in supply shocks, mainly from reduced food supply and disruptions to the distribution network due to floods early in the year. Another factor was public inflationary expectations, which as shown by several surveys, generally improved in 2002.

The Indonesian economy performed favourably in 2003 as indicated by the appreciation of the rupiah, lower interest and inflation rates, and higher economic growth. One key factor in this regard was the pursuit of mutually supportive monetary and fiscal policies, which helped maintain the momentum of economic recovery. Nevertheless, deeply rooted structural weaknesses remained, hampering a faster economic growth rate, which was vital to providing jobs for all new entrants into the labour force.

During 2003, the Indonesian economy had in fact been confronted with serious challenges. Among others, the major challenges were the impact of the Bali bombing tragedy of 2002, the plan to exit the International Monetary Fund (IMF) programme by the end of 2003, in addition to the subdued growth of the world economy. To cope with these, the government and Bank Indonesia adopted a series of policies to maintain the momentum and boost economic recovery while maintaining macroeconomic stability. These policies significantly contributed to improving Indonesia's macroeconomic performance in 2003, and resulted in the appreciation of the rupiah and the falling rate of inflation. The pursuit of an accommodative monetary policy at a time when international interest rates were declining and the risk associated with the country risk was improving had provided room for domestic interest rates to fall without adverse effects on its inflation and exchange rates. The world inflation rate, which had declined to a low level, also contributed to lowering domestic inflation. These, combined with continued efforts to improve the soundness and resilience of the banking system, and the reliability of the national payment system, led to improvements in banks' performance and the achievements in maintaining macroeconomic and financial system stability. Success in this regard was supported by heightened domestic security and public awareness of the importance of social stability. At the start of 2004, Indonesia's overall macroeconomic picture was stable and real GDP per capita returned to pre-financial crisis levels.

In 2004, though increasing, the pace of economic recovery continued to be hindered by various structural problems, especially in the areas of law enforcement, labour regulations, and the implementation of regional autonomy. These problems led economic growth to continue its reliance on consumption, whereas that on investment and exports was still limited. This situation was aggravated by the lack of an integrated policy strategy to foster a strong and highly competitive industrial sector; as a result, the growth of manufacturing (the largest sectored component of GDP) remained low compared with the pre-crisis period. Consequently, economic growth was inadequate to absorb the growing labour force and to raise per capita income to its pre-crisis level.

However, the year 2004 also presented new horizons for hope and optimism, in spite of its challenges. Sustained macroeconomic stability, improved international confidence, and clarity of the economic agenda, supported by enhanced institutional capacity, especially as regards policy formulation and decision making at the bureaucratic and political levels, provided a basis for higher growth in the following years. Concurrently,

2004 marked a new phase in national economic management following the completion of the IMF stabilization programme, Indonesia being the last of the Asian crisis countries to do so. The decision to exit from the IMF programme was triggered by improved macroeconomic developments and a strong commitment to continued economic restructuring on an autonomous basis.

The year 2004 was also a transitional year for Indonesia. With a strong government supported by all segments in the nation through direct general elections, Indonesia moved towards greater democracy. With the predicted, rapid and unanticipated changes during the transition period, the maintenance of macroeconomic stability had become essential. To this end, a number of short-term economic programmes were put on the post-IMF policy agenda (the White Paper). Within the broader policy framework, this short-term programme was a preliminary step in efforts to maintain consistency and continuity of the long-term policies.

The economy grew rapidly in 2004, reaching 5.1 per cent. Consumption continued to remain robust while investment started to rebound after three years of low growth. The sharp pickup in investment stemmed from strong domestic demand and lower financing costs. Exports of goods and services also expanded in line with higher world trade volume. Prompted by buoyant domestic demand and exports, imports of goods and services also expanded rapidly. These developments contributed to improving public welfare as reflected in a higher per capita income and a lower poverty rate. The higher economic growth in 2004 was achieved by keeping macroeconomic stability in check. Inflation did rise to 6.4 per cent but was still within the target range of 4.5 per cent to 6.5 per cent. The exchange rate weakened somewhat during the second quarter of 2004, but further weakening was arrested, hence limiting its volatility. The weakened exchange rate reflected the market's reaction to rising interest rates abroad, which triggered the reversal of short-term capital flows.

CONTINUOUSLY HIGHER ECONOMIC GROWTH

The Megawati administration introduced and implemented direct general elections in September 2004, resulting in Susilo Bambang Yudhoyono being Indonesia's first directly elected president After taking office on 20 October 2004, Yudhoyono moved quickly to implement a "pro-growth, pro-poor, pro-employment" economic programme. He appointed a respected group of economic ministers who announced a "100-Day Agenda" of short-term policy actions designed to energize the bureaucracy. The Yudhoyono administration targeted average annual economic growth of 6.6 per cent for 2004–09 to reduce unemployment and poverty significantly. Yudhoyono also announced an ambitious anti-corruption plan in December 2004. In 2009, at the end of his term, the economy was growing at only 4.5 per cent, lower than when he assumed power in 2004. The decrease in economic growth rate was because of the global crisis in 2008–09. But Indonesia's performance was one of the best in the world, the third highest after China and India, whereas a large number of countries experienced economic contraction. The poverty rate continued to decline, and was 14.1 per cent in 2009. The acceleration in economic development was also accompanied by a conducive business climate as well as political stability. The low inflation rate and steadier rupiah exchange rate were followed by a decrease in the government loans-GDP ratio to 28 per cent in 2009. Meanwhile, foreign exchange reserves continued to increase, reaching US$71.8 billion in March 2010.

In early 2005, the State Ministry of National Development Planning (BAPPENAS) released a Medium-Term Plan focusing on four basic objectives: creating a safe and peaceful Indonesia; creating a just and democratic Indonesia; creating a prosperous Indonesia; and establishing a stable macroeconomic framework for development. The year 2005 did not only witness a number of challenges confronting the economy, but also provided numerous lessons.

The Indonesian economy was still subject to many problems, such as excess liquidity, lack of coherence of strategy and policy implementation, and weak resilience of the economic infrastructure in dealing with external shocks which exposed the economy to greater risks. Global financial imbalances and soaring international oil prices brought home macroeconomic instability. The rupiah began to fluctuate and the threat of inflation loomed. Following the fuel price hike in October 2005, inflation soared to 17.1 per cent for the year.

This array of problems quickly overturned macroeconomic indicators which deviated markedly from earlier estimates. Mounting production costs triggered by high oil prices and falling investor confidence slowed down investment. Next, consumption, which had been the engine of growth in hard times, could no longer be relied on as a driving force because of escalating interest rates and the erosion of the public's purchasing power in the wake of the fuel price hike. Notwithstanding these setbacks, the economy still delivered a respectable performance as the growth in 2005 edged upwards to about 5.6 per cent.

To fend off the pressures bearing down on macroeconomic stability in 2005 and in anticipation of the persistent level of future high inflation rates, Bank Indonesia instituted a range of policies aimed at regaining macroeconomic stability. Bank Indonesia launched policy packages designed to curb exchange rate volatility through limiting speculative transactions to a maximum of 25 per cent of the net open position (NOP) of the bank's balance sheet; absorbing excess liquidity in the banking system; and coordinating with the government in managing foreign exchange needs. These courses of action succeeded in navigating the economy through various shocks, so that macroeconomic indicators regained stability by year end. Expectations of inflation once again eased and the exchange rate was brought back under control. At year end, the rupiah gained ground with less volatility.

Against the background of poor adjustments to global imbalances and the decline in purchasing power following the October 2005 fuel price hike, the Indonesian economy made gradual progress in 2006. The steep inflation in early 2006 progressively eased to 6.6 per cent (year-on-year). The sustained macroeconomic stability in turn made room for the economy to move ahead at a faster rate, bringing overall GDP growth to 5.5 per cent in 2006 (year-on-year). These developments were made possible by the consistent and prudent monetary and fiscal policies which complemented efforts to maintain macro stability and promote economic growth. Growth was driven primarily by the increased rate of consumption and exports. Investment growth, on the other hand, further slowed down from the lack of progress in handling various microstructural issues. As a result, the economic growth that was achieved in 2006 was not matched by significant improvements in workforce absorption and reduction in poverty.

Despite some mounting external pressures, the year 2007 witnessed remarkable achievements in the Indonesian economy. For the first time since the 1997–98 crisis, the economy grew at a rapid rate exceeding 6 per cent, with macroeconomic stability kept in check. The most favourable performances were reflected in a significant surplus of balance of payments which reinforced international reserves, stabilized the exchange rate, and kept strong credit expansion and inflation under control. Soaring international commodity prices, led by oil, and the unfolding of the subprime mortgage crisis, were among the largest challenges confronting the Indonesian economy during that year. In the face of these multiple adversities, the Indonesian economy appeared to show a higher level of resilience in supporting economic growth.

Economic expansion and other positive factors in 2007 succeeded in absorbing more workers than the number of new entrants to the workforce. As a result, open unemployment in 2007 fell to 10.5 million, compared with the 11.1 million recorded in 2006. At the same time, the number of people living in poverty declined from 39.30 million (17.8 per cent of the population) in 2006 to 37.17 million (16.6 per cent of the population) in 2007. This improvement in welfare had positive impacts on some of the targeted indicators in the 2015 Millennium Development Goals. The most important impacts were a reduction in poverty and hunger, lower child mortality rate, and more children receiving primary and secondary education.

GLOBAL RECESSION

Despite the significant slowing in the final quarter of 2008, economic growth in Indonesia reached 6.1 per cent for 2008. This growth was largely supported by the high growth in exports, which soared in line with escalating global prices for mining and agricultural commodities. Bolstered by the robust economic growth in China and India, Indonesia's exports charted buoyant growth in the first two quarters of 2008. Strong export growth then provided added momentum to purchasing power, especially in export-producing regions, which contributed to high levels of consumption and investment. As expected, import growth also soared in response to the need for raw materials and capital goods. However, Indonesia's economic growth began tapering off at the beginning of the second half of 2008, due to the steeper turn in the global economic slowdown and falling global commodity prices. These developments led to falling levels of export growth. In a similar vein, growth in household consumption, investment, and imports also registered a decline.

The steep downturn in the world economy was accompanied by mounting uncertainty and risk in global financial markets. The unstable conditions of financial markets subsequently triggered a negative sentiment that blunted the risk appetite of investors and set off a trend for a reshuffling of the global portfolio. In addition to the high levels of uncertainty, tight liquidity increasingly hampered efforts to boost exports and attract foreign investment.

Pressure from the world economic slowdown and turbulent global financial markets was also reflected in the deteriorating performance of Indonesia's balance of payments in the second half of 2008. During that year, the balance of payments recorded a US$2.2 billion deficit. At the end of calendar year 2008, Indonesia's international reserves stood at US$51.6 billion, equivalent to 4.0 months of imports and servicing of official external debt. However, these relatively advantageous external conditions deteriorated drastically in the second half of fiscal year 2008 triggered by massive losses from the subprime mortgage crisis in the United States and the impact on the U.S. real sector that far exceeded expectations. These changes led to a significant and rapid downturn in Indonesian exports. The current account surplus quickly evaporated due to falling exports and rising imports. In the capital and financial account, loss of foreign investor confidence in emerging markets led to capital outflows, pushing up the account deficit.

The impact of the global crisis was also reflected in the movement of the rupiah, which, since October 2008, had seen considerable volatility, combined with strong downward pressure. Heightened risks on a global scale triggered a rush to pull foreign portfolio investments out of Indonesia's financial market. On the other hand, the current account sustained pressure from falling commodity prices and declining economic activity in importing countries. These events led to increased pressure on the rupiah, which sank

TABLE 2.2
Indonesian Macroeconomic Conditions:
1997 Asian Crisis and 2008 Global Crisis

	1997	2008
GDP	4.7%	6.1%
Inflation	11.05%	11.1%
External		
– Current Account (% of GDP)	–2.3%	0.1%
– International Reserve (billions of USD)	21.4	31.6
(Month of Imports and Official Foreign Debt Repayment)	5.5	4.0
– Foreign Debt (% of GDP)	62.2%	29.0%
Fiscal		
– Fiscal Balance (% PDB)	2.2%	0.1%
– Public Debt (% PDB)	62.2%	32.0%
Banking		
– LDR (%)	111.1%	77.2%
– CAR (%)	9.19%	16.2%
– NPL (%)	8.15%	3.8%

Source: Bank Indonesia, various years.

to a low of Rp. 12,150 to the U.S. dollar in November, alongside sharply increased volatility at 4.67 per cent. On average for the year, the rupiah depreciated 5.4 per cent from Rp. 9,140 (2007) to Rp. 9,666 to the U.S. dollar (2008). At the same time, soaring global prices for crude oil and food commodities also affected the CPI inflation in Indonesia, which rose up to 11.06 per cent in 2008. This inflation was triggered by escalating world oil prices that forced the government to raise subsidized fuel prices in May 2008 by 28.7 per cent. The impact of the fuel price hike was exacerbated by supply shortages of relevant commodities, such as kerosene and bottled LPG in some regions. Rising world food prices, despite stable supplies, also increased food's contribution to inflation from 2.09 per cent to 2.59 per cent.

STRATEGIES IN 2009–14

Ten Steps to Economic Stabilization

In late October 2008, the government once again announced policies to mitigate the impact of the global financial crisis on the domestic economy and the national financial market. This was known as the government's ten steps to economic stabilization. There were two objectives for these ten steps. The first was to maintain undisrupted economic activity and preserve economic recovery and sustainability. The second was to respond to the constraints encountered by economic agents.

The first step was to maintain the sustainability of the balance of payment by making it mandatory for all state-owned enterprises to deposit their foreign currencies with a domestic bank in a clearing house. State-owned enterprises were required to report their foreign exchange revenues and expenses to the Ministry of State-Owned Enterprises and process the transactions through state-owned banks on a weekly basis and update their reports daily.

The second step was to maintain the sustainability of the balance of payment by expediting infrastructure projects that have obtained financing commitment, both bilateral and multilateral. The third step was to maintain liquidity stability and prevent price wars by prohibiting state-owned enterprises from shifting funds from one bank to another. The fourth step was to maintain market player confidence in government bonds by stabilizing the government bonds market. For that purpose, the government and Bank Indonesia could make gradual and measured purchases of government bonds in the secondary market. The government and Bank Indonesia instituted the policy by purchasing government bonds in the secondary market.[1] The fifth step was aimed at utilizing bilateral swap arrangements with the Bank of Japan, Bank of Korea, and Bank of China, when required, to maintain the sustainability of the balance of payments.

The sixth step was to maintain sustainability of exports by providing a guarantee against payment risk (post-shipment financing). In this regard, Bank Indonesia provided a facility for exporters to sell their export draft with recourse at a discounted rate, starting on 1 November 2008. The seventh step was to revoke CPO (Crude Palm Oil) export duty to maintain economic sustainability, and this also started on 1 November 2008. The eighth step was to maintain the sustainability of the 2009 State Budget.

The ninth step was to prevent illegal imports. The government has issued regulations on the import of certain commodities, garments, electronics, food, beverages, toys, and shoes. Only registered importers can import such commodities and they are subject to verification procedures at the loading port. The government also designated certain ports to be open to specific commodities, such as the ports of Tanjung Priok, Tanjung Mas, Tanjung Perak, Belawan, and Makassar, as well as the airports of Sukarno Hatta and Juanda Surabaya. This regulation came into effect from the first week of November 2008.

Finally, the tenth step was to establish an integrated taskforce among the relevant institutions to improve surveillance on circulation of goods starting from 1 November 2008.

2009: Election Year

Entering year 2009, the Indonesian economy was still shadowed with the global crisis, which created a number of significant challenges. These conditions brought instability in the monetary and financial system in the first quarter of 2009, while economic growth was also on a downward trend due to the contraction of export goods and services. These developments not only reduced confidence in economic agents, but also potentially reduced the positive economic performance achieved during the previous few years.

Facing these challenges, Bank Indonesia and the government implemented a number of policies to maintain macroeconomic stability and the financial system. They also prevented further decline in economic growth through monetary and fiscal stimulus policies. Various policies pursued were basically a continuation of a series of policies that had been taken by Bank Indonesia and the government in the fourth quarter 2008. Not only had these policies been successful in maintaining macroeconomic stability and financial system, but they had also strengthened the resilience of the domestic economy. The economy started to improve during the second quarter of 2009.

In general, the Indonesian economy in 2009 showed that it had been able to get through the recent challenging years. Slow economic growth amid the larger global economic contraction had been avoided because the Indonesian economic structure was driven more by domestic demand. After experiencing severe pressure in the first quarter 2009, financial markets and macroeconomic stability were also improving at the end of 2009. This is reflected in various indicators in the financial sector such as Currency Default Swap (CDS), Composite Stock Price Index (CSPI), yield (yield) SUN, and exchange rate. Inflation also went down to 2.78 per cent, the lowest in the last decade.

In the presidental election of July 2009, Yudhoyono was once again elected as president for the period 2009–14. His vision of the economy in 2009–14 was pro-growth, pro-employment and pro-poor. To realize this vision, high economic growth must be accompanied by equity and justice, as well as growth in the real sector. The growth in the real sector should depend on the continuous growth in agriculture, industrial services, tourism, and the creative economy. In the field of fiscal and monetary policies, it needs to re-create tax incentives and stimulus to re-excite the business world. The development of infrastructure, energy, food security, SMEs, transportation, industry, and services should not be forgotten either. The whole plan of development should be discussed together with local governments. All of these work programmes are expected to lead to an increase in new investment and, eventually, reduce unemployment and poverty. The policies are expected to provide a climate conducive to business for entrepreneurs and potential investors without sacrificing the feeling of justice in society.

National Medium-term Development Plan (RPJMN) 2010–14

In the documents of the National Long Term Development Plan (RPJPN) 2005–25, the process of achieving the national vision and mission will be implemented through five-year stages. The National Medium-term Development Plan (RPJMN) 2010–14, which is the second stage, has prioritized the improvement of the quality of human resources, including the development of science and technology capabilities, and strengthening economic competitiveness. This document has been set by the government through Presidential Decree no. 5/2010.

As shown in Figure 2.1, Indonesian Vision in 2014 is "Realizing Prosperous, Democratic, and Equitable Indonesia". To make it happen, the strengthening of the triple track strategy (pro-growth, pro-jobs, and pro-poor) will be continued with inclusive and equitable development. The embodiment of Indonesia will be reflected in the establishment of a society, nation, and state that is democratic, civilized, dignified, and upholds freedom with responsibility and human rights. These efforts are expected to consolidate democracy. Indonesia's latest vision of justice is to implement just and equitable development, with the active participation of the whole society so that the results can be enjoyed by the entire nation of Indonesia. The government plans to strengthen law enforcement and eradicating corruption, as well as reducing the social gap.

FIGURE 2.1
Indonesia's Development Plan, 2004–25

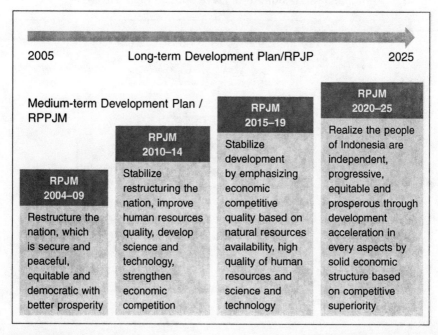

Source: Bappenas (2009).

Figure 2.2 shows that the 2010–14 RPJMN is arranged in three books. Book I (first) contains the vision, mission, objectives, macroeconomic framework, and national priorities. Book II (second) elaborates on the development strategies for nine development and cross-sector issues. The nine areas are: Socio-Cultural and Religious Life; Economy; Science and Technology; Facilities and Infrastructure; Politics, Defence and Security; Law and Apparatus; Regional and Spatial Planning; and Natural Resources and Environment. Book III (third) contains strategic issues and regional development strategies with the discussion organized for seven archipelagos: Sumatera, Java-Bali, Kalimantan, Sulawesi, Nusa Tenggara, Maluku, and Papua.

RPJMN 2010–14 focuses on two approaches. The first approach concentrates on national priorities. The RPJMN mentioned the implementation of eleven national priorities which consist of: reform of the bureaucracy and governance; education; health; poverty reduction; food security infrastructure; investment and business climate; energy; environment and

FIGURE 2.2
Indonesia's Medium-term Development Plan, 2010–14

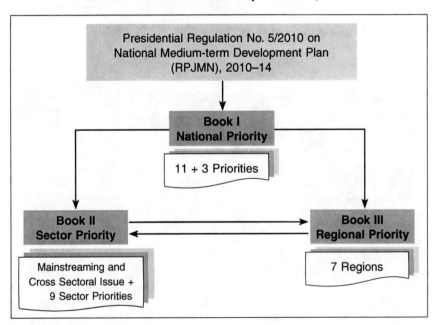

Source: Bappenas (2009).

disaster management; remote areas and post-conflict areas; and culture, creativity, and technological innovation. These eleven priorities are expected to be realized through hard work, such as accelerating the development of physical infrastructure, supported by additional government budget, and the development of cooperation between the government and private sector; soft infrastructure improvements supported by the deregulation and reform of the bureaucracy; strengthening the social infrastructure with poverty reduction; and creative development concerning the source of future growth. In addition, efforts to achieve the national vision will also be supported by other priorities in the three fields: political, legal and security; economy; and welfare.

The second approach is the implementation of business planning. The plans must be strategic and take into consideration all available resources. They must be accountable, with clear costs stated for implementing them. They must also have measurable indicators of achievement. Each programme must be clearly related to major goal.

The National Medium-term Development Plan (RPJMN) 2010–14 follows what the government called the "Development for All" strategy. This strategy is expected to be inclusive, have a regional dimension, and integrate national economies. The government also wants to produce economic growth accompanied by improved equity. This is a pro-poor policy which is expected to reduce the development gap between regions, improve quality of life, enhance quality of the environment, in conjunction with the Millennium Development Goals.

In his testimony to the Indonesian people on 11 December 2009, President Susilo B. Yudhoyono mentioned six basic policies in development strategies. First, development strategies must be inclusive, which means fair, balanced, and equitable. The development strategy in one region should not be targeted solely for the benefit of one group or certain parties. Development goals should be directed to be enjoyed by all classes and groups in the region.

Second, development strategies must have a territorial dimension. The development strategy in one area/region will not be the same as in other areas. Regional development strategies will be based on different land-based areas of islands. The regional development strategy in Java is different from those in Sumatera, Kalimantan, Sulawesi, Maluku, Papua, and so on. So with the territorial dimension, the development strategies would be more realistic and would optimize benefits.

Third, the strategy requires the development of national economic integration. With unity from a strong national economy for the next five years, and Indonesia's bargaining position in the globalization of the world economic arena, Indonesia's geo-economy is in a strong position and very competitive. Domestic economic integration will enhance its international competitiveness because the smooth domestic flow of goods and services will result in lower domestic costs. With efficiency in the production and distribution of its products, Indonesia will also be able to compete with imported goods. Furthermore, with improving transportation and distribution networks, the benefits and development outcomes are expected to be enjoyed equally by all communities because each region would have a better chance to participate in the process of production, distribution, and consumption.

The fourth policy is related to local economic development improvement in the various regions. Their governors, regents, and mayors have broad authority. They know their area condition best: the disadvantages, advantages, and business opportunities. With the development of good design, good implementation, and good synergy, local economies can grow and develop. Regional leaders are encouraged to eliminate blocks ("debottlenecking") in for example, interregional flows of goods, using state and local budgets effectively and efficiently, following the principles of good governance in decision making and budget management.

The fifth policy is that harmony between growth and equity should be maintained. High growth has no meaning if the income gap is too wide. In other words, during 2009–14, Yudhoyono would continue the pro-growth, pro-jobs, and pro-poor development strategy set in 2004.

And the final, sixth policy is in regard to the quality of its people. Human skill is very important because it can accelerate economic growth. Therefore, improving the quality of human life and society is a must.

Then, in a retreat in Tampak Siring, Bali, Indonesia from 19–21 April 2010, attended by cabinet members, governors, provincial legislative councils, and business communities, President Yudhoyono announced an economic road map. Among other things, he mentioned four economic targets for implementing his "pro-growth, pro-jobs, and pro-poor" programmes in his second term (2009–14). The first target is to achieve an annual economic growth rate of 7.0 per cent. The second is to reach a per capita income of US$4,500 by 2014. The third target is to reduce the unemployment rate to between 5.0 and 6.0 per cent by 2014. And the fourth target is to bring the poverty rate down to between 8.0 and

10.0 per cent by 2014. The "new" feature is the emphasis on the spirit of "justice for all" in the president's economic programmes.

Other targets include maintaining economic stability, strengthening domestic financing, raising food and water security, enhancing energy security, increasing economic competitiveness, and creating an environment friendly economy.

To achieve those targets, Indonesia is facing both challenges and opportunities. The development of the world economy shows the growing role of Asia in the global economic arena as the role of China and India is getting stronger. At the same time, the role of Indonesia in world economy is also increasing as it has been considered a member of the G-20.

CONCLUDING REMARKS

After enduring hyperinflation and economic decline during the final years of President Sukarno in the mid-1960s, Indonesia experienced rapid and sustained economic growth for three decades under the New Order government of President Soeharto. The good economic performance of those decades resulted in Indonesia being acknowledged as one of Southeast Asia's successful high performing and newly industrializing economies, following the success of the Asian tigers (Hong Kong, Singapore, South Korea, and Taiwan). Even though Indonesia's economy performed well during the 1980s and 1990s, it experienced downsizing during the financial crisis of 1997/98 which led to significant political reforms. Today, Indonesia's economy is performing steadily, but it still has some structural problems. To solve the problems, the government is designing a new Indonesian development policy road map. Yudhoyono, the president of the Republic of Indonesia for 2009–14, envisions an economic development strategy that is pro-growth, pro-employment and pro-poor poverty reduction, called "Development for All".

In other words, economic growth rate alone is not seen as being sufficient in Indonesia's current economic development planning. Growth must also be inclusive and equitable, meaning the development should involve and benefit everybody. The programmes must be pro-people, justice-oriented, and support the achievement of the targets of the Millennium Development Goals (MDGs). Pro-people programmes aim to improve the effectiveness of the three clusters of poverty reduction, namely social protection, community empowerment, and improvement of the people's economy. Justice-oriented programmes utilize planned measures for marginal groups, which focus on neglected children, orphans, street children, children in trouble with the law/bad boy, disabled children, poor, elderly people, victims of drugs, remote indigenous communities, and migrant workers displaced/Indonesian labour problems (TKIB).

The implementation of the MDGs is not simply to fulfil international commitments. Much more importantly, it will provide huge benefits for the people because it includes: eradicating poverty and hunger; achieving universal primary education; promoting gender equality and the empowerment of women; reducing child mortality; improving maternal health; controlling HIV and AIDS, malaria, and other infectious diseases; ensuring environmental sustainability; and developing partnerships at the global level of development. Furthermore, the MDGs should be achieved not only nationally, but also in each province and district.

NOTE

1. After adopting the policy, Bank Indonesia held two auctions and three bilateral purchases with banks. Total purchases amounted to Rp. 2.4 trillion. Meanwhile, in the same period, two buybacks by the government was able to absorb liquidity amounting to Rp. 368 billion. Purchases in the secondary market were effective in influencing the price of government bonds, particularly during the purchase period. In general, those various joint policies have provided sufficiently positive outcomes in the short run. This was reflected by a number of indicators such as a rise in the Stock Price Composite Index and the stabilization of the rupiah.

REFERENCES

Ahluwalia, Montek S. and Hollis Chenery. "The Economic Framework". In *Redistribution with Growth*, edited by Hollis Chenery et al. London: Oxford University Press, 1974.

Bank Indonesia. *Annual Report*. Jakarta: BI*a*, various years.

———. *Economic Report*. Jakarta: BI*b*, various years.

———. *Report for the Financial Year*. Jakarta: BI*c*, various years.

Bank Negara Indonesia. *Report for the Financial Year 1968, Unit I*. Jakarta: BNI, 31 December 1968.

Bappenas. *Rencana Pembangunan Jangka Panjang* (National Long Term Development Plan). Jakarta: Bappenas, 2005.

———. "Laporan Penyelenggaraan Musrenbangnas RPJPJMN 2010–14". A monograph. Jakarta: Bappenas, 2009.

Cassis, Youssef. *Capitals of Capital: The Rise and Fall of International Financial Centres 1780–2009*. Cambridge: Cambridge University Press, 2010.

Departemen Penerangan, Republik Indonesia. *GBHN (Garis-garis Besar Haluan Negara) Ketetapan MPR-RI No. IV/1978* [The Broad National Policy Guidelines]. Jakarta: Departemen Penerangan, 1978.

————. *Rencana Pembangunan Lima Tahun* 1969/70 – 1973/74 *REPELITA* [Five-Year Development Plan, 1969/70–1973/7]. Jakarta: Departemen Penerangan, 1969.

————. *Rencana Pembangunan Lima Tahun Kedua* [The Second Five-Year Development Plan, 1974/75–1978/79]. Jakarta: Departemen Penerangan, 1974.

————. *Rencana Pembangunan Lima Tahun Keempat* [The Fourth Five-Year Development Plan, 1984/85–1988/89]. Jakarta: Departemen Penerangan, 1984.

————. *Rencana Pembangunan Lima Tahun Kelima* [The Fifth Five-Year Development Plan, 1989/90–1993/94]. Jakarta: Departemen Penerangan, 1989.

————. *Rencana Pembangunan Lima Tahun Ketiga* [The Third Five-Year Development Plan, 1979/80–1983/84]. Jakarta: Departemen Penerangan, 1979.

Department of Information, Republic of Indonesia. *REPELITA VI. Indonesia's Sixth Five-Year Development Plan (1994/95–1998/99). A Summary.* Jakarta: Department of Information, no date.

Department of Legal Affairs, Bank Indonesia. "Act of The Republic of Indonesia Number 3 of 2004 Concerning Amendment to Act of The Republic of Indonesia Number 23 of 1999 Concerning Bank Indonesia". A booklet. Jakarta: Bank Indonesia, August 2005.

Hirawan, Fajar B. "Efektivitas Quantum Channel dalam Mekanisme Transmisi Kebijakan Moneter: Studi Kasus Indonesia tahun 1993–2005". *Jurnal Ekonomi & Pembangunan Indonesia* 7, no. 2, 2007.

International Monetary Fund. "The post-IMF policy agenda". The White Paper. Washington, D.C.: IMF, 2004.

————. *Year-End Report*. Washington, D.C.: IMF, various issues.

Sugiyono, F.X. and Ascarya. *Kelembagaan Bank Indonesia* [Bank Indonesia Institution]. Jakarta: Pusat Pendidikan dan Studi Kebanksentralan (PPSK), Bank Indonesia (Centre for Training and Central Banking Studies Bank Indonesia), 2003.

Sukada, Made. "Monetary Policy Response to Weather Global Financial Crisis: Indonesian experience". Paper presented at Bank Indonesia-ISEAS seminar on "Indonesia's Response to the Global Financial Crisis". Institute of Southeast Asian Studies, Singapore, 25 June 2009.

Triaswati, Ninasapti. "Pendahuluan". In *Pemikiran dan Permasalahan Ekonomi di Indonesia dalam Setengah Abad Terakhir. Paruh Pertama Ekonomi Order Baru, 1966–1982*, edited by Hadi Soesastro et al. Yogyakarta: Penerbit Kanisius, 2005.

Unit Kerja Presiden, Pengawasan dan Pengendalian Pembangunan. "Capaian Program
    100 Hari Kabinet Indonesia Bersatu II" [100 Day Programme Achievement
    of Indonesia's Unity Cabinet II]. A monograph. Jakarta: Unit Kerja Presiden,
    Pengawasan dan Pengendalian Pembangunan, 2010.
World Bank. *World Economic Report*. Washington, D.C.: World Bank, various
    years.

PART II
Monetary and Fiscal Policies

3
The Dynamics of Monetary Policy

Ascarya

INTRODUCTION

The implementation of monetary policy in Indonesia has passed through the dynamics of developments and structural changes since its independence in August 1945. However, in the early days of independence, the environment was preoccupied by political agenda, and monetary policy (as well as fiscal policy) was not yet viewed as a priority. Therefore, it was not surprising that despite the existence of Bank Indonesia (the central bank of Indonesia), the monetary policy could not assume its main function of controlling hyperinflation that was stemming from excessive money supply and government expenditures for the military and "beacon" projects. Hyperinflation reached 635 per cent in 1966.

Monetary policy received greater attention when the New Order government came into power. A new Bank Indonesia Act was stipulated in 1968 with multiple objectives, namely, to achieve and maintain price stability, stimulate economic growth, and create employment. Since then, economic stability and development have become the main priorities for the government and are pursued through periodic five-year development plans, known as *Rencana Pembangunan Lima Tahun* or REPELITA, which started in 1969. The monetary policy focused on controlling inflation and coordinating with the fiscal authority to achieve economic stability.

Inflation could finally and drastically be controlled to below 10 per cent in 1969. Thereafter, between 1969 and 1981, economic growth averaged about 7.86 per cent, with high revenue coming mainly from oil exports. Nevertheless, the inflation rate was significantly higher than growth rate, and averaged 15.76 per cent during that period. This was due in part to the international monetary crisis, in addition to both excess liquidity in the economy and the rupiah's devaluation in November 1978.

The most significant event that caused structural changes happened at the time of the Asian financial crisis in 1997/98. This prolonged financial crisis almost destroyed the Indonesian economy that was previously known as one of the Asian Tigers. Since this crisis, the monetary policy in Indonesia has been generally classified under two different eras: monetary policy in the pre-crisis era and monetary policy in the post-crisis era.

Since 1983, before the crisis began, significant structural changes had been taking place as Indonesia underwent financial liberalization, whereby direct monetary policies were replaced with indirect monetary policies. From 1966–83, Indonesia obtained abundant foreign exchange reserves from oil export revenues that were absorbed to control inflation. Bank Indonesia implemented a direct monetary policy using interest rate ceilings, credit

FIGURE 3.1
Growth, Inflation, and Unemployment in Indonesia

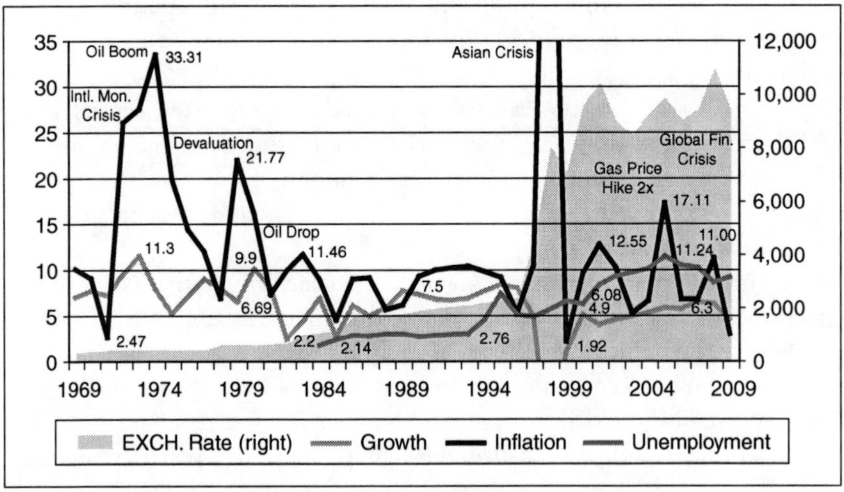

Note: In 1998, growth was −13.1 per cent and Inflation 77.63 per cent.

Source: Compiled and drawn from several Bank Indonesia and Badan Pusat Statistik publications (1969–2009).

ceiling, and selective credit. Moreover, high fiscal expenditures that were accelerating real economic activities were also controlled in order to maintain inflation at a level conducive to economic development. However, the period of high oil export revenues came to an end in the early 1980s when world oil prices dropped drastically. Consequently, economic growth dipped to 2.2 per cent in 1982. From then onward, economic development had to rely on non-oil and non-gas export revenues. To accelerate the development of the non-oil and non-gas sectors, the financial and banking sectors had to be deregulated and liberalized.

The first financial liberalization took place in June 1983. At this time the direct monetary policy was replaced with an indirect monetary policy through an open market operation using Bank Indonesia Certificate (Sertifikat Bank Indonesia or SBI) as its main instrument, coupled with intervention in money market when necessary. To achieve the multiple objectives stated before, Bank Indonesia implemented a base money (quantity) targeting framework. Further deregulation took place in October 1988, when the reserve requirement was significantly reduced from 15 per cent to 2 per cent and restrictions on permits to open new banks were eased. Since then, the banking sector has grown rapidly to participate as an agent of development. Non-oil and non-gas sectors have improved significantly to the point where oil and gas revenues are no longer dominant. Moreover, financial liberalization made other financial markets such as the equity market and bond market develop with increasing sophistication. As a result, short-term capital could flow freely in and out of the country and exposure to foreign exchange risk increased while the financial sector and real sector decoupled. Consequently, monetary management to control money supply became complex.

The 1997–98 Asian financial crisis hit Indonesia through a contagion effect from the currency crisis in Thailand in July 1997. This crisis struck Indonesia's economy so hard that it led to both a triple financial crisis (currency, banking, and foreign debt crisis) and a political crisis. (See Table 3.1 for a comparison of crises in some Asian countries.) This upheaval caused social unrest which then led to the fall of Soeharto's regime, resulting in both economic and political reforms. As a monetary authority, Bank Indonesia initially responded by adopting a free floating exchange rate regime. Previously, Bank Indonesia had adopted a managed floating exchange rate regime. However, the government decided to turn to the IMF for help and entered into a Standby Arrangement with it on 5 November 1997. Later, on 25 August 1998, this was stepped up and became known as an Extended Fund Facility.

TABLE 3.1
Asian Financial Crises

Country	Year	Type of Crisis	NPL (%)	Fiscal Cost (% GDP)	Output Loss (% GDP)	Growth (%)
Indonesia	1997	Banking, Currency, Debt	32.5	56.8	67.9	**-13.1**
Korea	1997	Banking, Currency	35.0	31.2	50.1	-6.9
Malaysia	1997	Banking, Currency	30.0	16.4	50.0	-7.4
The Philippines	1997	Banking, Currency	20.0	13.2	0.0	-0.6
Thailand	1997	Banking, Currency	33.0	43.8	97.7	**-10.5**
Vietnam	1997	Banking, Debt	35.0	10.0	19.7	4.8

Source: Laeven and Valencia (2008).

Economic restructuring also brought significant changes to Bank Indonesia. Under the new Act of 1999, Bank Indonesia became an independent (but still transparent and accountable) central bank that focused on the single objective of achieving and maintaining the stability of the rupiah. Bank Indonesia Act of 1999 was amended in 2004 to further refine the efficacy of monetary management. With fundamental changes in the new Act, Indonesia's monetary policy entered a new era of having a single objective, which was to maintain price stability or control inflation. A monetary policy with inflation as its final target is known as an inflation targeting framework (ITF). Initially, Bank Indonesia implemented inflation targeting lite (ITL), and later in July 2005, it implemented full-fledged inflation targeting (FFIT).[1] In the aftermath of these structural changes, interest rates, rather than money supply, took on an increasingly important role in influencing inflation.

Under the new act, Bank Indonesia was also given the mandate to either conduct monetary policy under the conventional system or/and under *shariah* principle. This was intended to accommodate the needs of the people who had not been officially accommodated under the previous act. As a result, Shariah banking and finance grew rapidly to provide alternative financial services which were also expected to help cope with future financial crises.

This chapter describes how Indonesia has been conducting its monetary policy from July 1953 — when Bank Indonesia was established as the monetary authority — up to 2009. It aims to provide a general picture of the dynamics of monetary policy in different eras while tracking national and global dynamics. Moreover, it provides documentation and descriptions of monetary policies that have taken place in each era that coped with economic conditions or problems faced at the time, complemented by associated fiscal policies, as well as foreign exchange policies, all in a single package of integrated policy.

The following section starts with discussions on the monetary policy during the pre-crisis era — the era before the Asian financial crisis — starting with the establishment of Bank Indonesia in July 1953. This pre-crisis era is organized into three different distinct periods, namely monetary policy in the early years of Bank Indonesia (1953–68) under the first Bank Indonesia Act of 1953; monetary policy in the second era of Bank Indonesia (1968–83) under the second Bank Indonesia Act of 1968; and finally, monetary policy after financial liberalization (1983–97) to anticipate a new era of non-oil/gas economic development priority.

The next section covers discussions on the monetary policy in the post-crisis era, which is also organized into three distinct periods, namely the monetary policy during the Asian financial crisis (1997–98), the monetary policy after the crisis (1999–2005), and the monetary policy under the Inflation Targeting Framework or ITF (2005–present). Moreover, one section discusses the introduction of monetary policy under the *shariah* principle as provided under the new Bank Indonesia Act of 1999. Lastly, some scenarios on probable future monetary policies in Indonesia under a dual monetary system — which maximizes the benefits and minimizes the cost of both the conventional and *shariah* monetary systems — are also discussed.

MONETARY POLICY IN THE PRE-CRISIS ERA

The Early Years of Bank Indonesia (1953–68)

Bank Indonesia was established in July 1953 under Undang-undang Pokok Bank Indonesia (Bank Indonesia Act) no. 11/1953 which replaced De Javasche Bank, the central bank in the colonial era that was created under Javasche Bank Wet of 1922. The establishment of Bank Indonesia was based on Undang-undang Dasar 1945, article 23, which stated that it was necessary to form a bank named Bank Indonesia to issue and manage paper currency. The stated goals were: to maintain the stability of the rupiah; to issue and circulate paper currency and ensure smooth domestic and international payment systems; to regulate and develop a sound bank and credit; and finally, to supervise bank and credit. Monetary authority was in the hands of the Monetary Board, which comprised the minister for finance as a chairperson and both the minister for economy and the governor of Bank Indonesia as members. Therefore, both monetary and fiscal authority were solely under the control of the minister for finance. In other words, Bank Indonesia was part of the government, rather than an independent monetary authority.

During the first twenty years of Indonesia's independence (1945–65), the political agenda remained dominant while economic policy (fiscal and monetary policies) was still not viewed as a priority. In fact, this early period witnessed economic turmoil and structural weaknesses, along with low growth and stagnation in some economic sectors; low income per capita; and a high rate of unemployment concurrent with the high rate of population growth. The current account (CA) of Balance of Payments (BOP) came under pressure due to sluggish exports, coupled with strong expansion in imports. Accordingly, foreign exchange reserves were depleted rapidly. This situation (under a fixed exchange regime and tight foreign exchange control) was further exacerbated by the flourishing foreign exchange black market, while the speculative activities and capital outflow increased.

Monetary stability was in serious trouble because the central bank had to monetize fiscal deficit, leading to excessive money supply. Budget deficits soared due to high government expenditures to finance military expenses and "beacon" projects, which were not supported by sufficient revenues. To finance the deficits, Bank Indonesia extended support in the form of an advance to the government. Consequently, at the end of 1966, the money supply increased by up to 1,000 per cent, which triggered hyperinflation of 635 per cent. Subsequently, the people's propensity to save (and therefore also bank deposits) decreased drastically. Banks could only depend on the central bank's fund to extend loans, which in turn, worsened the excess money supply and accelerated hyperinflation. This unfavourable situation impeded the development of banking sector very seriously.

As part of the government rehabilitation and stabilization programmes, Bank Indonesia then undertook several policies to address the internal and external problems. The most important monetary policies implemented in this period was to curb hyperinflation by raising the interest rate on deposits, in addition to the establishment of the rupiah as the official currency of the Republic of Indonesia, replacing the many different currencies circulating in various regions, as well as the redenomination of the rupiah from Rp. 1,000.00 to Rp. 1.00 in December 1965.

To improve the efficacy of its monetary policy, a new Banking Act no. 14/1967 was stipulated. Other measures taken by the government included undertaking fiscal and foreign exchange policies. In the fiscal sector, the government adopted a balanced budget policy to improve the budget deficit. In the external (foreign exchange) sector, the government eased foreign exchange controls and allowed private foreign investments. Foreign banks were given permission to open their branches in Indonesia. The results of coordinated policies in monetary, fiscal, and foreign exchange seemed positive. The inflation rate dropped significantly from 635.3 per cent in 1966 to 112.2 per cent in 1967, and further to 85.1 per cent in 1968. With the improvement in the inflation rate, the people's confidence with respect to the rupiah started to pick up. Table 3.2 provides a summary of the rehabilitation and stabilization programmes in this period.

TABLE 3.2
Rehabilitation and Stabilization Programmes

Monetary authority under Monetary Board chaired by minister for finance with governor of Bank Indonesia and minister for economy as members; fiscal authority under minister for finance.

Economic Conditions	Monetary Policies
• Many different currencies circulated in many different areas • Excessive money supply • Hyperinflation up to 635.3% • Drop in savings	• The issuance of the rupiah as formal currency of the Republic of Indonesia • Revaluation of the rupiah from Rp. 1,000 to Rp. 1 • Tight money policy; raised deposit interest rate to 72% • Extend direct credit to economic activities • New Banking Act no. 14/1967
Economic Condition	Fiscal Policy
• Budget deficit to finance military expenses and "beacon" projects	• Print money to finance budget deficit
Economic Conditions	Foreign Exchange Policies
• Current Account deficits • Tight foreign exchange control	• Ease foreign exchange control • Allow private foreign investment • Permit foreign bank to open branch • Exchange rate Rp. 45/US$1 in 08/1959; Rp. 250/US$1 in 04/1964

Results: Inflation dropped from 635.3 per cent in 1966 to 85.1 per cent in 1968 and confidence in rupiah improved.

Source: Compiled from several Bank Indonesia and other publications (1953–68).

The Second Era of Bank Indonesia (1968–83)

To further support the rehabilitation and stabilization, and in line with Banking Act no. 14/1967, a new Central Bank Act no. 13/1968 was stipulated to support the government's development programmes. Under this act, Bank Indonesia's objective was to assist the government in achieving and maintaining the stability of the rupiah, as well as promoting economic growth and improving employment. Monetary authority was still in the hands of the Monetary Board, meaning that monetary and fiscal authorities were still under the control for the minister for finance and Bank Indonesia was still part of the government.

The first development programme was initiated in 1969 in the form of a series of a five-year development plan (REPELITA or Rencana Pembangunan Lima Tahun), implemented as PELITA (Pembangunan Lima Tahun — Five-Year Development). The economic conditions during the early days of the first PELITA were characterized by continued economic improvement from rehabilitation and stabilization programs, which saw inflation further drop to 9.9 per cent in 1969, time deposits increased from Rp. 4.5 billion in 1968 to Rp. 33.6 billion in 1969, fiscal and monetary policies were well coordinated, and other macroeconomic indicators improved. However, the government gave less attention to prudent policies and there were no checks and balances on economic policies. Moreover, the government still ran budget deficits and foreign investors were still reluctant to invest in Indonesia.

To support the development plan, monetary policies focused on price stability in order to control inflation, encourage savings, and promote domestic investment. To achieve price stability, Bank Indonesia concentrated on managing inflation through controlling the money supply and shifting the sources of money supply from inflationary sources to non-inflationary sources. Thus, the sources of money supply were shifted from government sectors (stop printing money), to credit (domestic loan expansion) and external sectors (foreign investment).

To encourage savings, Bank Indonesia initiated a national savings movement in August 1971 in the form of a national development saving deposit (*Tabungan Pembangunan Nasional* or TABANAS) and a periodic insurance deposit (*Tabungan Asuransi Berjangka* or TASKA) which were insured by Bank Indonesia. All state-owned banks participated in this movement of offering these two products. To encourage domestic investment, Bank Indonesia introduced "investment loan facility" to domestic investors at a low interest rate. Moreover, in the fiscal sector, the government changed its budget deficit policy to a balanced budget policy. Furthermore, to provide sound business climate in the external sector, the government implemented free capital movement and a fixed exchange rate, where US$1 was fixed to Rp. 378 in December 1970, and Rp. 415 in February 1973.

The result of the first PELITA was that money supply could be managed and shifted to non-inflationary sources so that inflation could be controlled and decreased further to 2.47 per cent in 1971. However, due to the international monetary crisis because of the breakdown of the Bretton Woods Agreement in 1971, inflation jacked up again to 25.8

per cent in 1972 and 27.3 per cent in 1973. The new Banking Act and
Central Bank Act then improved the role of the banking system in the
economy. Savings increased dramatically from Rp. 4.5 billion at the end
of 1968, to Rp. 59.7 billion in March 1971, and Rp. 149.2 billion in
March 1973. Bank credit also increased dramatically from Rp. 121.3
billion (bank's own share = Rp. 29.3 billion) at the end of 1968, to Rp.
380.7 billion in March 1971 (bank's own share = Rp. 177.9 billion), and
Rp. 704 billion in March 1973. A summary of the monetary policy in
this period is shown in Table 3.3.

TABLE 3.3
Monetary Policies from 1968–73

Monetary authority under Monetary Board chaired by minister for finance with governor of Bank Indonesia and minister for economy as members; fiscal authority under minister for finance.

Economic Conditions	Monetary Policies
• Lower inflation • Improved savings • Well coordinated monetary and fiscal policies BUT • Lack of prudent monetary and fiscal policies • No check and balance on economic policies	• Focused on price stability (inflation) • Improved monetary-fiscal coordination • Controlled money supply • Creation of national savings movement • Gradually lower deposits rates • Low interest investment loan
Economic Condition	Fiscal Policies
• Budget deficit	• Stop printing money to finance budget deficit • Balanced budget
Economic Condition	Foreign Exchange Policies
• Lack of foreign investment	• Free capital movement • Fixed exchange rate US$1 = Rp. 378 (12/1970); Rp. 415 (2/1973)

Results: Economic stability; controlled money supply; non-inflationary money supply; improved banking role in the economy; improved savings; improved loan expansion; improved private investment; low inflation (before international monetary crisis).

Source: Compiled from several Bank Indonesia and other publications (1968–73).

The international economic environment in the early second PELITA (1974–78) was marked by a prolonged monetary crisis. It started when the United States unilaterally terminated the convertibility of U.S. dollar to gold. Under the Bretton Woods Agreements from 1950 to 1972, the U.S. dollar, with its strict fixed exchange rate and international monetary arrangements, was the world currency pegged to gold (one troy ounce of gold was equal to US$35). All other currencies were pegged to the U.S. dollar, with the guarantee that U.S. dollar would be exchangeable with gold at any time. The Bretton Woods era was known as the golden age where personal income, volume of world trade, and investment increased, while international economic stability was maintained. As discussed in Ascarya (2009*b*), there is no other period in time, in the past or present, comparable to or closely resembling the achievements (that is, high production, high productivity, low unemployment, and a just distributive income) of the Bretton Woods era.

Partly reflecting the international environment, inflation in Indonesia accelerated to 33.3 per cent in 1974. The sources of inflation were the hike in crude oil prices, which generated windfall revenues, short-term capital inflows, as well as credit expansion, stemming from increased liquidity credit from Bank Indonesia. To address this problem, the government launched a stabilization programme in April 1974. On the monetary front, to curb inflation, Bank Indonesia pursued a tight money policy by raising interest rates and reserve requirements, in addition to imposing a credit ceiling. To promote better income distribution and reduce unemployment, it introduced selected credit, with low interest in the form of small-scale investment credit (*Kredit Investasi Kecil* or KIK), along with permanent working capital credit (*Kredit Modal Kerja Permanen* or KMKP) for the less fortunate groups.

In the fiscal sector, the government launched a series of price controls for staple foods and selected commodities. To support staple food price stabilization, Bank Indonesia extended liquidity credit to the Bureau of Logistic (*Badan Urusan Logistik* or BULOG). In the external sectors, the government implemented statutory reserves to short-term capital flows, while the exchange rate was fixed at Rp. 415 to the U.S. dollar from 1973–78.

The money supply could be controlled in the second PELITA, resulting in the gradual decline of inflation from 14.2 per cent in 1976 to 6.7 per cent in 1978. The high interest rate policy brought in an increase in bank savings. A summary of the monetary policy in this period can be read in Table 3.4.

The economic condition in the early third PELITA (1979–83) was affected by both world recession and high oil prices. Domestically, there

TABLE 3.4
Monetary Policies from 1974–78

Monetary authority under Monetary Board chaired by minister for finance with governor of Bank Indonesia and minister for economy as members; fiscal authority under minister for finance.

Economic Conditions	Monetary Policies
• Continued international monetary crisis • Rising inflation in 1974 • Increased money supply from oil revenue and liquidity credit of Bank Indonesia	• Direct monetary policy since 1974: credit ceiling; interest ceiling; selected credit • Tight money policy: high interest rate policy; gradually lowered interest rate • Lower reserve requirement in 1978 • Direct credit to BULOG • Liquidity credit for KIK and KMKP
Economic Condition	Fiscal Policies
• General price increase	• Staple food price control • Selected commodities price control
Economic Conditions	Foreign Exchange Policies
• Short-term capital inflows • Windfall from oil revenues	• Statutory reserves • Fixed at Rp. 415/US$1 from 1973–78

Results: Controlled money supply; inflation gradually decreased to 6.7 per cent in 1978; savings increased.

Source: Compiled from several Bank Indonesia and other publications (1974–78).

was an overvaluation of the rupiah, due to the prolonged fixed rate of the rupiah at Rp. 415/US$1 from February 1973 to November 1978. Indonesia's commodity prices then became uncompetitive in world market. Also, its inflation was higher than those of its trading partners. The rupiah was then devalued to Rp. 625/US$1 and the fixed exchange regime was replaced by a managed floating regime in November 1978, with the rupiah value linked to a basket of foreign currencies. High oil prices resulted in high government revenues, Current Account Surplus, and excessive money supply.

To clear the excess money supply, Bank Indonesia implemented a tight money policy in 1979/80. In the fiscal sector, the government reduced the use of its account in Bank Indonesia to sterilize foreign exchange revenue from oil exports. It also raised the price of administered price commodities, such as gas and rice, to adjust to the new exchange rate. These measures resulted in another controlled money supply, which subsequently decreased the inflation rate to 7.1 per cent in 1981.

In 1982, economic conditions changed with the drop in oil prices, which decreased government revenue from its oil exports significantly. Consequently, Indonesia experienced the worst Current Account deficit and the lowest growth — at 2.2 per cent — in 1982. As government could not rely on oil or gas revenue any longer, non-oil and non-gas exports had to be boosted. To support this policy, Bank Indonesia provided export credit facilities for non-oil and non-gas commodities. As a result, the export of these commodities increased, which led to an increase in economic growth to 4.2 per cent in 1983. However, inflation also increased, reaching 11.5 per cent in 1983. A summary of monetary policy in this period is available in Table 3.5.

Overall, the monetary policy in the second era of Bank Indonesia (1968–83) was prioritized to support the government's long-term development plan. Although inflation could be brought down from hyperinflation, it could not be fully controlled at the time of the international monetary crisis resulting from the breakdown of the Bretton Woods Agreement in 1971, or during the world recession in 1979/80. The average inflation rate reached 15.07 per cent annually during the second era of Bank Indonesia (1968–83). Nevertheless, the development plan successfully maintained a relatively high economic growth rate, averaging 7.24 per cent a year, in this period. The overall results can be seen in Figure 3.2.

FIGURE 3.2
Growth and Inflation in the Second Era of Bank Indonesia, 1968–83

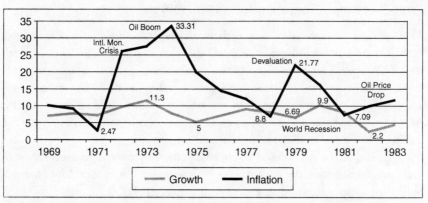

Source: Compiled and drawn from several Bank Indonesia publications (1968–84).

TABLE 3.5
Monetary Policies from 1979–83

Monetary authority under Monetary Board chaired by minister for finance with governor of Bank Indonesia and minister for economy as members; fiscal authority under minister for finance.

Economic Conditions	Monetary Policies
• World recession since 1979 • Inflation was higher than trading partners • Uncompetitive commodity price • Excessive money supply	• Controlled money supply • Export credit facilities for non-oil/gas
Economic Conditions	Fiscal Policies
• Increased oil price/revenues up to 1981, and decreased oil price/revenues since 1982 • General price increase	• Sterilization • Gas and rice price adjustments
Economic Conditions	Foreign Exchange Policy
• Devaluation of rupiah to Rp. 625/US$1 • Current Account surplus up to 1981, and worst Current Account deficit in 1982	• Managed floating exchange rate regime

Results: Controlled money supply; inflation decreased to 7.1 per cent in 1981, increased to 11.5 per cent in 1983; lowest growth of 2.2 per cent in 1982; increased non-oil/gas export.

Source: Compiled from several Bank Indonesia and other publications (1979–83).

Post-Financial Liberalization (1983–97)

This period started with some difficulties. Internationally, the world recession continued, oil price dropped significantly from US$35 per barrel to US$10 per barrel in mid-1980s, protectionism was widespread, and lastly, international non-oil commodity prices decreased. Furthermore, with additional BOP pressure, the domestic economy slowed down significantly. Also, structural weaknesses, such as the high-cost economy, inefficiency, and market distortion, made Indonesia's economy worse.

Because of the unfavourable external economic conditions and internal structural weaknesses, the government took a series of integrated fundamental policy measures in several sectors. These measures were undertaken as steps in financial liberalization which was divided into two stages. The first stage was financial deregulation in June 1983, and the second stage was monetary and banking deregulation in October 1988 and March 1989. Prior to financial liberalization, in March 1983, the initial anticipated policy taken by the government was to devalue the rupiah to Rp. 970/US$1 from Rp. 702.5/US$1.

The first-stage banking system deregulation in June 1983 was intended to improve the role of the banking system in the financial system, and to encourage people to be bank-minded. In the monetary sector, the direct monetary policy was replaced by an indirect monetary policy in controlling money supply. The banking deregulation had three main objectives: eliminate the credit ceiling; allow government-owned banks to set their own credit and deposit policies including interest rate policies; and, finally, phase out Bank Indonesia liquidity credit so that liquidity credit would only be provided to high priority sectors. This deregulation was intended to encourage banks to mobilize deposits and extend credit to productive and profitable sectors. By allowing banks to compete freely in the market, market distortion would be minimized and fund allocation would be more efficient. The deregulation was also intended to prevent capital outflow since the domestic interest rates would be in line with international interest rates.

In the monetary sector, direct monetary policies, such as credit ceiling and interest ceiling were replaced by indirect monetary policies, including reserve requirement, open market operation (OMO), discount facilities, and moral suasion. An indirect monetary policy means that Bank Indonesia could control base money (M_0) indirectly to affect broad money supply (M_1 and M_2), so that inflation could be controlled.[2] The conduct of OMO required monetary instruments. For this purpose, two monetary instruments were introduced. The first was the Bank Indonesia Certificate (*Sertifikat Bank Indonesia* or SBI), issued by Bank Indonesia, which was introduced in February 1984. The second were the Money Market Securities (*Surat Berharga Pasar Uang* or SBPU) issued by banks and introduced on February 1985. Hence, SBI as a liability-based monetary instrument, primarily served to contract money supply, while the SBPUs, as asset-based monetary instruments primarily served to expand the money supply. Moreover, discount facilities could be used either for contraction by raising the discount rate, or expansion, by lowering the discount rate.

The results from this first stage of financial deregulation were promising. In banking, fund mobilization and the number of bank customers increased significantly, reflecting the positive response from the general public. Money supply in term of M_2 increased significantly from Rp. 2.1 trillion in 1982/83 to Rp. 7.2 trillion in 1987/88. Inflation was controlled at an average of 7.25 per cent, which was lower than that of the previous period, while the economic growth rate reached 5.1 per cent on average. Moreover, unemployment could be maintained at a low level of 2.3 per cent on average. A summary of the monetary policy in this first stage of the financial liberalization period can be read in Table 3.6.

The second stage of financial, monetary, and banking deregulation in October 1988 (known as PAKTO'88), March 1989, and January 1990, was a continuation and refinement of the first-stage liberalization. The second stage, known as Sumarlin Move I, was intended to strengthen the control of inflation, further accelerate economic growth, and expand employment. Specifically those objectives would be achieved through the expansion of fund mobilization, acceleration of non-oil and non-gas exports, enhancement in efficiency of banks and other financial institutions, as well as development of equity market. The PAKTO'88 deregulation package included: permitting

TABLE 3.6
Monetary Policies from 1983–88

Monetary authority under Monetary Board chaired by minister for finance with governor of Bank Indonesia and minister for economy as members; fiscal authority under minister for finance.

Economic Conditions	Monetary Policies
• World recession continued • Oil price dropped from US$35 to US$10 per barrel • Economic slowdown • Structural weaknesses • Excessive money supply since 1987	• Eliminated credit and interest ceiling • Indirect monetary policy: OMO, discount facilities • Liquidity credit only for high priority sectors
Economic Condition	Fiscal Policy
• Speculative activities	• Sumarlin Move I in 06/1987
Economic Condition	Foreign Exchange Policy
• BOP pressure	• Devaluation from Rp. 702/US$1 to Rp. 970/US$1 in 03/1983; Devaluation from Rp. 1,134/US$1 to Rp. 1,644/US$1 in 09/1986

Results: Improved banking role in the economy; increased deposits; increased money supply; controlled average inflation to 7.3 per cent; lower average growth rate of 5.1 per cent; low average unemployment of 2.3 per cent;

Source: Compiled from several Bank Indonesia and other publications (1983–88).

the opening of new banks and new branches; encouraging participation in fund mobilization through the TABANAS and TASKA saving schemes; allowing state-owned enterprises to maintain their deposits in private banks; lowering reserve requirements from 15 per cent to 2 per cent; simplifying the requirements for corporations to go public; and, finally, establishing a parallel bourse.[3] In addition to lowering reserve requirements in the monetary sector, the tenure of monetary instruments (SBI and SBPU) was expanded to include longer maturity ranging from 30 days to 180 days. The lower reserve requirements were intended to allow the banking sector to expand its capacity to extend credit.

In March 1989, swap mechanism was also refined from a maximum six months to three years, while swap premium was determined by the interest spread between domestic and international interest rates. This policy was intended to improve the market's and people's confidence in the rupiah value so that the shock of exchange rates could be minimized and monetary stability improved.

In line with the advancement of the financial and banking sectors to support economic development, further enhancement of credit policy was introduced in January 1990. In this case, Bank Indonesia phased out direct credit. Liquidity credit would only be provided to support food self-sufficiency, development of cooperatives, and investments. This policy was intended to develop a stronger financial and banking sector, capable of mobilizing fund and extending credit without the support of liquidity credit. These concerted deregulations resulted in the acceleration of economic activities in both the real and the financial sectors. Innovations in financial instruments were developed in the banking sector and capital markets. However, due to the strong expansion in the demand for credit, interest rates increased and speculative activities in the money market heightened. To cope with this problem, in April 1990, a tight monetary policy stance was starting to be put in place. Furthermore, to halt speculation in the foreign exchange market, in February 1991, in the so-called Sumarlin Move II, the minister for finance ordered twelve state enterprises to withdraw their deposits amounting to Rp. 8.1 trillion from state-owned and private commercial banks and to have these converted to one-year special SBI, at the rate of 22 per cent.

The pursuit of a tight money policy gradually eased in 1993. In the following year, the persistently low interest rate caused a capital outflow. Thus, Bank Indonesia moved again to a tight monetary policy by raising the SBI rate. In the years of 1995 to 1996, investment was robust in view of the favourable prospects of the economy. Given the openness of the economy and the capital account, such a situation attracted capital inflow, which caused the rupiah to appreciate. Any sterilization move to arrest[4] appreciation would only accelerate the expansion of the money supply; therefore, to help contain the expansion of the money supply, Bank Indonesia raised reserve requirements from 2 to 3 per cent. This condition did not change much until the crisis hit the financial and banking sector in the second semester of 1997.

In summary, during this period, inflation could be controlled at an average of 8.6 per cent, while the economy grew at an average of 7.2 per cent and unemployment was maintained at a low level of 3.7 per cent. A summary of the monetary policy in this second stage of the financial liberalization period can be read in Table 3.7.

TABLE 3.7
Monetary Policies from 1988–97

Monetary authority under Monetary Board chaired by minister for finance with governor of Bank Indonesia and minister for economy as members; fiscal authority under minister for finance.

Economic Conditions	Monetary Policies
• Developed financial instruments • Increased credit demand and interest rate • Decoupling real and financial sectors • Overheated economy • Excess money supply in 1990 and 1994 • Low interest rate in 1994 • Increased money supply since 1995	• Tight monetary policy 04/1990; eased monetary policy in 1993; tight monetary policy since 1994 • Increased reserve requirement from 2% to 3%
Economic Condition	Fiscal Policy
• Speculative activities	• Sumarlin Move II in 02/1991
Economic Conditions	Foreign Exchange Policy
• Capital outflow in 1993 • Capital inflow and appreciation in 1995/96	—

Results: Improved financial sector role in the economy; increased deposits/credit; increased money supply; controlled average inflation to 8.6 per cent; higher average growth rate of 7.2 per cent; low average unemployment 3.7 per cent.

Source: Compiled from several Bank Indonesia and other publications (1988–97).

Overall, the monetary policy during the financial liberalization era and before the crisis — between 1983 and 1997 — was prioritized to develop a financial and banking system that was able to support economic development, as well as to improve monetary policy management. Inflation was controlled at an average of 8.1 per cent, while the economic growth rate was maintained at the rate of 6.4 per cent. Moreover, unemployment was maintained at the low rate of 3.2 per cent. The overall results can be read in Figure 3.3.

FIGURE 3.3
Growth, Inflation, and Unemployment after Financial Liberalization, 1983–97

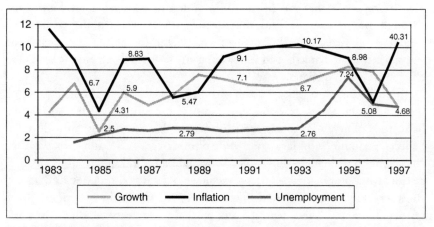

Source: Compiled and drawn from several Bank Indonesia and Badan Pusat Statistik publications (1983–98).

MONETARY POLICY IN THE POST-CRISIS ERA

During the Crisis (1997–99)

Southeast Asia encountered an appalling financial crisis since the attack on the baht in July 1997. This currency crisis in Thailand spread to other Southeast Asian countries, including Indonesia, through contagion. The crisis was triggered by external systemic events, including the overheating of the economies of the Asian Tiger countries, political instability, and massive currency devaluation. Alas, in Indonesia, structural weaknesses had been masked by high levels of economic growth during the years from 1988 to 1997.

What happened was that foreign investors withdrew their assets very suddenly, resulting in a drastic jump in demand for foreign exchange and causing the rupiah to depreciate significantly in a short period of time. Bank Indonesia responded to this situation by widening the intervention band (under a managed floating regime) in July 1997. But, foreign exchange reserve was drained very rapidly and so a free floating exchange rate regime was adopted on 14 August 1997. Subsequently, the value of the rupiah (which had been in the Rp. 2,600/US$1 range at the start of August 1997) plummeted to a low of Rp. 11,000/US$1 in January 1998. Due to the continued worsening of the crisis, in November 1997, the government asked the IMF for assistance. In this regard, Indonesia received financial assistance in the form of a Standby Arrangement (SBA) amounting to US$10 billion. The IMF programme was primarily intended to restore market confidence through maintaining sound macroeconomic fundamentals, addressing fundamental weaknesses in the financial sector (including the closure of sixteen insolvent banks), and embarking on structural reforms to enhance efficiency and transparency.

The decision to close banks without any deposit insurance in place brought about a loss in confidence among depositors which then led to bank runs. Therefore, to restore confidence, the government introduced a blanket guarantee[5] in January 1998. Some twenty-five ailing banks that could still be rescued were bailed out by Bank Indonesia and joined a restructuring programme set up by the newly established Indonesian Banking Restructuring Agent (IBRA) in February 1998. While this decision helped restore confidence, the central bank virtually lost control of the money supply. To keep the expansion of money supply under control, the central bank began to raise interest rates aggressively.

In these circumstances, acute excess liquidity (excessive money supply) resulted, which necessitated Bank Indonesia to pursue a tight money policy through aggressively raising SBI's rate from 8.63 per cent in July 1997 to as high as 69.57 per cent in August 1998. Monthly inflation jumped to 12.76 per cent in February 1998, while, year-on-year (see INFLATION in Figure 3.4) soared, reaching a peak of 64 per cent in September 1998. Economic growth contracted to −13.1 per cent in 1998, while unemployment persistently increased. Moreover public debt reached US$60 billion in November 1997, which imposed severe strains on the government's budget.

Within the banking sector, the increased interest rate caused NPLs (non-performing loans) to spread and mount and this was coupled with the deterioration of ROA (return on assets) and CAR (capital adequacy ratio).

Most national banks incurred losses in a short period of time, since they did not hedge their debt in foreign currency. Small and undercapitalized banks were weakened further. Only a few banks were able to survive without the help of Bank Indonesia, and among them was Bank Muamalat Indonesia, the only Islamic bank.

To restructure and recapitalize the banking system, the government issued debt instruments amounting to Rp. 665 trillion, with Rp. 433 trillion issued to the public, and the other Rp. 233 trillion given in the form of government debt securities (*Surat Utang Pemerintah* or SUP) to Bank Indonesia.

The financial crisis had also triggered a political crisis and social unrest which then forced President Soeharto to resign in May 1998. As part of structural reforms, a new Banking Act no. 10/1998 came into force in 1998 to support the banking restructuring, while new Bank Indonesia Act no. 23/1999 was brought out to support a more independent monetary policy with an increased focus on price stability.

With these concerted efforts, inflation dropped to 1.92 per cent and economic growth started to recover to 0.3 per cent in 1999. Nevertheless, Indonesia (as well as Thailand) suffered the most during this crisis, with fiscal cost reaching 56.8 per cent of GDP, while output loss reached 67.9 per cent of GDP (Laeven and Valencia 2008). It was not until 2004 that Indonesia's economy grew above 5.0 per cent again. A summary of

FIGURE 3.4
SBI Rate and Inflation during Financial Crisis

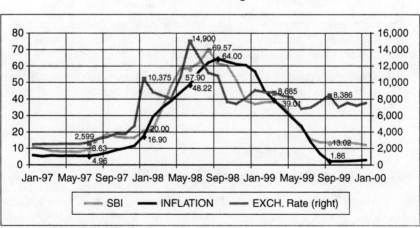

Source: Compiled and drawn from several Bank Indonesia and Badan Pusat Statistik data and publications (1997–2000).

monetary and other related policies in this financial crisis period can be read in Table 3.8.

TABLE 3.8
Monetary Policies in Financial Crisis Period of 1997–99

Monetary authority under Monetary Board chaired by minister for finance with governor of Bank Indonesia and minister for economy as members; fiscal authority under minister for finance.

Economic Conditions	Monetary Policies

• Overheated economy
• Structural weaknesses
• Unhedged foreign debt
• Contagion effect started from currency crisis in Thailand in July 1997
• Banking distress; NPL increased; margin, ROA and CAR became negative
• Bank runs in November 1997
	• Tight money policy
	• Closing of 16 hopeless ailing banks on 1 November 1997 (before implementing blanket guarantee)
	• LoI with IMF; SAP in 15 January 1998:
	   – Blanket guarantee in January 1998
	   – Bailout other ailing banks; established IBRA
	   – Aggressively raising interest rates
	• EFF I 05/1998; EFF II 01/2000
	• Banking Act 1998; Central Bank Act 1999

Economic Conditions	Fiscal Policies
• Budget deficits • Public Debt US$60 billion	• Cutting back government spending • Structural reforms
Economic Condition	Foreign Exchange Policies
• Speculation/rush in foreign exchange market caused rupiah to fall since August 1997	• Widen intervention band in July 1997 • Floating exchange rate regime in August 1997

Results: Inflation dropped to 1.92 per cent, growth improved to positive 0.3 per cent in 1999; inflation increased to 9.35 per cent, growth improved further to 4.9 per cent in 2000.

Source: Compiled from several Bank Indonesia and other publications (1997–2000).

Post-Southeast Asian Financial Crisis (2000–04)

The shocking financial crisis of 1997–98 raised the issue of central bank independence. This came up as the central bank was unable to undertake objective policies, and its policies were viewed to be contaminated with the political interests of the government. Therefore, central bank independence was included as one of fifty points agreed by the government and IMF in the Letter of Intent signed in January 1998. As a result, a new Central Bank Act no. 23/1999 entered into force in 1999, when Bank Indonesia became an independent (yet transparent and accountable) central bank, which focused on a single objective, which was to achieve and maintain rupiah stability. Since its independence, Bank Indonesia has had three primary tasks. Its first task is to set and implement monetary policy. Its second is to regulate and administer banks. And its third task is to regulate and maintain a sound and effective payment system.

Its independence as a central bank enabled Bank Indonesia to act as a monetary authority to formulate and conduct monetary policies independently without intervention from other parties, including the government. Bank Indonesia would also steer clear of intervention from other parties.

Since the exchange rate and capital movement systems are an integral part of the monetary policy, a new act on foreign exchange and exchange rate system was also introduced in May 1999. Act no. 24/1999 basically reaffirmed the maintenance of the free foreign exchange rate system that had been in place since 1998, and the floating exchange rate system in place since August 1997. Under this regime, Bank Indonesia could intervene in the foreign exchange market to smooth the movements of the exchange rate. Under the new Bank Indonesia Act, the monetary policy would focus on the single objective of price stability. Consequently, previous monetary policies based on a quantity targeting framework gradually shifted to a price targeting framework. In the early period, the target of inflation was achieved through an intermediate targeting of money supply, while the control of money supply was achieved through an operational targeting of base money which was determined by the government and IMF. Within the price targeting framework, the target of monetary policy would directly target the rate of inflation as determined by the government and Bank Indonesia. This transition towards the implementation of full-fledged inflation targeting used to be known as soft or light inflation targeting.

This period of economic restructuring and recovery started with optimism in early 2000. However, monetary conditions were still dominated by pressure from inflation and vulnerable exchange rates. Inflation increased again to 9.35 per cent in 2000 and the SBI rate increased slightly to 14.5 per cent, while the rupiah's exchange rate reached Rp. 8,400/US$1 on average. Moreover, unemployment had been increasing persistently and reached 6.08 per cent in 2000.

The monetary policy adopted in this period still focused on controlling excess money supply by tightening the monetary policy and keeping interest rate high. The intermediation function of the banking system had not improved much, with the loan to deposit ratio (LDR) at only 45.8 per cent, so that OMO with SBI and rupiah intervention were two main monetary instruments actively used to absorb excess liquidity, which became a burden to Bank Indonesia.

At the end of 2004, inflation was controlled at 6.4 per cent, economic growth had increased to new level of 5.1 per cent, the interest rate was lowered to 7.43 per cent, while the exchange rate stood at the rate of Rp. 8,940/US$1, and finally, unemployment persistently increased to 9.86 per cent. In the banking sector, the LDR improved slightly to 50 per cent, with NPL (non-performing loan) of only 1.7 per cent. A summary of monetary and other related policies in this economic restructuring and recovery period can be read in Table 3.9.

TABLE 3.9
Monetary Policies in Economic Recovery Period of 2000–04

Bank Indonesia as an independent monetary authority, with the single objective of achieving and maintaining the stability of the rupiah.

Economic Conditions	Monetary Policies
• Recovery optimism • New independent central bank • Inflation pressure; high interest rate • Banking restructuring (BLBI)	• Tight money policy; high interest rate – OMO with SBI – Rupiah intervention • Accommodative monetary policy in 2003 • Tight monetary policy in 2004
Economic Conditions	Fiscal Policies
• Foreign debt burden • Fiscal deficits	• Debt rescheduling in April 2000 (Paris Club II) • Fiscal sustainability
Economic Condition	Foreign Exchange Policies
• Vulnerable exchange rate	• Foreign exchange intervention • Sterilization of government foreign income

Results in 2004: Inflation dropped to 6.4 per cent, growth improved to 5.1 per cent; SBI rate lowered to 7.43 per cent; exchange rate stabilized at Rp. 8,900/US$1; unemployment increased to 9.86 per cent.

Source: Compiled from several Bank Indonesia and other publications (2000–04).

Under An Inflation Targeting Framework (2005–present)

The new Bank Indonesia Act of 1999 made a fundamental change in the conduct of monetary policy from multiple objectives using quantity targeting to single objective using price targeting, known as an inflation targeting framework. To further refine the efficacy of monetary management, the Bank Indonesia Act of 1999 was amended in 2004. Initially, Bank Indonesia implemented light ITF. Later, however, in July 2005, it implemented a full-fledged ITF, as a response to the aftermath of structural changes where interest rates started to take on an increasingly important role (compared with money supply) in influencing inflation.

ITF is a monetary policy framework marked by announcements to the public on the inflation target to be achieved over the next several periods. In explicit terms, a low and stable inflation is described as the overriding objective of this monetary policy. Under this framework, Bank Indonesia explicitly announces the government set inflation target to the public and monetary policy is geared towards achievement of this target. For the inflation target to be achieved, the monetary policy is implemented with a forward-looking approach, meaning that any change in the monetary policy stance is undertaken after evaluating whether future developments in inflation are on track to attain the established inflation target. Under this framework, monetary policy also operates with transparency and accountability to the public.

At the operational level, the monetary policy stance is reflected in the setting of the policy rate (BI Rate) with the expectation of influencing money market rates and, in turn, the deposit and lending rates in the banking system. Changes in these rates will ultimately influence output and inflation. There are four main characteristics of ITF. The first is an inflation target as one of its overriding objectives and a key contributor to monetary policy for improving the living standards of the population. The inflation target is determined with regard to the trade-off with economic growth. The second is an anticipative or forward-looking monetary policy in which the current policy is guided towards achieving an inflation target determined for a future period. The third is constrained discretion in determining the monetary policy stance. The central bank must consider the forecasts of inflation, economic growth, and various other variables, as well as take government economic policy within the framework of monetary policy coordination with other macro policies into account. The final and fourth characteristic is compliance with principles of good governance, such as clarity of objectives, consistency, transparency, and accountability.

The selection of the ITF monetary policy framework is based on the following considerations: compliance with sound monetary policy principles; consistency with the mandate of Act no. 23/1999 concerning Bank Indonesia as amended by Act no. 3/2004; awareness of the growing difficulty of controlling monetary aggregates; and finally the success stories of the countries in curbing inflation without increasing output volatility. This framework could strengthen Bank Indonesia's credibility as an institution responsible for inflation control through its commitment to achieve the target.

The adoption of the ITF does not mean that the central bank pays attention to only inflation and no longer takes economic growth and overall policy and economic trends into consideration. Moreover, ITF does not have a rigid rule, but is a comprehensive framework for formulating and implementing monetary policy. Thus, the focus on inflation targeting does not mean guiding the economy towards a condition of zero inflation.

A low and stable inflation rate in the long term will in fact provide support for sustainable growth. The reason is that inflation has a positive correlation with fluctuations in the inflation rate. When inflation rises, so does the rate of fluctuation and the public no longer has any assurance regarding the existing level of inflation. As a result, long-term interest rates will rise because of the high-risk premium brought on by the inflation. Business planning will become more difficult and investors will lose interest. Faced with uncertainty over inflation, investors will prefer short-term financial assets over long-term real investment. For these reasons, monetary authorities frequently put forward the argument that an anti-inflation policy is in fact a pro-growth policy. Monetary instruments used include: open market operations (OMO) with SBI, standing facilities, intervention on the foreign exchange market, establishment of the minimum statutory reserve requirement, and moral suasion.

At the beginning of the ITF implementation (2005), economic conditions were viewed with optimism because of signs of economic recovery. However, in the second semester of 2005, the situation changed quickly as external factors and global imbalances put pressure on the domestic economy, especially the drastic increase in price of oil to US$70 per barrel (the highest in twenty-five years), and the rise of Fed fund rate (and subsequent U.S. dollar appreciation), which caused Current Account pressure, rupiah depreciation, and high inflation. The upward adjustments of domestic oil prices (in March by 29 per cent and in October by 126 per cent) were in tandem with the depreciation of rupiah to almost

Rp. 12,000 in August 2005 leading to an accelerating inflation of 17.1 per cent in 2005 (see INFLATION2 in Figure 3.5).

FIGURE 3.5
SBI Rate, Inflation, and Exchange Rate since ITF, 2005–07

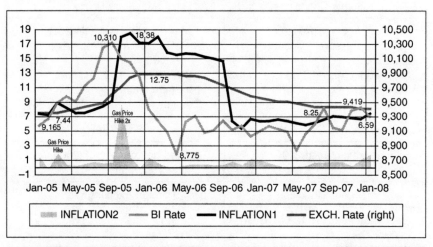

Source: Compiled and drawn from several Bank Indonesia and Badan Pusat Statistik data and publications (2005–07).

Bank Indonesia responded with a tight monetary policy by aggressively raising the BI rate up to 12.75 per cent in December 2005. It started to lower it gradually only after May 2006. Moreover, to absorb the excess liquidity, Bank Indonesia also raised the statutory reserve requirements of banks. In the foreign exchange market, Bank Indonesia responded with foreign exchange intervention so as to ease further pressure on the rupiah. Finally, inflation was controlled in 2006 and 2007 and the BI rate was gradually lowered to 8.0 per cent in December 2007. In the meantime, economic growth improved to 6.3 per cent in 2007, and unemployment decreased slightly to 10.01 per cent in 2007 (see Table 3.10).

In order to improve the operational framework of the ITF monetary policy, on 9 June 2008, Bank Indonesia replaced the operational target from a weighted average of the one-month SBI rate to the overnight (O/N) interbank rate. With this change, the implementation of all monetary instruments was directed towards optimums financial liquidity management so that the O/N interbank rate could move inside the narrower corridor of

TABLE 3.10
Monetary Policies since ITF and before Global Financial Crisis, 2005–07

Bank Indonesia as an independent monetary authority, with the single objective of achieving and maintaining the stability of the rupiah by taking into account the general economic policies of the government.

Economic Conditions	Monetary Policies

• Continued optimism in 2005
• External pressures; global imbalances
• Oil price increased; Fed fund rate increased
• High inflation of 17.1% in 2005
	• Tight monetary policy in 2005
	  – Raised BI rate to 12.75% in 12/2005
	  – Raised statutory reserve requirements
	• Ease monetary policy in 2006–07

Economic Condition	Fiscal Policy
• Budget pressures in 2005	• Raised gas price in 03/2005 (29%) and in 10/2005 (126%)
Economic Condition	Foreign Exchange Policy
• Depreciation to Rp. 12,000/US$1 in 08/2005	• Foreign exchange intervention in 2005

Results in 2007: Inflation dropped to 6.59 per cent; growth improved to 6.3 per cent; SBI rate lowered to 8.0 per cent; stable exchange rate at Rp. 9,419/US$1; unemployment increased to 10.01 per cent.

Source: Compiled from several Bank Indonesia and other publications (2005–07).

the BI rate (policy rate). This change, which adopts the ITF, was in line with international best practices, as most countries, including Canada, New Zealand, Australia, Korea, and Malaysia, use the interbank O/N rate as their operational target. Nevertheless, there were a few countries including the United Kingdom and Thailand that have not used the interbank O/N rate as their operational target.

The implementation of the ITF monetary policy has further improved since March 2010 (and became fully effective starting June 2010) when the weekly SBI/SBIS regular auction was changed to a monthly SBI/SBIS regular auction.[6] Meanwhile the tenure of instruments that are to be auctioned will focus on three-month and sixth-month (rather than one-month) SBI/SBIS. The purpose of this change is to encourage banks to manage their liquidity over a longer period of time, so that the interbank money market will become more active, and monetary operations will become more effective. Moreover, it will improve financial deepening.

MONETARY POLICY DURING THE GLOBAL FINANCIAL CRISIS

In July 2007, the global economy witnessed a financial crisis precipitated by the subprime mortgage crisis in the U.S. banking system. The situation worsened in 2008, with oil price soaring up to more than US$100 per barrel, which further escalated to $147 per barrel by July 2008 but fell soon after that. Moreover, in the second half of 2008, the prices of most commodities fell drastically because of market expectations of diminished demand during the global recession. The crisis reached a new level of global banking systemic contagion in September 2008. It contributed to the failure of key businesses and substantial financial commitments incurred by governments, the decline in consumer wealth, and a significant decline in economic activity.

The crisis was first transmitted to Indonesia through the capital market. The composite stock index or Indeks Harga Saham Gabungan (IHSG) and Jakarta Islamic Index (JII) started to slide rapidly in March 2008 from their highest index in December 2007 and February 2008, when they were around 2,700 and 500 respectively. Both stock market indices (IHSG and JII) reached their lowest level of 1,241.54, and 194.33 respectively in November 2008. The value of IHSG and JII thus decreased by 55 per cent and 61 per cent, respectively. The fall in these indices was due to the reaction of foreign investors who chose to exit from the Indonesian stock market. The ownership share of foreign investors decreased significantly from 66.3 per cent in December 2007 to 63.2 per cent in August 2008, which was equal to a decrease of Rp. 123 trillion. This movement of IHSG and JII can be seen in Figure 3.6. Capital outflows and flight to quality[7] had caused persistent pressure on the rupiah since September 2008. About ten months later, in October 2008, the rupiah was brought down to Rp. 10,995 to the U.S. dollar and continued to weaken further to Rp. 12,151 in November 2008. To prevent further negative sentiment, Bank Indonesia entered into a Bilateral Currency Swap Arrangement (BCSA) with the Central Bank of China

In May 2008, the crisis started to have a negative impact on Indonesia's economy which was intensified after the Lehman Brothers' bankruptcy in September 2008. This bankruptcy caused the banking system to face tight liquidity problems, not because of scarce liquidity (since the loan to deposit

FIGURE 3.6
Stock Market Indices Movement during Global Financial Crisis

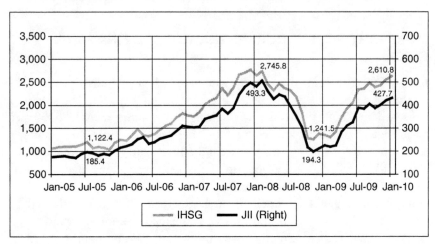

Source: Compiled and drawn from several BAPEPAM data and publications (2005–10).

ratio or LDR of the banking system was less than 80 per cent, and only 72.8 per cent in May 2008), but rather because of psychological factors and uneven interbank liquidity. SBIs held by banks started to deplete from Rp. 211.18 trillion in April 2008 to Rp. 116.56 trillion in September 2008, a decrease of Rp. 94.62 trillion or 44.8 per cent (see Figure 3.9). However, the capital adequacy ratio of the banking system was a strong 16 per cent in August 2008, which was far above the minimum CAR of 8 per cent. Moreover, world oil price jumped to US$130 per barrel in September 2008. Monthly inflation (month-on-month) jumped to 2.42 per cent in June 2008, because of the upward adjustment to domestic oil prices in May 2008. Bank Indonesia responded to this pessimistic economic outlook by implementing a tight money policy and by gradually raising the BI rate, starting in May 2008. To improve liquidity, Bank Indonesia eased the statutory reserve requirement, eased the short-term funding facilities (Fasilitas Pendanaan Jangka Pendek or FPJP), as well as lowered the capital adequacy ratio (CAR) of banks. Moreover, to lessen the volatility of the rupiah exchange rate, Bank Indonesia implemented a stabilization policy in the foreign exchange market.

To maintain confidence in the banking system, the government through Lembaga Penjamin Simpanan (LPS, a Deposits Insurance Institution), increased the minimum deposit guarantee twenty times from Rp. 100

million to Rp. 2 billion. In relation to creating a financial safety net, the government established the Komite Stabilitas Sistem Keuangan or KSSK (Financial System Stability Committee), with the Ministry of Finance and Governor of Bank Indonesia as members, and also issued and prepared its necessary regulations.

Worsening financial conditions forced Bank Indonesia to raise the BI rate continuously and gradually, letting it reach 9.5 per cent in October 2008, and keeping it unchanged in November 2008. This policy was intended to dampen the expectation of accelerated inflation. Bank Indonesia consistently implemented calculated and prudent monetary policy strategies to maintain financial stability without sacrificing the economic development momentum, and to achieve the mid-term inflation target.

Many critics regard Bank Indonesia's BI policy in raising the BI rate during the months of October and November as an overly prudent policy since other central banks had started to lower their policy rates from October 2008. In the meantime however, monthly inflation (year-on-year) started to decrease from 12.4 per cent in September 2008 to 12.0 per cent in October 2008 (see INFLATION1 in Figure 3.7).

Finally BI started aggressively to lower BI rate in December 2008. This policy signalled an optimistic economic outlook for the market. The

FIGURE 3.7
SBI Rate, Inflation, and Exchange Rate during Global Financial Crisis, 2007–09

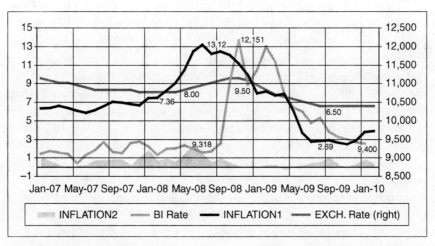

Source: Compiled and drawn from several Bank Indonesia and Badan Pusat Statistik data and publications (2007–10).

CPI (consumer price index) inflation reached 11.06 per cent, while core inflation attained 8.29 per cent in 2008. Since then, inflationary pressure has decreased and Bank Indonesia has continued to lower the BI rate which reached 6.5 per cent in August 2009, and was kept constant until at least early 2010, when this chapter was written.

Although the crisis was able to be contained, there was one small troubled bank that had to be bailed out in November 2008 in order to prevent it from having a systemic risk. This policy also invited many critics who saw it as an overly prudent and unnecessary policy that led to political questioning. Nevertheless, the results in 2009 were surprisingly positive. The banking system escaped systemic risk and economic growth turned out to be better than expected, hitting 4.4–4.5 per cent. Furthermore, inflation rate was brought down to a much lower level of only 2.78 per cent, instead of the previously predicted 5.0–7.0 per cent. Nevertheless, unemployment increased slightly to 9 per cent. Indonesia was among a few countries (such as Brazil, India, and China) that registered positive economic growth. A summary of monetary and other related policies during the global financial crisis can be read in Table 3.11.

THE INTRODUCTION OF ISLAMIC MONETARY POLICY

The stipulation of the new Bank Indonesia Act of 1999 provides room for Bank Indonesia to act as a monetary authority in conducting its monetary operation on conventional as well as *shariah* principles.

The basic concept of monetary management in Islam is to achieve stability in money demand and to direct money demand towards important productive activities needed by the society. Chapra (1985) stated that the demand for money in an Islamic economy would arise from transactions and precautionary needs that are largely determined by the level of income and its distribution. Islamic monetary policy minimizies the speculative demand for money, so that the demand for money would essentially be stable. Consequently, monetary instruments that lead to instability and misallocation of resources (funds) would be left out (Karim 2007).

Chapra (1985, p. 1) mentioned that the main objectives of Islamic monetary policy include: full employment and economic growth, socio-economic justice and equitable distribution of income and wealth, and stability in the value of money. Moreover, Ascarya (2009*b*) argues that the monetary policy in Islam is a response to activities in the real sector and is a policy that can speed up the velocity of money and discourage the hoarding of money. Therefore, there is no parallel dichotomy between the

TABLE 3.11
Monetary Policies during Global Financial Crisis, 2007–09

Bank Indonesia as an independent monetary authority, with the single objective of achieving and maintaining the stability of the rupiah by taking into account the general economic policies of the government.

Economic Conditions	Monetary Policies
• Global Financial Crisis started in 07/2007. • Stock market index started to slide since 03/2008; oil price continued to increase drastically and reached $147 in 07/2008. • Global banking systemic contagion worsened in 09/2008; tight liquidity problems in the banking system. • Inflation pressure lessened in 09/2008; many central banks started to lower their policy rates.	• Tight monetary policy; gradual BI rate increase since 05/2008 • Eased statutory reserve requirement and FPJP; lowered Capital Adequacy Ratio • BI rate increased 25 BP in 10/2008 and kept unchanged in 11/2008. • Bailed out one troubled small bank in 11/2008 • Eased monetary policy aggressively from 12/2008 until early 2010
Economic Condition	**Fiscal Policies**
• Fiscal sustainability pressure since early 2008; increased cost of subsidies	• Budget tightening by 10% in 2008; decreased subsidy; raised gas price in 05/2008 • Increased minimum deposit insurance twenty times • Established KSSK and necessary regulations and lowered it again in 12/2008 • BCSA with BOC; BSA with Japan • Lowered gas price in 12/2008
Economic Conditions	**Foreign Exchange Policy**
• Capital outflows since early 2008 • Depreciation to Rp. 12,150/US$1 in 11/2008; increased volatility	• Stabilization policy in FX market

Results in 2009: Inflation dropped to 2.78 per cent; growth reached 4.4 per cent; SBI rate lowered to 6.5 per cent; strong exchange rate at Rp. 9,300/US$1; unemployment decreased to 9.0 per cent.

Source: Compiled from several Bank Indonesia and other publications (2005–09).

monetary and real sectors, since monetary sector always links and follows the real sector as the characteristic of Islamic finance is based on the real sector. There is no chance for market actors to profit from transactions that have no value added to the economy.

Under the dual monetary system, the design of monetary instruments should satisfy two main principles, namely consistency and equality (Astiyah et al. 2006). Consistency between instruments is necessary to align the monetary policy in the Islamic money market or the conventional money market with the policy stance of the monetary authority. Therefore, there would not be any confusion in market perceptions of monetary policy signals that could decrease the efficacy of the monetary policy. Equality in monetary instruments would provide fair accessibility and pricing to both actors in both markets. Moreover, fair treatment would eliminate arbitrage between the two markets if there is no clear barrier between the two.

With the new mandate, giving it dual monetary authority, Bank Indonesia started to introduce several Islamic monetary instruments comparable to conventional monetary instruments, which comply with *shariah* laws in 2000. These are statutory reserve requirements for Islamic banks, a *shariah* interbank money market, with *Sertifikat Investasi Mudharabah Antarbank* or SIMA (Interbank *Mudharabah* Investment Certificate), issued by Islamic banks as its instrument, and *shariah* open market operations with *Sertifikat Wadi'ah Bank Indonesia* or SWBI (Bank Indonesia *Wadi'ah* Certificate). As the last resort lender of Islamic banks experiencing a mismatch, Bank Indonesia in 2003 introduced standing facilities for Islamic banks known as *Fasilitas Pembiayaan Jangka Pendek Syariah* or FPJPS.

The statutory reserve requirements for Islamic banks is similar to statutory reserve requirements for a conventional bank, which serves as a direct instrument. SIMA in the Islamic money market is similar to interbank call money in a conventional money market. Conventional banks can enter the Islamic money market, but Islamic banks cannot enter the conventional money market.

The SWBI is not similar to the SBI in conventional OMO. The SWBI was first introduced by BI as a facility for Islamic banks to place their excess liquidity. The trading of SWBI was not conducted through a usual auction, but through a window so that it was similar to central bank deposit facilities. The SWBI could be considered a passive monetary instrument, as opposed to the SBI, which is considered an active monetary instrument. Transactions in SWBI used a *wadi'ah* contract, which is essentially the safekeeping of one's deposits, with a tenure of seven days, fourteen days, or one month. For these deposits, Bank Indonesia would reward an Islamic bank with a bonus (in money), which was determined at the time of maturity. As a proper monetary instrument under the dual monetary system, SWBI had two drawbacks. The first was that the SWBI was a passive monetary instrument, thus, BI could not use it as actively as an OMO instrument. The second was that SWBI lacked equality characteristics with its counterpart, the SBI, since the return on SWBI as a *wadi'ah* or safekeeping contract was much lower than the return on SBI.

As the share of Islamic finance (especially Islamic banking) continued to increase, the need to conduct an active monetary policy using a proper active monetary instrument became more important. Therefore, in April 2008, BI replaced SWBI with the SBIS (*SBI Shariah* or Bank Indonesia Shariah Certificate). The SBIS as an Islamic monetary instrument is a comparable counterpart to the SBI as a conventional monetary instrument. The SBIS is an active monetary instrument using a *ju'alah* contract, which is a promise or commitment (*iltizam*) to award certain returns ('*iwadh* or *ju'l*) for an attainment (*natijah*) determined for a piece of work. The reward on the SBIS is benchmarked to the return on SBI, so that both consistency and equality requirements are satisfied. The rates for the SBI and SWBI/SBIS can be seen in Figure 3.8.

With the introduction of SBIS, dual monetary management where each system (conventional and Islamic) is equipped with comparable instruments can be conducted fully. However, the equalization of SBIS and SBI could result in a kind of Islamic monetary management that deviates from its real

FIGURE 3.8
Returns on SBI and SWBI/SBIS

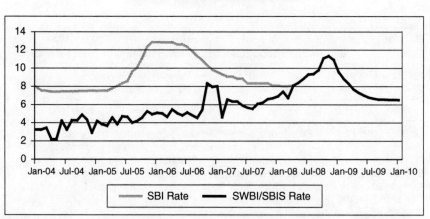

Source: Compiled and drawn from several Bank Indonesia data and publications (2003–10).

essence and objectives since the return on SBIS does not reflect the real return of the economy. Moreover, the monetary sector and real sector will be decoupled since they each have their own prices and commodities. Thus, further and continuous studies should be conducted to find a proper dual monetary policy benchmark and instruments that satisfy all requirements and can also achieve the intended objectives.

Current Islamic monetary instruments are not as complete as conventional monetary instruments yet. For example, Islamic monetary operations do not have any instruments for an irregular monetary policy (fine-tuning operation instruments) or an instrument for deposit facilities. As Islamic financing and banking grows, Islamic monetary instruments must evolve accordingly. However, the development of Islamic monetary instruments should not have to mirror conventional monetary instruments. The distinct Islamic characteristics should always be embedded and intact in every Islamic monetary instrument. In summary, the current dual monetary policy and instruments can be seen in Table 3.12.

TABLE 3.12
Current Dual Monetary Policies and Instruments

Purpose	Instrument	Conventional	Islamic
Fractional Reserve Banking	Statutory Reserve Requirement	Reserve Requirement	
Lender of Last Resort	Standing Facilities	– FPJP – FLI – Repo of SBI	– FPJPS – FLIS – Repo of SBIS
	Deposit Facilities	FASBI (ON – 14-day)	N/A
Regular Monetary Policy	Open Market Operations (OMO)	– SBI (1 & 3 month)	– SBIS (1 month)
Irregular Monetary Policy	Fine Tune (FT) Operation	– FT Expansion – FT Contraction	– N/A – N/A
FOREX Stabilization	Intervention	FOREX Intervention	

Notes: FPJP: Fasilitas Pendanaan Jangka Pendek (short-term credit facilities); FPJPS: Fasilitas Pembiayaan Jangka Pendek Syariah (short-term shariah financing facilities); FLI: Fasilitas Likuiditas Intra-hari (intraday liquidity facilities); FLIS: Fasilitas Likuiditas Intra-hari Syariah (intraday shariah liquidity facilities); ON: Overnight; SBI: Sertifikat Bank Indonesia (Bank Indonesia certificate); SBIS: Sertifikat Bank Indonesia Syariah (Bank Indonesia Shariah Certificate); FASBI: Fasilitas Simpanan Bank Indonesia (Bank Indonesia's deposit facilities); FOREX: Foreign Exchange; N/A: Not Available.

Source: Author's own compilation.

FIGURE 3.9
Outstanding SBI, SBI Rate, Deposit Rate, and Inflation Rate

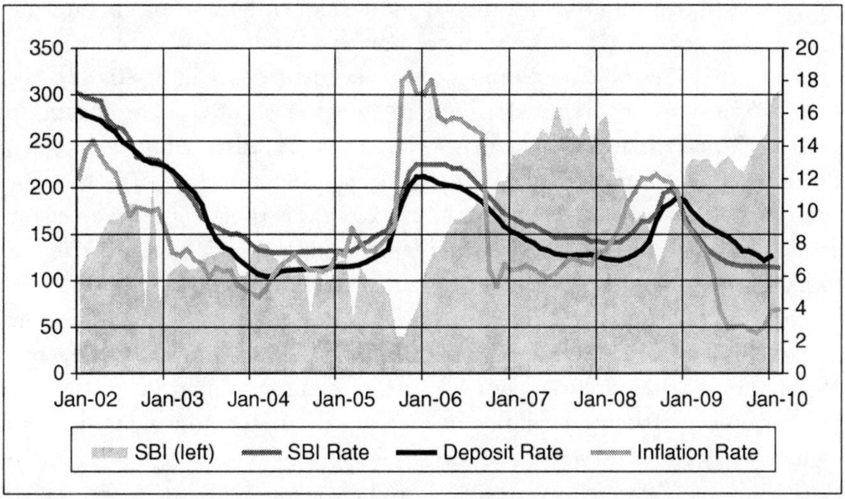

Source: Compiled and drawn from several Bank Indonesia data and publications (2002–10).

THE FUTURE OF MONETARY POLICY IN INDONESIA

Financial crises have occurred one after another since the demise of gold standard regime in 1915. The crises started with a depression in Japan (1920), followed by hyperinflation in Germany (1922–23) and culminated in the Great Depression of 1929–30 (Davies and Davies 1996). Subsequently, a financial crisis hit Austria (banking crisis in 1931), France (hyperinflation in 1944–46), Hungary (hyperinflation and monetary crisis in 1944–46), German (hyperinflation in 1945–46), and Nigeria (banking crisis in 1945–55).

The crises subsided in the period under Bretton Woods Agreement from 1950–72, under which there was a strict fixed exchange rate international monetary arrangement whereby the U.S. dollar was the world currency pegged to gold (one troy ounce of gold was equal to US$35) while other currencies were pegged to U.S. dollar, with the guarantee that the U.S. dollar was exchangeable to gold any time. That was the golden age. No other eras have come even close to the economic performance during the Bretton Woods era.

However, the Bretton Woods agreement finally collapsed in 1971, when the United States unilaterally terminated the convertibility of the U.S. dollar to gold. The United States enjoyed huge *seigniorage* from printing fiat currency without any gold backup. Other countries finally followed the U.S. example in using fiat money and adopted different exchange systems, including the floating exchange rate system. Following the collapse of Bretton Woods Agreement, financial crises resurfaced more frequently, starting in England (banking crisis in 1973–74) and then moving to industrial countries (deep recession in 1978–80), developing countries (debt crises in 1980–82), the United States and the United Kingdom (great crash of stock exchange in 1987), Mexico (financial crisis in 1994), as well as Asian countries, Russia, Brazil, and Argentina (financial crisis and hyperinflation in 1997–99). The latest global financial crisis of September 2008 was triggered by the August 2007 subprime mortgage crisis in the United States which has been referred to as the worst financial crisis since the Great Depression of the 1930s.

Since the collapse of Bretton Woods Agreement there have been more than 96 financial crises and 176 monetary crises (Caprio and Klingebiel 1996). These crises occurred not because of cyclical or managerial failures, but because of structural failures in various countries under very different regulatory systems, as well as at different stages of economic development (Lietaer et al. 2009). However, the conventional solutions that were taken have only dealt with the symptoms rather than the root of the problem. A new database of financial crises in 1970–2007 can be found in Laeven and Valencia (2008), which covers 395 episodes of financial crises (banking crises, currency crises and sovereign debt crises), including 42 twin crises and 10 triple crises (see Figure 3.10).

It seems that we have not yet learnt our lessons on how to eradicate and/or control financial crisis and inflation, which is a subject that is so much discussed, but so little understood (Hazlitt 1978). Therefore, repeated

FIGURE 3.10
Frequency of World Financial Crises

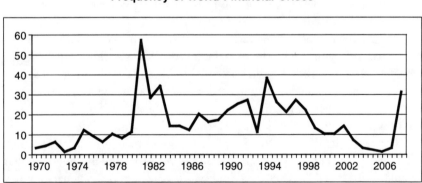

Source: Compiled and drawn from Laeven and Valencia (2008) and other 2008–09 articles.

financial crises and unresolved problems of inflation have triggered paradigm shifts and posed new challenges on how to conduct an effective monetary policy in the future.

After the eruption of the current global financial crisis, opinions on restructuring the current global financial and monetary system became widespread. Among the proposed options is a return to the Bretton Woods Agreement, suggested by the European Union in October 2008, and to be called Bretton Woods II. Options for alternative financial and monetary systems can be derived from different economic views, such as New Keynesian, Austrian, Lietaer, Binary economics, and Islamic economics. The proposed solutions from non-mainstream paradigms can be seen in Table 3.13.

Mainstream economic paradigms have been criticized on the ground that their fundamental flaws have resulted in repeated financial crises, with shorter time lags, larger magnitude, and wider destruction. The most recent global recession was the largest financial crisis since the Great Depression of the 1930s. The remedies taken have not touched the root structural causes, but have only touched the symptoms — surfaces or the tip of the iceberg. Among the root structural causes mentioned by most non-mainstream economic paradigms are: an international money system based on multiple fiat currencies dominated by the U.S. dollar; banking systems based on fractional reserves; speculative behaviour of economic actors; and the existence of business cycles or credit cycles (Hazlitt 1978; El-Diwany 2002; Rab 2002; Shakespeare and Challen 2002; Lietaer et al. 2002, 2009; Meera 2004; Siregar 2009; and Ascarya 2009a).

Given the various views on the shortcomings of the current economic system and proposed solutions there are some convergences on the structural problems of the current economic system (most notably, money system and speculation) and their alternative solutions. All views tend to agree on the use of gold as a resolution to the current money system and a move towards a stable and just global monetary system. Every school of economics also agrees to limit or prohibit speculative behaviours or products. Moreover, economists of different paradigms also agree to dampen or remove artificial business cycles.

The question now is what are the options for a future monetary policy in the short to medium terms. Since the revival of Islamic economics and finance in the 1970s, many countries have adopted Islamic finance to exist side by side with its current conventional finance. This trend occurs not only in countries with a majority of Muslims in the population (including

TABLE 3.13
Alternative Solutions to Various Economic Paradigms

	Mainstream Economics	Lietaer's View	Austrian Economics	Binary Economics	Islamic Economics
Riba				Interest free	Prohibition (PLS/Trade)
Money System	Bretton Woods II	*Terra* – Complementary Currency	Gold Standard	Gold/Counter-Inflationary Currency	Gold and Silver Based
Banking System			Free Banking	No money creation	100% Reserve Banking
Speculation	Limitation	Limitation	Limitation	Limitation	Prohibition
Business Cycle	Government Intervention	Automatically Dampened	Automatically Removed	Automatically Removed	Automatically Removed

Source: Author's own compilation.

Malaysia, Kuwait, Saudi Arabia, United Arab Emirates, Kingdom of Bahrain, Qatar, Brunei Darussalam, Indonesia, South Africa, Morocco, Turkey, and Pakistan), but also in countries with a majority of non-Muslims in the population such as the United Kingdom, Germany, Singapore, the United States, and Australia. Moreover, there also exists countries that adopt full-fledged Islamic economics and finance, such as Sudan and Iran.

Although most codes of conduct and subsystems of economy may be converging between mainstream economics and Islamic economics in the long run, three main pillars of the monetary system are still largely in opposition to principles of Islamic economics, namely, an interest system as opposed to a PLS (Profit/Loss Statement)/trade system, a fractional reserve banking system as opposed to a 100-per-cent reserve banking system, and a fiat money system as opposed to a gold or silver based system. These circumstances pose a challenge to economists on both sides to find an integrated system which will be productive for both economic systems. However, two things have been agreed, namely, a restriction or prohibition on speculation activities and products, as well as counter-cyclical policies which will dampen business cycles.

The above analysis shows that options for a monetary policy framework and instruments in the near future would ideally contain six characteristics. First, that a monetary policy should not induce speculative behaviour from market actors so that economic bubbles would be minimized. Second, a monetary policy should be counter-cyclical to dampen the impact of business cycles, especially in avoiding a financial crisis and recession. Third, a monetary policy should be counter-inflationary to be able to achieve sustainable price stability. Fourth, monetary policy should not be costly and not put a burden on society. Fifth, a monetary policy should be able to benefit from converging elements of the mainstream and Islamic monetary systems, as well as minimize the counter-productive effects of opposing elements of both systems. Sixth, a monetary policy should be able to capitalize on the superiority of each opposing element of the mainstream and Islamic monetary systems, whenever applied.

In a nutshell, following the introduction of the new Bank Indonesia Act no. 23/1999, Indonesia has allowed for a dual monetary system whereby a conventional monetary policy coexists with *shariah* principles. The implementation of the dual monetary policy has developed gradually in line with the development and growth of the Islamic financial system. The people in democratizing Indonesia have the freedom to conduct their financial transactions either through the conventional financial system or the Islamic financial system, or both.

NOTES

1. According to Stone (2003), full-fledged inflation targeting (FFIT) is the best known form of inflation targeting monetary policy regimes, and it requires a country (that wants to adopt it) to have a medium to high level of credibility, clearly commit to its inflation target, and institutionalize this commitment in the form of a transparent monetary framework that fosters accountability of the central bank to the target. Inflation targeting lite (ITL) is an inflation targeting monetary policy regime where the country adopting it has relatively low credibility, so that even though the country announces a broad inflation objective, it is not able to maintain inflation as its foremost policy objective.

2. M or money supply is the total amount of money available in an economy at a particular point in time. M can be defined in several ways from narrowly defined (M_0) to broadly defined (M_1, M_2, and so on). In Indonesia, M_0 is defined as base money or currency (notes and coins) in circulation; M_1 is M_0 plus demand deposits; and M_2 is M_1 plus saving deposits and time deposits.

3. The Parallel Bourse is the Indonesian Parallel Stock Exchange (IPSX). The main bourse is the Jakarta Stock Exchange (JSX) or Bursa Efek Jakarta (BEJ) in Jakarta. The Surabaya Stock Exchange (SSX) or Bursa Efek Surabaya (BES) was established in Surabaya in June 1989. In July 1995, SSX was successfully merged with IPSX. In October 2007, SSX was merged to JSX to become the Indonesian Stock Exchange (IDX) or Bursa Efek Indonesia (BEI).

4. Sterilization is a policy of a central bank to control currency appreciation from foreign capital inflows by buying foreign exchange in the domestic market, so that the (domestic) money supply would increase.

5. A blanket guarantee is a guarantee to all bank depositors that their deposits will be fully covered by government insurance.

6. SBI (Sertifikat Bank Indonesia-Bank Indonesia Certificate) is regular conventional monetary instrument, while SBIS (Sertifikat Bank Indonesia Syariah — Bank Indonesia Syarih Certificate) is a regular Islamic monetary instrument.

7. Investors' move/exchange of their assets/funds into better assets.

REFERENCES

Ascarya. *Instrumen-instrumen Pengendalian Moneter.* Buku Seri Kebanksentralan No. 3. Pusat Pendidikan dan Studi Kebanksentralan, Bank Indonesia, 2002.

———. "Lessons Learned from Repeated Financial Crises: An Islamic Economic Perspective". *Buletin Ekonomi: Moneter dan Perbankan.* Bank Indonesia 12, no. 1, July 2009*a*.

———. "Toward Optimum Synergy of Monetary Policy in Dual Financial/Banking System". *Journal of Indonesian Economy and Business*, 24, no. 1, 2009*b*.

Astiyah, S., Wahyu A. Nugroho, and Donni F. Anugrah. "Kebijakan Moneter Tepadu dalam Dual Banking System". *Working Paper*, WP/07/2006. Jakarta, Indonesia: Biro Riset Ekonomi, Direktorat Riset Ekonomi dan Kebijakan Moneter, Bank Indonesia, 2006.

Bank Indonesia. *Data Perbankan Indonesia*. Jakarta, Indonesia: Direktorat Perizinan dan Informasi Perbankan (DPIP) Bank Indonesia, several annual publications, 2000–04.

———. *Laporan Bulanan Ekonomi, Moneter dan Perbankan*. Jakarta, Indonesia: Direktorat Riset Ekonomi dan Kebijakan Moneter(DKM) Bank Indonesia, several monthly publications, 2003–05.

———. *Laporan Kebijakan Moneter*. Jakarta, Indonesia: Bank Indonesia, several quarterly publications, 2005–09.

———. *Laporan Perekonomian Indonesia*. Jakarta, Indonesia: Bank Indonesia, several annual publications, 2003–08.

———. *Laporan Tahun Pembukuan*. Jakarta, Indonesia: Bank Indonesia, several annual publications from 1953/54 to 1960/65.

———. *Laporan Tahun Pembukuan*. Jakarta, Indonesia: Bank Indonesia, several annual publications from 1969/70 to 1983/84.

———. *Laporan Tahunan*. Jakarta, Indonesia: Bank Indonesia, several annual publications from 1984/85 to 1998/99.

———. *Laporan Tahunan*. Jakarta, Indonesia: Bank Indonesia, several annual publications, 2000–08.

———. *Tinjauan Kebijakan Moneter*. Jakarta, Indonesia: Bank Indonesia, several monthly publications, 2005–09.

———. *Statistik Perbankan Indonesia*. Jakarta, Indonesia: Direktorat Perizinan dan Informasi Perbankan (DPIP) Bank Indonesia, several monthly publications, 2005–09.

Bank Negara Indonesia Unit I. *Laporan Tahun Pembukuan Bank*. Jakarta, Indonesia: Bank Negara Indonesia Unit I, several annual publications from 1966/67 to 68.

BAPEPAM-LK. *Statistik Pasar Modal*. Jakarta, Indonesia: Departemen Keuangan RI, BAPEPAM-LK, Biro Riset dan Teknologi Informasi, several weekly publications, 2005–10.

Caprio, Gerard and Daniela Klingelbiel. "Bank Insolvencies: Cross Country Experience". Policy Research Working Papers no. 1620. Washington, D.C.: World Bank, Policy and Research Department, 1996.

Chapra, M. Umer. *Towards a Just Monetary System*. Islamic Economics Series 8. United Kingdom: The Islamic Foundation, 1985.

El-Diwany, Tarek. "History of Banking: An Analysis". In *Stable and Just Monetary System: Viability of the Islamic Dinar*, edited by International Islamic University Malaysia. Kuala Lumpur, Malaysia: IIUM Research Centre, 2002.

Gray, Simon, Glenn Hoggarth, and Joanna Place. *Introduction to Monetary Operations*. Revised, 2nd ed. Handbook in Central Banking no. 10, Centre for Central Banking Studies, Bank of England, 2000.

Harahap, Sofyan S. "Ekonomi Syariah, Bretton Woods, KTT ASEM, dan AS". *Republika*, 3 November 2008, p. 6.

Hazlitt, Henry. *The Inflation Crisis, and How to Resolve it*. New York, USA: Arlington House, 1978.

Karim, Adiwarman A. *Ekonomi Makro Islami*. Jakarta, Indonesia: Rajawali Pers, 2007.

Laeven, Luc and Fabian Valencia. "Systemic Banking Crises: A New Database". IMF Working Paper WP/08/224. Washington, D.C.: International Monetary Fund, 2008.

Lietaer, Bernard and Gernot Nerb. "Terra: A Counter-cyclical Reference Currency to Stabilize the Business Cycle". In *Stable and Just Monetary System: Viability of the Islamic Dinar*, edited by International Islamic University Malaysia. Kuala Lumpur, Malaysia: IIUM Research Centre, 2002.

Lietaer, Bernard, Robert Ulanowicz, and Sally Goerner. "Options on Managing a Systemic Banking Crisis". *Sapiens-journal* 2, no. 1, March 2009.

Meera, Ahamed Kameel M. *The Theft of Nations: Returning to Gold*. Selangor Darul Ehsan, Malaysia: Pelanduk Publications, 2004.

Pohan, Aulia. *Kerangka Kebijakan Moneter dan Implementasinya di Indonesia*. Jakarta, Indonesia: Rajawali Pers, 2008.

―――. *Potret Kebijakan Moneter Indonesia*. Jakarta, Indonesia: Rajawali Pers, 2007.

Pohan, Aulia, Achjar Ilyas, C. Harinowo, Erman Munzir, and Tarmiden Sitorus. "Indonesia's Monetary Policy in the More Market Based System". Paper presented at the "SEACEN-IMF Conference", Jakarta, Indonesia, 26–28 January 1991.

Rab, Hifzur. "Problems Created by the Fiat Money, Islamic Dinar and Other Available Alternatives". In *Stable and Just Monetary System: Viability of the Islamic Dinar*, edited by International Islamic University Malaysia. Kuala Lumpur, Malaysia: IIUM Research Centre, 2002.

Rizaldy, Ryan and Diah Esti Handayani. "Bank Indonesia System of Models for Forecasting and Policy Analysis". Country Paper presented at the "SEACEN Workshop on Economic Forecasting Frameworks and Performances in SEACEN Member Economies". Seoul, Korea, 27–30 April 2004.

Siregar, Hermanto. *Kebijakan Makroekonomi Berbasis Mikro*. Bogor, Indonesia: Institut Pertanian Bogor Press, 2009.

Stone, Mark R. "Inflation Targeting Lite". IMF Working Paper No. WP/03/12, January 2003.

Warjiyo, Perry and Juda Agung, eds. *Transmission Mechanisms of Monetary Policy in Indonesia*. Jakarta, Indonesia: Bank Indonesia, 2002.

Widodo, Triono and Erwin Haryono. "Implementasi Kerangka Kerja Kebijakan Moneter Bank Indonesia menurut UU No. 23 Tahun 1999". Paper presented at the Conference "Kerangka Kebijakan Moneter Menurut UU No. 23/1999 Tentang Bank Indonesia" in Fakultas Ekonomi Universitas Diponegoro, Semarang, 15 November 2000.

4

The Financial System: Balancing Financial Stability and Economic Growth

Suhaedi and Pungky P. Wibowo

INDONESIA'S FINANCIAL SECTOR IN THE ERA OF GLOBALIZATION

As shown in Figure 4.1, commercial banks own the largest share (79.5 per cent) of the total assets of Indonesia's financial institutions. Like in many other countries, the domination of the banking industry has become a challenge in Indonesia, especially during the recent global financial crisis when the world economy was slowing down and uncertainty was rampant. The increase in banks' aversion to risk, and the lack of banks' confidence in the economy's prospect have made securing funding difficult for the private sector. This in turn has had an impact on the performance of the banking sector itself as well as the overall economic growth of the country.

During the crisis, the pressures in the global financial market (due to the lack of liquidity and disintermediation) triggered and accelerated the "deleveraging process" in financial institutions. Financial institutions sought an expansion in funding sources to compensate for the lack of interbank funding and securitization activities. Several banks sold their liquid assets

FIGURE 4.1
Asset Composition in Indonesia's Financial Institutions, December 2008

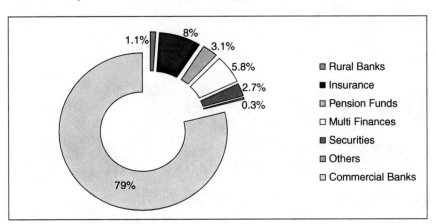

Source: Bank Indonesia (2010).

to absorb off-balance sheet losses to mitigate financial risks, as well as to strengthen their liquidity reserves.

The deleveraging process in the United States was reflected by the drastic drop in assets acquired by asset backed securities (ABS) issuers and main broker-dealers since mid-2007. The International Monetary Fund (2008) estimated that the deleveraging process would continue until the end of this decade.

Total sales of liquid assets from mid-2007 to Q3-2008 is estimated at $580 billion, with 95.0 per cent of this done by banks in North America and Europe. Consequently, there was an increase in banks' capital of about $430 billion during this period. Also, the deleveraging process mainly involved only a few banks (twenty of the biggest banks contributed to 75.0 per cent of the total sales).

The sale of liquid assets and increase in capital did not only occur in the United States and Europe, but in Asia as well. However, compared with many other countries, Indonesia's financial sector has been relatively "immune".

This phenomenon raised up two "schools of thought" on the issue of financial stability versus economic growth. One argues that this situation shows that Indonesia's financial sector is relatively robust (not affected by) against global economic shocks or even a global economic crisis. On the other hand, the other thought is that such a situation could only happen because Indonesia's financial sector is "shallow", meaning that it is conservative and highly bank dominated.

The second school of thought, therefore, also argues that it is important to boost the financial sector's performance with more advanced financial products and highly innovative financial solutions that will in turn generate higher economic growth. The concern about balancing financial stability and economic growth became more profound during the 2009 global financial crisis since there was an indication of a rising financial stability index (FSI) in Indonesia. Because of the global crisis, the FSI reached its peak at 2.43 in November 2008, a rapid increase from 1.60 in June 2008. Since then, it has been declining, but still remains above the 2.0 indicative level.[1] The FSI was still at 2.08 in February 2009. This indicated that Indonesia's financial stability was slightly unstable.

This chapter examines the issue of balancing financial stability with economic growth in Indonesia's financial system by concentrating on two important questions. The first is whether financial liberalization in Indonesia had in any way contributed to the cause of the 1997 economic crisis. In the years prior to 1997, following the government's new policy of opening up its financial sector, Indonesia experienced a period of stable and strong growth. Economic activities were booming, fuelled by both domestic and foreign funds. However, many argued that the liberalization also brought instability to the financial system, which further led to a catastrophic economic crisis in mid-1997.

The second question is whether there were "structural weaknesses" present in the financial system that could have amplified the adverse impact of liberalization. Thus, liberalization on its own would have caused less damage than what actually occurred during the 1997 economic crisis.

The answers to the two questions provide a good foundation to understanding the evolution of financial sector in Indonesia, especially how it struggles to balance stability and growth. This chapter also offers strategies on ways to maintain financial stability while continuing to promote economic growth.

FINANCIAL LIBERALIZATION AND 1997 ECONOMIC CRISIS

It is clear that over the decades between 1970 and 2000, the financial systems in several developed and developing countries moved towards liberalization.[2] Many developing countries, including Indonesia, started to make this move by allowing their central banks to lift the bank interest rate ceilings,[3] lowering compulsory reserve requirements and entry barriers,[4] and reducing government interference in credit allocation decisions.

Such liberalization has been designed for a modern central bank to provide financial stability as its core function. Financial stability can be established based on the following four main foundations: a stable macroeconomic environment; a well managed financial institution within a sound framework of prudential regulations; efficient and smooth functioning financial markets; and finally, safe and robust payment systems (Sinclair 2002).

Since the 1970s, Indonesia has experienced a period of structural adjustments through the implementation of a variety of packages of economic liberalization reforms. This has put in place all the essential elements for sustainable economic development in the long run.

In order to focus solely on the significant changes in the Indonesian banking system, we have split the discussion of financial liberalization into six distinct periods: 1967–80, 1980–83, 1983–88, 1988–91, 1991–September 1997, and September 1997–2001. The periodization is attributed to the characteristics of the banking business, which moved from a distressed financial situation that resulted from heavy regulation and limitation, to a more optimistic and "prudent" atmosphere, due to the deregulatory measures adopted by Bank Indonesia (BI).

First, we discuss the two periods of 1967–80 and 1980–83. During the first period, Indonesian monetary policy was governed by the need to restore the economy to a low inflation level through controlling credit and deposit interest rates. The high inflation that Indonesia experienced during this period was caused by the monetary expansion of liquidity credit, following the oil boom. In this case, credit control was imposed by directing credit allocation extended by state banks to various sectors and enterprises, in particular, key manufacturing industries and agriculture sectors. This policy was then followed by a reform in the capital account of the balance of payments in 1970. Evidently, liberalization was aimed primarily at attracting foreign capital, especially foreign direct investment (henceforth FDI).[5]

In the period 1980–83, a drastic decline in oil prices hit the export figures of Indonesia. The government responded by deregulating the financial sector in order to boost domestic savings to finance development and to increase the efficiency and competitiveness of the financial sector.

Bank Indonesia introduced its first deregulation to the Indonesian banking system in June 1983. The package of reforms aimed to make a greater degree of competition between state and private banks. It removed many of the subsidized lending programmes, lifted credit quotas, and allowed state banks to provide market-based interest rates on deposits. Moreover, the government decided to reduce the pre-financing export credit for small and medium enterprises, and simultaneously introduced new indirect instruments, namely open market operations through discount window facilities, such as Bank Indonesia Certificates (henceforth SBI), and Money Market Commercial Paper (henceforth SBPU). The SBI was designed to absorb banks' excess liquidity, while SBPU was designed to provide an instrument for money market operations and liquidity management for banks.[6]

The next period, between the years of 1983 and 1988, experienced a fall in oil prices, specifically in mid-1986. This second decline in oil prices forced the Indonesian Government to undertake more intensive macroeconomic adjustment measures as well as structural and financial sector reforms, which were implemented by a series of banking deregulations.

The process of financial sector liberalization was taken further by the introduction of Pakto, a policy package, in October 1988. This second deregulation is often considered to be the most important step in the liberalization of the Indonesian economy. The Indonesian banking industry was to be made much more liberal through removing restrictions on the establishment of new private banks; opening of branch offices of banks, including non-bank financial institutions and rural credit banks; permitting foreign banks to form joint ventures with local partners; and lastly, branching out to six major provincial cities outside the capital city, Jakarta.

Furthermore, to promote the mobilization of funds, the deregulation encouraged banks to introduce various attractive saving schemes. The package also included a reduction of reserve requirements for commercial banks from 15.0 per cent to 2.0 per cent of current liabilities.

As a result, the Indonesian banking industry experienced a massive growth in the number of banks and bank offices (see Figures 4.2 and 4.3), asset size (see Figure 4.4), deposits (see Figure 4.5), and the variety of their products.

The banks' successes in collecting and mobilizing funds, introducing financial innovations, and accessing foreign funds finance, were soon followed by the rapid increase in credit extensions (see Figure 4.6). In short, the structure of the economy had undergone a fundamental change. Financial deepening and diversification of banking products through innovation had resulted in a considerably larger role for the Indonesian banking industry.

FIGURE 4.2
Number of Indonesian Banks by Groups

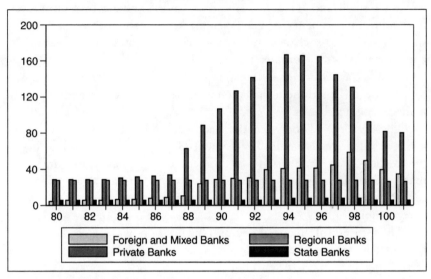

Source: Bank Indonesia (*Indonesian Financial Statistics,* various editions).

FIGURE 4.3
Number of Indonesian Bank Offices by Groups

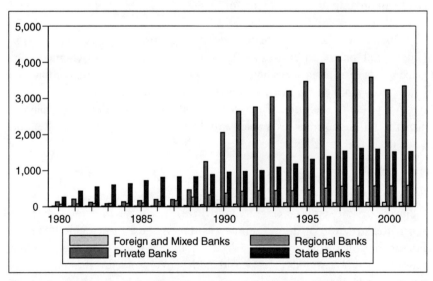

Source: Bank Indonesia (*Indonesian Financial Statistics,* various editions).

FIGURE 4.4
Total Assets of Indonesian Banks by Groups

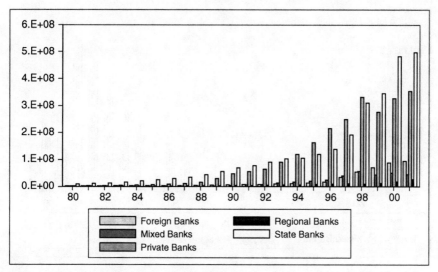

Note: E refers to 10.

Source: Bank Indonesia (*Bank Monthly Reports*, various editions).

FIGURE 4.5
Total Deposits of Indonesian Banks by Groups

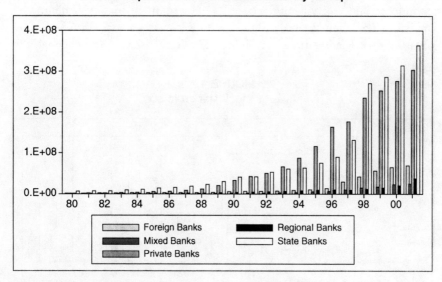

Note: E refers to 10.

Source: Bank Indonesia (*Bank Monthly Reports*, various editions).

FIGURE 4.6
Total Loans Extended to Indonesian Banks by Groups

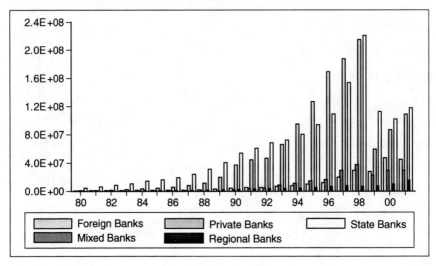

Note: E refers to 10.

Source: Bank Indonesia (*Bank Monthly Reports*, various editions).

Simultaneously, reform was introduced in the non-bank sector which energized the capital market in 1987 and 1988, in order to boost investor confidence and create a more conducive environment for investment. The capital market then showed a rapid increase in performance (as reflected by Jakarta Stock Market Index in Figure 4.7). It also started to challenge the

FIGURE 4.7
Jakarta Stock Market Index

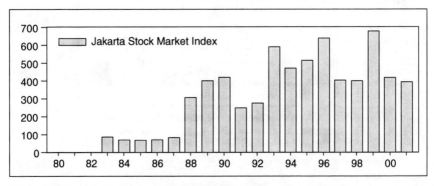

Source: Bank Indonesia (*Indonesian Financial Statistics*, various editions).

dominance of Indonesian commercial banks as the main source of external finance, especially in long-term financing.

It can be seen that a series of banking reforms in the period from January 1980 to December 1988 was aimed specifically at strengthening the banking structure in Indonesia as a consequence of financial liberalization, such as ownership and management, the capital adequacy requirement, and the legal lending limit. Moreover, the banking reforms were introduced to strengthen all groups of Indonesian banks[7] and for them to perform their role as financial intermediaries.

The years of 1988–91 can be considered the acceleration period, following the impact of extensive banks reforms in October 1988. Subsequently, from 1991–97, prudential banking principles were introduced, including capital adequacy and bank ratings (Djiwandono 1997). Moreover, the government continued to roll out a series of reform packages. These were designed to improve the effectiveness of banks as financial intermediaries and to stabilize the banking system.[8] In this period BI granted many new licences for commercial banks and new branches.

As shown in Figure 4.8, Indonesia's structural adjustments have also encouraged banks to access foreign funds. Furthermore, Indonesian commercial banks began to raise foreign borrowings actively through obtaining commercial bank lending and various portfolio financial instruments. Thus, foreign capital, especially long-term funds, was a necessary

FIGURE 4.8
Total Foreign Liabilities of Indonesian Banks by Groups

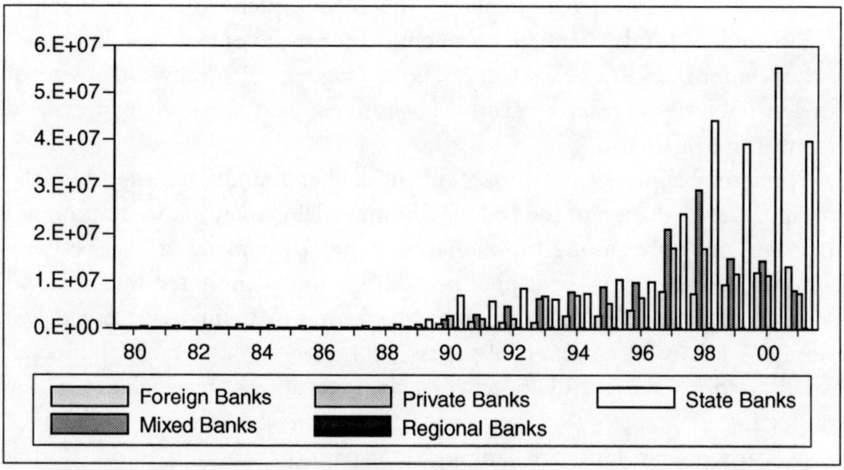

Source: Bank Indonesia (*Bank Monthly Reports*, various editions).

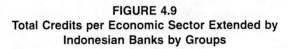

FIGURE 4.9
Total Credits per Economic Sector Extended by
Indonesian Banks by Groups

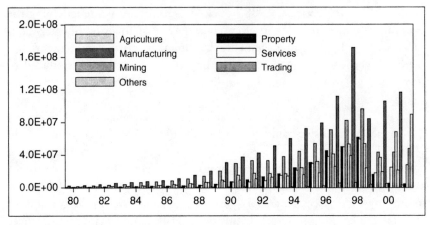

Note: E refers to 10.

Source: Bank Indonesia (*Bank Monthly Reports*, various editions).

means to financing economic activities to a degree beyond the capacity of domestic financial resources.

Most incoming funds were used to finance long-term investments such as import-intensive mega projects in the manufacturing, trading, and property sectors.[9] Figure 4.9 shows the extension of credit per economic sector by all the banking groups.

At the same time, confidence in the economy encouraged companies to tap foreign funds. Foreign borrowings by private enterprises and state-owned enterprises increased very rapidly. Figure 4.10 shows the size of foreign liabilities carried by banks, government and state enterprises, and private enterprises.

Structural adjustments, through financial liberalization, have substantially changed the landscape of the Indonesian financial markets. Competition has increased not only among Indonesian commercial banks, but also between commercial banks and the capital market. Hence, as proposed by Glen and Pinto (1994), the alternative sources of external financing have diversified through bank loans, commercial papers, rupiah bonds, and equity. However, as indicated in Figure 4.11, other financial institutions only make up a tiny proportion of financing compared with commercial banks.

Clearly, the Indonesian banking industry experienced a boom during the period 1988–97. This encouraged banks to become more aggressive in

FIGURE 4.10
Total Foreign Liabilities of Indonesian Banks, Government and State Enterprises, and Private Companies

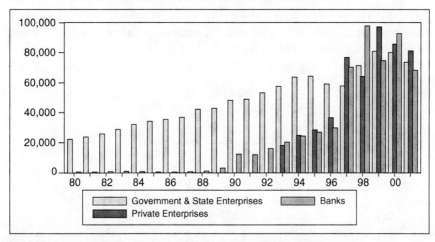

Note: The data of private foreign enterprises liabilities are not available in the 1980s since the obligation to inform the BI of their foreign liabilities was not compulsory. It was only since 2000 that the new regulation was imposed on private enterprises to inform BI of their foreign liabilities monthly.

Source: Bank Indonesia (*Bank Monthly Reports*, various editions) and Bank Indonesia (*Annual Reports*, various editions).

FIGURE 4.11
Comparison between Banks and Non-Bank Financial Institutions in Extending Loans (percentage)

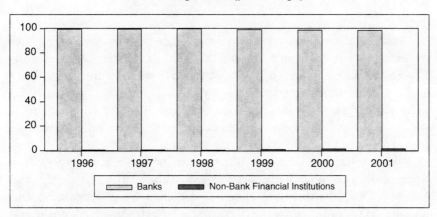

Source: Bank Indonesia (*Bank Monthly Reports*, various editions) and Bank Indonesia (*Annual Reports*, various editions).

tapping the deposit market and extending loans without exercising sufficient prudential measures.

In September 1997, the financial crisis hit Indonesia as well as Thailand, South Korea, the Philippines, and Malaysia. It abruptly reduced the growth in deposits and bank loans, and even the number of Indonesian commercial banks, as illustrated in Figure 4.12.

FIGURE 4.12
Rupiah to USD Exchange Rates

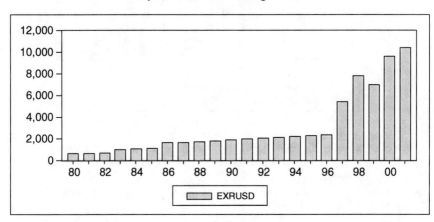

Note: The data of private foreign enterprises liabilities are not available in the 1980s since the obligation to inform BI of their foreign liabilities was not compulsory. It was only since 2000 that the new regulation was imposed on private enterprises to inform BI of their foreign liabilities monthly.
Source: Bank Indonesia (*Indonesian Financial Statistics*, various editions).

As a result, Indonesia experienced sudden and unprecedented pressures on exchange rates and inflation, as illustrated in Figures 4.13 and 4.14. Due to the large exposures of the rupiah to external debt, the rupiah/USD exchange rate became weak and highly volatile. Furthermore, social and political instability occurred. Inflation increased astronomically because of the combination of a weakening exchange rate, a hike on administered prices, and a jump in inflationary expectations.

Many researchers saw this situation as inevitable after a period of financial deregulation and liberalization (McKinnon 1973; Shaw 1973; and Crockett 1997). Furthermore, they found that financial deregulation and liberalization could increase the opportunity for extending bank credit and deepening financial markets in which more funds were mobilized among

FIGURE 4.13
Indonesia's Consumer Price Index

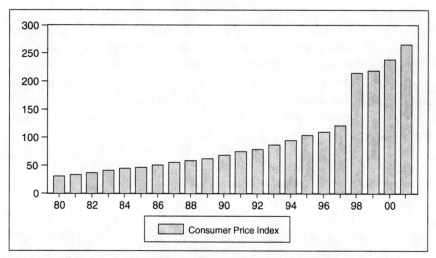

Source: Bank Indonesia (*Indonesian Financial Statistics*, various editions).

FIGURE 4.14
Total Credits and NPL of Groups of Banks

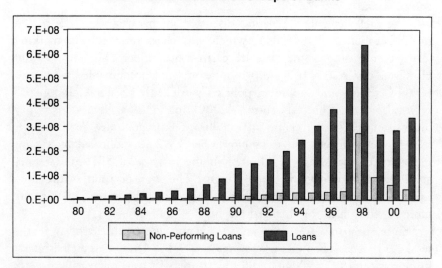

Note: E refers to 10.

Source: Bank Indonesia (*Bank Monthly Reports*, various editions).

economic agents. On the other hand, they also argued that it could create fragility in the banking system, which would eventually lead to financial instability.

Many other studies also confirmed the existence of a link between financial liberalization and financial instability in emerging economies. One particular study by Weller (2001) showed that emerging economies are systematically becoming more susceptible to both currency and banking crises after financial liberalization. Liberalization also allows more liquidity to enter an emerging economy, which finds its way into both productive and speculative projects.

Indonesia's experience is a testimony on how financial deepening stimulates economic growth in the long run but that in the short run, the misallocation of funds during the lending boom actually creates a financial collapse.

On the fiscal aspect, the cost in resolving the Indonesian financial crisis has been the highest among Asian countries, amounting to Rp. 654 trillion or 51.0 per cent of annual GDP, while in other countries the figures are 32.8 per cent (Thailand), 26.5 per cent (South Korea), 20.0 per cent (Japan), 16.4 per cent (Malaysia), and 0.5 per cent (the Philippines) (Honohan and Klingebiel 2000). Thus, in order to overcome the weaknesses in the Indonesian banking industry, BI attempted to develop more prudent regulation and supervision while continuing the banking deregulation.

The final deregulation period discussed in this chapter is the period from October 1997 to 2001, which was characterized by a banking restructuring programme that BI carried out under IMF supervision. However, this restructuring programme was not accompanied by a well planned strategy and supported policies, particularly because of Indonesia's political intervention.[10] Nasution (2000) found that there were policy inconsistencies in the economic stabilization programme. For example, the closure of sixteen banks in November 1997 was followed by a tight monetary policy. This was reflected in the increase of SBI interest rates and interbank money market overnight. The monetary authorities even squeezed market liquidity by shifting deposits into BI instead of injecting more liquidity into the financial system.

Since the banks were not yet adequately supervised, the delay in the results of Indonesia Bank Restructuring Agency (IBRA), from its establishment in November 1997 to March 1999 led to deposit runs on perceived weak banks and a quality flight to perceived good banks (Batunanggar 1996). As a consequence, this forced BI to provide liquidity support to the banks on which depositors were doing a run, most of which were private banks. The increase in BI liquidity support can be seen from the liabilities to BI, as illustrated in Figure 4.15.

Radelet and Sachs (1998) provided early diagnosis of the 1997 financial crisis in Asia. They showed that at the core of the crisis, the large-scale foreign capital inflows into financial system were what had become vulnerable to panic. A combination of panic on the part of international investment community, policy mistakes at the onset of the

FIGURE 4.15
Total Loans Extended by Indonesian Banks by Groups

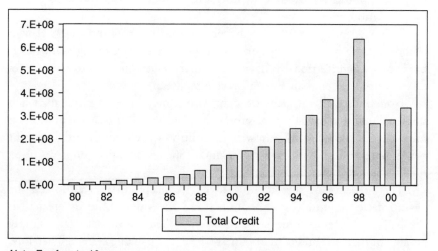

Note: E refers to 10.
Source: Bank Indonesia (*Bank Monthly Reports*, various editions).

crisis by Asian governments, and poorly designed international rescue programmes turned foreign capital withdrawal into a full-fledged financial panic and deepened the crisis.

STRUCTURAL WEAKNESSES IN THE FINANCIAL SYSTEM

The adverse impact of liberalization on financial stability was believed by most to have worsened due to a number of factors: lax banking supervision, highly concentrated ownership of banks, and consequently, weak corporate governance in the banking system. The laxity in banking supervision is often identified as one of the major causes of financial instability. Prior to the

1997 crisis, the central bank experienced a serious lack of resources (that is, shortage of supervisors), relative to the scale and scope of the banking industry it had to supervise.

This situation was further aggravated by the central bank's reluctance to evaluate the extent of banks' problems earlier in the crisis, but rather preferring to apply temporary policies as a quick remedy.[11] One example of this was when BI provided banks with emergency loans for both liquidity and capital purposes. The policy was based on the idea that a "bank run effect" should be avoided at all costs.

An evidence of this situation can be found in the closure of Bank Summa,[12] one of the largest Indonesian private banks. In this case, BI supplied a limited guarantee deposit while Bank Suma's owner provided the resolution costs.

This evidence is similar to the observation by Kiggundu (1996) who found that the monetary authority management in developing countries is frequently characterized by having quick remedies and reactive responses to the crisis, rather than taking preventive actions.

Nonetheless, this strategy brought with it moral hazard problems when implemented due to its lack of supervision and the clear absence of an "exit mechanism". Failed banks as well as politically well connected insolvent banks were still allowed to remain open. Such a situation only nurtured fragility in the Indonesian banking system.

The existence of the "too big to fail" concept further reinforced the vicious cycle of moral hazard conduct and the vulnerability it created in the banking system. Some large banks were "not allowed to fail" simply because of their size and connectedness within the banking system. Therefore, the imprudent and risky behaviour of commercial banks was structurally tolerated.

Structural weaknesses were also present in the ownership structure of Indonesian banks prior to the 1997 crisis. Despite the dramatic increase in the number of banks, especially private banks, during the period 1988–97, the ownership of Indonesian banks remained highly concentrated.

The top ten banks (seven state banks[13] and three private banks[14]) accounted for almost 72.0 per cent of the total bank assets in the country. Moreover, the top ten private banks,[15] plus the six state banks, accounted for almost 80.0 per cent of the total bank assets. Furthermore, most of the shares of these private banks were still owned by the original owners. In the case of private banks, such a concentration of share holdings resulted in "information asymmetries" between the majority and minority shareholders (investors and creditors).[16]

Evidently, such an unfavourable ownership structure had a damaging impact on the corporate governance conduct of Indonesian banks. Political pressure had caused state banks to extend loans to a particular sector or group of debtors without any proper and comprehensive evaluation.[17] This pressure was more prevalent in the oil boom years (as previously discussed), during the first period of financial liberalization, but nonetheless, it remained to be the case, though to a lesser extent, in the post-1998 reform period. The key issues for Indonesia are the resolution of banks engulfed with financial problems; continued improvement of supervision and regulation; and the maintenance of a competitive and efficient market structure.

Rajan and Zingales (1998) offered a different perspective on the issue of structural weaknesses in the banking system. They found that financial instability may be caused by the incompatibility between East Asian banking systems and foreign inflows into this area. East Asian banking systems are characterized by underdeveloped institutional infrastructure (lack of contract law, bankruptcy law, and weak supervision), while foreign investors demand protection for their investments. As a result, foreign investors prefer to place their funds in short-term loans that can be withdrawn at any time, no matter what the economic environment is.

It is, therefore, reasonable to conclude that beyond promising growth figures that it generated, financial liberalization was actually also a nurturing seed to the 1997 financial crisis due to its inadequate prudential regulations and lack of central bank supervision.

On a separate note, due to several adjustments during the financial liberalization and deregulation process, interest rates had increased which, in turn, brought about structural weaknesses. Such increase contributed to financial instability through adverse selection or via balance sheet channel to borrowers (Stiglitz 1994). This financial instability then led to a financial crisis in which the adverse selection and moral hazard problems worsened much. Subsequently, financial markets were unable to channel funds efficiently to those who have the most productive investment opportunities.

The adverse selection problem further caused credit rationing, a significant decline in loan supply, and even helped bring the collapse in the loan market as illustrated in Figure 4.16. It indicates that in the aftermath of the 1997 financial crisis, extended loans were still increasing in 1998 (perhaps due to the loan commitments that banks made before the crisis). However, soon after that, in 1999, loans growth dropped almost 54.0 per cent from the previous year.

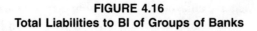

FIGURE 4.16
Total Liabilities to BI of Groups of Banks

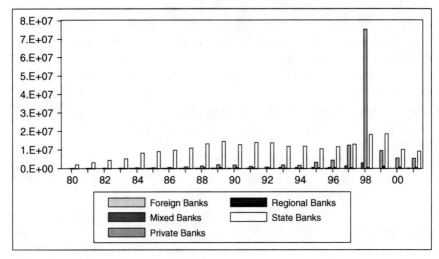

Note: E refers to 10.

Source: Bank Indonesia (*Bank Monthly Reports*, various editions).

Gertler and Rose (1996) also found that the increase in the interest rates as a result of financial deregulation may have caused a decline in a firm's net worth, leading to an increase in the premium for external finance, even for good borrowers. Figure 4.7 indicates that, in the Indonesian case, high domestic interest rates had encouraged domestic banks and private companies to raise foreign external funds in 1997 and 1998. This was accompanied by an implicit government guarantee of a predictable exchange rate movement. There was a strong incentive for Indonesian commercial banks and private companies to go unhedge[18] with their foreign borrowings.

Since the capital inflows were essentially induced by mere interest rate differentials, it is not surprising that most of the foreign borrowings were short run, leaving the economy vulnerable to liquidity problems in the event of sudden outflows.

THREE ASPECTS OF PROMOTING FINANCIAL STABILITY AND ECONOMIC GROWTH

Having examined two important issues above on the struggle to balance stability with growth, this section discusses three strategies in maintaining financial stability while continuing to promote economic growth.

Improving Bank Capital

One of the Indonesian Banking Architecture's (API) initiatives is strengthening bank capital by requiring both the conventional and *shariah* commercial banks (including regional government banks or BPDs) to provide at least Rp. 80 billion Tier 1 capital by the end of 2008, and at least Rp. 100 billion Tier 1 capital by the end of 2010.

This initiative was envisaged as a "market-driven" process. However, since the launching of API in early 2004, such a market-driven process has yet to be realized. Reflecting this is the result of stress test conducted in 2005–07 on the business plan of several small banks. The test showed that these banks, which had capital of less than Rp. 100 billion, had not made sufficient effort to comply with the minimum capital requirements.

The initiative to increase Tier 1 capital was motivated by the fact that capital is important in bank risk management. It functions as a cushion to absorb loss and is thus paramount in a bank's ability to conduct risk taking activities. The higher the capital, the better the bank is in performing, as well as contributing to the economy. It is difficult to achieve high growth in bank loans without any improvement in the capitalization of the banks themselves.

The need to have higher Tier 1 capital is dictated by future challenges in terms of international regulations and economic globalization. Compared with other countries in Asia, Indonesia needs to put a lot more effort in accumulating bank capital. Limited growth of Tier 1 capital would result in Indonesian bank loans contributing a lower rate to GDP, compared with that in other countries. Therefore, in order to improve economic growth through bank loans while keeping banking stability in check, it is imperative to increase Tier 1 capital.

Strengthening Governance and Performance

Despite the healthy situation in the overall banking industry in Indonesia today, there is still much room for improvement. One of its most visible weaknesses is the lack of good corporate governance and core banking skills at most banks.

Banks need to improve their capability in handling rising operational risks, particularly in the areas of internal control and compliance with prudential banking principles. One reference for prudential banking principles is the *25 Basel Core Principles for Effective Banking Supervision* published by the Basel Committee on Banking Supervision (BCBS).

Banks also need to improve their operational performance. Current levels of profitability and operating efficiency in the banking system are not adequate enough to be sustainable because of lingering difficulties with their earning assets structure. Although the Net Interest Margin (NIM), Return On Equity (ROE), and Return On Assets (ROA) of the Indonesian banking industry can be classified as "high", compared with other countries, the ratio of operational costs to income costs is also among the highest. This condition suggests that most banks' non-interest income is derived from trading activities susceptible to fluctuation. The low ratio of assets per customer also means that banks in Indonesia carry higher operating expenses in comparison to other countries.

To increase their contribution to the economy, banks have to find ways to improve their operational efficiency. Their stability should be improved to raise their current profitability and efficiency level.

Improving the Effectiveness of Banking Supervision

Complementing the two aspects above, bank supervision is another aspect that needs to be updated and improved. The need to improve is based on past experience where there was a lack of proper implementation of some prudential regulations. For instance, there were difficulties in enforcing some regulations simply because bank supervisors were not equipped with the best knowledge and skills.

The goal to build capacity in bank supervision is consistent with BI's effort in implementing the 25 Basel Core Principles for effective banking supervision, including improved use of supervision technology. Because of the extremely broad scope and dynamic nature of bank supervision, quality improvement in banking supervision should be managed as part of a routine and ongoing process.

The issue of banking fraud represents another challenge for the banking system. It directly affects most members of the Indonesian banking sector, as well as Indonesia's society. Hence, it is recommended that clear and easily understood standards be created that are not only for conducting banking supervision, but also for receiving and treating customer complaints, as well as releasing information on bank products (transparency). Transparency is indispensable to a healthy financial sector.

To ensure a sustainable and meaningful contribution from the banking industry to the economy, it is a necessity to manage various risks in the banking system through effective supervision. The capacity of banking supervision should always be updated to keep pace with advancement in the fields of technology, social development, and business.

CONCLUDING REMARKS

This chapter discusses the process of financial liberalization and its impact on the economy as well as on financial stability. The discussion is centred on the issue of balancing financial stability and economic growth in Indonesia's financial system.

Several conclusions are made in this chapter. The first is that financial liberalization has helped the economy accelerate by allowing more money to circulate in the system. However, the occurrence of the financial crisis in 1997 indicated that such liberalization also nurtured vulnerabilities in the financial system since much of the liquidity entering the economy found their way into both productive and speculative projects. Second, the adverse impact of liberalization on financial stability has worsened due to a number of factors: lax banking supervision, the highly concentrated ownership of banks, and weak corporate governance in the banking system. Liberalization proved to be hazardous when it was implemented in an environment lacking a robust prudential system.

In order to continue promoting economic growth while maintaining financial stability, this chapter proposes three strategies: improve bank capital, strengthen governance and performance of banks, and improve the effectiveness of banking supervision. These three strategies are in line with current initiatives at Bank Indonesia to ensure a safe and sound banking industry that also contributes to the economy.

NOTES

1. The indicative level of 2.0 is derived from 1990–2005 historical data. Based on this data, the crisis takes place in Indonesia when the FSI is above 2.0.
2. According to Kunt and Detragiache (1998, p. 9), in a tightly controlled financial system, bank lending interest rates are usually subject to ceiling rates which prevent the banks from charging high risk premia. Hence, loans to high-risk borrowers cannot be profitable.
3. The lift of the credit ceiling rates by central banks as a result of financial liberalization enabled the banks to support riskier borrowers in return for higher future yield (Kunt and Detragiache 1998).
4. Laeven (2003) argued that barriers to entry in the banking sector have often been lowered as well and the development of securities markets has been stimulated.

5. McKinnon (1991) and Edwards (1984) proposed that the sequence for Indonesian financial liberalization, that is, the liberalizing of the capital account of its balance of payments prior to the domestic financial sector, implies that financial liberalization has been applied in a different order to that propounded by literature on the sequencing of financial reform. However, Soesastro (2006) stated that the Indonesian financial liberalization was driven by pragmatism and necessity, rather than by a theory or ideology.

6. The introduction of SBIs and SBPUs in this case is aimed to set indirect monetary operations since the government does not issue treasury bills like in many other countries as the basis of open market operations and repurchase agreement policies. Besides SBIs, as an open market operation instrument, are not only aimed at managing the short-term liquidity of banks, firms, and individuals, but also as an alternative investment.

7. State banks are large banks in terms of total assets owned by the government and have access to foreign sources of funds. Private banks are owned by domestic private entrepreneurs and almost 90 per cent of them has access to foreign funds as well. Foreign banks are owned by foreign investors and have access to foreign sources of funds. Mixed or joint banks are owned by joint ventures between domestic and foreign investors and also have foreign fund access. While regional banks — as relatively small banks in terms of total assets owned by regional governments — may even have foreign fund access, they are not really able to seek the foreign funds due to their asset size.

8. The packages aimed at promoting fair competition among banks by allowing new entry, widening the network, reducing segmentation between state banks and private banks, and permitting more independence in decision making.

9. See Nasution (1994).

10. Some examples of political intervention in Indonesia are described later in this chapter. Unfortunately, the issue of political and social constraints faced by policy-makers when they attempt to overcome the financial crisis has often been ignored in the literature on banking crisis (De Luna-Matinez 2000). De Luna-Martinez found that Indonesia's strategy for the 1997–98 crisis was closer to that of Mexico, which had adopted a gradual approach to all stages of crisis resolution. Indonesia's strategy was different from that of South Korea, which follows a rapid "big bang" approach.

11. Since the 1997 financial crisis, the International Monetary Fund (IMF) has been involved in the Indonesian banking crisis resolution by focusing more on financial variables than on financial restructuring. Stiglitz (2002) argued that the IMF strategy failed to manage fully the adverse impact of policy on the real economy problems. In addition, he suggested that the strategy for dealing with the financial goal in resolving the crisis was to maintain credit flows.

12. Bank Suma belonged to one of the Indonesian conglomerates (owned by Edward Suryajaya) that owned the Astra Group. It experienced massive non-performing loans (especially in the property sector) and large losses in 1991.

13. There were seven state banks that were involved: Bank Negara Indonesia (henceforth BNI), Bank Rakyat Indonesia (BRI), Bank Export Import Indonesia (BEII), Bank Dagang Negara (BDN), Bank Bumi Daya (BBD), Bank Pembangunan Indonesia (Bappindo), and Bank Tabungan Negara (BTN).

14. The three private banks that were among the top ten Indonesian banks, based on their total assets, prior the crisis were Bank Central Asia (BCA), Bank Danamon, and Bank International Indonesia. These three banks were owned by the biggest conglomerates in Indonesia. BCA, in particular, was owned by the biggest conglomerate in Indonesia (belonging to Liem Su Liong, who was very close to the central politic power at that time).

15. The top ten private banks involved were Bank Central Asia (BCA), Bank Danamon, BII, BDNI, Lippo, Bank Bali, Bank Niaga, Bank Umum Nasional, Panin, and Bank Duta. The top ten private banks were linked to major business groups as well as politically powerful groups. Both Bank Central Asia (BCA) and Bank Umum Nasional (BUN) have shareholders linked to former President Soeharto's children, and Bank Duta is known to hold the funds of the former president's foundations and of Badan Urusan Logistik Negara (BULOG), the state logistics agency.

16. Despite the legal lending limits to affiliated groups or one group, there was gross violation of this requirement as evident in the post audits undertaken on banks taken over by the government after the crisis.

17. One example of this is the Timor National Car, owned by former President Soeharto's youngest son. Timor National Car was favoured by the special status of being permitted to import their car parts and components, and later, fully built-up vehicles from Kia in Korea, duty free. In this case, a group of banks involving state and some private banks were asked to extend loans for this project. Another example is the clove monopoly, a private body, again owned by Soeharto's youngest son, was given monopoly to buy the cloves from farmers and resell them to cigarette manufactures, and was also favoured with low interest credit directly from the central bank.

18. Roughly, "to go unhedge with foreign currencies" means having no protection from fluctuations in foreign currencies.

REFERENCES

Bank Indonesia. *Annual Reports*. Jakarta: Bank Indonesia, various years.
———. *Bank Monthly Reports*. Jakarta: Bank Indonesia, various years.
———. *Financial Stability Review* 14, March 2010.
———. *Indonesian Financial Statistics*. Jakarta: Bank Indonesia, various years.
Batunanggar, S. "Strategic Management in Action: The Case of Bank Indonesia". Unpublished MBA dissertation. England: University of Nottingham, 1996.

Crockett, A. "Why is Financial Stability a Goal of Public Policy?". *Economic Review*, issues Q IV, 1997.

de Luna-Matinez, Jose. "Management and Resolution of Banking Crisis: Lessons from the Republic of Korea and Mexico". Discussion Paper no. 43. Washington, D.C.: World Bank, 2000.

Djiwandono, J.S. "The Banking Sector in Emerging Markets: The Case of Indonesia". In *Banking Soundness and Monetary Policy*, edited by C. Enoch and J. Green. Washington, D.C: International Monetary Fund, 1997.

Edwards, S. "The Order of Financial Liberalisation of External Sector in Developing Countries". Essays in International Finance no. 156. Princeton, N.J.: Department of Economics, Princeton University, 1984.

Gertler, M. and A. Rose. "Finance, Public Policy and Growth". In *Financial Reform: Theory and Experience*, edited by G. Caprio Jr., I. Atiyas, and J.A. Hanson. New York: Cambridge University Press, 1996.

Glen, J. and B. Pinto. "Debt or Equity? How Firms in Developing Countries Choose". International Finance Corporation Discussion Paper no. 2. Washington, D.C: World Bank, 1994.

Honohan, P. and D. Klingebiel. "Controlling Fiscal Costs of Banking Crisis". Policy Research Working Paper no. 2441. Washington, D.C.: World Bank, 2000.

International Monetary Fund. *Global Financial Stability Report: Containing Systematic Risks and Restoring Financial Soundness*. Washington, D.C.: IMF, April 2008.

Kiggundu, M.N. "Integrating Strategic Management Task into Implementing Agencies: From Firefighting to Prevention". *World Development* 24, no. 9 (1996): 1417–30.

Kunt, A. and E. Detragiache. "The Determinants of Banking Crises in Developing and Developed Countries". IMF Staff Papers 45, no. 1 (1998): 81–109.

Laeven, L. "Does Financial Liberalization Reduce Financial Constraints?". *Financial Management* 32, no. 1, Spring 2003.

Mc Kinnon, J.G. "Critical Values for Cointegration Tests". In *Long Run Economic Relationships: Reading in Cointegration*, edited by R.F. Engle and C.W.J. Granger. Oxford: Oxford University Press, 1991.

Mc Kinnon, R.I. *Money and Capital in Economic Development*. Washington, D.C.: Brookings Institution, 1973.

Nasution, A. "Banking Sector Reform in Indonesia, 1983–1993". In *Indonesia Assessment 1994: Finance as a Key Sector in Indonesia's Development*, edited by R. Mc Leod. Canberra: Research School of Pacific and Asian Studies, Australian National University, 1994.

———. "Recent Issues in the Management of Macroeconomic Policies in Indonesia". *Rising to the Challenge in Asia: A Study of Financial Markets* 6. Manila: Asian Development Bank, 2000.

Radelet, S. and J. Sach "The Onset of the East Asian Financial Crisia ". National Bureau of Economic Research (NBER) Working Paper no. W6689, August 1998.

Rajan, R. and L. Zingales. "Which Capitalism? Lessons From the East Asia Crisis". *Journal of Applied Corporate Finance* 11, no. 3, Fall 1998.

Shaw, E.S. *Financial Deepening in Economic Development.* New York: Oxford University Press, 1973.

Sinclair, P. "International Financial architecture: The Central Bank Governors". *Bank of England Quaterly Bulletin* 42, no. 3, 2002.

Soesastro, H. "Regional Integration in East Asia: Achievement and Future Prospects". *Asian Economic Policy Review* 1, issue 2, December 2006.

Stiglitz, J. *Globalization and Its Discontents.* New York: W.W. Norton & Co., 2002.

————. "The Role of the State in Financial Market". Proceedings of World Bank Annual Conference on Development Economics 1993. Washington, D.C.: World Bank, 1994.

Weller, C.E. "Financial Crises after Financial Liberalization: Exceptional Circumstances or Structural Weakness?". *Journal of Development Studies* 38, no. 1, 2001.

5

Economic Crisis and Fiscal Policy Management

Silvia Mila Arlini and Yohanes Eko Riyanto

INTRODUCTION

The year 2008 was marked by a major global financial and economic crisis on an unprecedented scale that had not been seen since the Great Depression of 1929. In the aftermath of the crisis a global recession ensued. This crisis dragged many countries, including Indonesia, into a recession limbo. Export revenues fell dramatically as global demand weakened and consumer confidence hit rock bottom. Financial institutions collapsed, thousands of people became unemployed, and companies went bust. However, even though Indonesia was affected by the negative impact of the crisis, the impact was relatively mild compared with that on many other countries, including ASEAN countries. This was essentially due to the country's relatively low reliance on exports and strong domestic consumption.

To put the brakes on this downward pressure on the economy, several policy measures were introduced. Furthermore, in addition to the active monetary policies pursued by the central bank, the government launched an emergency fiscal stimulus package to stimulate the economy and help it avoid the recession.

This chapter gives an overview of the fiscal policy adjustments during the global economic crisis and provides an evaluation of the measures taken.

The next section, Section 2, will start by providing a brief historical synopsis of Indonesian fiscal conditions. Such a synopsis throws light on how the crisis impacted Indonesia's fiscal conditions and also provides a discussion on how the country managed its fiscal policy, and what budgetary problems it faced during the global financial crisis. Section 3 discusses the government budget in detail, starting with government revenue items, the moving on to government expenditure items, and finishing with the government's financing options. Subsequently, Section 4 of this chapter scrutinizes the contents of the Indonesian fiscal stimulus package and provides a brief analysis of the advantages and disadvantages of this package. Section 5 concludes the chapter.

A HISTORICAL OVERVIEW OF INDONESIAN FISCAL CONDITIONS

In late 1960s and early 1970s, the Indonesian economy underwent a fundamental transformation.[1] Soeharto's New Order government at that time took significant actions directed at stabilizing the depressed economy that had been plagued by extreme inflationary pressure. The government thus launched several fiscal and monetary initiatives that were aimed at combating high inflation, opening up the economy to international trade, attracting foreign investors and development, as well as promoting the oil and gas sectors to become major revenue generators. Consequently, with help from these major initiatives, the Indonesian economy awoke from its slumber. Unfortunately however, the major initiatives also brought with them an undesirable consequence. The economy had become heavily dependent on revenue generated by the oil and gas sector. Thus, the share of revenue from this sector to the total government revenue increased dramatically from only about 20 per cent in the early 1970s, to more than 50 per cent in the mid-1970s (see Table 5.1).

Naturally, such a heavy reliance on the oil and gas sector made the Indonesian economy susceptible to any major external shock that affected this sector. This was indeed what happened in the early 1980s as world oil prices plummeted. The impact of this oil price shock on the Indonesian economy was huge and government revenue dwindled, thereby creating a major fiscal imbalance in the economy. Realizing the danger, the government responded swiftly to this negative external shock by taking several measures, including the diversification of its revenue base. Thus, it boosted revenues from the non-oil and non-gas sectors in order to reduce the heavy reliance on the oil and gas revenue. This swift response bore fruit as the government was able to boost its tax and non-tax revenues from the non-oil and non-gas sectors. The revenue from the value added tax (VAT) generated from these other sectors surged dramatically. In 1990s, it contributed to about one third of total government revenue (see Table 5.1).

Despite its ability to boost some of these tax-based revenues, the Indonesian Government was still relatively unsuccessful at mobilizing revenue from corporate and personal income taxes. Prior to 1990s, the contribution of these income tax revenues to total government revenue was meagre, mainly due to inefficiencies in tax enforcement and collection system and also due to the presence of pervasive tax evasions. It was not until the mid-1990s that revenue from the income tax increased significantly.

On the expenditure side, both routine and development expenditure items experienced a steady increase over time.[2] As the economy grew, government expenditure also moved in tandem. It accounted for nearly 27 per cent of GDP in the period 1980–81, which represented a significant increase from a mere 12 per cent of GDP in the period of 1970–71.

The rapid increase in expenditure called for more financial support. The government could no longer rely solely on existing sources of revenue to finance its expenditure. Hence, this triggered its decision to diversify its revenue base further. Since the domestic financial sector was not yet strong enough to provide the necessary financing support, the government decided to tap into foreign aid and borrowings.

In the New Order era, the government's main budgetary aim was to maintain a balanced budget (*Anggaran Berimbang-Dinamis*). This was primarily done by keeping government expenditure in balance with revenue from all sources, including those from foreign aid and borrowings (Asher and Booth 1990). When the level of government expenditure soared, the government counterbalanced it with higher foreign aid and borrowing in order to maintain a balanced budget.

The government's decision to increase foreign aid and borrowing, coupled with the increasingly globalized world financial market in 1990, led to a dramatic increase in the foreign aid and borrowing components of the budget. While foreign borrowings were helpful as a catalyst for rapid economic growth and a buffer mechanism to maintain a balanced budget at the time, they also created an additional burden to the government budget in the form of debt and interest obligations. As the level of foreign borrowings went up, the amount of debt and interest payments also escalated, putting the Indonesian economy at risk of being insolvent should the economy face global financial turmoil. Rising debt and interest obligations could expose the country to myriads of problems in the form of a severe budget deficit,

TABLE 5.1
Government Budget from 1970/71 to 1999/2000 (in IDR trillion)

	1970/71	1975/76	1980/81	1985/86	1990/91	1995/96	1997/98	1999/2000
Rupiah (in trillion)								
Income Tax	0.05	0.30	1.11	2.07	8.25	21.01	34.39	59.68
Oil and Gas Revenue, including Tax	0.07	1.20	6.77	12.92	17.74	16.05	30.56	58.48
Value Added Tax	0.17	0.59	1.70	4.09	12.98	25.78	33.91	49.06
Other Revenues	0.00	0.04	0.09	0.16	0.79	1.89	2.64	4.07
Non-Tax Revenue	0.05	0.11	0.25	1.69	2.44	8.27	10.78	17.13
Total Government Revenue	0.34	2.24	9.93	20.94	42.19	73.01	112.28	188.43
Rupiah (in trillion)								
Personnel Expenditure	0.12	0.55	1.78	3.93	7.09	13.00	17.27	32.11
Material Expenditure	0.08	0.28	0.69	1.35	1.84	5.18	9.00	9.97
Fuel Subsidy	0.00	0.00	1.02	0.45	3.31	0.00	9.81	40.92
Other Subsidies	0.06	0.07	0.29	0.46	0.18	1.92	11.35	19.13
Interest Payments	0.01	0.03	0.27	1.20	4.57	6.73	10.90	42.85
Other Expenditures	0.00	0.00	0.00	0.00	0.00	0.00	0.00	3.39
Development Expenditure	0.14	1.44	5.45	11.74	18.25	28.78	38.34	52.62
Transfer to Local Government for								
personnel expenditure	0.00	0.17	0.70	2.25	3.64	7.81	10.52	16.57
material expenditure	0.00	0.09	0.27	0.24	0.25	0.42	0.54	0.77
Total Government Expenditure	0.41	2.63	10.48	21.62	39.13	63.84	107.74	218.32

Source: Compiled from Ministry of Finance (several editions) and Arlini and Suatmi (2006).

depressed capital formation, the slowing down of long-run economic growth, and a rising fear of increasing future taxes to service the debts. All these could hamper and discourage economic activities.

Indeed such global financial turmoil took place during 1997–98, with its effects felt primarily by Asian countries. Indonesia was among the countries that was badly affected by the crisis. The 1997–98 crisis exposed Indonesia's currency to massive downward pressure against the U.S. dollar and put the Indonesian economy under heavy inflationary pressure. Anxious to provide some short-run fiscal stimulus to stimulate the economy and prevent it from going into a deeper contraction (Corden 1998), the government increased its expenditure. Fuel subsidy and and other subsidies were also increased, mainly to help the middle and low income groups who suffered most from the crisis.

Unfortunately, the massive depreciation of the Indonesian currency by nearly 250 per cent severely escalated the amount of foreign debt obligations. Thus, a huge budget deficit ensued. Furthermore, because about 84 per cent of Indonesia's budget deficit was still financed by foreign borrowing (Lane et al. 1999), Indonesia experienced difficulties in repaying its foreign debts. This forced the government to request a moratorium and a rescheduling of its debt payments, and to avoid any development programmes that would "lock the country into future commitments" (Hill 1999). In addition, the government took the initiative to reduce the fiscal strain by selling the recapitalized assets of failed banks and financial institutions to strategic domestic and foreign investors. It also decided to privatize some of the state-owned enterprises.

Subsequently, the Indonesian parliament took the bold initiative to pass constitution laws on decentralization, regional autonomy, and fiscal budget (UU no. 22/1999 and no. 25/1999). The laws effectively granted autonomy to local governments to manage their own fiscal administration and budgetary systems without any intervention from the central government. The central government also provided regional governments with a "balance fund" in the form of revenue sharing funds, general allocation funds, and specific allocation funds, in order to finance the needs related to the implementation of the decentralization policy.

Since regional governments were also required to generate their own revenues, there had been some cases in which they tapped into the balance fund to generate more revenue through investing money in the central bank debt certificates (SBI-*Sertifikat* Bank Indonesia), rather than supporting the implementation of decentralization and boosting their own regional development. Investments in SBI, while they are relatively risk-free, clearly did not generate multiplier effects nor add value to their regional economies. This misallocation in the use of balance fund was clearly apparent from the low share of budget absorption in the regional development expenditure posts. In addition, most of these expenses on the development expenditure posts occurred only towards the end of the fiscal year. It is, however, also possible that the low share of budget absorption in regional development expenditure was caused by other factors other than the misallocation of the balance fund. One of these factors could be the late disbursement of the approved funds to regional governments due to excessive bureaucratic procedures.

In 2002, the government also took the initiative to generate publicly financed funds by issuing government bonds (SUN — *Surat Utang Negara*) and selling them in the domestic market. This move was quite successful not only in generating more funds, but also in reducing the dependency of the Indonesian economy on foreign borrowing. Table 5.2 shows that from 2005 onward, government bonds generated funds of more than 20 IDR trillion. The peak was in 2008 with funds of more than 85 IDR trillion. The proceeds from the sale of government bonds exceeded the amount of foreign borrowing, thereby reducing the country's dependency on foreign financing. Thus, from 2004 onward, the amount of foreign financing decreased significantly, resulting in a negative net value. The gross foreign debt drawing had been lesser than its amortization. Consequently, the World Bank applauded Indonesia's achievement and regarded the country as one of the successful countries in making a remarkable fiscal turnaround and in reducing its foreign debt obligations significantly.

Throughout the 2000s, despite facing fiscal deficit, Indonesia was able to maintain its deficit at a manageable level. In 2008, the budget deficit was only around 4 IDR trillion, around 0.1 per cent of the GDP. This was the lowest level of deficit seen since the 1997–98 Asian financial crisis. The government was thus able to accumulate surplus balance of financing (SILPA) of around 80 IDR trillion.

As the economy recovered from the Asian financial crisis in the early 2000s, government revenue increased steadily. Private consumption also followed the same pattern. The latter contributed significantly to boosting government tax revenue. The revenue from value added tax (VAT) and income tax grew at an annual rate of 18.5 per cent in the period 2002–07. All these positive developments resulted in the better than expected realization of government revenue.

However, the increase in government revenue did not seem to lead to an increase in government expenditure since this was lagging behind its

TABLE 5.2
Government Financing from 2000–08 (in IDR billion)

	2000	2001	2002	2003	2004	2005	2006	2007	2008
Surplus/Deficit	**-16,132**	**-40,485**	**-23,652**	**-35,109**	**-23,810**	**-16,390**	**-28,220**	**-49,844**	**-4,121**
Government Financing	**16,132**	**40,485**	**23,652**	**35,109**	**20,793**	**11,116**	**29,412**	**42,452**	**84,072**
Domestic Financing	**5,936**	**30,218**	**17,024**	**34,561**	**48,851**	**45,326**	**93,044**	**66,305**	**102,478**
Domestic Bank	-12,964	-1,227	-8,140	10,705	22,710	21,388	55,978	8,420	16,159
Domestic Non-Bank	18,900	31,445	25,164	23,856	26,141	23,938	37,066	57,885	86,319
Privatization		3,465	7,665	7,300	3,519	6,564	-1,600	3,000	82
Recovery of Bank Assets	18,900	27,980	19,438	19,661	15,751	6,564	2,680	2,413	2,820
Government Bonds			-1,939	-3,105	6,871	22,575	35,986	57,172	85,917
Foreign Financing	**10,195**	**10,267**	**6,628**	**548**	**-28,057**	**-10,272**	**-26,566**	**-23,853**	**-18,406**
Gross Drawings	17,818	26,152	18,887	20,360	18,434	26,840	26,115	34,070	45,029
Amortization	-7,623	-15,885	-12,259	-19,812	-46,491	-37,112	-52,681	-57,923	-63,435
SILPA (Financing Balance)					**-3,017**	**-5,274**	**1,192**	**-7,392**	**79,951**

Source: Bank Indonesia (2009).

TABLE 5.3

Realization of Government Revenue and Expenditure from 2001–07

(in IDR trillion)

	2001	2002	2003	2004	2005	2006	2007
Rupiah (in trillion)							
Tax Revenues	185.5	210.1	242.0	280.6	347.0	409.2	491.0
Income Tax	94.6	101.9	115.0	119.5	175.5	208.8	238.4
Value Added Tax	56.0	65.2	77.1	102.6	101.3	123.0	154.5
International Trade Taxes	9.6	10.6	11.1	12.7	15.2	13.2	20.9
Land and Building Tax	5.2	6.2	8.8	11.8	16.2	20.9	23.7
Duties on Land and Building	1.4	1.6	2.1	2.9	3.4	3.2	6.0
Exercise Duties	17.4	23.2	26.3	29.2	33.3	37.8	44.7
Others Domestic Taxes	1.4	1.5	1.7	1.9	2.1	2.3	2.7
Non-Taxes Revenues	115.1	88.4	98.9	122.5	146.9	227.0	215.1
Grants	0.5	–	0.5	0.3	1.3	1.8	1.7
Total Government Revenue	301.1	298.5	341.4	403.4	495.2	638.0	707.8
Personnel Expenditure	38.7	39.5	47.7	52.7	54.3	73.3	90.4
Material Expenditure	9.9	12.8	15.0	15.5	29.2	47.2	54.5
Capital Expenditure	–	–	–	–	32.9	55.0	64.3
Interest Payment	87.1	87.7	65.4	62.5	65.2	79.1	79.8
Oil Subsidies	–	–	30.0	69.0	104.4	64.2	83.8
Non-Oil Subsidies	–	–	13.9	22.5	16.3	43.2	66.4
Social Assistance	5.7	3.1	15.0	13.7	34.0	37.4	15.4
Development Expenditures	41.6	37.3	69.2	61.5	–	–	–
Regional Budget Expenditures (Balance Funds)	81.1	98.2	120.3	129.7	150.5	226.2	253.3
Total Government Expenditure	341.6	322.2	376.5	427.2	511.6	666.2	757.7

Source: Bank Indonesia (2009).

expenditure budget. Thus, the government faced the problem of inefficient budget absorption. In the period 2004–06, actual government expenditure in the first semester was consistently less than 30 per cent of the expenditure budget. These expenditures were mainly in the form of subsidies, interest payments, and personnel related expenses rather than in the form of capital or development expenditure.

THE INDONESIAN FISCAL OUTLOOK DURING THE GLOBAL FINANCIAL CRISIS

General Overview

Being an open economy, Indonesia was unable to escape from the damaging impact of the global financial crisis that swept the world in late 2008. As a result, the economy experienced a contraction and faced strenuous fiscal burdens. Economic growth in the first semester of 2009 fell to 4.2 per cent, way below the 6.3 per cent growth achieved in the first semester of 2008. Exports and industrial output plummeted significantly, consumer confidence was low, and financial institutions were reluctant to lend money.

FIGURE 5.1
Economic Growth of Southeast Asian Countries — Year-on-Year (per cent)

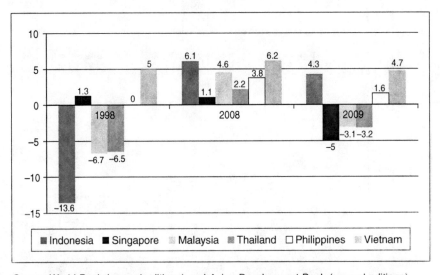

Source: World Bank (several editions) and Asian Development Bank (several editions).

TABLE 5.4
Government Budget and Realization from 2007–09 (in IDR trillion)

	2007				2008				2009		
	Budget APBN-P	Realization Sem. I	Realization Total	% to Budget	Budget APBN-P	Realization Sem. I	Realization Total	% to Budget	Budget APBN	Realization Sem. I	% to Budget
Government Revenues and Grants	**694.1**	**292.6**	**707.8**	**102.0**	**895.0**	**425.1**	**981.6**	**109.7**	**848.6**	**367.3**	**37.4**
1. Tax Revenues	492.0	205.3	491.0	99.8	609.2	307.5	658.7	108.1	661.8	288.6	43.8
Income Tax	251.7	113.3	238.4	94.7	305.0	164.0	327.5	107.4	319.6	163.7	50.0
i. Non-Oil and Gas	214.5	20.3	194.4	90.7	251.4	34.4	250.5	99.6	280.8	136.3	54.4
ii. Oil and Gas	37.3	93.0	44.0	118.1	53.7	129.7	77.0	143.6	38.8	27.4	35.6
Value Added Tax	152.1	58.5	154.5	101.6	195.5	87.1	209.6	107.3	233.6	81.0	38.6
Land and Building Tax	22.0	1.3	23.7	107.7	25.3	10.4	25.4	100.3	23.9	4.6	18.1
Duties on Land and Building	4.0	1.6	6.0	150.1	5.4	2.2	5.6	102.6	7.2	2.1	37.7
Exercise Duties	42.0	21.1	44.7	106.3	45.7	23.6	51.3	112.1	54.4	26.3	51.3
Other Domestic Taxes	2.7	1.3	2.7	100.7	3.4	1.4	3.0	90.5	3.5	1.4	46.1
International Trade Taxes	17.5	8.1	20.9	119.9	29.0	18.8	36.3	125.4	19.5	8.9	24.5
2. Non-Tax Revenues	198.3	87.0	215.1	108.5	282.8	117.1	320.6	113.4	185.9	78.6	24.5
3. Grants	3.8	0.4	1.7	44.4	2.9	0.5	2.3	78.1	0.9	0.1	4.3
Government Expenditures	**752.4**	**275.2**	**757.7**	**100.7**	**989.5**	**363.6**	**985.7**	**99.6**	**988.1**	**372.7**	**37.8**
1. Central Government Expenditures	498.2	168.0	504.4	101.2	697.1	246.9	693.4	99.5	691.5	233.0	33.6
Line Ministries Expenditure	244.6	69.9	224.6	91.8	290.0	81.8	259.7	89.5	314.7	101.0	38.9
Non-Line Ministries Expenditure	253.6	98.1	279.8	110.3	407.0	165.0	433.7	106.5	376.8	132.0	30.4
Interest payment	83.6	39.1	79.8	95.5	94.8	45.2	88.4	93.3	110.6	49.6	56.1
Subsidies	105.1	38.8	150.2	143.0	234.4	91.7	275.3	117.4	123.5	34.2	12.4
Other Expenditures, incl Social Assistances	65.0	20.2	49.8	76.6	77.8	28.1	70.0	89.9	142.6	48.2	33.8
2. Regional Budget Expenditures	254.2	107.2	253.3	99.6	292.4	116.8	292.4	100.0	303.1	139.7	47.8
Deficit/Surplus	-58.3	17.4	-49.8	n.a.	-94.5	61.5	-4.1	n.a.	-139.5	-5.4	n.a.
Government Financing	58.3	11.8	42.5	72.8	94.5	62.0	84.1	89.0	139.5	48.0	34.405
1. Domestic	70.8	36.9	66.3	93.6	107.6	80.5	102.5	95.3	109.4	70.4	64.351
2. Foreign	-12.5	-25.1	-23.9	n.a.	-13.1	-18.5	-18.4	n.a.	30.1	-22.4	n.a.
Balance of Financing	0.0	29.2	-7.4	n.a.	0.0	123.5	80.0	n.a.	0.0	42.6	n.a.

Note: n.a. = not applicable.

Source: Ministry of Finance (several editions).

Nevertheless, compared with other ASEAN countries, Indonesia fared much better. In 2009, Indonesia's economic growth was the second highest among other ASEAN countries, after Vietnam. This relatively better performance was mainly due to the fact that the share of its domestic consumption in GDP was larger than that of exports. Indonesia is regarded as the economy which is not as highly trade dependent as most other ASEAN countries, particularly Singapore. This fact effectively cushioned the adverse effects of shrinking global demand on the Indonesian economy.

Another important reason behind the relatively mild impact of the global economic downturn on the Indonesian economy was the presence of huge domestic consumption linked to the parliamentary and presidential elections held in 2009.[3] The scale of these elections was huge as they involved about 140 million eligible voters. This spike in domestic consumption helped to stimulate the economy and to lessen the negative impact of the global financial crisis on the Indonesian economy.

Nevertheless, despite the better than average performance of the Indonesian economy compared with other ASEAN countries, the global financial crisis exerted a negative impact on the government's budgetary conditions. The slowdown in world demand put a brake on domestic economic activities, reduced the national income, and shrank the income tax base so government income tax revenue also fell.

Subsequently, the government responded to this by lowering its revenue and expenditure projections, and also by launching a fiscal stimulus package to boost the domestic economy. Fortunately, the Indonesian Government had relatively ample room to administer the stimulus package given that, by the end of 2008, it had an actual cash surplus of more than 61 IDR trillion.

Government Revenue

In 2007 and 2008, the Indonesian Government experienced a significant increase in revenue. During these periods, the realized revenue was also higher than the budgeted revenue. This increase in realized revenue could be attributed to the increase in various tax and non-tax revenues, including VAT revenue.

In particular, tax and non-tax oil and gas revenue benefited from the soaring world crude oil price in 2008, which reached its peak at around US$134 per barrel in July 2008 (see Figure 5.2). Although the price dipped in the third quarter of 2008, the overall impact of the increasing crude oil price on government revenue was still positive. The tax and non-tax

FIGURE 5.2
Crude Oil Price, 2008–09 (US$/barrel)

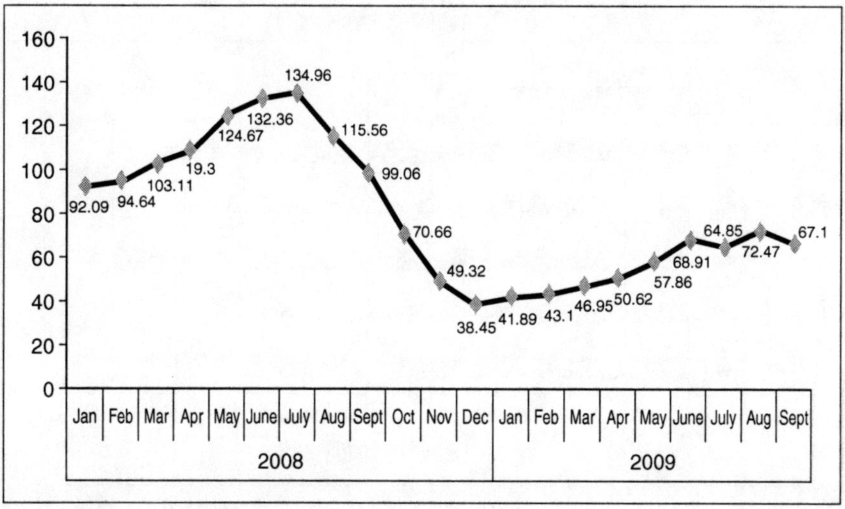

Source: Ministry of Finance (several editions).

oil and gas revenue grew about 75 per cent in 2008 compared with the previous year.

Income tax revenue from non-oil and non-gas sectors also increased significantly in 2008 due to the successful implementation of the "sunset policy" and the "taxpayer registration policy".[4] Many previously unregistered tax subjects came forward to register and to self-report their assets. Likewise, numerous existing taxpayers took advantage of the sunset policy. These policies significantly increased the tax collection rate to about 29 per cent in 2008.

Unfortunately, the occurrence of the global economic crisis in late 2008 and early 2009 put a brake on the momentum. The slowing down of economic activity shrunk the tax base and reduced the tax revenue significantly. Furthermore, as part of its fiscal stimulus package, the government provided cuts in personal income tax rates and also increased the tax-free income base which led to further reductions in tax revenue. Compared with the first semester of 2008, government tax revenue and non-tax revenue fell by 18.9 IDR trillion and 38.5 IDR trillion respectively in the first semester of 2009. As a result, the total realization of government revenue was only about 40 per cent of the total budgeted revenue (see Figure 5.3).

FIGURE 5.3
Share of Actual Government Revenue in Budget Revenue:
First Semester, 2007–09 (in IDR trillion)

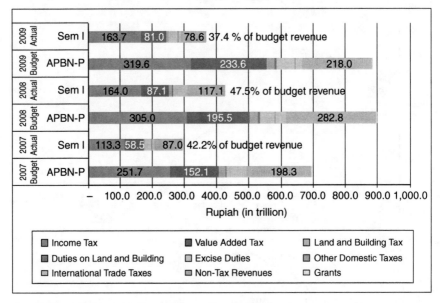

Source: Compiled from Ministry of Finance (several editions).

Total income tax revenue can be broken down into two main categories, namely income tax revenue from the oil and gas sector as well as income tax revenue from non-oil and non-gas sectors. Compared with the first semester of 2008, the former fell by about 317 IDR billion in the first semester of 2009. Interestingly, the latter did not decrease, but instead increased nearly threefold. This was probably what best reflected the positive impact of the sunset and taxpayer registration policies. Thus, in sum, the implementation of these two policies came at the right time as they helped a little in absorbing the negative impact of the global economic crisis on the government budget.

Government Expenditure

In the wake of the global economic meltdown, the Indonesian Government was fairly conservative in its spending. At the end of 2008, the realized expenditure was much lower than the budgeted expenditure. This low level of spending was caused by the fear that the global economic crisis would give the country a large budget deficit and any large amount of spending would worsen the deficit (Fengler 2009). In a way, it was probably a wise decision to be cautious, as it did indeed result in a much lower than expected level of deficit. Specifically, the actual deficit was only 4.1 IDR trillion, a much lower figure than the budgeted level of deficit of 94.5 IDR trillion.

However, given that the difference between the actual deficit and budgeted deficit was very large, that is, about 90 IDR trillion, it does seem to suggest that apart from the cautious approach in spending, there may also have been a deeper structural problem that caused such a wide gap, in the form of say, inefficiency in absorbing the budget. For example, if we take a look at the proportion of development expenditure that went into the capital expenditure, the actual figure was always lower than the budgeted figure. In 2008, the actual capital expenditure was only 71.2 IDR trillion, while the budgeted capital expenditure was 79.1 IDR trillion.

Another way of looking at the problem of absorbing the budget is by examining the proportion of budget that went into the various line and non-line ministerial budget posts.[5] The actual amount of expenditure allocated to line ministerial posts was always lower than its budgeted amount. Moreoever, the share of expenditure allocated to line ministerial posts was also lower than that allocated to non-line ministerial posts. Budget items that were categorized under non-line ministerial posts were, among other items, subsidies and interest debt payments. These non-line ministerial expenditure posts constituted about 69 per cent of the overall government expenditure.

In 2008, the expenditure allocated to non-line ministerial posts amounted to nearly 60 per cent of total government expenditure. Around 58 per cent of this expenditure, or approximately 234.4 IDR trillion, was allocated to the provision of various forms of subsidies, including fuel, electricity subsidies, and a direct cash transfer to the poor in order to lessen their hardship amidst the economic crisis of 2008. Overall, the amount of expenditure on subsidies spent in the first semester of 2008 rose more than twofold from the amount spent in the first semester of 2007. Even though towards mid-2008 the government reduced the amount of fuel subsidies, the overall amount of subsidies still increased from the previous year because of direct cash transfers. It should be noted that in that year the actual amount of subsidies had been larger than their budgeted amount.

As for line ministerial expenditure, it was mainly allocated to administrative, material, and personnel expenses, rather than development related project expenses.[6] In 2008, development project (capital) expenditure only received about 27.3 per cent (that is, 79.1 IDR trillion) of total line ministerial expenditure. This allocation was even lower in 2009, when it was only about 22.9 per cent (that is, 72 IDR trillion) of total line ministerial expenditure. However, in 2008 and 2009, the budgeted expenditure allocated to both administrative and personnel expenses constituted about 65.8 per cent and 73.7 per cent (that is, 191 IDR trillion and 231.9 IDR trillion) of total line ministerial expenditure respectively. Thus, from the above observation, we can conclude that the Indonesian Government tended to allocate a larger budget for consumption spending, rather than for investment spending. This imbalance in budget allocation for consumption spending and investment spending could have put a brake on the growth of productive capacity.

In 2009, the government increased the budget allocated to line ministerial expenditure by 8.5 per cent or 24.7 IDR trillion more than the amount allocated in the previous year. Furthermore, it cut the budget allocated to non-line ministerial expenditure by 7.4 per cent or 30.2 IDR trillion less than the amount allocated in the previous year. Most of the increase in the budget allocation for line ministerial expenditure went to the Ministry of Education, the Ministry of Defence, the Ministry of Health, and the Ministry of Public Works. In particular, the Ministry of

FIGURE 5.4
Absorption of Government Expenditure in Semester I, 2007–09
(in IDR trillion)

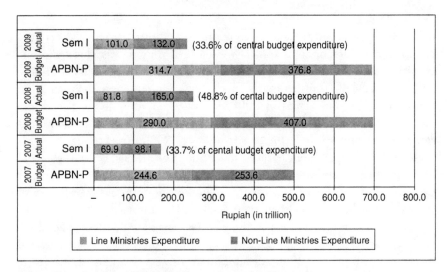

Source: Compiled from Ministry of Finance (several editions).

Education received around 19.3 per cent of the total budget allocated to line ministerial expenditure. This amount was roughly the same as the one committed by the government to support the enactment of the law on the national education system (UU no. 20/2003).[7] The Ministry of Public Works, which is responsible for developing infrastructure projects, received nearly 11 per cent of the budget allocated to line ministerial expenditure. The remaining two ministries received 7.7 per cent and 6.3 per cent respectively of the budget allocated to line ministerial expenditure. The government expected the increase in this budget allocation to stimulate the acceleration of physical and human capital investments that would then further enhance national productive capacity. As argued by Domar (1947), the increase in physical and human capital investments could increase the national productive capacity and generate further economic growth.

Government Financing

As mentioned earlier, in an attempt to diversify its source of funding to finance its expenditure, the government has since 2002 been issuing bonds to domestic investors (financial institutions and individual investors). However, the domestic demand for these bonds has been primarily low because of the domestic bond market's underdevelopment. Consequently, this forced the government to look for an opportunity beyond selling to domestic investors, and in 2006, it decided to offer its bonds to foreign investors. In line with the better credit rating given by Fitch and Moody to Indonesian bonds, government bonds picked up interest from many foreign investors. Most of these foreign investors, however, preferred to hold government bonds with a short-term maturity.

As Table 5.5 shows, the amount of government bonds held by foreign investors increased significantly by about 17 per cent annually from 2007–09. In 2007, the proportion of government bonds held by foreign investors was around 40 per cent, and it fell slightly to 35 per cent in 2008–09. The presence of foreign investors stimulated the interest of domestic investors. Thus, slowly but surely, more domestic investors, primarily domestic insurance and mutual fund companies, decided to invest in government bonds as well. In recent times, individual domestic investors have started to feel more interested in holding government bonds. In 2007–09, the proportion of government bonds held by individual domestic investors grew by 41.6 per cent annually (see Table 5.5).

The amount of government funding generated from the bond market has significantly reduced the dependency of the Indonesian economy on

TABLE 5.5
**Amount of Government Bonds According to Ownership from 2007–09
(in IDR billion)**

Ownership	2007	2008	2009	Growth (%) 2007–09
Bank	**268.5**	**258.75**	**254.36**	**–2.7**
Bank of Indonesia	**14.86**	**23.01**	**22.50**	**23.1**
Non-Bank	**194.24**	**243.93**	**304.89**	**25.3**
Foreign Investors	78.16	87.61	108.00	17.5
Domestic Investors	116.08	156.32	196.89	30.2
1. Insurance Companies	43.47	55.83	72.58	29.2
2. Mutual Fund Companies	26.33	33.11	45.22	31.1
3. Pension Funds	25.5	28.55	37.50	21.3
4. Individuals	20.5	30.21	41.12	41.6
5. Securities	0.28	8.62	0.47	29.6

Source: Debt Management Office Statistics, Ministry of Finance <http://ww.dmo.go.id> (accessed 17 May 2010).

foreign borrowings. In 2008, the revenue generated from government bonds stood at 85.9 IDR trillion or about 83.8 per cent of total revenue. The proceeds from selling government bonds were mostly generated in the first semester of 2008. Alas, the ensuing global financial crisis towards the end of 2008 brought a halt to the promising role of government bonds. As a result, the crisis destroyed investor confidence.

The Indonesian Government tried to revitalize the proceeds from selling bonds by diversifying its bond products with Islamic compliant bonds, that is, *sukuk* and *samurai bonds*. The latter are basically yen-denominated bonds sold in the Japanese capital market to institutional buyers that include insurance companies and banks. The government expected the bond equivalent products to be quite appealing to the investors who would otherwise not be interested in buying existing government bonds. Other than issuing these new products, the government also made an effort to shift foreign investors' holding of government bonds from short-term ones to long-term ones, that is, those with a maturity longer than five years. All these innovations helped the Indonesian Government maintain a reasonably high level of expenditure in 2010.

As the actual amount of budget deficit in 2008 was very low, that is, around IDR 4.1 trillion, while the generated amount of government financing was relatively high, the government enjoyed a large surplus in its "financing balance" (SILPA — *Sisa Lebih Pembayaran Anggaran*). In 2008, the amount of SILPA stood at IDR 80 trillion. The presence of this large surplus (SILPA) enabled the government to finance its fiscal stimulus package.

FISCAL STIMULUS PACKAGE

The choice between monetary policy and fiscal policy as an instrument of stabilization policies is a long-standing issue in economic discourses among academics and policy-makers (Beetsma and Jensen 2005; Eggertsson and Woodford 2004; and Aarle et al. 2008). The former refers to the use of money supply, exchange rates, and interest rates to expand or contract aggregate demand and supply, while the latter refers to the use of tax structure, government spending, and government borrowing to expand or contract aggregate demand and supply. The advantage of monetary policy over fiscal policy is in its immediacy (DeLong 2002). Monetary policy changes can be implemented in a relatively short period of time. In contrast, the implementation of fiscal policy changes often takes a long time to materialize. In practice, most countries facing economic slowdown would adopt a mixture of monetary and fiscal policies. This is exactly what Indonesia did when responding to the recent economic crisis. The central bank lowered its lending rate in order to stimulate the economy. Unfortunately, this policy alone was not enough, especially considering that banks were reluctant to lend in the first place, fearing that the financial crisis would undermine their liquidity and solvency.

The macroeconomic downturn that took place as a result of the global financial crisis in 2008 called for fiscal stimulus to combat the ensuing decline in the economic activity and labour market conditions (Blanchard and Cottarelli 2008; Corsetti 2008; Martens 2009). In line with this reasoning, the Indonesian Government launched a countercyclical fiscal stimulus package aimed at resuscitating the domestic economy in order to prevent it from slipping into a worse situation. As mentioned earlier, Indonesia's relatively prudent fiscal policies allowed the country to finance this stimulus package, using a reasonably large surplus in its financing balance (SILPA) without excessively straining its budget.

The current stimulus package that has been implemented by the Indonesian Government clearly follows a standard Keynesian response to an economic crisis. Without the stimulus, the inability of the economy to move back to full employment equilibrium can cause the economy to spiral into severe recession (Mankiw 2000). The Indonesian package includes a substantial cut in taxes as well as an increase in government spending, both of which are needed in response to insufficient demand for goods and services in the economy brought about by the crisis and to push the economy back towards full-employment equilibrium.

The package was specifically aimed at meeting the following goals (Ministry of Finance 2009):

(a) Increasing people's purchasing power so that they can maintain a steady growth in consumption, thereby stimulating the real economy. This is done by cutting personal income tax rates and increasing the tax-free income base.
(b) Giving incentives to corporations, in the form of tax cuts, import duties relief, payroll tax incentive, and encouraging entrepreneurship.
(c) Creating jobs and mitigating job losses using government spending on labour-intensive infrastructure projects in the areas of public works, communications, energy, and housing.

The value of the fiscal stimulus package that was committed by the Indonesian Government in 2009 was on par with other countries (see Table 5.6) as it amounted to about 1.4 per cent of its GDP. The economy itself is projected to grow around 4.5 per cent in 2009. Some critics argue that the stimulus package was implemented simply because the government felt the need to conform to the approach adopted by

TABLE 5.6
GDP Growth and Fiscal Stimulus Package as a Percentage of GDP

Country	2009 GDP Growth Projection (%)	Fiscal Stimulus as % of GDP
Malaysia	0.2	4.4
Thailand	2	1.8
Australia	1.7	1.5
Indonesia	**4.5**	**1.4**
US	−0.8	1.2
UK	−1.3	1.1
Singapore	−5	1.1
Japan	−0.2	1.0
South Korea	2.5	0.9
India	6	0.9
China	8	0.6

Source: CEIC financial and economics database, ISI emerging markets.

many countries experiencing the wrath of the financial crisis, and not because the country actually needed it. We believe that this argument is rather misguided. We do not think that the circumstances surrounding the financial crisis allowed Indonesia to adopt alternative approaches. The economy experienced contraction and thus, exports and industrial production declined. Not only did the fear of financial contagion discourage banks and other financial institutions from lending, but it also inflicted a massive blow to consumer confidence. Active monetary policies alone were not sufficient enough to lift an economy that had been plagued with high uncertainty. The government simply had to intervene and provide sufficient incentives for firms and consumers to invest and spend in order to boost aggregate demand and kick-start the recovery process.

Table 5.7 shows the breakdown of the fiscal stimulus package according to the three broad aims mentioned above. The major part of the budget in the package was spent on efforts to increase people's purchasing power

TABLE 5.7
Fiscal Stimulus, 2009

Description	Allocation (IDR trillion)
1. Tax Savings	43.0
• Reductions in income tax rates	32.0
○ Lower corporate tax rate	18.5
○ Lower personal income tax rate	13.5
• Income tax-free band raised to 15.8 IDR million	11.0
2. Tax/Import Duty Subsidies for Business/Targeted Households	13.3
• VAT on oil/gas exploration, cooking oil	3.5
• Import duties on raw materials and capital goods	2.5
• Payroll tax	6.5
• Geothermal tax	0.8
3. Pro-business/Jobs Subsidies and Budget Expenditures	15.0
• Reduced price for automotive diesel	2.8
• Discounted electricity billing rates for industrial users	1.4
• Additional infrastructure expenditures, subsidies and government equity injection	10.2
• Upscaling community block grants (PNPM)	0.6
Total Stimulus	**71.3**

Source: Ministry of Finance, <http://www.fiskal.depkeu.go.id> (accessed 5 March 2009).

through reductions in income tax rates and an increase in the tax-free income base.

Obviously, the jury is still out on whether it was really the fiscal stimulus package, or rather other factors such as the low reliance of the Indonesian economy on international trade, the high domestic consumption (particularly during the Indonesian legislative and presidential elections), the relatively less developed domestic financial market, and the prudential monetary policy that contributed positively to the ability of the Indonesian economy to cope with the crisis. It is definitely still too early to conclude whether the Indonesian fiscal stimulus package really did play a large role in expanding aggregate demand and stimulating economic activities. Nevertheless, early indicators do seem to suggest that the economy has slowly awakened from its slumber. Also, an intercountry study on the fiscal stimulus by the IMF has shown that a countercyclical fiscal stimulus package, complemented by accommodative monetary policies, could indeed have long-run multiplier effects on the economy (Freedman et al. 2009). However, this study also stresses that fiscal stimulus packages should ideally be considered only when countries are not facing strict financing constraints in the form of high borrowing costs and severe budget deficits. For Indonesia, these two constraints, although remaining a concern, did not really cause serious hindrances. In fact, as was mentioned earlier, Indonesia enjoyed a cash surplus of around 80 IDR trillion, and a relatively low fiscal deficit of around 0.1 per cent of GDP at the end of 2008. Figure 5.5 shows an intercountry comparison of fiscal deficit as a percentage of GDP at the end of 2008. Nevertheless, a more thorough and careful empirical econometrics analysis would certainly be needed to settle the issue.

In spite of the useful nature of the countercyclical fiscal stimulus package in alleviating the economy, policy-makers must also bear in mind that such a package could also bring some unwanted consequences. Firstly, huge government spending that comes with the fiscal stimulus package could potentially crowd out private consumption and private investment, and thus may fail to increase the level of economic activity. This is essentially a conservative economist's argument refuting the Keynesian based fiscal stimulus package (Reuss 2009). To avoid this crowding out effect, they argue that an increase in government spending must be financed either through higher taxes or increased government borrowing (Corden 2009). However, we think otherwise. Increasing taxes and government borrowing in the wake of an economic crisis would not solve the problem. In fact, the increase in foreign borrowing would bury the economy further with the need to service its debts. It is hard to see how the country will service

FIGURE 5.5
Comparative Fiscal Deficits, 2008 (percentage of GDP)

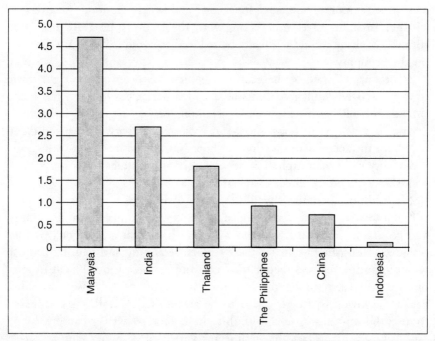

Sources: Ministry of Finance and Standard Chartered Bank (2009).

its debts when its economy has already been stretched thin by the crisis. Also, more importantly, it is hard to find foreign creditors in a time of crisis like this. Increasing taxes to finance government spending would also not be viable as higher taxes would create a heavier burden for domestic companies which are already badly affected by the crisis.

Secondly, huge government spending may exert an inflationary pressure, and this is one thing that the government wants to avoid. This fiscal inflationary pressure may lead to stagflation instead of recovery (Cochrane 2009). In order to avoid slipping into stagflation, a solid monetary policy would also be needed.

Thirdly, cuts in personal income taxes may not always lead to higher private consumption as individuals will expect the government to raise its taxes eventually in order to finance the deficit. This is the well known Ricardian equivalence argument (Mankiw 2000).

The key to a successful stimulus package is to avoid all these potential pitfalls. For this reason, in general, fiscal stimulus packages should only be seen as a temporary measure. It is best used when economic recovery is still not in sight. Over time, along with the recovery progress, the fiscal stimulus package should gradually be reduced to avoid inflationary pressure on the economy.

The current state of the economy, which has been on the right track towards recovery, still needs a fiscal stimulus package. However, the focus should probably be shifted towards sustaining long-term growth, rather than creating a quick fix to boost short-run economic activity. The government could, for instance, focus on efforts to boost infrastructure as well as increase the quality of human capital, rather than giving subsidies for consumption goods and providing direct cash transfers.

In addition, perhaps it would be better if Indonesia retailored its fiscal stimulus package so that it could also focus on stimulating some sectors and geographic areas (such as those outside Java) that are plagued by idle resources. Boosting output for these sectors, retraining and rehiring laid-off workers, and developing better infrastructure in these geographical regions outside Java seem to be the obvious way to utilize this fiscal stimulus package. Obviously, we also have to be aware that in reality it is difficult to use the stimulus package to hit these targets with great precision, especially given the fact that politicians with vested interests play a great role in influencing the direction of the fiscal stimulus package. Because of this, it would unfortunately not be surprising to see a politically popular package in place that may have little impact in stimulating the depressed real sector.

CONCLUDING REMARKS

The Indonesian economy was certainly affected by the recent global economic crisis. Nevertheless, the negative impact on the country was relatively mild in comparison to that on other countries. This was due to the relatively low contribution of exports to GDP and strong domestic demand. These two factors helped insulate the vastly negative impact of the crisis from hitting the Indonesian economy. Nevertheless, it was crucial for the government to act promptly to tackle the potential repercussions as the real sector was depressed and unemployment and bankruptcy levels soared. The government introduced a mixture of monetary and fiscal policies and also implemented a countercyclical fiscal stimulus package, a widely popular policy adopted by virtually all countries affected by the crisis.

Indonesia's budgetary condition was quite conducive in supporting the implementation of the fiscal stimulus package. Thus, the country enjoyed a relatively large positive surplus in its financing budget and a consistently low level of budget deficit. Therefore, there was ample room for the government to manoeuvre with the fiscal stimulus package.

The government had a good record of prudent fiscal policy. Over time, it was able to reduce the dependency on foreign borrowings by diversifying its revenue base. Several innovative actions were launched, including the sale of a variety of government bonds to domestic and foreign investors. The government was also successful in increasing tax revenue. Two recent tax policy measures, the sunset and taxpayer registration policy, deserve applause. The dependency on revenue from the oil and gas sector also diminished over time, thus reducing the susceptibility of the country to an external oil price shock.

However, the current budget also seems to indicate that the government had difficulty in absorbing the budget as the actual expenditure was below the budgeted expenditure. This may either indicate inefficiency in the implementations of various government projects, or it may be related to bureaucratic inefficiency. Over the long-term period, such inefficiency in absorption could escalate the costs of implementing projects. Usually, by the time the projects are ready to take off, the costs of implementing the projects will have increased to a higher level than the one previously budgeted.

Perhaps it is too early to evaluate the performance of the fiscal stimulus package fully, given that such a package usually takes a long time to take effect. However, early indications show that it has been quite successful. Therefore, the economy, although not yet fully recovered, seems to be on the right track.

Finally, this chapter has argued that the fiscal stimulus package should be used only as a temporary measure and be gradually reduced and abolished when the economy starts to recover steadily. This is because this package could also bring some unwanted consequences by crowding out private consumption, investment, and exerting inflationary pressure. A Ricardian equivalence effect may also kick in. That is, instead of spending the tax-cut money for private consumption, people might just use it as additional saving for fear that they will face higher tax rates in the future. As a result, these various tax cuts that are part of the fiscal stimulus package may fail to boost domestic economic activity As long as the economy remains depressed, such a countercyclical fiscal stimulus package may be warranted.

NOTES

1. See Booth and McCawley (1981) for a more detailed overview of changes in the fiscal system during this period.
2. Routine expenditures consist of personnel and material expenditures and subsidies for both fuel and other items such as foods and fertilizer.
3. The parliamentary election was held in April 2009, and the presidential election was held in July 2009.
4. The sunset policy gave tax amnesty to taxpayers who voluntarily reported any unpaid tax payable before April 2009. The taxpayer registration policy required all tax subjects to have a tax number (NPWP — *Nomor Pokok Wajib Pajak*).
5. Ministerial budget post refers to all expenses related to personal, material, and development projects administered by various government ministries. Non ministerial budget post refers to all expenses used to finance subsidies, interest debt payments, and other expenditures unrelated to any specific government ministry.
6. See The Budget Memorandum and APBN, 2009, p. III.10.
7. UU no. 20/2003 governs Indonesia's education system. To support the implementation of this law, the government committed to allocate 20 per cent of their line ministerial expenditure to developing the national education system.

REFERENCES

Aarle, Bas van, L. Bovenberg, and M. Raith. "Monetary and Fiscal Policy Interaction and Government Debt Stabilization". *Journal of Economics* 62, no. 2, June 1995.

Arlini, Silvia M. and B.D. Suatmi. *Makro Ekonomi Indonesia*. Jakarta: Lembaga Penelitian IBiI, 2006.

Asher, Mukul G. and Anne Booth. "Fiscal Policy". In *The Oil Boom and After: Indonesian Economic Policy and Performance in the Suharto Era*, edited by Anne Booth. Singapore: Oxford University Press, 1992.

Asian Development Bank. *Asian Development Outlook*. Manila: ADB, several editions.

Bank of Indonesia. *Indonesian Financial Statistics*. Jakarta: BI, several editions.

Beetsma, R.M. and H. Jensen. "Monetary and Fiscal Policy Interactions in a Microfounded Model of a Monetary Union". *Journal of International Economics* 67 (2004): 320–52.

Blanchard, Oliver and Carlo Cottarelli. "IMF Spell Out Need for Global Fiscal Stimulus". *IMF Survey Magazine*, 29 December 2008.

Booth, Anne and Peter McCawley. "Fiscal Policy". In *The Indonesian Economy During the Soeharto Era*, edited by Anne Booth and Peter McCawley. Kuala Lumpur: Oxford University Press, 1981.

Cochrane, John. "Fiscal Theory, and Fiscal and Monetary Policy in the Financial Crisis". Paper prepared for the conference on "Monetary-Fiscal Policy Interactions,

Expectations, and Dynamics in the Current Economic Crisis". Princeton University, 22–23 May 2009. <https://www.princeton.edu/economics/seminar-schedule-by-prog/macro-s09/monetary-fiscal-policy-co/schedule/pdfs/Cochrane-paper-2.pdf> (accessed 6 January 2010).

Corden, W.M. *The Asian Crises: Is There a Way Out?* Singapore: Institute of Southeast Asian Studies, 1998.

———. "The Theory of the Fiscal Stimulus: How Will a Debt-Financed Stimulus Affect the Future?" Melbourne Institute Working Paper No. 15/09, 2009. <http://melbourneinstitute.com/wp/wp2009n15.pdf> (accessed 5 January 2010).

Corsetti, Giancarlo. "The Rediscovery of Fiscal Policy". <www.voxeu.org> (accessed 11 February 2008).

DeLong, Bradford. *Macroeconomics*. New York: McGrawHill, 2002.

Domar, Evsey D. "Capital Expansion, Rate of Growth, and Employment". *Econometrica* 14, no. 2 (1947): 137–47.

Eggertsson, Gauti B. and M. Woodford. "Optimal Monetary and Fiscal Policy in a Liquidity Trap". NBER Working Paper No. 10840, October 2004.

Fengler, Wolfgang. "Imagine a New Indonesia: Spending to Improve Development". <http://blogs.worldbank.org/eastasiapacific/imagine-a-new-indonesia-spending-to-improve-development> (accessed 4 June 2009).

———. "Indonesia's $100 Billion Budget: Is Debt an Issue?". <http://blogs.worldbank.org/eastasiapacific/indonesias-100-billion-budget-is-debt-an-issue> (accessed 23 April 2009).

Financial Times. "Indonesia Sells $3bn in Debt at Discount". 27 February 2009.

Freedman, Charless, Michael Kumhoff, Douglass Laxton, and Jaewoo Lee. "The Case for Global Fiscal Stimulus". *IMF Research Department Working Paper*, 2009.

Hill, Hal. "Fiscal Policy". In *The Indonesian Economy*, edited by Hal Hill. New York: Cambridge University Press, 2000.

———. *The Indonesian Economy in Crises: Causes, Consequences and Lessons*. Singapore: Institute of Southeast Asian Studies, 1999.

International Monetary Fund. *World Economic Outlook 2000*. Washington, D.C.: IMF, 1999.

Jakarta Post. "Sukuk' Success Stories in Indonesia and Beyond". <http://www.thejakartapost.com/news/2009/11/20/sukuk039-success-stories-indonesia-and-beyond.html> (accessed 20 November 2009).

Lane, T. et al. "IMF Supported Programs in Indonesia, Korea, and Thailand: A Preliminary Assessment". IMF Occasional Paper No. 178. Washington, D.C.: International Monetary Fund, 1999.

Mankiw, Gregory. *Macroeconomics*. New York: Worth Publisher, 2000.

Ministry of Finance. *Financial Memorandum and Revised Budget*, several editions.

———. "Realization of Macroeconomic Assumption and Budget Realization up to September 2009". <http://www.anggaran.depkeu.go.id/Content/09-10-26,%20narasi%20real%202009%20sd%20September%20(Inggris).pdf> (accessed 5 January 2010).

————. "The 2009 Revised Budget Fiscal Stimulus Programme: Mitigating the Impact from the Global Crisis and State Budget 2008 and 2009". <http://www.fiskal.depkeu.go.id> (accessed 5 March 2009).

Reuss, Alejandro. "Fiscal Policy and Crowding Out, in the General Theory and the Current Crisis: A Primer on Keynes' Economics". <http://www.dollarsandsense.org/archives/2009/0509reusskeynespartI.html> (accessed 6 January 2010).

Roubini, Nouriel. "Indonesia: Fiscal Policy". <http://www.roubini.com/briefings/58213.php> (accessed 6 January 2010).

Standard Chartered Bank. "Analysis of Economic and Financial Markets Development", 2 September 2009.

World Bank. *World Economic Outlook*. Washington, D.C.: World Bank, several editions.

6

Understanding the Role of Fiscal Stimulus in Maintaining Economic Resilience

Haris Munandar and Iskandar Simorangkir[1]

EXITING THE 2008–09 CRISIS: A POLICY-DRIVEN RECOVERY

The 2007–08 global financial turbulence originated from the subprime mortgage crisis in the United States which had spread across both developed and developing countries. This financial turmoil not only touched the financial sector, but also the real sector as well. In the financial sector, global financial institutions reported a series of losses; thus, confidence in financial institutions eroded and the level of granted credit dropped significantly. Meanwhile, in the real sector, world trade volume and economic growth dropped drastically and unemployment level and poverty rates rose sharply. The IMF had downgraded the forecast for world economic growth 2009 from 2.2 per cent in November 2008 to 0.5 per cent in January 2009, and to –1.4 per cent in July 2009. However in its October 2010 update, the IMF announced the actual growth rate in 2009 to be –0.6 per cent (International Monetary Fund 2010).

World output and trade started to improve in the second half of 2009. Confidence significantly bounced back up in both the real and financial sectors as extraordinary policy responses have prevented another Great Depression. Governments and central banks introduced a number of measures to deal with liquidity and solvency problems.[2] Central banks eased monetary policy by reducing interest rates to unprecedented levels, with some interest rates slashed down close to zero to offset the increase in private sector premium and to prevent a further decline in economic activity. In spite of these policies, credit markets remained very tight, and economic growth and employment in many countries continued to weaken. With limited room for further stimulus through monetary policy, attention switched to the fiscal side, such as improving direct fiscal spending and temporarily cutting taxes to push domestic aggregate demand. Therefore, following the G-20 consensus, the Indonesian economy maintained its resilience throughout the turbulence by cutting interest rates and running a fiscal stimulus package.

Notably, the governments in many countries used fiscal stimulus package to prevent their economies from falling into recession. Developed countries, such as the United States, the United Kingdom, and Germany introduced such packages for the real sector to push their domestic aggregate demand. Asian countries, such as China and India, also introduced fiscal stimulus support. Theirs consisted of an increase in infrastructure expenditure, along with a simultaneous tax cut.

In spite of these government responses, there is still an ongoing debate on the role of *ad hoc* fiscal policy in managing business cycles. The Keynesian school of thought argues that fiscal stimuli can be used to enhance output as long as the price is rigid and the economy has excess capacity; the Classical school, on the other hand, argues that fiscal stimuli only increase prices and do not have any effect on output.

Indonesia was among the economies that were applying for such fiscal support. The country was certainly affected by the global financial crisis, as reflected in the decline of growth from 6.01 per cent in 2008 to 4.55 per cent in 2009. However, its economic performance was still relatively remarkable, compared with the negative growth experienced by most economies. Nevertheless, to maintain the resilience of the Indonesian economy and cushion it from the global crisis, in addition to its monetary and financing policies, the Indonesian Government provided substantial fiscal stimulus packages to push household consumption and infrastructure investments. In 2009, the Indonesian Government launched a fiscal package of Rp. 73.3 trillion (1.4 per cent of GDP), which consists of expenditure, tax cuts and tax subsidies. This countercyclical policy was introduced to sustain public purchasing power, maintain business competiveness, and reduce unemployment, and hence, boost economic growth. For 2010, the government has planned to allocate a budget of Rp. 36.3 trillion (0.6 per cent of GDP) for the same purpose.

An interesting and important question is how effective the fiscal stimuli have been in lessening the depth of the slowdown in Indonesian economy, particularly in 2009. This chapter studies the importance of the fiscal stimuli in preventing the Indonesian economy from weakening further. To explore the impact of fiscal supports on the economy, a computable general equilibrium model of the Indonesian economy is constructed and utilized. In both developed and developing countries, computable general equilibrium models have become a standard tool for policy analysis.

The remainder of this chapter is divided into four sections. First, the role of fiscal policy in an economy is analysed with the 2007/08 global crisis as the background. Second, the development of the Indonesian economy in 2009 is examined. Third, the impact of the fiscal stimuli on the national account, industrial sectors, and income distribution is analysed. Finally, some concluding remarks and lessons learned are offered.

ECONOMIC SLUMP AND PRINCIPLES OF FISCAL STIMULI

With the global growth declining from 3.0 per cent in 2008 to –0.6 per cent in 2009, IMF confirmed the sluggishness of 2009 world economy in its April 2010 World Economic Outlook (International Monetary Fund 2010). Such a record was confirmed by the data in which both production and consumption decreased tremendously, both in developing and developed countries. A decline in GDP took place in almost all countries in 2009. A number of facts pointed to such declines, including a series of losses reported by world commercial financial institutions, worsening risk perception, and sliding world commodity prices.

The slowdown of the global economy, attributed to the widespread impact of the global financial crisis, had decreased inflationary pressures by reducing aggregate demand. This situation had encouraged central banks in most countries to ease their monetary policies. The Federal Reserve of the United States had significantly cut its key Fed Funds rate to a level very close to zero (0.25 per cent). Moreover, similar policies were followed by central banks in other countries including Australia, the United Kingdom, the Eurozone, and Asia to avest an even greater deteriorating impact of the crisis on their economies. These central banks lowered their key interest rates to between 0.4 per cent and 5.3 per cent in 2008–09 (see Figure 6.1).

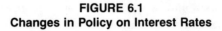

FIGURE 6.1
Changes in Policy on Interest Rates

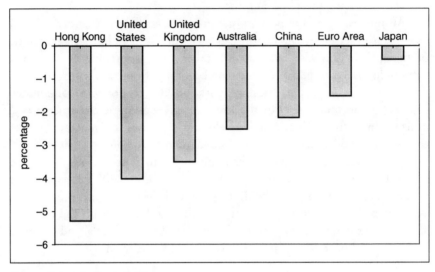

Source: Drawn by the authors.

Such monetary easing was crucially supported by policies that were directed at removing the liquidity shortage in financial markets. Thus, the U.S. Government announced a US$838 billion bailout package directed at saving a number of important financial institutions and preventing panic and systemic damage in housing markets. Besides that, a US$250 billion Troubled Assets Relief Program (TARP) was also launched in an attempt to take over problematic assets through the Capital Purchase Program. In the banking sector, governments across countries issued various types of guarantee schemes for bank deposits and loans, and injected capital into banks with liquidity problems. These measures were taken to boost confidence in the banking sector. For instance, in an attempt to improve its banking sector, the U.K. Government made £50 billion in liquidity assistance available (see Table 6.1).

Nevertheless, due to the limitations of monetary and financing policies in stimulating the economy, there have been renewed calls for governments to use fiscal policy actively to prevent sharp declines in economic activity.[3] Governments in many countries provided substantial fiscal stimulus packages to push household consumption up and increase infrastructure investments. For instance, this was done by providing a temporary tax cut on investments. The type and scale of stimulus packages issued by developed and developing

TABLE 6.1
Policy Responses in a Number of Countries

Countries	Recapitalization	Deposit Guarantee	Liquidity
Australia	Buying up residential mortgage-backed securities by the government of up to 4 billion dollars	Guarantee all new and existing bank deposits of up to A$1 million for three years	$2.71 billion for mortgage-backed securities
Germany	A maximum of 80 billion euros is available for recapitalization, 20 billion set aside as a provision for the guarantee offer	Unlimited guarantee (worth 1 trillion euro)	
Malaysia	Capital into banks if needed	Guarantee deposits in all currencies until December 2010	Broader access to liquidity facility
Netherlands	Inject 20 billion euros into financial institutions	Guarantee up to 100,000 euros with total prepared fund worth 200 billion euros	
Poland	Inject fresh capital into banks, if needed	Boost bank deposit guarantees of up to 175,000 zlotys	Use of currency swaps and introduction of repo operations
South Korea	Government to provide $30 billion to domestic banks and exporters and help small enterprises to take 12 billion won ($9 billion) as loan and an other $4 billion for debt laden builders	Government guarantees $100 billion. Injection of up to 1 trillion won ($960.7 million) on securities for banking industries in Korea	

TABLE 6.1 *(Cont'd)*

Countries	Recapitalization	Deposit Guarantee	Liquidity
United Kingdom	Provide 50 billion pounds for domestic banking and financial institutions, and 25 billion in addition to support capital improvement	Insured up to 50,000 pounds for all deposits and short-term and medium-term debt; insured up to 250 billion pounds for qualified financial institutions	Term Securities Lending Facilities worth at least 200 billion pounds
United States	Set up US$250 billion Troubled Assets Relief Program (TARP) Fund to take over toxic assets through Capital Purchase Program	Insured up to $250,000 for all deposits until 31 December 2009	$900 billion liquidity injection

Sources: Bank Indonesia, *Indonesian Economic Outlook 2009–2014.*

countries obviously varied (see Table 6.2). Thus, the 2009 fiscal deficit in advanced economies increased to around 7 per cent, far higher than that of developing countries which was approximately 2 per cent. A number of countries in the Asian region such as China, India, and Indonesia, designed economic stimulus packages aimed at increasing infrastructure expenditure while cutting tax simultanously; on the other hand, the economic stimulus packages from Malaysia, Taiwan, and South Korea were directed only at increasing infrastructure spending. In Australia, the fiscal stimulus package came in three forms: funding assistance for low- and middle-income households (to increase their disposable income), infrastructure spending

TABLE 6.2
Fiscal Interventions in Selected Asian Countries

Countries	Fiscal Measures
China	Economic stimulus package worth $586 billion, which includes spending on various areas such as roads, airports, and other infrastructure, health and education, environmental protection, high technology, and housing; also covers tax deductions for exporters.
India	Economic stimulus package that includes additional government spending worth 200 billion rupees (US$4 billion), a cut on value added tax, credit support for textile, leather, handlooms and other labour-intensive sectors, and infrastructure financing.
Malaysia	Economic stimulus package worth 7 billion ringgit ($2 billion) to be spent on "high-impact" construction projects, including roads, schools, hospitals, and low-cost housing.
Korea	Economic stimulus package worth at least 14 trillion won ($11 billion), which covers spending on regional infrastructure and providing tax benefits, mainly on investments in factories.
Taiwan	Economic stimulus package of NT$500 billion ($15 billion), which includes a shopping voucher programme, the launch of public construction projects, urban renewal plans, and incentives to encourage private investment and industrial upgrading.
Indonesia	Economic stimulus package with Rp. 73.3 trillion, consisting of Rp. 60.5 trillion in cuts on personal income tax, value added tax, and import duty guaranteed by government, and Rp. 12.8 trillion for expenditure increases, mostly for infrastructure financing.

Source: Bank Indonesia (2009*b*).

increase, and temporary tax cuts related to private investments. Table 6.3 shows the percentage contributions of these stimulus packages to GDP in the various regions.

There has been a long debate about the appropriate role of fiscal policy in managing business cycles, especially during an economic downturn. One school of thought argues that taxes, transfers and fiscal spending can be used to counter fluctuations in economic activity, especially to the

TABLE 6.3
Fiscal Stimulus Package Announced as a
Proportion of GDP in the Region,
January 2009

Economic Region	2009	2010
United States	**1.9**	**2.9**
Tax cuts	0.9	1.2
Infrastructure	0.3	0.8
Other	0.6	1.0
Euro area	**0.9**	**0.8**
Tax cuts	0.3	0.3
Infrastructure	0.4	0.0
Other	0.2	0.4
Japan	**1.4**	**0.4**
Tax cuts	0.1	0.1
Infrastructure	0.3	0.1
Other	1.0	0.2
Asia excluding Japan	**1.5**	**1.3**
Tax cuts	0.1	0.1
Infrastructure	1.1	0.0
Other	0.3	1.2
Rest of G-20	**1.1**	**0.3**
Tax cuts	0.5	0.1
Infrastructure	0.2	0.1
Other	0.4	−0.1
Total (PPP-weighted)	**1.4**	**1.3**
Tax cuts	0.4	0.4
Infrastructure	0.5	0.3
Other	0.5	0.7

Source: Freedman et al. (2009).

extent that economic fluctuations are mainly due to the market falling out of equilibrium. The simplest way to explain this argument is with the Keynesian approach. Keynesians assume price rigidity and excess capacity, so that output is determined by aggregate demand. Hence, a tax cut or increased government spending is thought to lead to an increase in aggregate demand, either through consumption or investment.

Though government spending on infrastructure increases investment, the way the government finances its increased spending may affect the final outcome of the stimulus. If the increase in government spending is followed by an increase in tax, then the rising government expenditure would lead to a change in consumption because it will affect private sector tax burdens. For a given income before tax, a tax increase implies a decline in consumers' current income after tax. Because of the decline in their current income, consumers then respond by reducing consumption.

On the other hand, if an increase in government spending is financed by debt, the government will have to repay its debt in the future, implying that future taxes will have to rise. If taxpayers are smart enough to understand that increased government spending today means higher taxes in the future, thus lowering expected future incomes, they will again reduce their desired consumption. In addition to reducing consumption, an increase in government spending crowds out investment spending. Crowding out occurs when expansionary fiscal policies cause interest rates to rise, thereby reducing private spending, particularly investment.

On the other hand, a tax cut directly increases current incomes, so a tax cut should increase desired consumption. However, the current tax cut should also lead people to expect lower after-tax incomes in the future. The reason is not that the government has changed its spending, but rather it has increased its current borrowing in order to cut taxes today. Since the extra debt will have to be repaid with interest in the future, future taxes will have to be higher, which in turn implies lower future disposable incomes for households. Assuming other things are equal, the decline in expected future incomes will cause people to consume less today, offsetting the positive effect of increased current income on desired consumption. Some economists argue that the positive effect of increased current income and the negative effect of decreased future income on desired consumption should cancel each other out, so that the overall effect of a current tax cut on consumption is zero (Ricardian Equivalance applies).

There are many empirical studies conducted to measure the role of fiscal stimuli in improving economic activities. Studies by Blanchard and Perotti (2002) and Romer and Romer (2008) showed that a fiscal stimulus of 1 per cent of GDP was found to increase GDP by close to 1 percentage point, and by as much as 2 to 3 percentage points of GDP when the effect peaks a few years later. Perotti (2005) found much smaller multipliers for European countries. Recently, Freedman et al. (2009) found that neither government expenditure nor targeted transfers have a sizeable multiplier effect on the economy.

In a situation where a fiscal stimulus has been global and supported by monetary accommodation, and where financial sectors that are under pressure have been supported by governments, every dollar spent on government investment can increase GDP by about a dollar. Therefore, in countries in which room for fiscal measures is limited, it will be particularly important to select measures that will have the largest effect on aggregate demand, such as a targeted transfer and government investment. Meanwhile, intercountry studies conducted by Christiansen (2008) found small fiscal multipliers for the economy and, in some cases, multipliers with negative signs. The studies with negative multipliers of fiscal stimuli were conducted by Giavazzi and Pagano (1990) and surveyed in Hemming, Kell, and Mahfouz (2002). In the international context, Corsetti et al. (2010) theoretically examined the role of various factors, including the size and openness of the economies, financial imperfections, and trade elasticities. They found that coordinated short-term stimulus measures are the most effective when designed and implemented with credible, medium-term consolidated plans featuring at least some spending constraints.

Fiscal stimulus can also be helpful in defending an economy against an economic slowdown (Elmendorf and Furhan 2008). If a sharp economic downturn appears imminent, and well designed tax or spending changes can quickly be implemented, then such fiscal stimuli could instantly boost economic activity. Fiscal stimuli could provide greater confidence about the economic outcome, though their effect is still uncertain. However, it would be better not to have any fiscal stimulus packages at all than to have to cut taxes or increase spending when they are poorly timed, badly targeted, and/or would permanently increase the budget deficit. Based on this idea, Elmendorf and Furman (2008) analysed three principles, namely timely, targeted, and temporary, that have been advocated by Summers (2007), Sperling (2007), and Stone and Cox (2008) to maximize the benefits from fiscal stimulus packages.

In this case, timely means policy-makers should act in a timely manner to lessen any impact on economic growth. Thus, fiscal stimuli should not be enacted prematurely, delayed too long, or consist of tax cuts or spending increases that would take too long to be implemented. Targeted means policy-makers should ensure that each dollar from tax cuts or higher spending raises output in the short run by the maximum amount. From the perspective of households, policy-makers should ensure that the money ends up in the pockets of families that are the most vulnerable in a weakening economy. Temporary means taxes should be cut or spending should be increased to raise output in the short run, but the stimuli should not increase a budget deficit in the long run.

THE INDONESIAN ECONOMY AND CRISIS-INDUCED FISCAL INTERVENTION

Amid pressures from the global economy, in 2009, the Indonesian economy still managed to achieve higher growth compared with other countries in the region. This performance was supported by the resilience of its domestic demand, which in turn provided the primary driving force for national economic growth. During that year, economic growth reached 4.55 per cent on a year-on-year basis. Although less vigorous than in the preceding year, domestic demand recorded a 5.29 per cent expansion. The growth in domestic consumption was an impressive 6.21 per cent. At this level, consumption helped prevent further losses in economic growth. Bolstering the brisk pace of consumption were a number of fiscal and structural initiatives such as direct cash transfers, a pay rise for civil servants, and increases in the minimum wage in some regions. This added momentum to household consumption came from a flurry of activities surrounding the general elections, including extra spending in advertisement, communications, food processing, hotels and restaurants, and the printing business.

Expectations of an improvement in the global economy had imbued market actors with a positive sentiment which had in turn benefited the Indonesian economy. The spread of Credit Default Swap (CDS) for Indonesia, an indicator of risk perceptions, eased from as high as 713 basis points in the first quarter of 2009 to 160 at the end of 2009. On the domestic side of the market, capital inflows were spurred by positive sentiment in the world economy and the gradual recovery of liquidity in global financial markets. This in turn led to an appreciation of the rupiah, renewed growth in the composite stock index, and improved yield on Indonesian Government securities. Capital inflows also strengthened Indonesia's international reserves to US$66.1 billion, sufficient for 6.5 months of imports and the servicing of government external debt.

Despite the signs of improvement, most developed economies had not recovered or even continued to show signs of slowing down. Furthermore, the global economy remained fraught with risk and uncertainty. As a result, pressure continued to bear down on the performance of the Indonesian economy. Indonesia's exports weakened further, despite indications of improvement in some export commodity prices. Counterbalancing this were falling imports because of both weakening domestic demand and plunging imports of oil-based fuels. Indonesia has been moving forward with kerosene energy conversion and energy diversification programmes.

At the same time, pressure on the Indonesian economy in 2009 was evident from its falling investment growth. This decline was primarily explained by a softening demand for its exports and weakening domestic consumption, followed by a tightening of financial sources. Investment in the construction sector maintained momentum with limited ongoing work on infrastructure construction. On the other hand, investment in other sectors recorded negative growth rates.

As a result of the weak conditions in the domestic economy, low inflation in trading partner nations, and improved food supplies, annual inflation continued on a downward trend. Headline inflation in 2009 was remarkably low at 2.78 per cent on a year-on-year basis. This low inflationary pressure was largely explained by the falling pressure on non-fundamentals, with low levels of volatile food prices and administered prices.[4] Similarly, favourable developments in fundamentals helped lower the pressure on core inflation. Appreciation of exchange rate, continual soft domestic demand, and the downward trend in inflation expectations, were all factors that contributed to low inflation.[5]

The financial and monetary sectors were slowing in 2009. Cash held outside banks, that so-called "real M1", and banking transactions in the RTGS (Real Time Gross Settlement) as well as clearing systems in 2009, all recorded a declining trend in growth. On top of all this, there was a further tapering off in credit expansion. Amid brisk growth in depositor funds, the low credit expansion rate freed up liquidity in the banking system. Although bank lending expanded at a very limited rate, some corporate sectors had began seeking alternative funding sources on stock and bond markets and this activity was projected to grow in view of tax incentives and the ease of launching initial public offerings (IPOs).

At the micro level, the Indonesian banking system was in a comparatively stable condition. The downward movement in BI rate since December 2008 met with a positive response in the banking system, albeit on a limited scale. Supporting this were various indicators. The capital adequacy ratio (CAR) recorded in December 2009 was 17 per cent. At the same time, the gross non-performing loans (NPLs) ratio was held below 4 per cent.

TABLE 6.4
Selected Macroeconomic Indicators

Macro Indicators	Unit	2008					2009				
		Q1	Q2	Q3	Q4	Total	Q1	Q2	Q3	Q4	Total
Real GDP Growth	%y-o-y	6.21	6.30	6.25	5.27	6.01	4.53	4.08	4.16	5.43	4.55
Consumption Growth	%y-o-y	5.47	5.49	6.34	6.42	5.94	7.28	6.27	5.44	5.91	6.21
Investment Growth	%y-o-y	18.58	10.88	9.65	11.22	12.42	-0.92	3.01	4.35	4.49	2.77
Export Growth	%y-o-y	13.64	12.36	10.63	1.99	9.53	-18.73	-15.52	-7.79	3.67	-9.70
Import Growth	%y-o-y	17.99	16.11	11.10	-3.73	10.00	-24.42	-21.04	-14.67	1.62	-14.97
Headline Inflation	%y-o-y, EoP	7.10	11.03	12.14	11.06	11.06	7.92	3.65	2.83	2.78	2.78
Core Inflation	%y-o-y, EoP	8.07	7.36	8.08	8.29	8.29	7.15	5.56	4.86	4.28	4.28
Exchange Rate	Avg	9,256	9,259	9,224	10,937	9,666	11,578	10,527	9,973	9,459	10,374
BI Rate	%pa, EoP	8.00	8.50	9.25	9.25	9.25	7.75	7.00	6.50	6.50	6.50

Notes: y-o-y: year on year; EoP: End of Period; Avg: Average; pa: per annum.
Source: Bank Indonesia (2010).

Liquidity in the banking system, including in the interbank money market, had improved progressively alongside growth in third party funds.

The government predicted that the domestic economy in 2010 would expand further in line with earlier projections. As of April 2010, the government expected the 2010 growth to be in the region of 5.5–6.0 per cent. Meanwhile, a series of accommodative monetary policies during 2009 supported the performance of the national economy. Bank Indonesia had consistently and mindfully lowered the BI rate between January and August 2009. It had successfully lowered the BI rate by 50 basis points per month from January to March 2009, by 25 basis points per month from April until August 2009, and then keeping it at the level reached then of 6.5 per cent since September 2009. This series of loose policies was further supported at the operational level by strengthening open market operations and improving the structure of the interest rates. Thus, such a monetary stance seemed to support the resilience of the national economy. Furthermore, this series of monetary policy decisions was also expected to provide support for other measures to sustain the domestic economic growth momentum while continuing to safeguard price stability and financial system stability in the medium term.

In Indonesia the government designed a fiscal package of Rp. 73.3 trillion (US$7.33 billion) which consisted of expenditure and revenue components. This countercyclical policy was introduced with four goals: to sustain public purchasing power, to bolster business competitiveness and resilience, to mitigate the impact of mass employee dismissals, and to reduce unemployment through increased spending on labour-intensive infrastructure. The outline of the Indonesian 2009 planned fiscal stimulus of Rp. 73.3 trillion is presented in Table 6.5.

The revenue aspect of the stimulus package was in the form of various tax cuts (corporate income tax, individual income tax, value added tax, and import duty) amounting to a total of Rp. 60.5 trillion (US$6.05 billion), while the expenditure aspect had a size of Rp. 12.8 trillion. The idea was to increase the ability of corporations and individuals to save through a decrease in income tax of Rp. 30.0 trillion and Rp. 24.5 trillion respectively. Compared with income tax revenue in 2008, the change in corporate income tax would be –9.3 per cent and individual income tax, –7.7 per cent. The alleviation of Value Added Tax was to the tune of Rp. 3.5 trillion (a 1.8 per cent decrease) and was planned to be directed towards oil and gas exploration, as well as cooking oil production. Lastly, an alleviation of import duty for material and capital goods was scheduled to be instituted to the tune of Rp. 2.5 trillion, constituting a decrease of 14 per cent compared with the 2008 import duty.

The expenditure aspect of the package was set to amount to Rp. 12.8 trillion (US$1.28 billion), in which Rp. 11 trillion would be dedicated to infrastructure projects and the rest to non-infrastructure projects. The main projects would be managed by the Department of Construction (Rp. 6.6 trillion), Department of Transportation (Rp. 2.2 trillion), Department of Energy and Mineral Resources (Rp. 0.5 trillion), and State Ministry of Housing (0.4 trillion). Non-infrastructure projects would include additional funding for training in Labour Training Units, additional loan funding for Small Business Credit, and additional State Equity Participation in PT Asuransi Ekspor Indonesia (Indonesian Export Insurance Corporation).

The implementation of the government fiscal package required synergy between the central government and regional governments. This synergy would involve synchronization of central and regional government budgets and improvements in the regulatory or policy framework in order to support regional economies through rescinding counterproductive regulations. In the preceding years, regional government budget outcomes were still marked by a concentration of expenditures in the final quarter, but this pattern had seen a gradual improvement. To this end, the support from regional governments in promoting economic activity can also be extended in the form of accelerated expenditure disbursements, accomplished through changes in the structure and magnitude of these regional expenditures.

Despite the various efforts taken by central and regional governments, the realization of the 2009 fiscal stimulus package only reached 52.1 per cent by the end of 2009. Table 6.6 compares the planned and realized figures of

TABLE 6.5
Composition of 2009 Planned Fiscal Stimulus

2009 Planned Fiscal Stimulus	Value (Rp. T)	Changes compared with 2008 (%)
Corporate income tax decrease	30.0	−9.3
Individual income tax decrease	24.5	−7.7
Value added tax decrease	3.5	−1.8
Import duty decrease	2.5	−14.0
Expenditure increase	12.8	15.6
Total	73.3	

Source: Personal communication with Ministry of Finance.

the fiscal stimulus package. From these, two explanations for the deviation between planned and realized stimulus can be offered. First, most eligible corporations did not take the opportunity to decrease their employees' income tax (and hence increase their disposable income) temporarily since these corporations were reluctant to face the risk of being asked by the workers to make the higher income permanent. Second, the revenue side of the stimulus was executed based on requests from firms but there were only a few of such requests because the firms were worried that their employees would expect the policies to be permanent. Therefore, the only component of the package that could be pushed by the government was the expenditure side. This effort was quite successful, as indicated by the fact that it registered the highest realization rate among the stimulus components (79.7 per cent). Out of the realization of Rp. 10.2 trillion, Rp. 6.6 trillion was disbursed to various infrastructure projects, mainly roads, bridges, and irrigation, coordinated by the Department of Construction. In addition, Rp. 2.2 trillion was channelled to a number of railroad revitalization projects, under the management of the Department of Transportation.

TABLE 6.6
Plan and Realization of Fiscal Stimulus

Fiscal Stimulus Components	Plan (Rp. T)	Realization (Rp. T)	Proportion
Corporate income tax decrease	30.0	17.5	58.3%
Individual income tax decrease	24.5	7.7	31.4%
Value added tax decrease	3.5	2.5	71.4%
Import duty decrease	2.5	0.3	12.0%
Expenditure increase	12.8	10.2	79.7%
Total	73.3	38.2	52.1%

Source: Personal communication with Ministry of Finance.

SIMULATED IMPACT OF THE FISCAL STIMULUS PACKAGE ON THE NATIONAL ECONOMY

The fiscal policy response mentioned above constituted a policy "shock" to the economy, and hence generated a new picture different from the one that would have been if there had not been such a stimulus package.[6]

The implications of this fiscal support on Indonesian output and other components of the national account are important and interesting, not only to see how the policy action contributed to the resilience of the economy, but also to analyse the possible different impacts to various industries and household categories. In order to conduct such an analysis, a computable general equilibrium model is employed. This model, namely Bank Indonesia's SEMAR (Social Economic Model for Analysis of Real Sector), makes use of the Indonesian 2005 Social Accounting Matrix (SAM).[7,8] (See Appendix for technical descriptions of SEMAR.) The focus of this analysis is on the simulated impact of the fiscal stimulus package on GDP and its components, government fiscal balance, industrial performance, as well as household income and consumption.

The analysis is conducted to understand the role of fiscal stimulus in helping the national economy in the midst of a global crisis. The analysis on the impact of planned and realized fiscal stimulus is performed in three stages that are designed to measure and compare the effectiveness of each type of fiscal stimulus. First we will focus on the simulated impact of the planned Rp. 60.5 trillion and realized Rp. 28.0 trillion savings from tax cuts. Second we will concentrate on the simulated impact of the planned Rp. 12.8 trillion and realized 10.2 trillion increases in government expenditure. And third we will combine the impact from tax cuts and increases in expenditure. See Table 6.7.

Thus, a series of simulation is conducted using SEMAR. The impacts of various types of fiscal stimuli on output and the components of the national accounts, as well as core inflation, are depicted in Table 6.7. Furthermore, the corresponding influence of various stimuli on government fiscal balance is presented in Table 6.8.

TABLE 6.7
Fiscal Stimulus and Macro Variables
(change in percentage points)

a. Planned Fiscal Stimulus

Macro Variables	Fiscal Stimulus Scenario		
	Tax Cut	Expenditure Increase	Combination of Tax Cut and Expenditure Increase
GDP	0.438	0.051	0.488
Consumption	0.448	0.055	0.502
Investment	0.510	0.054	0.563
Gov. Expenditure	0.454	0.052	0.505
Export	0.384	0.045	0.428
Import	0.460	0.056	0.516
Inflation	0.0004	–0.014	–0.014

Source: Created by the authors.

b. Realized Fiscal Stimulus

	Fiscal Stimulus Scenario		
Macro Variables	Tax Cut	Expenditure Increase	Combination of Tax Cut and Expenditure Increase
GDP	0.324	0.042	0.365
Consumption	0.332	0.046	0.376
Investment	0.376	0.045	0.420
Gov. Expenditure	0.336	0.043	0.378
Export	0.284	0.037	0.320
Import	0.341	0.046	0.386
Inflation	0.000	−0.012	−0.011

Source: Created by the authors.

TABLE 6.8
Fiscal Stimulus and Government Fiscal Balance
(change in percentage points)

a. Planned Fiscal Stimulus

	Fiscal Stimulus Scenario		
Government Fiscal Balance	Tax Cut	Expenditure Increase	Combination of Tax Cut and Expenditure Increase
Revenue	−4.814	0.034	−4.783
Expenditure	0.195	0.086	0.279
Saving	−27.582	−0.226	−27.791
Deficit	−1.181	−0.010	−1.191

b. Realized Fiscal Stimulus

	Fiscal Stimulus Scenario		
Government Fiscal Balance	Tax Cut	Expenditure Increase	Combination of Tax Cut and Expenditure Increase
Revenue	−2.791	0.028	−2.766
Expenditure	0.145	0.071	0.213
Saving	−16.136	−0.186	−16.304
Deficit	−0.695	−0.008	−0.703

Source: Created by the authors.

The simulation of the planned decrease in income tax which amounted to Rp. 54.5 trillion and was transmitted through an increase in disposable income has shown that households consumption would increase by about 0.45 per cent. However, the income tax only declined by Rp. 25.2 trillion. As a result, the total consumption simulated would increase only slightly by 0.33 per cent. Also, additional savings of households and firms resulting from the tax cut were scheduled to push aggregate investment forward by about 0.51 per cent. However, the investment was only up by 0.38 per cent because of the smaller realization of the decrease in income tax. Apart from being motivated by domestic consumption, the easing of import duty on materials and capital goods would also play a role in pushing import value to about 0.34 per cent, which is smaller than the planned increase of 0.46 per cent. Furthermore, exports would also rise by only 0.284 per cent, rather than the 0.38 per cent initially estimated, due to a slight increase in each of the industries and incentives in value added tax of Rp. 2.5 trillion (Rp. 1 trillion less than planned).

For the government, the realized cuts in those various taxes would decrease government revenue rather sharply, that is by –2.79 per cent, but this is still smaller than planned. Since government expenditure tends to stay the same, only moving by 0.14 per cent which is largely due to government consumption and subsidy, this situation would increase the government deficit by –0.69 per cent, relative to the original budget, which is without the fiscal stimuli.

With such a transmission, the overall fiscal stimulus in the form of tax cuts was predicted to support growth by 0.32 per cent. However, although this type of fiscal stimulus would push aggregate demand up, inflation would be almost unchanged. The transmission mechanism of a tax-cut-only fiscal stimulus can be found in Figure 6.2.

Rather different from tax cuts which aimed at giving more cushion to the economy by increasing aggregate demand, the development of infrastructure by government targets production and distribution, which is the aggregate supply side of the economy. The simulation shows that the expenditure increase amounting Rp. 10.2 trillion (of the initially planned Rp. 12.8 trillion) would increase government expenditure by 0.071 per cent (see Table 6.8*b*). This additional investment would increase productivity and efficiency, as well as imports (especially materials and capital goods) such that exports would increase, but only by 0.037 per cent (see Table 6.7*b*). Next, such an increase in production would be accompanied by improvements in household income which can boost aggregate consumption by 0.046 per cent. Given the rather small scale of expenditure stimulus

FIGURE 6.2
Transmission Mechanism of Tax Cuts

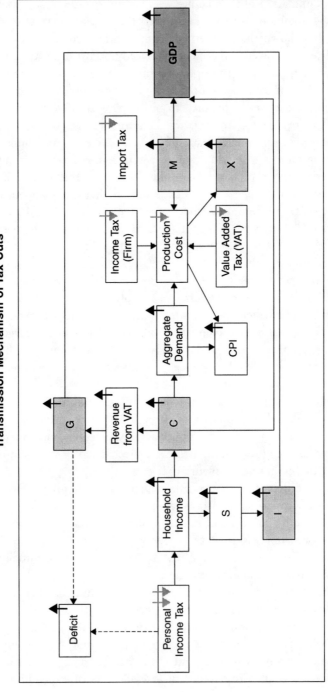

Source: Created by the authors.

(actual figure of Rp. 10.2 trillion, compared with realized tax cut stimulus of Rp. 28 trillion), GDP was predicted to increase only by 0.042 per cent. And since fiscal stimulus of this type was more to increase the aggregate supply, inflation was expected to go down by 0.012 per cent. As shown in Table 6.8, the increase in government expenditure would only increase the government budget deficit by 0.008 per cent, much lower than the 0.695 per cent from the tax cut. The transmission mechanism of the expenditure fiscal stimulus is shown in Figure 6.3.

Lastly, the simulated impact of the total Rp. 38.2 trillion fiscal stimulus package (against the planned 73.3 trillion) from the simultaneous increases in both tax cuts and expenditure is analysed. Such a combined strategy would certainly perform better, not only because of the bigger size of the package compared with the sizes of its components, but also because of its attempt to move both aggregate demand and aggregate supply at the same time. With the two transmission mechanisms taking place in tandem with each other (see Figures 6.2 and 6.3), the total fiscal stimulus package was predicted to be able to increase GDP by 0.365 per cent, supported by an increase in corporate and household consumption, investment, export, and government spending. The figure of a 0.365 per cent additional increase in GDP was in fact lower than the initial target of about half a per cent.

It is imperative to mention here that SEMAR is a static and deterministic simulation model; hence the expected incremental growth of 0.365 per cent would mean that such a fiscal stimulus package would support an increase of GDP by 0.365 per cent relative to the original 2009 outlook (without the package). The reality is that the economy grew by 4.55 per cent in 2009. Without the stimulus package, the economic growth rate would have been only 4.19 per cent in 2009, lower than the real figure of 4.55 per cent. Furthermore, had the total fiscal budget been realized, the economic growth rate would have been 4.68 per cent in 2009. See Table 6.7.

In the case of determining the inflation, an increase in aggregate demand, particularly due to an increase in consumption, could be neutralized by an increase in aggregate supply such that inflation would be expected to go down by 0.011 per cent. However, such a combined fiscal stimulus gives additional pressure to the government budget, increasing the deficit to 0.70 per cent, relative to the original budget.

Next, using the CGE model, the impact of the combined fiscal stimuli on the performance of each industry in terms of production, that is, export and import, is presented in Table 6.9 and analysed. The fiscal stimuli would cause an increase of production for all sectors. Since the majority of the funding was directed at infrastructure investment, the

FIGURE 6.3
Transmission Mechanism of Government Expenditure Increases

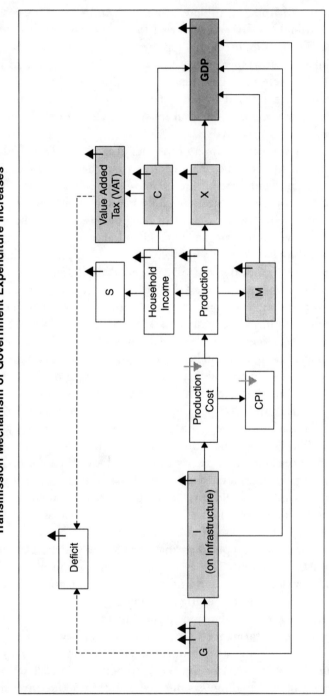

Source: Created by the authors.

TABLE 6.9
Fiscal Stimulus and Industrial Sectors
(change in percentage points)

a. Planned Fiscal Stimulus

Industrial Sector	Production	Export	Import
Agriculture	0.50	0.44	0.51
Mining	0.42	0.35	0.52
Oil and Gas	0.52	0.55	0.48
Non-oil and Gas	0.49	0.43	0.52
Utilities (water, electricity, gas)	0.46	0.00	0.00
Construction	0.56	0.00	0.00
Trades	0.49	0.43	0.51
Transportation and Communication	0.48	0.44	0.50
Financial Institution	0.50	0.44	0.51
Others	0.50	0.44	0.52

b. Realized Fiscal Stimulus

Industrial Sector	Production	Export	Import
Agriculture	0.37	0.33	0.39
Mining	0.31	0.26	0.39
Oil and Gas	0.39	0.43	0.35
Non-Oil and Gas	0.36	0.32	0.39
Utilities (water, electricity, gas)	0.34	0.00	0.00
Construction	0.42	0.00	0.00
Trades	0.37	0.32	0.38
Transportation and Communication	0.36	0.33	0.37
Financial Institution	0.37	0.33	0.38
Others	0.38	0.33	0.39

Source: Created by the authors.

construction sector would receive the highest impact of 0.42 per cent. The trigger from the construction sector would raise the production of other sectors on average by 0.36 per cent. With the revenue stimulus in the form of a cut in the value added tax for the oil and gas sector, the production of oil and gas sector would increase by 0.39 per cent. This was also influenced by an increase in aggregate demand due to the household income tax cut.

The above simulation increase in domestic production, combined with the alleviation of import duty of around Rp. 1.5 trillion, would have boosted imports of materials and capital goods by 0.38 per cent on average. Furthermore, exports would also have been pushed upward by 0.33 per cent on average due to declining production costs resulting from expenditure generated aggregate supply increases, especially in the oil and gas sector (0.43 per cent increase in export, see Table 6.9*b*).

The simulation result depicted in Table 6.10 shows that enterprises and all types of households would have indeed benefited from the realized fiscal stimuli. In fact, households and firms would have seen their revenue improving between 0.28 per cent and 0.34 per cent (*vis-a-vis* the baseline scenario without the stimuli). As a result of the tax cut, the total tax paid to the government, especially in the form of income tax, would decrease rather significantly by between 4.5 per cent and 5.1 per cent. Among the various types of households, the highest relative increase in consumption would have been enjoyed by the urban-poor category (0.50 per cent), most

TABLE 6.10
Fiscal Stimulus and Income Distribution
(change in percentage points)

a. Planned Fiscal Stimulus

Category	Revenue	Expenditure		
		Tax Payment	Consumption	Savings
Enterprise	0.424	−8.92	0.00	6.51
Rural Poor Household	0.377	−7.35	0.52	2.48
Rural Non-Poor Household	0.464	−7.27	0.45	2.54
Urban Poor Household	0.378	−7.35	0.72	2.70
Urban Non-Poor Household	0.420	−7.31	0.50	2.70

b. Realized Fiscal Stimulus

Category	Revenue	Expenditure		
		Tax Payment	Consumption	Savings
Enterprise	0.317	−5.10	0.00	3.88
Rural Poor Household	0.282	−4.63	0.37	1.56
Rural Non-Poor Household	0.347	−4.57	0.34	1.61
Urban Poor Household	0.282	−4.63	0.50	1.70
Urban Non-Poor Household	0.314	−4.60	0.37	1.71

Source: Created by the authors.

likely for fulfilling their basic needs. This is then followed by the rural-poor, the urban-non-poor, and the rural-non-poor categories. Although further characterization of the impacts of the fiscal stimulus package on income distribution requires a more detailed study, the current results indicate that the income distribution within and between rural and urban areas have improved. In addition, the resulting simulated increases in disposable income seemed to have added savings of between 1.5 per cent and 1.7 per cent across all household classifications.

CONCLUDING REMARKS

As part of its policy responses to maintain the resilience of the domestic economy and to combat the downward pressure on economic growth, the Indonesian Government launched a series of policy stimuli. The fiscal stimuli have been largely implemented in a timely manner and on a sufficient scale. Combined with monetary easing which had been implemented since the last quarter of 2008, the fiscal stimuli were mainly expected to prevent the economy from deteriorating further, an experience which many countries in the region already had. With a growth of 4.55 per cent in 2009, the Indonesian fiscal stimuli were indeed successful in preventing the growth rate from deteriorating any further, *vis-a-vis* the 2008 growth of 6.01 per cent.

To examine the impact of the stimulation package, a simulation to investigate the impact of the planned Rp. 73.3 trillion and the realized Rp. 38.2 trillion Indonesian 2009 fiscal stimulus package on the national economy has been conducted. The study is divided into three stages, namely, the investigation of the impact of planned and realized tax cuts, expenditure increases, and simultaneous increases in both tax cuts and expenditure. With both transmission mechanisms functioning in parallel (see Figures 6.2 and 6.3), the simulation model predicts that the stimulus package has improved economic growth by 0.365 percentage point relative to the situation where there had not been a stimulus package. This positive impact was mainly the direct result of a significant increase in the consumption of firms and households, as well as a surge in investment, exports, and government expenditure. In other words, the fiscal support managed to contribute around 0.32 percentage points to the recorded 2009 growth of 4.55 per cent.

The impact of the fiscal stimulus package on the real sectors may have included an increase in production across all industrial sectors by 0.36 per cent on average, and a surge in exports of the magnitude of 0.33 per cent.

Also, the revenue of households and firms was believed to have increased by between 0.28 per cent and 0.32 per cent. On the other hand, revenue transfers to the government, especially in the form of income tax, decreased significantly due to the tax cuts. The highest relative consumption increase was posted by urban-poor households (0.50 per cent), followed by the rural-poor and urban-non-poor with the same impact (0.37 per cent), and then the rural-non-poor households. Furthermore, there has been an argument supporting the suggestion that this stimulus package was in fact a pro-poor fiscal stimulus package. Moreover, the disposable income increase contributed to the rise of household savings of between 1.5 per cent and 1.7 per cent on average.

Finally, despite its significantly lower-than-planned size, the 2009 fiscal stimulus package may have had a favourable impact on the overall performance of the Indonesian economy.

NOTES

1. The authors wish to thank Muchamad Barik Bathaluddin and Justina Adamanti, both economists at the Bureau of Economic Research of Bank Indonesia (Central Bank of Indonesia), for their excellent research assistance.
2. Examples of extraordinary policy responses include those mentioned in Table 6.1
3. For instance, during the G-20 London Summit on financial markets and the world economy, held on 2 April 2009, the G-20 heads of state wanted a large financial stimulus. The leaders reached an agreement which, in principle, provides US$1.1 trillion to various programmes designed to improve international finance, credit, trade, and overall economic stability and recovery.
4. The components of headline inflation are threefold: core (also regarded as fundamental, generated by the gap between aggregate demand and aggregate supply — popularly known as output gap), administered prices, and volatile food prices (the last two are considered as non-fundamental since they are driven by non-aggregate demand force).
5. Inflation expectation is the future level of inflation as predicted by economic agents, that is, households and firms. Evidence shows that (current) inflation expectation significantly influences the (actual) level of future inflation through the self-fulfilling principle.
6. A "shock" to an economy is meant here as a big, exogenous change to the economy.
7. A technical description of the model is relegated to the appendix.
8. The analysis makes use of the 2005 SAM. The Indonesian SAM is constructed on a five-year basis. It is assumed that the industrial structures does not change significantly during each of the five years. This is a plausible assumption since we

deal here with data from the real sector which is characterized by low volatility and high rigidity, not data from financial sectors which have the opposite features.

REFERENCES

Bank Indonesia. *2008 Economic Report on Indonesia*. Jakarta; BI, March 2009*a*.

———. *Indonesian Economic Outlook 2009–2014*. Jakarta: BI, July 2009*b*.

———. *2009 Economic Report of Indonesia*. Jakarta: BI, March 2010.

Blanchard, O. and R. Perotti. "An Empirical Characterization of Dynamic Effects of Changes in Government Spending and Taxes on Output". *Quarterly Journal of Economics* 117 (2002): 1329–68.

Christiansen, L. "Fiscal Policy for the Crisis". IMF Staff Position Note 08/01. Washington: International Monetary Fund, 2008.

Corsetti, G., M. Meier, and G.J. Gerno. "Cross-Border Spill over from Fiscal Stimulus". *International Journal of Central Banking* 6 (March 2010): 5–37.

Elmendorf, D. and J. Furhan. "If, When, How: A Primer on Fiscal Stimulus", The Hamilton Project, Strategy Paper, The Brookings Institution, Washington, D.C., January 2008.

Freedman, C., M. Kumhof, D. Laxton, and J. Lee. "The Case for Global Fiscal Stimulus". IMF Staff Position Note No. SPN/09/03, March 2009.

Giavazzi, F. and M. Pagano. "Can Severe Fiscal contractions be Expansionary? Tales of Two Small European Countries". *NBER Macroeconomics Annual 1990*. Cambridge, Massachusetts: NBER, 1990, pp. 75–122.

Hemming, R., M. Kell, and S. Mahfouz. "The Effectiveness of Fiscal Policy in Stimulating Economic Activity — A Review of the Literature". IMF Working Paper 02/208. Washington, D.C.: IMF, 2002.

International Monetary Fund. "World Economic Outlook April 2010". Washington, D.C.: IMF, 2010.

Perotti, R. "Estimating the Effects of Fiscal Policy in OECD Countries". CEPR Discussion Paper No. 4842. London: Centre for Economic Policy Research, 2005.

Romer, C. and D. Romer. "The Macroeconomic Effects of Tax Changes: Estimates based on a New Measure of Fiscal Shocks". Unpublished manuscript. University of California, Berkeley, 2008.

Sperling, G. "Ways to Get Economic Stimulus Right This Time". Bloomberg.com, 17 December 2007.

Stone, C. and K. Cox. "Economic Policy in a Weakening Economy: Principles for Fiscal Stimulus". Washington, D.C.: Centre on Budget and Policy Priorities, 8 January 2008.

Summers, L.H. "The State of the US Economy". Presentation at Brookings Institution Forum. Washington, D.C., 19 December 2007.

Appendix: Technical Descriptions of SEMAR

A. Price Block Key Equations

1. Import Price

$$PM_c = (1 + tm_c - subc).pwm_c.EXR$$

$$\begin{bmatrix} \text{import} \\ \text{price} \\ \text{(dom. cur.)} \end{bmatrix} = \begin{bmatrix} \text{tariff} \\ \text{adjustment} \end{bmatrix} \cdot \begin{bmatrix} \text{import} \\ \text{price} \\ \text{(for. cur.)} \end{bmatrix} \cdot \begin{bmatrix} \text{exchange rate} \\ \text{(dom. cur per} \\ \text{unit of for. cur.)} \end{bmatrix} \quad c \in CM$$

2. Export Price

$$PE_c = (1 - te_c).pwe_c.EXR$$

$$\begin{bmatrix} \text{export} \\ \text{price} \\ \text{(dom. cur.)} \end{bmatrix} = \begin{bmatrix} \text{tariff} \\ \text{adjustment} \end{bmatrix} \cdot \begin{bmatrix} \text{export} \\ \text{price} \\ \text{(for. cur.)} \end{bmatrix} \cdot \begin{bmatrix} \text{exchange rate} \\ \text{(dom. cur per} \\ \text{unit of for. cur.)} \end{bmatrix} \quad c \in CE$$

3. Domestic Demand Price

$$PDD_c = PDS_c$$

$$\begin{bmatrix} \text{domestic} \\ \text{demand} \\ \text{price} \end{bmatrix} = \begin{bmatrix} \text{domestic} \\ \text{supply} \\ \text{price} \end{bmatrix} \quad c \in CD$$

4. Absorption

$$PQ_c.(1 - tq_c).QQ_c = PDD_c.QQ_c + (PM_c.QM_{c'})_{|c \in CM} \quad c \in C$$

$$\begin{bmatrix} \text{adsorption} \\ \text{(an demand prices} \\ \text{net of sales tax)} \end{bmatrix} = \left(\begin{bmatrix} \text{domestic sales price} \\ \text{times} \\ \text{domestic sales quantity} \end{bmatrix} + \begin{bmatrix} \text{import price} \\ \text{times} \\ \text{import quantity} \end{bmatrix} \right)$$

5. Commodity Prices

$$PX_c.QX_c = PDS_c.QD_c + (PE_c.QE_{c'})_{|c \in CE}$$

$$\begin{bmatrix} \text{producer price} \\ \text{times} \\ \text{domestic output quantity} \end{bmatrix} = \left(\begin{bmatrix} \text{domestic sales price} \\ \text{times} \\ \text{domestic sales quantity} \end{bmatrix} + \begin{bmatrix} \text{export price} \\ \text{times} \\ \text{export quantity} \end{bmatrix} \right) \quad c \in CX$$

6. Production Activity Price

$$PA_a.(1 + suba_a) = \sum_{c \in C} PXAC_{a,c}.\theta_{ac}$$

$$\begin{bmatrix} \text{activity} \\ \text{price} \end{bmatrix} = \begin{bmatrix} \text{producer prices} \\ \text{times yields} \end{bmatrix} \quad a \in A$$

7. Production Cost and Output

$$PQ_a . QA_a = PVA_a . QVA_a + PINTA_a . QINTA_a \quad c \in C$$

$$\begin{bmatrix} \text{activity price} \\ \text{(net of taxes)} \\ \text{times acivity level} \end{bmatrix} = \begin{bmatrix} \text{value-added} \\ \text{price time} \\ \text{quantity} \end{bmatrix} + \begin{bmatrix} \text{aggregate intermediate} \\ \text{input price times} \\ \text{quantity} \end{bmatrix}$$

8. Consumer Price Index

$$\overline{CPI} = = \sum_{c \in C} PQ_c . cwts_c$$

$$\begin{bmatrix} \text{consumer} \\ \text{price index} \end{bmatrix} = \begin{bmatrix} \text{prices times} \\ \text{weights} \end{bmatrix}$$

B. Production and Trade Block Key Equations

1. CES Function for Production Activity

$$QA_a = \alpha_a^a . \left(\delta_a^a . QVA_a^{-\rho_a} + (1 - \delta_a^a) . QINTA_a^{-\rho_a} \right)^{-\frac{1}{\rho_a}} \quad a \in A$$

$$\begin{bmatrix} \text{activity} \\ \text{level} \end{bmatrix} = CES \begin{bmatrix} \text{quantity of aggregate value added,} \\ \text{quantity of aggregate intermediate input} \end{bmatrix}$$

2. Output Transformation Function (CET

$$QX_c = \alpha_c^t . \left(\delta_c^t . QE_c^{\rho_c} + (1 - \delta_c^t) . QD_c^{\rho_c} \right)^{\frac{1}{\rho_c}}$$

$$\begin{bmatrix} \text{aggregate marketed} \\ \text{domestic output} \end{bmatrix} = f \begin{bmatrix} \text{export quantity, domestic} \\ \text{sales of domestic output} \end{bmatrix}$$

3. Composite Commodity Supply Function (ala Armington)

$$QQ_c = aq_c . \left(\delta_c^q . QM_a^{-\rho_c} + (1 - \delta_c^q) . QD_a^{-\rho_c} \right)^{-\frac{1}{\rho_c}} \quad c \in CM$$

$$\begin{bmatrix} \text{composite} \\ \text{supply} \end{bmatrix} = f \begin{bmatrix} \text{import quantity, domestic} \\ \text{use of domestic output} \end{bmatrix}$$

C. Institution Block Key Equations

1. Non-Government Domestic Revenue

$$YI_i = \sum_{f \in F} YIF_{i,f} + \sum_{f \in F} TRII_{i,i} + tr_{i,gov} . CPI + tr_{i,row} . EXR$$

$$\begin{bmatrix} \text{revenue of} \\ \text{institution} \\ i \end{bmatrix} = \begin{bmatrix} \text{factor} \\ \text{income} \end{bmatrix} + \begin{bmatrix} \text{transfers from} \\ \text{other domestic} \\ \text{non-government} \\ \text{institution} \end{bmatrix} + \begin{bmatrix} \text{transfers} \\ \text{from} \\ \text{government} \end{bmatrix} + \begin{bmatrix} \text{transfers} \\ \text{from} \\ \text{RoW} \end{bmatrix} \quad i \in INSDNG$$

2. Intra Industry Transfer

$$TRII_{i,j} = shii_{i,j}.(1 - MPS_i)(1 - TINS_i).YI_i$$

$$\begin{bmatrix} \text{transfer} \\ \text{from} \\ \text{institution} \\ i' \text{ to } i \end{bmatrix} = \begin{bmatrix} \text{share of net} \\ \text{income of} \\ \text{institution } i' \\ \text{transferred to } i \end{bmatrix} + \begin{bmatrix} \text{income of} \\ \text{institution } i', \\ \text{net of savings} \\ \text{and direct taxes} \end{bmatrix} \quad i \in INSDNG \quad i' \in INSDNG$$

3. Household Expenditure for Consumption

$$EH_{i,j} = \left(\left(1 - \sum_{i \in INSDNG} shii_{i,h}\right)\right).(1 - MPS_h).(1 - TINS_h).YI_h\right) - tr_{row,h}.EXR$$

$$\begin{bmatrix} \text{household income disposable} \\ \text{for consumption} \end{bmatrix} = \begin{bmatrix} \text{household income, net of direct taxes, savings,} \\ \text{and transfers to other non-government} \\ \text{institutions} \end{bmatrix} \quad h \in H$$

4. Government Revenue

$$YG = \sum_{i \in INSDNG} TINS_i.YI_i + tr_{gov,gov}.CPI +$$

$$\sum_{c \in C} tq_c.PQ_c.QQ_c + \sum_{c \in CM} tm_c.pwm_c.QM_c.EXR + tr_{gov,row}.EXR$$

$$\begin{bmatrix} \text{government} \\ \text{revenue} \end{bmatrix} = \begin{bmatrix} \text{direct taxes} \\ \text{from institutios} \end{bmatrix} + \begin{bmatrix} \text{transfers} \\ \text{from gov.} \end{bmatrix} + \begin{bmatrix} \text{sales tax} \end{bmatrix} + \begin{bmatrix} \text{import} \\ \text{tariffs} \end{bmatrix} + \begin{bmatrix} \text{transfers} \\ \text{from RoW} \end{bmatrix}$$

5. Government Expenditure

$$EG = \sum_{i \in INSDNG} tr_{INSDNG,gov}.\overline{CPI} + tr_{gov,gov}.\overline{CPI} + \sum_{c \in C} PQ_C qg_C +$$

$$\sum_{a \in A} suba_a.PA_a.QA_a + \sum_{c \in C} subc_c.pwm_c.QM_c.EXR + tr_{row,gov}.EXR$$

$$\begin{bmatrix} \text{government} \\ \text{Expenditure} \end{bmatrix} = \begin{bmatrix} \text{transfers to domestic} \\ \text{non gov. institution} \end{bmatrix} + \begin{bmatrix} \text{transfers to} \\ \text{government} \end{bmatrix} + \begin{bmatrix} \text{government} \\ \text{consumption} \end{bmatrix} + \begin{bmatrix} \text{subsidies for} \\ \text{activities} \end{bmatrix} +$$

$$\begin{bmatrix} \text{subsidies for} \\ \text{commodities} \end{bmatrix} + \begin{bmatrix} \text{transfers} \\ \text{from RoW} \end{bmatrix}$$

D. System Constraints Key Equations

1. Factor Market

$$\sum_{a \in A} QF_{fa} = \overline{QFS}_f \quad f \in F$$

$$\begin{bmatrix} \text{demand for} \\ \text{factor } f \end{bmatrix} + \begin{bmatrix} \text{supply of} \\ \text{factor } f \end{bmatrix}$$

2. Composite Commodity Market

$$QQ_c = QG_c + \sum_{h \in H} QH_{ch} + \sum_{a \in A} QINT_{ca} + QINV_c$$

$$\begin{bmatrix} \text{composite} \\ \text{supply} \end{bmatrix} = \begin{bmatrix} \text{government} \\ \text{consumption} \end{bmatrix} + \begin{bmatrix} \text{household} \\ \text{consumption} \end{bmatrix} + \begin{bmatrix} \text{intermediate} \\ \text{use} \end{bmatrix} + \begin{bmatrix} \text{fixed} \\ \text{investment} \end{bmatrix}$$

3. Saving-Investment Equilibrium

$$\sum_{i \in INSDNG} MPS_i.(1 - TINS_i).YI_i + EZR.\overline{FSAV} = \sum_{c \in CINV} PQ_c + QINV_c$$

$$\begin{bmatrix} \text{non government} \\ \text{savings} \end{bmatrix} + \begin{bmatrix} \text{government} \\ \text{savings} \end{bmatrix} + \begin{bmatrix} \text{foreign} \\ \text{investment} \end{bmatrix} = \begin{bmatrix} \text{fixed} \\ \text{investment} \end{bmatrix} \quad i \in INSDNG$$

PART III
Domestic Economy

7

Regional Heterogeneity of the Large Market and Production Base

Evi Nurvidya Arifin

LARGE AND HETEROGENEOUS POPULATION: AN EMERGING ASSET

Indonesia is the world's largest archipelagic country with more than 17,000 islands sprawling from the province of Aceh at its northern tip to the eastern province of Papua. In between the two are eight million square kilometres of land and sea. In terms of population and GDP (income), Indonesia is the largest country in ASEAN. In the more than six decades since its independence in 1945, Indonesia underwent a huge rise in population which has tripled from 73.3 million in 1945 (Badan Pusat Statistik 2005*b*) to 237.6 million in 2010 (Badan Pusat Statistik 2010). In 2010, Indonesia accounted for 13 per cent of the world's population and was the world's fourth populous country after China, India, and the United States.

It is not surprising then that many countries have eyed Indonesia as a country with emerging opportunities and that Indonesia has been one of the incentives for the creation of the 2015 Asian Economic Community which is to make ASEAN a single market and production base. Indonesia is a very promising market due to its huge number of potential customers who have rising incomes and aspirations. It is also a large pool of potential human resources as Indonesians have beome more educated, healthy, and mobile.

This chapter examines the Indonesian population in order to shed more light on the country's potential as a market and production base. The information given is also very important for development planning. Another feature of this chapter is its focus on the regional variations within Indonesia. Democratization in Indonesia, since 1998, has been accompanied by decentralization through the regional autonomy policy, which transferred much of the decision making power to regional, in particular, district governments. Since its decentralization, it has become more difficult to speak of "Indonesia" as a whole because one region can be very different from another and the country as a whole can also be very different from its past because many changes have occurred administratively, geographically, and demographically. Nonetheless, the large country of Indonesia had already shown its heterogeneity well before decentralization took place.

The novelty of this chapter lies in its discussion of the many new faces within Indonesia's population. The following section starts with a discussion on what is called the "Big Bang" decentralization. This was a new paradigm in the country's history which basically showed how excessive proliferation of administrative units had been taking place in this archipelagic huge country that is both multi-ethnic and multi-religious. The process of and timing for creating these new areas is crucial to understanding the population statistics presented throughout this chapter, as the changes in administrative borders have significantly affected the size and composition of the markets and production bases, as well as the country's development planning.

This section is then followed by a discussion on the regional variations of population dynamics across provinces from Aceh to Papua. Then the subsequent section examines the changes that took place within Indonesian families in terms of the number of children. At the beginning of the Reform era, the family planning programme was no longer an important issue for the central government. In fact, the family planning programme had by then become the local government's responsibility. On the other hand, since 1980s, Indonesians have been much more mobile across regions within the country and beyond. Thus, the section after family issues discusses migration, in particular, migration within the country.

Later, using the gender lens, the chapter discusses the shift in sex composition in Indonesia. Furthermore, Indonesia being a big market, the chapter discusses age structure of the populations across provinces. Ethnic and religious landscapes are also examined. Finally, education programmes — especially educational attainment across provinces — which have been mandated to the local governments, are examined. Another novel aspect of this chapter is its analysis of the educational attainment among the working age population in relation to their religious affiliation. The chapter then ends with some concluding remarks.

THE BIG BANG DECENTRALIZATION

Laws on Regional Autonomy

Particular care should be exercised when discussing the regional variations of Indonesia's population, especially during the Reform era starting in 1998. The first democratic election in the Reform era was conducted in 1999. This was the same year that the people in the province of East Timor voted to be independent from Indonesia through a United Nations-sponsored referendum. The province has popularly been known as Timor-Leste after its independence. With the independence of East Timor, the number of Indonesian provinces declined to twenty-six.

Pressure was also mounting to decentralize political and economic powers away from the central government. Thus, two important laws were enacted: Law no. 22/1999 on Regional Governance and Law no. 25/1999 on the Fiscal Balance between the central government and the regions.

Under Law no. 22/1999, the Central Government of Indonesia decentralized its power and resources to local governments — regencies and municipalities, rather than provinces.[1] As stipulated in article no. 4, provinces and local (district) governments shall be independent and not possess hierarchical relationships to one another. The local governments were no longer obligated to report to the provinces as they could now communicate directly with the central government. Thus, today the districts are autonomous regions that are in charge of administering the subdistricts (*kecamatan*).

For the sake of accountability, heads of local governments were elected by local parliaments, whose members in turn were directly elected by the people. The local parliaments were entrusted with the task of "implementing democracy". This law puts people at the centre. As a result, information on the size of the population in the regions has become increasingly more crucial to the democratization process.

Since the official implementation of regional autonomy laws in January 2001, the number of provinces has increased and some new proposed provinces are still in the process of being debated. In the meantime, the number of districts has increased even faster, making it possible for local actors to control both the local people and local natural resources for political and economic reasons. New administrative borders need to be fully understood in order to comprehend the changes to the geographical distribution in Indonesian population especially since 2001.

In September 2004, the two laws were revised and the national assembly legislated Laws nos. 32 and 33 on Regional Administration and Fiscal Balance between the centre and the regions which came into effect in October 2004. Less than a year later, in June 2005, political decentralization took place, with Indonesians having their first ever direct regional elections for governors, mayors, and regents. Since then, a series of local elections have taken place throughout the country (Sulistiyanto forthcoming). In April 2009, Indonesians held the third democratic elections in the Reform era to elect members of parliaments, followed by a presidential election in July. These elections were successfully run with a relatively smooth process, but left an important lesson: that an accurate and regularly updated registration of the population is very crucial to the democratisation process.

Predecentralized Period

In the predecentralization period of 1998–2000, there were already four new provinces. It started with the creation of the autonomous province of North Maluku, a split from Maluku, in October 1999. Maluku was divided into two provinces after the outbreak of "religious" violence between Muslims and Christians in August 1999.[2] The conflict actually included disputes over ethnicity, religion, natural resources, economics, political power struggles, and frictions between internally displaced persons and hosting communities. As described in Law no. 46/1999, North Maluku consisted of two regencies (Central Halmahera, and North Maluku) and one city (Ternate). By 2003, North Maluku had created another six new districts.

In 1971, Maluku was home to Muslims and non-Muslims in equal numbers. After the split, the religious compositions of the two provinces became starkly different, with North Maluku being predominantly Muslim, but Maluku containing almost equal numbers of Muslims and Christians. (In this chapter, Maluku refers to the Maluku with its "new" administrative boundary after its split with North Maluku.)

In 2000, three other provinces were created, namely Bangka Belitung, Banten, and Gorontalo. The province of Bangka-Belitung was formerly part of South Sumatera, while Banten was part of West Java. As discussed by

Kurniawan (2005), a strong factor driving Bangka-Belitung to separate from South Sumatera was the feeling among some Bangkanese that Bangka was only Palembang's economic plantation for the benefit of both Palembang and Jakarta.[3] Since becoming an autonomous province, it has transformed into a dynamic economic and business centre. The province initially consisted of three districts, namely regencies of Bangka, Belitung, and the city of Pangkal Pinang. Later in 2003, four regencies (West Bangka, Central Bangka, South Bangka, and East Belitung) were established. In total, it consisted of seven districts.

Banten is the only new province on the most densely island of Java. It was established in October 2000, signed under Law no. 23/2000. The province consisted of four regencies (Serang, Pandeglang, Tangerang, and Lebak) and two municipalities (Cilegon and Tangerang). Since its establishment, the number of districts remained the same until 2007 when the city of Serang[4] was established as autonomous and acted as its capital. This province is the home province of the Bantenese, who in 2000 formed 46.9 per cent of its population. Nevertheless, other ethnic groups such as the Sundanese, Javanese, and Betawi have had quite a significant presence in the province's population. The Sundanese comprised 22.7 per cent, or less than half of the Bantenese. This separation has made the province of West Java predominantly Sundanese, as they contribute to 73.7 per cent of the population (Suryadinata, Arifin and Ananta 2003).

The province Gorontalo was established in December 2000. It used to be part of the province of North Sulawesi, a long peninsula, and part of the islands to the north of the island of Sulawesi, called Sangihe Talaud. Gorontalo is known as Minahasa Peninsula, which stretches from west to east to take a horizontal form bordering with North Sulawesi on the eastern part, and Central Sulawesi on the western part. The Sulawesi Sea is to the north and Tomini Gulf is to the south with some islands surrounding it.

There have been sharp differences among regions in North Sulawesi. The separation was characterized by a contrasting feature of the people, as Gorontalo's population is exclusively Muslim, and North Sulawesi is predominantly Christian. When it was established in 2000, there were only two regencies and one city in the province. Several splittings of regencies occurred in 2003 and 2007. As of 2007, it has five regencies (Gorontalo, North Gorontalo, Boalemo, Bone Bolango, and Phuwato) and one city (Gorontalo).

Gorontalo was relatively isolated until it gained road access when Manado was built at the end of the 1970s (Jones 1989). Jones further observed that economic growth in Gorontalo had been sluggish and the economy of Sangihe Talaud had contracted in 1980s. The municipality of Gorontalo failed to attract young people from staying as its economy was not able to absorb them. Yet, on gaining its autonomy, Gorontalo's economy started to take off. Since then, a dynamic economic growth has been seen in this province.

In general, a profound increase in the number of local governments was seen, from 314 in 1998 to 341 in 1999 when there were no more changes until 2000. In the first year of decentralization, the number of local governments proliferated to 353 due to the creation of municipalities (see Figure 7.1). Figure 7.1 shows the changes from 1998 which was predecentralization to 2008.

FIGURE 7.1
Number of Districts (Regencies and Municipalities) and Sub-districts: Indonesia, 1998–2008

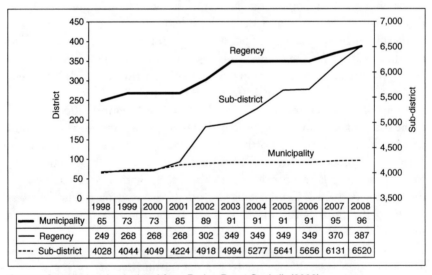

	1998	1999	2000	2001	2002	2003	2004	2005	2006	2007	2008
Municipality	65	73	73	85	89	91	91	91	91	95	96
Regency	249	268	268	268	302	349	349	349	349	370	387
Sub-district	4028	4044	4049	4224	4918	4994	5277	5641	5656	6131	6520

Source: Compiled and calculated from Badan Pusat Statistik (2008).

Full Decentralization Period

The years 2001–03 constituted Indonesia's full decentralization period, with "big bang" decentralization bumping up the number of local governments from 353 in 2001 to 483 in 2003, a rapid growth rate of 7.3 per cent annually. Yet, during this time, only two new provinces were created.

One of these provinces was the Riau Archipelago, popularly known in Indonesian as Kepri (Kepulauan Riau), which was created in 2002. This province has international borders with Vietnam and Cambodia in the north, Malaysia and West Kalimantan in the east, Singapore and Malaysia in the west, and the provinces of Bangka Belitung and Jambi in the south. These borders make the province of Kepri the most internationally exposed, especially with the creation of the specific economic zones of Batam, Bintan, and Karimun.

"Papua" is the other province that was divided into two provinces when granted Special Autonomy in 2001. Its western part became the province of West Irian Jaya or Irian Jaya Barat in 2003. It was renamed West Papua on 7 February 2007, with Manokwari as its capital. The separation was not without controversy. Some analysts have comprehensively discussed the challenges of Papua's economic development (Resosudarmo et al. 2009), public administration, and public policy under Special Autonomy (Resosudarmo, Manning and Napitupulu 2009).

The period 2003–06, as seen in Figure 7.1, was a stable period since only one province, West Sulawesi, under Law no. 26/2004[5] was created. Nevertheless, within the local governments, the creation of new subdistricts and villages continued. The number of these subdistricts grew rapidly from 4,994 in 2003 to 5,656 in 2006, while the number of villages increased from 70,921 to 71,563 respectively. In the period 2007–08, as indicated in Figure 7.1, new local governments, in particular, new regencies, were established. As of December 2008, the number of local governments totalled 483. In other words, the growth in the creation of local governments during the period of full decentralization from 2001–08 was 4.5 per cent annually. Figure 7.1 shows that although the creation of municipalities contributed to the proliferation of the number of local governments, the establishment of new regencies, or *kabupaten* (regency), has contributed most to the swelling number.

As can be concluded from Table 7.1, most of the new districts that were created were outside Java. In other words, the provincial and district geographical borders have been more stable in Java than in other parts of the country. Yet, the possibility of having more new districts in Java remains important as may be seen in the next several years. More new provinces are likely to emerge as some submissions and requests are currently still under consideration. They are namely the provinces of Cirebon,[6] Tapanuli,[7] Aceh Leuser Antara (ALA), Aceh Barat Selatan (ABAS),[8] North Kalimantan,[9] and Central Papua.[10]

TABLE 7.1
Number of Districts: Indonesia, 1996–2007

Island	Number of Regions				
	1996	1999	2002	2005	2007*
Sumatera	74	96	110	132	136
Java/Bali	116	119	124	124	125
Nusa Tenggara	20	21	23	25	28
Kalimantan	29	38	48	52	53
Sulawesi	40	45	50	62	69
Maluka/Papua	18	22	36	45	45
Indonesia	297	341	391	440	456

Note: * End of January 2007
Source: BPS, Statistik Indonesia, various years.

In a nutshell, the creation of new local governments has been motivated by various backgrounds, ranging from the feeling of being neglected by the central government to geographic isolation, leadership ambition, and claims over natural resource revenues. Other motivations include administrative dispersion, preference of homogeneity, fiscal spoils, as well as bureaucratic and political rent seeking (Fitriani, Hofman and Kaiser 2005).

FROM ACEH TO PAPUA: POPULATION SIZE ACROSS PROVINCES

The large size of Indonesia's population hides a significant number of important pieces of information in terms of its market and production base. One of these is the "imbalance" in the distribution of the population,[11] in particular between the more crowded and smaller Island of Java, and the larger, more sparsely populated islands of Java and Outer Islands. This "imbalance" can be traced back to the colonization era when activities in Java had led to the growing number of urban centres such as Jakarta, Semarang, and Surabaya.

In 2010, the Island of Java remained the most densely populated island, comprising 57 per cent of Indonesia's total population. But, as seen in Figure 7.2, its share of the country's population has been slowly declining since 1961, partly due to government-sponsored transmigration policies, in tandem with the aggressive family planning programme that was implemented

FIGURE 7.2
Population of Java and Outer Islands, 1900–2010

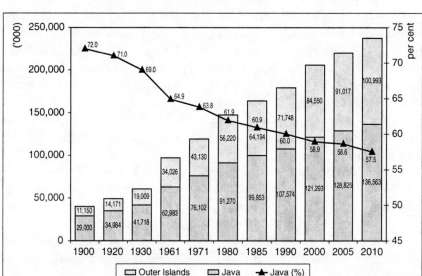

Source: Compiled and drawn from Hugo (1997), Suryadinata, Arifin and Ananta (2003), and Badan Pusat Statistik (2007, 2010).

under the New Order era. At the same time, the relatively more advanced infrastructure and economic advancements on the Island of Java have not been successful in countering the declining trend of its population growth so that the growth rate of the population on the Island of Java has been lower than that of the Outer Islands.

The transmigration programme, as argued by Tirtosudarmo (2009), had important demographic, social, economic, and political impacts in some places, although it did not have an important impact in the places of origin. These impacts, in the destination areas, have been stronger during the decentralization era, and are discussed in more detail later in this chapter.

At the provincial level in 2000, the size of the population in Aceh, at the northern tip of the Island of Sumatera, in the most western part of Indonesia, needs special examination. Though the size of the population in Aceh has been gradually increasing, the growth rate has been declining for more than two decades. Its population was 3.9 million in the year 2000, reflecting an annual growth rate of only 1.5 per cent from a decade earlier when it was 3.4 million. This was a big decline from the 1980–90 growth rate of 2.7 per cent.

Apart from decentralization, the prolonged local conflict in Aceh should be considered when analysing population issues in this province. In the 2000 population census, some districts were underreported and the data for the regency of Pidie was not reported at all since the area was not considered safe. Therefore, the Indonesian Central Board of Statistics (Badan Pusat Statistik 2001) only managed to enumerate 1.7 million as its population. Moreover, they recorded 0.2 million for the population that did not respond to the census, and an estimated 2.0 million for the unenumerated population.

Later, Aceh obtained a Special Autonomy law, Law no. 18/2001 which transferred an unprecedented amount of power and financial resources from Jakarta to Aceh.[12] In terms of development in administrative structure, the province of Aceh has changed tremendously. In 2000, the province consisted of eleven regencies and two cities. Several new districts were then created in the province after 2001. In 2005, it had seventeen regencies and four cities.[13] Two years later, the regency of Pidie Jaya was created which gave it a total of eighteen regencies, plus the city of Subussalam was created from the Aceh Singkil regency. Thus, as of 2007, Aceh consisted twenty-three districts. As a consequence, the population size in each fragmented districts has become smaller.

The devastating earthquake followed by the tsunami in 2004 brought the opportunity to have more complete information on the population through the Post-tsunami Population Census in Aceh and Nias in 2005 (Badan Pusat Statistik 2005). As of 15 September 2005, the census date, the size of Aceh's population was 4,031,589. This number included 60,736 individuals without fixed places of residence (Badan Pusat Statistik 2005).

The annual population growth rate further declined to only 0.8 per cent in the period 2000–05. This slow growth rate was caused by the culmination of three demographic phenomena (Arifin, Ananta and Siagian 2007). First, the fertility rate in Aceh continued to decline. Second, the mortality rate rose due to the tsunami disaster in 2004, and the conflict between 2000 and 2005. Third, there was heavy emigration from Acheh due to the conflict and the natural disaster between 2000 and 2005.

It was not long after the 2004 tsunami that media reports mentioned various numbers for dead and missing persons. These numbers ranged from about 100,000 to 170,000.[14] Ananta (2007) estimated that the loss of population due to earthquake/tsunami related deaths or outward migration from 2000–05 could range between 250,000 and 300,000 people.

Nonetheless, further studies should examine the extent of the impact from each of these phenomena. Since 2005, Aceh has entered a new era where peace finally reigns and its political and economic situations have gained momentum. It recently also attracted more people to live it, as suggested by the preliminary results of 2010 population census, which shows a higher population growth rate of 1.9 per cent in this province for the period 2005–10.

Situated in the eastern most part of Indonesia, Papua had been the largest province as it covered the entire western part of New Guinea Island until 2003. In 2000, Papua had an estimated population of 2.2 million, which was smaller than that of Aceh. The number was only an estimate because about 23 per cent of the population was estimated to be unenumerated due to local conflicts in several areas of Papua. In 2005, this number became even smaller at 1.9 million, mainly because Papua split into two provinces in 2003, the province of Papua and the province of West Irian Jaya. As in Aceh, these two provinces had been experiencing fragmentation within themselves by creating smaller districts. However, Papua, as revealed by the preliminary result of 2010 population census, grew the fastest among the provinces, with its current population (2.8 million) outnumbering the population in Papua in 2000, before the fragmentation.

Between Aceh and Papua, as indicated in Table 7.2, the population size in 2000 across provinces ranged from as tiny as 0.73 million in North Maluku to as large as 35.72 million in West Java. However, these two extreme sizes of population are still much bigger than some countries in Southeast Asia. The population of North Maluku is double that of Brunei Darussalam, the second richest country in the region. Meanwhile, the population in West Java is slightly larger than the combined size of the two neighbouring countries of Malaysia and Singapore. This pattern shows how big Indonesia is in terms of its population size, which in turn creates many different regional and international development potentials.

For instance, Ternate, the capital of North Maluku, is closer to Manila than it is to Jakarta. Trade activities between Ternate and Manila will be more efficient and productive than between Ternate and Jakarta. Since its creation, North Maluku saw its economy continue to grow at an accelerating rate from 2.4 per cent in 2002, to 3.8 per cent in 2003, and up further to 6.0 per cent in 2008. Its population grew the fastest among the provinces, at 4.4 per cent annually for 2000–05 (see Table 7.2), mostly because of its relatively high fertility rather than in-migration to the province. The total fertility rate in Ternate was still 3.2 during

TABLE 7.2
Indonesia's Population, Pre- and Post-Decentralization, 2000 and 2005

No.	Code	Province	2000*a*	2005*b*	Rate of growth
1	11	Nanggroe Aceh Darussalam	3,929.2	4,083.5	0.77
2	12	North Sumatera	11,624.5	12,418.0	1.32
3	13	West Sumatera	4,248.5	4,567.2	1.45
4	14	Riau	4,948.0*	4,835.9	–
5	15	Jambi	2,407.2	2,650.5	1.93
6	16	South Sumatera	6,899.1	6,815.9	–0.24
7	17	Bengkulu	1,563.8	1,566.1	0.03
8	18	Lampung	6,730.8	7,087.4	1.03
9	19	Bangka Belitung Islands	900.0	1,074.8	3.55
10	21	Riau Archipelago	na	1,278.9	–
		Sumatera (per cent)	**21.0**	**21.1**	–
11	31	Jakarta	8,361.2	8,892.3	1.23
12	32	West Java	35,724.1	39,150.6	1.83
13	33	Central Java	31,223.3	31,873.5	0.41
14	34	Yogyakarta	3,121.0	3,365.5	1.51
15	35	East Java	34,766.0	36,481.8	0.96
16	36	Banten	8,098.3	9,071.1	2.27
		Java (per cent)	**58.9**	**58.6**	–
17	51	Bali	3,150.1	3,405.4	1.56
18	52	West Nusa Tenggara	4,008.6	4,149.1	0.69
19	53	East Nusa Tenggara	3,823.2	4,279.5	2.25
		Bali and Nusa Tenggara (per cent)	**5.3**	**5.4**	–
20	61	West Kalimantan	4,016.4	4,037.2	0.10
21	62	Central Kalimantan	1,855.5	1,969.7	1.19
22	63	South Kalimantan	2,984.0	3,296.6	1.99
23	64	East Kalimantan	2,452.0	2,887.1	3.27
		Kalimantan (per cent)	**5.5**	**5.5**	–
24	71	North Sulawesi	2,000.9	2,143.8	1.38
25	72	Central Sulawesi	2,176.0	2,312.0	1.21
26	73	South Sulawesi	8,050.8*	7,489.7	–
27	74	Southeast Sulawesi	1,820.4	1,945.1	1.33
28	75	Gorontalo	833.5	936.3	2.33
29	76	West Sulawesi	na	985.7	–
		Sulawesi (per cent)	**7.2**	**7.2**	–
30	81	Maluku	1,163.1	1,264.8	1.68
31	82	North Maluku	732.5	914.1	4.43
32	91	West Irian Jaya	na	688.2	–
33	94	Papua	2,213.8*	1,934.7	–
		Maluku and Papua (per cent)	**2.0**	**2.2**	–
		INDONESIA	205,843.2	219,852.0	1.32

Note: * These provinces experienced fragmentation in the period 2000–05.

Sources: a. Table 1.1.2, Suryadinata, Arifin and Ananta (2003).
          b. Compiled from Badan Pusat Statistik (2007).

the period 1996–99, though it declined to 2.9 in 2001–04. The national figure stood at an average of 2.3 for these periods. Table 7.5 shows that North Maluku had a negative net migration rate, meaning more people migrated out than into the province. During the period 2000–05, the number of people migrating out from North Maluku was 16,500, larger than those coming into this province (10,400).

West Java's population grew slower than that of Banten, a province that was created from West Java in 2000. The former grew at 1.8 per cent annually, while the latter grew at 2.3 per cent during the period 2000–05. Furthermore, Banten has grown even faster since, and registered a 3.2 per cent annual population growth rate for the latest period from 2005–10. All other provinces in the most populous island of Java grew slower, at less than 1.5 per cent. Central Java grew even less, at only 0.4 per cent annually from 2000–05. A possible reason for this slow growth was its relatively low fertility rate. Moreover, Central Java is a migrant sending province — a province which is a source of out-migration to other provinces and other countries (see Tables 7.3 and 7.5).

In 2005, during the full decentralization period with thirty-three provinces, the imbalance in population size became even wider, with the lowest in West Irian Jaya at 0.69 million, and the largest in West Java at 39.15 million. The gap was even wider in 2010, ranging from 0.76 million to 43.0 million. However, assuming that current proposals to create new provinces will be accepted, these further splits will narrow the gap in population sizes. The province of West Java, the largest province, will become smaller; while the smallest province will not be smaller than West Irian Jaya.

Geographically, West Irian Jaya has a bigger land mass than that of West Java and there is an extreme difference in population density between the two. In 2007, it was estimated that there were six people per square kilometre in West Papua, versus 1,092 in West Java. Since 2007, West Irian Jaya, or West Papua, has established eight regencies and one city. Therefore, with a smaller population, West Papua's local leaders are expected to manage their resources better to improve the welfare of their people.

Figure 7.3 provides a glance of the population sizes across the districts in 2005 and the differences between Java and Outer Java, as well as between regencies and municipalities. The population sizes in the districts in Outer Java are generally smaller than those in Java, while the number of districts in Outer Java is much larger. The average population size at the regency level in Java was more than four times that of Outer Java, while the mean at the municipality level in Java was near three times that of Outer Java.

Evi Nurvidya Arifin

FIGURE 7.3
Scatter Plot of Population Size at District Level: Indonesia, 2005

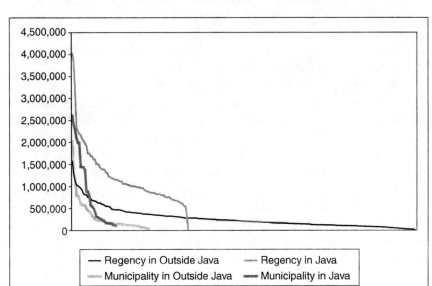

Source: Compiled and drawn from various publications of Badan Pusat Statistik.

This is reflected in the range of population sizes among regencies in Java, compared with those outside Java. Outside Java, the population ranged from 1.5 million in the regency of Deli Serdang, North Sumatera, to slightly more than 12,000 in the regency of Supiori, Papua. In Java, the population ranged from 4.0 million in the regency of Bandung to 18,000 in the regency of Kepulauan Seribu, which split from North Jakarta in 2001. In a nutshell, Figure 7.3 shows the large variations in the size of the market and production base among the districts.

FROM BIG FAMILY TO "NO" FAMILY

The national family planning programme started in 1969, with the primary focus on the crowded islands of Java and Bali. In the second stage, covering 1975–79, the family planning programme was implemented in ten provinces. The last stage, which took the remaining provinces into account, began in 1980. The different starting points of the different stages of the family planning programme partly contributed to the large geographical variations in fertility rates and, therefore, in the age structure of the regional population.

In turn, this difference in the age structure of the population hints at some variations in market and production base from one to another.

Since the Reform era took place in 1998, there has been no clear path in Indonesia's population policy. The responsibility for controlling population growth was transferred to the local governments. At the central government level, there was no longer a Ministry of Population. Furthermore, the branches of the family planning division in many local governments had disappeared.

Together with other development policies, such as improving women's education, along with improving women's participation in the labour market, as well as health facilities and services, many provinces in Java had successfully lowered their fertility rates within a relatively short period of time compared to many developed countries. Generally, Indonesians shifted from having a big family to having a smaller family. From a political perspective, Ananta (2006) discussed the emerging latent demand for democracy in Indonesia that accompanied the demographic transition. The accentuation of individual autonomy and self-actualization will gain more emphasis as family sizes become smaller. The Government of Indonesia used to be able to engineer individual behaviour, but this is no longer the case. Furthermore, decentralization is going on in tandem with democratization, where people participate more in the process of development.

As seen in Table 7.3, since the beginning of the 1990s, Yogyakarta, Jakarta, East Java, and Bali have below replacement fertility rates with women having just enough babies to replace themselves — below 2.1 as measured by TFR (total fertility rate). In Outer Java, North Sulawesi has been the only province with a fertility rate below replacement. Yet, Hartanto and Hull (2009) estimated that the adjusted total fertility in North Sulawesi was 2.2 in 2002–03, which increased slightly to 2.3 in 2007 above the replacement level.

It should be noted that the recent fertility rate in Yogyakarta has been very low. It was 1.6 or even 1.5 in the newest data (Hartanto and Hull 2009). This low fertility rate, that was unimaginable in the past, puts Yogyakarta equal to many developed countries demographically.[15] The low rate may also result in shrinking the Javanese population in the future. In the meantime, the fertility rate in East Java, another home province of the Javanese, reached 1.9 and is very likely to go further down.

Moreover, although marriage is still quite universal among Indonesians, the trend to remain single has been emerging. Jones (2003) found that the percentage of women staying single in their thirties has increased faster than those in their forties. Furthermore, Jones and Gubhaju (2008) showed that

TABLE 7.3
Trend in Total Fertility Rates by Province:
Indonesia, 1966–2007

Province	(1966–70)	(1970–75)	(1975–79)	(1980–84)	(1985–89)	(1990–94)	(1995–99)	(1998–2002)	2007
Indonesia	5.61	5.20	4.68	4.05	3.33	2.80	2.34	2.27	2.30
Nangroe Aceh Darussalam	6.26	5.00	5.24	4.79	4.37	3.29	2.81	2.44	2.80
North Sumatera	7.20	6.72	5.93	5.12	4.29	3.53	3.10	2.84	3.50
West Sumatera	6.18	5.97	5.75	4.80	3.89	3.35	3.06	2.95	3.00
Riau	5.94	6.06	5.43	4.71	4.09	3.25	2.77	2.45	2.60
Jambi	6.39	5.91	5.57	4.62	3.76	3.11	2.67	2.37	2.40
South Sumatera	6.33	5.55	5.58	4.78	4.22	3.14	2.88	2.33	2.30
Bengkulu	6.71	6.57	6.20	5.13	3.97	3.19	2.68	2.49	2.30
Lampung	6.36	6.46	5.75	4.79	4.05	3.29	2.65	2.42	2.40
Bangka Belitung	na	na	na	na	na	na	2.60	2.53	2.40
Riau Archipelago	na	na	na	na	na	na	na	na	2.60
Jakarta	5.17	4.78	3.99	3.25	2.33	1.93	1.63	1.66	1.80
West Java	6.33	5.64	5.07	4.30	3.47	2.87	2.51	2.28	2.30
Central Java	5.33	4.92	4.37	3.82	3.05	2.58	2.06	2.14	2.10
Yogyakarta	4.75	4.47	3.42	2.93	2.08	2.00	1.44	1.79	1.50
East Java	4.72	4.32	3.56	3.20	2.46	2.27	1.71	1.87	1.90
Banten	na	na	na	na	na	na	2.72	2.37	2.50
Bali	5.96	5.23	3.97	3.09	2.27	2.01	1.89	2.03	2.10
West Nusa Tenggara	6.66	5.75	6.49	5.74	4.97	3.68	2.92	2.69	2.70
East Nusa Tenggara	5.96	na	5.54	5.12	4.61	4.01	3.37	3.46	3.70
West Kalimantan	6.26	5.54	5.52	4.98	4.44	3.47	2.99	2.62	2.30
Central Kalimantan	6.83	6.49	5.87	4.76	4.03	3.16	2.74	2.21	2.50

TABLE 7.3　(*Cont'd*)

Province	(1966–70)	(1970–75)	(1975–79)	(1980–84)	(1985–89)	(1990–94)	(1995–99)	(1998–2002)	2007
South Kalimantan	5.42	5.26	4.59	3.74	3.24	3.09	2.33	2.30	2.50
East Kalimantan	5.41	5.69	4.99	4.16	3.27	2.96	2.50	2.32	2.30
North Sulawesi	6.79	6.16	4.91	3.58	2.69	2.66	2.12	2.10	2.30
Central Sulawesi	6.53	6.29	5.90	4.86	3.85	3.28	2.75	2.81	3.30
South Sulawesi	5.71	5.71	4.88	4.12	3.54	3.04	2.56	2.55	2.30
Southeast Sulawesi	6.45	6.82	5.82	5.66	4.91	3.69	3.31	3.14	3.00
Gorontalo	na	na	na	na	na	na	2.70	2.63	2.30
West Sulawesi	na	na	na	na	na	na	na	na	3.10
Maluku	6.88	na	6.16	5.61	4.59	3.68	3.39	3.29	3.70
North Maluku	na	na	na	na	na	na	3.17	3.04	2.90
Papua	7.20	na	5.35	4.83	4.70	3.78	3.28	2.38	2.90

Note: na = not available because the provinces were not yet created.

Sources: Badan Pusat Statistik (2006a), and Hartanto and Hull (2009).

the number of those remaining single among people between the ages thirty-five and thirty-nine was quite significant in several provinces. As shown in Table 7.4, among women who are at their old reproductive ages, namely between the ages of thirty-five and thirty-nine, in South Sulawesi, there were fourteen singles per 100 of them. The rates were even higher in two

TABLE 7.4
Percentage of Never Married, Ranked by Province (Age Group 35–39):
Indonesia, 2005

Women		Men	
South Sulawesi	14.0	Jakarta	12.5
Jakarta	10.6	Yogyakarta	11.8
East Nusa Tenggara	10.1	North Sulawesi	11.8
Yogyakarta	8.4	Bangka-Belitung	10.3
North Sulawesi	7.3	East Nusa Tenggara	8.7
Bali	6.4	South Sulawesi	8.4
Maluku	6.0	East Kalimantan	8.4
Bangka-Belitung Islands	5.7	Riau Islands	7.8
Central Sulawesi	5.3	Maluku	7.8
North Maluku	4.9	Bali	7.7
Southeast Sulawesi	4.8	West Kalimantan	7.5
West Kalimantan	4.5	South Kalimantan	6.8
Gorontalo	4.5	North Maluku	6.3
INDONESIA	4.3	Central Sulawesi	6.1
North Sumatera	4.2	East Java	5.7
South Sumatera	4.1	South Sumatera	5.7
South Kalimantan	4.1	INDONESIA	5.7
East Kalimantan	3.9	Central Java	5.4
Central Java	3.8	North Sumatera	5.3
Riau Islands	3.7	West Sumatera	5.0
East Java	3.5	Jambi	4.9
West Nusa Tenggara	3.4	Papua	3.8
Jambi	2.9	Gorontalo	3.7
West Java	2.6	Banten	3.7
Lampung	2.5	West Nusa Tenggara	3.7
Banten	2.3	Southeast Sulawesi	3.5
Central Kalimantan	2.1	Riau	3.5
Bengkulu	2.1	Central Kalimantan	3.4
West Sumatera	2.0	West Java	3.4
Riau	2.0	Lampung	3.3
Papua	1.5	Bengkulu	0.9

Source: Jones and Gubhaju (2008).

Javanese provinces. In Yogyakarta, it was eight in ten people in the same age group, and three or four out of ten in East Java.

MIGRANT-SENDING AND MIGRANT RECEIVING PROVINCES

The movement of people from one place to another has occurred throughout human history. People can either choose to move (voluntary migration), or be forced to move (involuntary migration). Migration occurs on a variety of scale, namely, international and internal migration. A variety of reasons for migration include environmental, political, economic, and cultural causes which pull or push people to move, sometimes at the price of leaving other members behind. In short, Indonesians have been on the move beyond their geographical and social boundaries to enhance their capabilities to increase their welfare.

Migration is also a selective process. Not everyone has the urge to overcome its various barriers. People voluntarily migrate in search of a better life, a higher education, or perhaps a family reunion. However, in other cases, people involuntarily migrate when faced with unexpected choices as seen in the various forms of forced migration. In such cases, people are forced to move in search of an escape from natural disasters, wars, or fear of social conflicts.

Regardless of the type of migration, the movements of people affect population characteristics in destinations and places of origin. This movement's impact is not only affected by their numbers, but their cultural traits and the ideas diffused along with them. It produces, creates, modifies, and affects cultural landscapes in both places of origin and in particular, destinations. It creates large and various business opportunities.

This section briefly examines the migration pattern of Indonesians, focusing on migration across provinces within the country in the last four decades.[16] It should be noted, however, that Indonesians have also been crossing national borders for economic reasons. They are now spread out over more than fourteen countries, with Malaysia and Saudi Arabia as the most popular destinations (Ananta and Arifin 2008).

The discussion here is based on information on recent migration, which is defined by comparing the province of residence at the time of the survey with the province of residence five years prior to the census/survey year. Table 7.5 provides net migrants, measuring the difference in the number of in- and out-migrants in each province. The negative sign indicates that the number of out-migrants surpasses that of in-migrants; therefore,

TABLE 7.5
Recent Interprovincial Net Migrants:
Indonesia, 1975–2005 (in thousands)

Province	Net Migrants			
	1975–80[a]	1985–90[a]	1995–2000[b]	2000–05[c]
Nanggroe Aceh Darussalam	23.0	6.9	−146.2	n.a.
North Sumatera	−81.7	−169.7	−218.6	−94.6
West Sumatera	−60.1	−44.2	−124.9	−20.5
Riau	44.9	152.6	435.4	115.1
Jambi	71.1	72.4	26.2	14.9
South Sumatera	89.2	13.4	11.3	−40.8
Bangka Belitung	−	−	2.7	2.1
Bengkulu	51.0	54.2	33.0	2.7
Lampung	462.2	76.4	−0.3	−19.0
Riau Archipelago	−	−	−	145.7
Jakarta	384.1	−160.4	−148.1	−159.4
West Java	83.6	854.9	465.2	287.9
Banten	−	−	412.9	158.0
Central Java	−724.5	−774.9	−663.3	−334.6
Yogyakarta	26.0	40.9	67.1	102.2
East Java	−367.4	−318.7	−343.0	−94.1
Bali	−15.1	9.9	39.8	37.6
West Nusa Tenggara	−12.8	0.5	9.3	−5.4
East Nusa Tenggara	−8.7	−18.5	14.9	3.1
West Kalimantan	11.0	−0.9	3.5	−16.6
Central Kalimantan	33.7	41.8	99.5	−15.8
South Kalimantan	15.6	21.9	26.7	20.8
East Kalimantan	92.3	126.3	112.7	101.8
North Sulawesi	7.2	−16.6	15.7	−2.9
Gorontalo	−	−	−24.1	−4.5
Central Sulawesi	66.3	42.0	44.7	24.8
South Sulawesi	−82.7	−41.6	−89.9	−36.1
Southeast Sulawesi	21.4	34.4	88.0	10.0
Maluku	19.9	29.8	−74.1	−20.8
North Maluku	−	−	−13.7	−6.1
Papua	17.2	42.2	33.6	17.7
Total	166.7	75.0	96.1	173.3

Note: n.a. — not available

Sources: [a] Compiled and calculated from Muhidin (2002), Table 2.21.
    [b] Compiled and calculated from Badan Pusat Statistik (2001), Table 12a.9.
    [c] Compiled and calculated from Badan Pusat Statistik (2006*b*).

a province with a negative net migration is an indication of a migrant-sending province. The positive sign indicates the opposite: the number of in-migrants exceeds that of outmigrants, thus making the province a migrant-receiving province.

Using this definition, within four decades there have been many changes and continuity of migration patterns in the provinces in Indonesia. Some provinces have changed from being migrant-receiving provinces to being migrant-sending provinces. These include Lampung, Jakarta, Aceh, West Kalimantan, and Maluku. Some others have changed the other way round. On the other hand, Bali, West Nusa Tenggara, and East Nusa Tenggara have transformed from migrant-sending provinces to migrant-receiving ones.

This changing pattern of migration is one of the signs showing Indonesia's rapid population mobility transition. This transition is partly due to the regional variations in fertility-mortality transitions and economic development across regions in Indonesia. In addition, the vast development in road networks and other transport infrastructure, together with investments in information, communication, and technology, may have greatly facilitated the ease of movement across regions.

Furthermore, Hugo (1997) concluded that there was a shift in the pattern of interprovincial migration in Indonesia in the mid-1980s, indicated by the reversal of the earlier pattern of out-migration from the Island of Java to the Outer Islands. Previously, the transmigration programme and government policies emphasized exploitation and export of natural resources, which contributed to the significant outflow of migration from Java to the Outer Islands. However, with the declining emphasis on transmigration and shift of investment to manufacturing industries, most of which were found in Java (particularly around Greater Jakarta), the pattern of migration changed. The flow from Java to Outer Java declined while the flow from Outer Java to Java and, particularly, to the areas around Jakarta, rose. Lampung is an example of this case.

The province of Lampung, which used to be the main destination for transmigration[17] was already saturated and no longer a destination point for transmigration since the early 1980s. Unsurprisingly, in the period 1995–2000, there were slightly more out-migrants than in-migrants to Lampung. In the period following that, the deficit in net migrants became larger, meaning that there were increasingly larger numbers of people leaving Lampung to the neighbouring provinces of the island, that is, South Sumatera, and provinces in Java, in particular, Banten and West Java.

Tirtosudarmo (1996) described this shift as a change in paradigm from the transmigration paradigm before 1985 to the "human resource paradigm" after 1985. He argued that the rising mobility that happened before 1985, especially from 1975–85, followed the "transmigration paradigm", a migration that was engineered by the Government of Indonesia. The government was very active in determining the areas of origin and destination and in bringing the people to areas of destination with the main purpose of advancing the economic development of these areas. The migration was mostly to rural areas.

In the human resource paradigm, the decision to migrate was mostly made by the people themselves, rather than because of government intervention. In other words, the market mechanism of supply and demand in the labour market played a stronger role in determining the migration decisions. Thus, the economic attractiveness of a region, rather than directions from the government, has become a much more important factor in inducing migration.

The pattern of migration in some provinces during the post-Soeharto era can be explained as a product of local conflicts based on ethnic or religious issues. These are the forced migrants. For example, Nanggroe Aceh Darussalam used to be a destination for the migrants; however, the number of out-migrants from this province was slightly more than ten times that of in-migrants in the period 1995–2000. Between 1990 and 1998, Aceh was under the DOM, *Daerah Operasi Militer* — Military Operations Zone. Throughout this period, sympathy towards GAM (Gerakan Aceh Merdeka — Free Aceh Movement) grew alongside the rising distrust of the central government and the deepening perception that the military had conducted human right violations. After the fall of Soeharto in 1998, the degree of distrust of the government accelerated. The clashes between the military and GAM continued to cause loss of lives of civilians, especially in the regencies of Pidie, Bireuen, and North Aceh (Hamid 2006). The conflict in Aceh was probably one of the reasons for leaving this province as some people moved out and into the neighbouring provinces of North Sumatera, Riau, Bengkulu, South Sumatera, and West Java. All these provinces received more than 10,000 migrants from Aceh. Since the peace and reconstruction programme started in 2005, this pattern of migration has reversed again, and there is now much more in-migration than out-migration from Aceh.

Central Kalimantan has also changed its migration pattern recently after being a migrant-receiving province for a long time. Perhaps, the most violent conflict between the Madurese and Dayak ethnic groups of Central Kalimantan in March 2001 is an explanation for the shift in the migration pattern in Central Kalimantan from being migrant-receiving to migrant-sending. It started in 1996 when the Dayak attacked a migrant, who was a Madurese. The killing was brutal and fears of being victimized sent many Madurese back to East Java, their home province. They might also have gone somewhere else and become internally displaced persons.[18] Today, there may be no more Madurese in the province as they fled to escape from the violence.

North Maluku is also a migrant-sending province, with the number of out-migrants exceeding in-migrants by 13,700 in 1995–2000. This number declined to 6,100 in 2000–05. North Sulawesi, which is predominantly Christian, was the major destination for North Malucans, the people from North Maluku. In 1995–2000, 45.8 per cent of the out-migrants went to North Sulawesi.[19] However, in the period 2000–05 the people from North Maluku moved a bit farther, namely East Java, which accounted for 31.1 per cent of the total outmigrants. Yet, 23.2 per cent of the outmigrants continued migrating to North Sulawesi.[20]

Maluku is another province that experienced intercommunal violent conflicts and thus changed from being a migrant-receiving to a migrant-sending province. However, the nature of the conflicts in Maluku was different from that in Central Kalimantan. The conflict here was between religious groups. In the past, Maluku had been well known as the Spice Islands, which became a home to Muslim and non-Muslim population in about the same proportions. Ambon, the capital city of Maluku, has been home to the Ambonese who profess Christianity. Meanwhile the northern part of Maluku, which was dominated by Muslims, broke off to form a new province, North Maluku, in 1999.

Another province which was considered a migrant-sending province was Gorontalo, which separated from North Sulawesi in 2000. Like in the case of North Maluku, Gorontalo's population was mostly Muslims. As shown in Table 7.5, the number of out-migrants from Gorontalo exceeded that of in-migrants by 24,100 in 1995–2000, although the gap then declined to 4,400 in 2000–05. The predominantly Christian North Sulawesi was the major destination among the migrants from Gorontalo, accounting for 38 per cent of the province's out-migrants in 1995–2000, which increased to 47.7 per cent in 2000–05.[21]

FROM A SURPLUS WOMEN TO A SURPLUS MEN POPULATION

Do women consume differently compared with men? Do women work differently compared with men? It is not easy to answer these questions, as their answers may be very locality-specific. Yet, it is quite safe to conclude that women and men constitute different markets and production bases, that a woman is supposed to consume different things in comparison to a man, and that some jobs still remain female or male specific. Therefore, it is important to learn the gender composition within the Indonesian population and to understand the potential market and production base in different regions of Indonesia and the country as a whole.

Indonesia has changed from having a population with a surplus of women to one with a surplus of men. Although the process of masculinization has occurred for at least thirty years, it still has not caught the demographer's attention. The sex ratio has continued rising since 1971, though it was always below 100 before the year 2000. A ratio of below 100 indicates a surplus of women and a ratio above 100 indicates a surplus of men. A rising man to woman ratio, but still kept under 100, means that a surplus of women still exists, but in a declining percentage. In other words, a rising sex ratio implies a trend of masculinization in the population.

A turning point was reached around 2000. The sex ratio hit 100.6 that year (Siagian and Dasvarma 2005) — meaning that the surplus of women had already disappeared and had been replaced with a surplus of men. Furthermore, the sex ratio rose to 101.2 in 2010, implying a continuation of the masculinization of the population, with a rising surplus of men in Indonesia. Does this mean that the population of men will become a more lucrative market in Indonesia?

As shown in Table 7.6, the phenomenon of masculinization is seen in most of the provinces, regardless of whether they are comprised of men or women surplus populations. In Java, where more than 55 per cent of the Indonesian population resides, the sex ratios in its provinces, except for Jakarta, have been increasing since 1971. This could provide an explanation for the change in sex ratio of the overall population. In 2010, in thirty-three provinces in Indonesia, the sex ratio ranged from as low as 94.1 in West Nusa Tenggara to as high as 112.6 in Papua. This range was narrower than that in 1971 when the highest sex ratio was 141.4 in Papua, a "land of men". In other words, although Papua is a "land of men", this province has been feminizing its population.

Feminization has also occurred in a few other provinces such as North Sumatera and West Nusa Tenggara, most probably because of the heavy flow of male out-migration from these provinces. Feminization also seemed to happen in Aceh in 2005, but this was only a temporary phenomenon. As discussed by Arifin, Ananta, and Siagian (2007), the phenomenon in Aceh

TABLE 7.6
Sex Ratio by Province: Indonesia, 1971–2005

Province	Sex ratio					
	1971	1980	1990	2000	2005	2010
Nanggroe Aceh Darussalam	100.2	101.5	101.1	101.0	99.0	100.0
North Sumatera	101.3	100.7	99.8	99.8	99.6	99.6
West Sumatera	93.7	95.5	95.9	96.1	97.5	98.5
Riau	104.6	104.0	105.2	104.4	104.2	106.2
Jambi	107.5	105.7	104.3	104.2	105.9	104.5
South Sumatera	99.5	102.0	101.2	101.0	102.4	103.6
Bengkulu	102.0	103.2	105.6	103.2	104.1	104.5
Lampung	102.3	107.3	105.5	106.2	107.6	105.8
Bangka Belitung	–	–	–	104.0	109.0	107.9
Riau Archipelago	–	–	–	–	99.9	105.2
Jakarta	102.1	102.6	102.0	102.5	98.7	102.8
West Java	96.8	96.6	100.5	102.1	102.7	103.5
Central Java	95.3	96.2	97.5	99.2	99.8	98.7
Yogyakarta	94.3	95.5	96.7	98.3	100.2	97.6
East Java	94.3	97.4	96.0	97.9	98.7	97.4
Banten	–	–	–	101.5	103.8	104.6
Bali	98.0	98.4	99.5	101.0	103.1	101.6
West Nusa Tenggara	97.5	98.3	95.5	94.2	93.5	94.1
East Nusa Tenggara	102.0	99.6	98.3	98.6	100.4	98.6
West Kalimantan	104.2	103.5	103.8	104.7	105.0	104.4
Central Kalimantan	101.8	106.3	106.6	106.8	106.5	108.8
South Kalimantan	96.3	94.9	99.6	100.5	101.8	102.1
East Kalimantan	107.0	96.9	110.9	109.7	109.7	111.0
North Sulawesi	100.6	102.7	102.7	104.9	103.9	104.4
Central Sulawesi	104.6	105.1	105.1	104.7	105.2	105.1
South Sulawesi	94.8	95.5	95.5	95.1	94.8	95.4
Southeast Sulawesi	91.3	99.7	99.7	100.7	101.6	100.9
Gorontalo	–	–	–	101.0	101.3	100.6
West Sulawesi	–	–	–	–	–	100.7
Maluku	103	104.4	103.8	102.8	103.1	102.1
North Maluku	–	–	–	104.7	105.2	104.7
West Irian Jaya	–	–	–	–	–	112.4
Papua	141.4	109.3	110.5	110.4	112.3	112.6
INDONESIA	97.2	98.8	99.4	100.6	101.1	101.2

Sources: Compiled from Siagian and Dasvarma (2005), except for the statistics in 2005 and 2010, which were calculated from Badan Pusat Statistik (2005, 2006*b*, 2010).

could be the result of the suffering from long conflicts and/or devastating tsunami disasters. They also observe a distinct "marriage market", given a surplus of men in the western coastal districts of Aceh, the districts badly hit by the tsunami, and a surplus of women in the eastern and central coastal districts, where internal conflicts had occured.

In general, the new provinces established in decentralized Indonesia comprise different population compositions in terms of sex ratios. For example, Riau Archipelago in 2005 has more women than men, while Riau has more men than women. The development of Batam as part of the industrial park under the Growth Triangle (Singapore, Johor, and Riau) and the recent creation of Batam, Bintan, and Karimun as Free Trade Zones in the Riau Archipelago, may have attracted more female migrants to the province. However, as seen in Table 7.6, a different pattern was observed in 2010, when men outnumber women in the Riau Archipelago. This reversed pattern needs further investigation. In 2010, West Sulawesi has a surplus of men, but South Sulawesi remains a women-surplus province. Bangka Belitung and South Sumatera have a sex ratio above 100, with the ratio in Bangka Belitung higher than that of South Sumatera. Furthermore, North Maluku also has a sex ratio above 100, higher than Malukus.

CONTINUITY OF A RISE IN ADULT POPULATION

Age is an important factor to take into account when differentiating between the supply and demand of goods and services since different age groups have different needs. The discussion on the age structure of population in this chapter is broadly divided into three groups: the young group (those younger than 15 years old), the adult or working age population (aged 15–59 years), and the old group (60 years and above). With Indonesia experiencing a relatively fast demographic transition, Ananta and Arifin (forthcoming) have described some new faces in the country's population as the product of past transformations. One of these groups of new faces is Indonesia's increasing number and percentage of older persons, baby boomers turning into elderly boomers. Another new phenomenon is that Indonesia and the world as a whole have become smaller for Indonesians. This is indicated by the rising population mobility both in and outside Indonesia, as well as the rising number of foreigners migrating into Indonesia. Ananta and Arifin argue that the changing faces of the Indonesian population may have important social, economic, and political implications. For instance, the increasing number of older persons will bring about financial and political ramifications.

Some provinces have been turning into ageing societies even earlier than Indonesia as a whole and some have achieved a high life expectancy of above seventy years. The province of Yogyakarta, for example, already had an old population in 2000, with older persons accounting for 14.2 per cent of its population, while Central Java, East Java, Bali, North Sulawesi, West Sumatera, and South Sulawesi had a transitional population. On the other hand, as seen in Figure 7.4, some provinces still contained a small percentage of older persons — they are still at the stage of having a youthful or even very young population. A population is considered to be very young when the percentage of older persons is less than 6.0 per cent; a youthful population has between 6.0 and 8.0 per cent of older persons; a transitional population has between 8.0 and 12.0 per cent of older people; and an old population has above 12.0 per cent of older persons. Arifin and Ananta (2009) has a more detailed discussion on this subject. In other words, there is a wide gap among the provinces with regard to the pace of population ageing.

The possibility of an increasing number of older persons in the future will probably be a challenge to the financial condition of the country because of its limited social security system and/or scope of welfare assistance. The out-migration of young people, especially migration from rural to urban areas, may weaken the traditional support for older persons. As a consequence, the agriculture sector may suffer from a lack of young workers and have the more fragile generation work the fields. Ananta and Arifin (2009) argued that older persons should be actively involved in various aspects of life, including economic, social, and cultural activities. Active ageing should be seen as one of the important objectives in development. Furthermore, they argue that active ageing will help transform a growing number of older persons into assets as they become a comparative advantage for economic development.

Alongside the declining fertility rate, the proportion of the young population has also been declining. Again, regional variations exist, with the smallest share of young people in 2005 seen in Yogyakarta, and the largest share seen in East Nusa Tenggara (see Figure 7.4). In terms of an absolute number, the young population group aged below fifteen years ranged from 0.3 million in Gorontalo to 11.4 million in West Java. This regional variation can affect how funding in each area is allocated in terms of education and infrastructure, including health infrastructure, for all ages. Despite the declining share of the young population and the rising percentage of older persons in numerous areas, the population in many provinces are currently still dominated by the working age group between

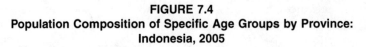

FIGURE 7.4
Population Composition of Specific Age Groups by Province:
Indonesia, 2005

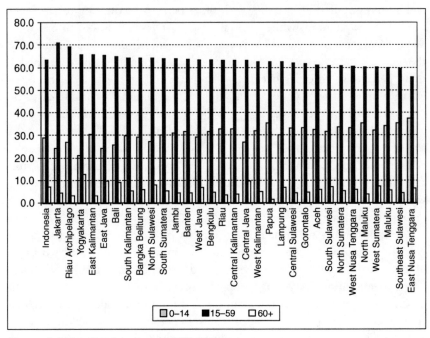

Source: Calculated and drawn from Table 7.7.

the ages of fifteen and fifty-nine. In 2005 Indonesia had a population of more than 135 million in the potentially productive working age group. Figure 7.4 shows that this group comprised 70 per cent of the population in Jakarta and in the Riau Archipelago. Only in East Nusa Tenggara did this share fall below 60 per cent, though the productive working age group remained the largest component of the population. In absolute numbers, the working age population across provinces in 2005 ranged from 0.53 million in North Maluku, to 24.7 million in West Java (see Table 7.7). The expansion of the population in the working age group provides a golden opportunity to boost the economy. Indonesia will still experience a continual increase in its workforce in the next several decades. This is in contrast to some countries, especially advanced economies, that have been anticipating a declining working age population, while yet other countries, such as Japan and Italy, are already facing a situation with a shrinking working population.

TABLE 7.7
Number of Young and Old People in the Population in Comparison with Working Age People by Province: Indonesia, 2005

Province	YOUNG (0–14)	WORKING AGE (15–59)	OLD (60 and above)
Indonesia	61,965,192	135,872,285	15,537,810
Aceh	1,292,953	2,435,062	242,838
North Sumatera	3,936,957	7,120,456	631,574
West Sumatera	1,465,370	2,743,866	346,574
Riau	1,496,814	2,892,986	173,606
Jambi	820,080	1,683,736	123,400
South Sumatera	2,046,404	4,345,593	375,648
Bengkulu	491,710	981,153	73,423
Lampung	2,157,907	4,449,925	496,740
Bangka Belitung	307,051	672,693	63,084
Riau Archipelago	345,736	884,959	42,316
Jakarta	2,159,576	6,275,661	404,010
West Java	11,446,933	24,700,323	2,739,719
Central Java	8,609,920	20,154,680	3,131,514
Yogyakarta	711,691	2,199,824	425,580
East Java	8,839,512	23,697,668	3,520,927
Banten	2,869,014	5,739,230	399,907
Bali	875,143	2,191,515	311,434
West Nusa Tenggara	1,390,163	2,522,652	256,880
East Nusa Tenggara	1,592,597	2,372,265	278,320
West Kalimantan	1,292,819	2,539,035	210,963
Central Kalimantan	626,426	1,211,752	74,848
South Kalimantan	979,881	2,110,727	180,805
East Kalimantan	870,988	1,872,138	97,748
North Sulawesi	579,293	1,367,647	174,077
Central Sulawesi	762,608	1,421,430	106,931
South Sulawesi	2,678,607	5,163,624	614,892
Southeast Sulawesi	696,718	1,173,804	90,175
Gorontalo	306,914	567,460	45,641
Maluku	427,673	750,476	71,063
North Maluku	314,279	532,741	34,847
Papua	866,408	1,532,296	41,134

Sources: Data for Aceh are compiled and calculated from Table 2.1 (Badan Pusat Statistik 2005). Data for other provinces are compiled and calculated from Tables 10.9 and 35.3 (Badan Pusat Statistik 2006).

As consumers, they are a potential target group as they have income through their participation in the labour market. As factors of production, they are the potential drivers for creating goods and services.

BETWEEN A JAVANESE MAJORITY AND A CHINESE MINORITY

When Soeharto's New Order regime collapsed in May 1998, "ethnic and religious violent conflicts" became the biggest and most unpleasant surprise for Indonesians. They were "ethnic conflicts" because the conflicts involved people from different ethnic backgrounds. The underlying cause of this conflict lay with political elites in Indonesia who used the tension among different ethnic and religious groups as their political means. It started with the anti-Chinese riots in May 1998, which also contributed to the overthrow of Soeharto and the New Order era. Other ethnic conflicts in various provinces were sparked off since. The conflict between the Dayak and Madurese in West Kalimantan occurred in 1999. Then, another conflict between the Madurese and Dayak in the neighbouring province of Central Kalimantan occurred in 2001. In addition, in January 1999, an ethnic and religious conflict in Maluku originally started as a small conflict between a local Ambonese and a migrant. But later, it changed into a religious war as Christian Ambonese turned against all the Muslims in the area, regardless of whether they were migrants or not. Although not necessarily because of ethnic conflicts, several areas under regional autonomy law split up based on ethnic differences. Therefore, ethnicity plays an important role in the Indonesian society.

Yet, the first statistics on Indonesia's multi-ethnicity were only collected in 1930 by the Dutch Government. Then, for seventy years since 1930, information on ethnicity was never again collected in any population censuses/surveys that were conducted in the country. Literature examined ethnicity, but there was still no reliable statistics on ethnic groups, although there are many different ethnic groups in the country spreading from Sabang, the westernmost part of Indonesia, to Merauke, its easternmost part. At the same time the tourism industry has often marketed the rich ethnic cultures all over Indonesia as an attraction. Even existing statistics had for the most part been based on small scale surveys, "guestimates" or extrapolations from the 1930 census. The reason for this lack of statistics on multi-ethnicities during Old and New Order eras was that it was a political taboo to discuss differences in religion and ethnicity. Therefore, the statistics were not collected, because it was feared that such information would cause social and political disturbances.

Nevertheless, the collapse of the New Order era created a breath of fresh air for Indonesian statistics on ethnicity. The Government of Indonesia, through its National Statistics Agency (BPS), made a breakthrough in its 2000 Indonesian Population Census by collecting statistics on ethnicity. It again continued collecting BPS statistics on ethnicity in its 2005 Intercensal Population Survey and the 2010 Indonesian Population Census. However, the publication of the 2005 Intercensal Population Survey results did not include statistics on ethnicity.

The statistics on ethnicity have produced a much clearer picture on Indonesian ethnic groups. There have been a lot of changes in ethnic composition in Indonesia as a whole between 1930–2000, unlike in the case of its religious composition. For example, before the availability of the 2000 population census, Chinese Indonesians were speculated to comprise between 3.0 and 10.0 per cent of the total Indonesian population. However, using the statistics from the census, Suryadinata, Arifin, and Ananta (2003) showed that these percentages were too high and that the number was actually only between 1.5 and 2.0 per cent. In fact, using the results of the 2005 Intercensal Population Survey, Ananta, Arifin, and Bakhtiar (2008) found that the percentage could be even lower and declining from 2000–05. Meanwhile, the Chinese Indonesians, who had limited political roles in the Soeharto era, have gained their momentum during the Reform.

In contrast to the Chinese Indonesians, the Javanese has been perceived as the majority since more than 50 per cent of Indonesia's population resided on the island of Java, namely in Central Java, East Java, and Yogyakarta, the home provinces of the Javanese. Yet, no precise number was available prior to 2000 except for the 1930 population census, which revealed that the Javanese formed 47.0 per cent of the total Indonesian population. With the 2000 population census, the second time Indonesia had any statistics on ethnicity, the population of Javanese was found to have declined to 41.7 per cent (Suryadinata, Arifin, and Ananta 2003). As shown in Table 7.8, the Javanese contributed a significant share of the ethnic composition in every province. Moreover, they migrated everywhere within the country too. In addition, the Javanese significantly built up the Malay Muslim society in Singapore and Malaysia (Sekimoto 1994). As of 2000, the Singapore population census showed there were 80,339 Javanese among the 455,207-strong Malay resident population (Leow 2001*b*).[22] In other words, the Javanese comprised 17.6 per cent of the Malay Singapore society. In recent decades, the Javanese have also been migrating overseas as labour migrants, and Malaysia is the main destination in the region. And finally at the district level, Ananta, Arifin, and Suryadinata (2004) found that the percentage of the Javanese ranged

TABLE 7.8
The Javanese and their Concentration in Each Province:
Indonesia, 2000

Province	Number	Concentration
Central Java	30,287,197	98.0
Yogyakarta	3,020,157	96.8
East Java	27,232,103	78.4
Lampung	4,113,731	61.9
Jakarta	2,927,340	35.2
North Sumatera	3,753,947	32.6
East Kalimantan	721,351	29.6
Jambi	664,931	27.6
South Sumatera	1,851,589	27.0
Riau	1,190,015	25.1
Bengkulu	348,505	22.3
Central Kalimantan	325,160	18.1
Nanggroe Aceh Darussalam	274,926	15.9
South Kalimantan	391,030	13.1
Papua	211,663	12.5
Banten	986,146	12.2
West Java	3,939,465	11.0
West Kalimantan	341,173	9.1
Central Sulawesi	166,013	8.3
Southeast Sulawesi	124,686	7.0
Bali	214,598	6.8
Bangka Belitung	52,314	5.8
Maluku	53,552	4.7
West Sumatera	176,023	4.2
North Maluku	21,211	3.2
South Sulawesi	212,273	2.7
Gorontalo	20,427	2.5
North Sulawesi	44,192	2.2
West Nusa Tenggara	56,340	1.5
East Nusa Tenggara	30,795	0.8
Total	83,752,853	41.7

Source: Suryadinata, Arifin and Ananta (2003).

from as low as 0.8 per cent in East Nusa Tenggara, to as high as 98.0 per cent in Central Java.

It should be mentioned that Javanese culture and politics were closely related and, in fact, very dominant, particularly during the New Order (1966–98) era. All six Indonesian presidents, except Habibie, the third president, who is a mix of Javanese and Buginese, were Muslim and Javanese.

As revealed by Suryadinata, Arifin, and Ananta (2003), the Sundanese remained the second largest ethnic group, rising from 14.53 per cent in 1930 to 15.41 per cent in 2000. From the revised figures, the percentage of the Madurese dropped substantially from 7.28 per cent in 1930 to 3.37 per cent in 2000, thus shifting this ethnic group from third place to fifth (Ananta, Arifin, and Bakhtiar 2005). Furthermore, they found that the concentration of Malays rose from 1.61 per cent in 1930 to 4.45 per cent in 2000, and was actually the third largest ethnic group in 2000.

This change in ethnic composition is mostly due to differences in fertility. Ananta, Arifin and Bakhtiar (2005) estimated and found that the Javanese had the lowest fertility with TFR at 1.96, which is below the replacement level. This might explain the drop in the percentage of the Javanese to the population as a whole. The Madurese also reached below replacement fertility level, with a TFR equal to 2.08. On the other hand, the Sundanese's and Malay's fertility rates were still above the replacement level fertility, with TFRs of 2.55 (Sundanese) and 2.86 (Malay).

Among the minorities, Chinese Indonesians comprised the majority share. As with other indigenous ethnic groups, the Chinese Indonesians[23] have been living in Indonesia for many generations, and experienced many and different political attitudes towards them. Everything related to their Chineseness had been viewed with suspicion under the New Order era. Not surprisingly, from 1967–98, the political system produced an unwillingness and lack of confidence among Chinese Indonesians to identify themselves publicly as Chinese. This attitude towards the Chinese and Chineseness aggravated the problem in identifying Chinese Indonesians. Soeharto's fall from power created an opportunity for Chinese revival in Indonesia. Furthermore, President Abdurrahman Wahid took a positive step by abolishing some of the discriminatory laws against Chinese Indonesians.

With this new and positive attitude towards the Chinese and Chineseness, Chinese Indonesians now have the confidence to state who they are. Nevertheless, they may themselves be confused about their own ethnicity. Therefore, the statistics on Chinese Indonesians, particularly after 2000, might not have understated their numbers. The statistics has correctly excluded the "Chinese" who, without any political or social pressure, did not feel they were Chinese. Many studies have discussed the debate on the identity of Chinese Indonesians in the post-Soeharto era (Chua 2004; Koning 2006; Turner and Allen 2007). Meanwhile, some others have discussed the demographics of Chinese Indonesians. For example, Suryadinata, Arifin, and Ananta (2003) and Ananta, Arifin, and Bakhtiar (2008) found that ethnic Chinese are declining in relative and absolute numbers. In 2000, the percentage was, at most, 1.60 per cent (Suryadinata, Arifin, and Ananta 2003). They argued that it could be even lower than 1.60 per cent. Further studies conducted by Ananta, Arifin, and Bakhtiar (2008) found that this percentage seemed to have declined from 2000–05, but the question is to what extent this decline has been. It may have declined to 1.18 per cent in 2005, and in numbers, from about 3.22 million in 2000 to about 2.57 million in 2005.

BETWEEN THE VERANDA OF MECCA AND VERANDA OF JERUSALEM

Indonesia is a country with the largest number of Muslims in the world, totalling 177.5 million in 2000. However, although efforts towards it remain alive and the idea to be an Islamic country still lingers in the minds of some Indonesian Muslims, Indonesia is not an Islamic country, but a multi-religious one. However, it officially only recognizes six religions, namely Islam, Protestantism, Catholicism, Buddhism, Hinduism, and Confucianism. Thus, other religions are not allowed. Indonesians are forced to choose one of the six listed official religions. Furthermore, not having a religion is not an option and is considered politically incorrect. Because individuals are obliged to choose a religion, some may just embrace one of the six religions for the sake of having an identity card (*KTP — Kartu Tanda Penduduk*). Therefore, some may be seen as KTP Muslim, while others are KTP Christian, KTP Buddhist, KTP Hindus, or KTP Confucian. Thus, they may say it is their religion, but they may not practise it. "Anecdotal" observations also show that there has been an increasing number of "free thinkers", though on their KTPs, they must still belong to one of the six official religions.

Kaharingan is an example of a local religion, practised by a number of Dayak ethnic groups in Kalimantan. However, they had to be registered as Hindus. Nevertheless, progress has been made to change this especially since the implementation of regional autonomy. Thus, the local government in the province of South Kalimantan has now recognized Kaharingan as a religion and attempts have been made to gain recognition from the national government, as is stipulated in the Constitution guaranteeing religious freedom. The people in South Kalimantan can mention Kaharingan as their religion in the KTP.

The limited choice of religions in Indonesia is in contrast to the religious options in its neighbouring countries, Malaysia and Singapore. In the Malaysia 2000 population census, there were nine options available: Islam, Buddhism, Hinduism, Christianity, Confucianism/Taoism/Others, Tribal/Folk religion, Others, No religion, and Unknown. In Singapore, the religious affiliations are: Buddhism, Taoism/Chinese traditional beliefs, Islam, Hinduism, Sikhism, Catholicism, other schools of Christianity, Other religions, and No Religion (Leow 2001*a*).

The religion of Confucianism in Indonesia has a unique history. Long before the twentieth century, Confucianism existed in Indonesia as an uninstitutionalized religion. However, Confucianism became an institutionalized religion, just like Christianity and Islam, in 1967 when Sukarno recognized six Indonesian religions as mentioned above. Soon after the regime changed though, at the end of 1978, under strong political pressure, Confucianism was derecognized as one of the religions in the country. Thus, by early 1979, Confucianism was no longer a religion and thus no longer appeared on Indonesian identity cards. Instead, followers of Confucianism had to be registered as Buddhists. It was not until the Habibie administration in post-Soeharto era that Confucianism was verbally recognized again as a religion, and since then, it has been officially recognized as a religion under the Gus Dur (Abdurrahman Wahid) presidency.[24]

As Islam has the largest number of followers in Indonesia as a whole, many provinces and districts comprise a Muslim majority. Figure 7.5 provides the variations in religious composition among provinces in 2000, with Gorontalo being the most exclusively Muslim province. On the other hand, Hindus are dominant in the province of Bali, forming 87.4 per cent of the population in 2000. In the province of East Nusa Tenggara, Christians accounted for 87.7 per cent of the population. Other provinces with large percentages of Christians are Papua (75.5 per cent), North Sulawesi (69.27 per cent), and Maluku (50.19 per cent). However, no province contains a majority of Buddhism or Confucianism adherents. At the lower administrative level, many regencies were almost exclusively Muslims (with more than 99.0 per cent). These regencies are located in

FIGURE 7.5
Religious Composition in the Provinces: Indonesia, 2000

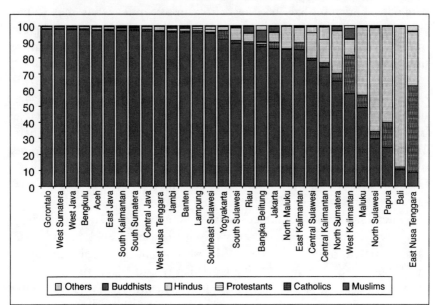

Source: Compiled and drawn from Badan Pusat Statistik (2001).

Nanggroe Aceh Darussalam, West Sumatera, West Java, Central Java, East Java, West Nusa Tenggara, and South Sulawesi.

The percentage of Muslims in Indonesia increased from 1971–2000 as did the percentage of Christians, consisting of Protestants and Catholics. On the other hand, the percentage of Hindus, Buddhists, and others declined. Other religions have even declined in absolute numbers. Yet, in terms of size, the numbers of all religious followers (except "others") in Indonesia have been increasing at different annual growth rates. The number of Christians grew the fastest at 2.5 per cent in the period 1971–2000, while the number of Muslims grew at a slower rate of 1.9 per cent, Hindus at 1.6 per cent, and Buddhists at 1.5 per cent. It should be noted here that, regardless of the official religions, the Indonesian census provided an option of "Others" to record the non-official religions, although we cannot really know what they are. What could be some of the reasons for the differences in growth rate among religious groups?

Though rare, conversions may have occurred among the Indonesian population. Yet, differences in fertility and mortality rates, as well as the flow of in-migration and out-migration among various regions, may have been important determinants in the change in religious composition within regions in Indonesia.

The highest growth, registered by the Christians, is attributable to the differences in fertility level among the religious groups. Data show that from 2000–05, Christians had the highest fertility rate, measured by the TFR of 2.71. This means that on average, Christian women have two to three children over their reproductive period. Meanwhile the fertility rate among Muslims was lower (2.32), and it was much lower still, at 1.98, among those of "Other Religions".[25]

Geographically, Christians have mostly lived in provinces where the fertility rate was relatively high. As shown by Suryadinata, Arifin, and Ananta (2003), more than half of the Christians lived in the provinces of North Sumatera, East Nusa Tenggara, Papua, and West Kalimantan, where the families on average, still have about three children.[26] In addition, most Christians lived in the provinces where the family planning programme started the latest. However, the popularly known Christian province of North Sulawesi is an exception. This province has a low fertility rate (TFR = 1.99), but is home to only 7.6 per cent of the Christians in Indonesia. As mentioned earlier, the highest concentration of Christians is seen in East Nusa Tenggara. On the other hand, most of the Indonesian Muslims lived on the most populous island of Java. This is the island where the government first started the family planning programme. In 2000 fertility rates in many provinces on this island have reached or were approaching below replacement level.[27]

Local governments have also been used as a vehicle for legitimizing religious symbols and establishing the hegemony of particular groups. For example, Aceh, known as Veranda Mecca, was granted a special autonomy law, under Law no. 18/2001. The Law transferred unprecedented amounts of power and financial resources from Jakarta to Aceh. This law allows the province to have more freedom in running its internal affairs, and to establish Islamic *shariah* as the base of the legal system and to redesign the local government with regard to local traditions. Under this law, the province is given the provision to change its name from Daerah Istimewa Aceh to Nanggroe Aceh Darussalam.

Several districts also apply *shariah* by-law, although the law on regional autonomy clearly stipulates that regions (including districts) cannot make their own regulation on religions.[28] As a reaction to the application of *shariah* by-law, Manokwari, a city in West Papua, was declared the Gospel City in March 2007 (Adeney-Risakotta 2008). This move is part of the effort of Christians to establish their Christian identity amid the continuous flow of Indonesian Muslims to this area. Adeney-Risakotta further observed that the policies that were adopted were similar to those in Aceh. These policies included prohibiting alcohol, requiring Christians to follow the gospel, calling Manokwari the veranda of Jerusalem, and limiting the development of other religions. Thus, like Islam in Aceh, the Christian identity was asserted through political power.

BETWEEN LOW AND HIGH EDUCATION

Democratization also means empowerment of the people. One means to empower the people is through enhancing their educational attainment. In Indonesia, the literacy rate has been improving significantly. However, the educational profile of Indonesia's labour force (aged fifteen years and above) is still dominated by those with primary education as their highest attainment level. In 2000, 60 per cent of the working age population attained at most primary education; nearly 4 per cent held a tertiary education certificate; while those in between, with junior and secondary school certificates, each comprised a nearly even share of the population at about 18 per cent.[29]

A large proportion of the younger groups in this labour force cohort will remain in the labour market long into the future. Since there is a lesser likelihood for the existing cohort to upgrade their educational attainment over time, the education profile of the future Indonesian labour force will be very much influenced by the education attainment of new entrants into the labour force. The fact is that the educational attainment of these entrants aged between nineteen and twenty-four years old have had a different educational background from those in the older groups. The cohort of 19–24-year-olds in 2000 has more education. This group has had at least a secondary school education, with 34 per cent of them holding secondary school certificates, and about 3 per cent having had a tertiary education. On the other hand, this figure also indicates a limited pool of the labour force with a tertiary education.

The delivery of education in Indonesia has also been decentralized, meaning that it is now the regional government's responsibility to maintain schools, pay teacher salaries, as well as collect student fees. This decentralization of education policy may have increased the large regional variations in educational attainment. Figure 7.6 shows that many provinces with better education are located outside Java. There were thirteen out of thirty provinces in 2000 that had a relatively better education, as measured by the percentage of those who only finished primary school. Among these

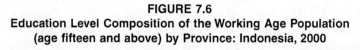

FIGURE 7.6
Education Level Composition of the Working Age Population
(age fifteen and above) by Province: Indonesia, 2000

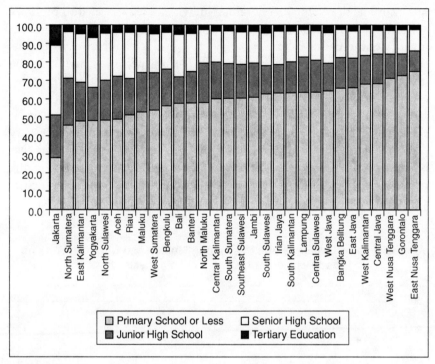

Source: Author's calculations from raw data of the 2000 population census.

thirteen provinces, Jakarta was the best, with only less than 30 per cent having at most primary education, while Yogyakarta and Banten were the other two provinces in Java having relatively better human resources. The remaining ten provinces are located in Outer Java. Meanwhile, the three most populous provinces in Java, namely West Java, Central Java, and East Java, have more than 60 per cent of their working age population with only a primary education. However, the least developed province is still East Nusa Tenggara, in Outer Java.

Taking religion into account, Arifin (2009) found that the educational achievement also varied across religious groups with the majority of Muslims finishing only primary school, while Christians attain education above primary school level. Enjoying a tertiary education is still a luxury service for Muslims in Indonesia, as only 3.4 per cent could complete a higher level of education, in contrast with 7.8 per cent among Christians. Arifin argued that the education discrepancy between Muslims and non-Muslims can bring further discrepancies in the economic conditions of Muslims and non-Muslims since only highly skilled individuals are expected to optimize opportunities in a globalized and liberalized economy. Therefore, there is an urgent need to continue to narrow the gap in education between Muslims and non-Muslims to avoid social unrests. The urgency is heightened by the fact that the ASEAN Economic Community only allows free movement of skilled labourers.

The provincial variations in religion and educational attainment is shown in Figure 7.7, where in many cases the percentage of tertiary education attainment among the Muslim population is lower than that of the Christian population. Provinces here are arranged based on the percentage of their Muslim population, from Gorontalo with the highest

FIGURE 7.7
Percentage of Tertiary Graduates among Muslim and Christian Working Aged Population by Province: Indonesia, 2000

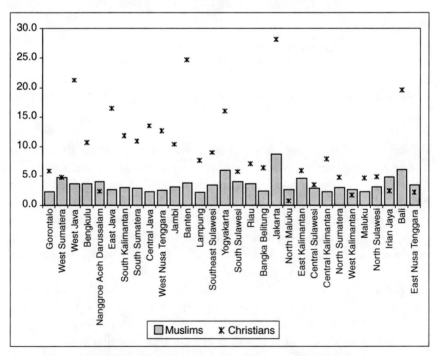

Source: Author's calculations from raw data of the 2000 population census.

percentage of Muslims to East Nusa Tenggara, with a mostly Christian population. Some exceptions in educational attainment are observed in Aceh, North Maluku, West Kalimantan, Papua, and East Nusa Tenggara where the Muslims are more educated than Christians. The educated Muslims in Papua and East Nusa Tenggara are probably the migrants. This figure deserves further investigation in order to understand the role of religion and other factors in determining educational attainment. In summary, the level of education varies according to province and religion.

CONCLUDING REMARKS

One of the problems in understanding regions of Indonesia is the dynamics in the development of its administrative units during the democratizing era, in particular, with the rising tendency of provinces and districts to split themselves further. As of 2008, the latest data used show there were seven new provinces, namely Bangka Belitung, Riau Archipelago, Banten, Gorontalo, West Sulawesi, North Maluku, and West Papua, since the regional autonomy laws took effect in 1999. No new province had been created since August 2010. But, some requests are still being reviewed. In this chapter, it has been shown that the imbalance of population size has become wider in 2010 compared with 2000, with the lowest population in 2010 standing at 0.76 million for West Irian Jaya, and the largest at 43.0 million for West Java.

Furthermore, a "big bang" decentralization occurred at a lower (district) level. The number of local governments increased tremendously in the period 2001–03, making the annual growth rate as high as 11.0 per cent. In the period following 2003–08, it grew more slowly. Thus, there has been a huge inequality in terms of the size of populations among districts.

Until 2000, Indonesia was perceived as a women dominated population. Though masculinization has occurred since, at least, 1971, Indonesia still had a surplus of women before the year 2000. Yet, the period of 2000–10 witnessed a change from the population of "a surplus of women" to "a surplus of men". The shift is also observed among provinces. Regionally, the gender imbalance varies greatly.

Looking beyond 2010, if the population growth rate remains the same as the rate for 2000–10, at 1.47 per cent annually, by 2015, Indonesia's market will definitely reach more than a quarter billion, a huge single market. Among the provinces in the 2010–15, the Riau Archipelago will have the highest population growth rate (see Table 7.9). Furthermore, the Indonesian population in the next several years will remain dominated by the adult working age group, which is a favourable condition for the economy. At the same time, Indonesia's population is ageing, with Yogyakarta showing an old population structure even in 2000. By 2015, when the ASEAN Economic Community is expected to be created, Indonesia's market will continue to grow and approach 250 million potential customers.

As one of the important objectives of human development, education has improved. It is often perceived that the populations outside Java suffer from a lack of human resources. However, this chapter shows the opposite. Many provinces outside Java have about 30 per cent of their working age population holding high secondary school or tertiary educational certificates, while the most populous provinces of East Java, Central Java, and West Java only have about 20 per cent with this educational attainment. It should be noted that Jakarta and Yogyakarta are exceptions. This chapter also concludes that although Muslims are the majority in many provinces, they are not better in terms of education compared with the Christians.

Apart from fragmentation within decentralizing Indonesia, this chapter has shown a number of important transitions that have been occurring in the Indonesian population. Generally, Indonesian families have changed from having a big family to adopting a small family size or even to not having a family at all, a current emerging trend. The majority of the Javanese provinces have reached a below replacement level of fertility since the 1990s. From a population balance equation point of view, this means that other ethnic groups will grow faster than the Javanese.

Javanese mobility has changed in terms of numbers and geographical coverage. However, not only the Javanese, Indonesians in general have become more mobile. This chapter has also shown a number of changes at the provincial level in the past four decades, with some provinces changing from labour-receiving to labour-sending provinces, and vice versa. Meanwhile, some provinces remain labour-sending provinces or labour-receiving provinces. Some of the changes occurred during the decentralization period, triggered by ethno-religious conflicts. Although the dynamics could be felt stronger across districts, evidence-based analysis cannot be done due to the unavailability of published information. Yet, this deserves further research through analysis on raw data gathered by Badan Pusat Statistik (National Statistical Agency). In short, this chapter shows that decentralization so far has created a more homogenous market in certain areas along ethnic and religious lines.

TABLE 7.9
Estimated Population Size by Province: Indonesia, 2005–15

No.	Code	Province	2005a	2010b	2015a	Growth Rate 2005–10	Growth Rate 2010–15
1	11	Nanggroe Aceh Darussalam	4,083.5	4,486.6	4,765.6	1.88	1.21
2	12	North Sumatera	12,418.0	12,985.1	14,435.9	0.89	2.12
3	13	West Sumatera	4,567.2	4,846.0	5,205.6	1.19	1.43
4	14	Riau	4,835.9	5,543.0	5,988.7	2.73	1.55
5	15	Jambi	2,650.5	3,088.6	3,103.8	3.06	0.10
6	16	South Sumatera	6,815.9	7,446.4	7,802.3	1.77	0.93
7	17	Bengkulu	1,566.1	1,713.0	1,811.0	1.79	1.11
8	18	Lampung	7,087.4	7,596.1	8,082.2	1.39	1.24
9	19	Bangka Belitung Islands	1,074.8	1,223.0	1,226.1	2.58	0.05
10	21	Riau Archipelago	1,278.9	1,685.7	1,933.2	5.52	2.74
		Sumatera (per cent)	**21.1**	**21.31**	**21.95**	—	—
11	31	Jakarta	8,892.3	9,588.2	9,581.1	1.51	-0.01
12	32	West Java	39,150.6	43,021.8	44,891.3	1.89	0.85
13	33	Central Java	31,873.5	32,380.7	34,116.4	0.32	1.04
14	34	Yogyakarta	3,365.5	3,452.4	3,686.9	0.51	1.31
15	35	East Java	36,481.8	37,476.0	38,258.6	0.54	0.41
16	36	Banten	9,071.1	10,644.0	10,886.7	3.20	0.45
		Java (per cent)	**58.6**	**57.49**	**57.11**	—	—
17	51	Bali	3,405.4	3,891.4	3,735.1	2.67	-0.82
18	52	West Nusa Tenggara	4,149.1	4,496.9	4,830.6	1.61	1.43
19	53	East Nusa Tenggara	4,279.5	4,679.3	5,125.5	1.79	1.82
		Bali and Nusa Tenggara (per cent)	**5.38**	**5.50**	**5.53**	—	—

TABLE 7.9 (*Cont'd*)

No.	Code	Province	2005a	2010b	2015a	Growth Rate	
						2005–10	2010–15
20	61	West Kalimantan	4,037.2	4,393.2	4,723.0	1.69	1.45
21	62	Central Kalimantan	1,969.7	2,202.6	2,245.4	2.24	0.38
22	63	South Kalimantan	3,296.6	3,626.1	3,781.6	1.91	0.84
23	64	East Kalimantan	2,887.1	3,550.6	3,588.0	4.14	0.21
		Kalimantan (per cent)	**5.54**	**5.80**	**5.79**	–	–
24	71	North Sulawesi	2,143.8	2,265.9	2,345.2	1.11	0.69
25	72	Central Sulawesi	2,312.0	2,633.4	2,724.1	2.60	0.68
26	73	South Sulawesi	7,489.7	8,032.6	8,498.8	1.40	1.13
27	74	Southeast Sulawesi	1,945.1	2,230.6	2,372.8	2.74	1.24
28	75	Gorontalo	936.3	1,038.6	1,050.6	2.07	0.23
29	76	West Sulawesi	985.7	1,158.3	1,138.5	3.23	-0.34
		Sulawesi (per cent)	**7.19**	**7.31**	**7.32**	–	–
30	81	Maluku	1,264.8	1,531.4	1,451.5	3.83	-1.07
31	82	North Maluku	914.1	1,035.5	1,069.0	2.49	0.64
32	91	West Irian Jaya	688.2	760.9	825.3	2.01	1.62
33	94	Papua	1,934.7	2,852.0	2,342.9	7.76	-3.93
		Maluku and Papua (per cent)	**2.18**	**2.60**	**2.3**	–	–
		INDONESIA	219,852.0	237,556.4	247,623.2	1.55	0.83

Note: Growth rate is calculated exponentially.

Sources: a = Compiled from Badan Pusat Statistik (2007); b = Compiled from Badan Pusat Statistik (2010).

NOTES

1. Placing power in local governments has partly been motivated by concern over the possible agitation for separation from Indonesia by provinces — especially the provinces with rich natural resources, as in the case of East Timor — if large power is delegated to the provinces.
2. The violent conflict in North Maluku started out as an ethno-religious conflict between Muslim Makianese and Christian Kaonese because of a local territorial dispute. The scope of the conflict was widened when external actors with competing interests got involved. It was declared a state of civil emergency on 27 June 2000 and the status of civil emergency was lifted in May 2003. A more detailed history of the conflict in North Maluku is available in Cutura and Watanabe (2004).
3. Palembang is the capital of the province of South Sumatera.
4. According to Law no. 32/2007, the city of Serang consisted of six subdistricts (Serang, Klasemen, Walantaka, Curug, Cipocok Jaya, and Taktakan).
5. The province of West Sulawesi was created in 2004 and was formerly part of South Sulawesi. It consisted of five regencies: Polewali Mandar, Mamasa, Majene, Mamuju, and North Mamuju. Its capital is Mamuju. Ethnically the two are different, as West Sulawesi has a majority of Mandar, while South Sulawesi has a majority of Makasarese and Buginese.
6. "Deklarasi Provinsi Cirebon Diundur 8 Maret", *Antara*, 14 February 2009. <http://www.antara.co.id/view/?i=1234586224&c=NAS&s>.
7. <http://niasonline.net/2007/01/15/propinsi-tapanuli-sudah-pasti/>.
8. "Megawati Dukung Pembentukan Propinsi Ala, Abas Segera", *Antara*, 24 July 2008, <http://www.antara.co.id/view/?i=1216913053&c=NAS&s=>.
9. Bakker (2009) discussed in *Inside Indonesia* that the attempt to create a new province of North Kalimantan (Kalimantan Utara or Kaltara) from the northern part of East Kalimantan was not yet successful. One of the reasons is that there are issues over both ethnic identity and control over land.
10. "Papua Tengah Dideklarasikan", *Papua Pos*, 14 May 2008, <http://papuapos. com/index2.php?option=com_content&do_pdf=1&id=230>.
11. The term "imbalance" is debatable. If seen simply from the variations in the number, the word "imbalance" may be appropriate. However, seen within the social, economic, and political contexts, the term may not sufficiently describe the situation in Indonesia. This chapter does not go into this debate, and therefore it puts "........" to the term.
12. The law allows the province to have more freedom to run its internal affairs, to establish Islamic *shariah* as the basis of its legal system, and to redesign the local government with regard to local traditions. Under this law, the province was given the provision to change its name from Daerah Istimewa Aceh to Nanggroe Aceh Darussalam (NAD). Since April 2009, the governor of Aceh through the Peraturan Gubernur (Pergub) Aceh no. 46/2009 renamed NAD to Aceh.

13. The city of Langsa split from the regency of East Aceh under Law no. 3/2001. The regency of Aceh Tamiang, the only Malay-majority district in the province, was also separated from East Aceh. The regency of Southwest Aceh (known as Abdaya/Aceh Barat Daya) was established under Law no. 4/2002 after splitting from South Aceh. Two new districts were also created in 2002 from West Aceh: Aceh Jaya and Nagan Raya. In the same year, Gayo Lues was separated from Southeast Aceh. Later in 2003, Bener Meriah split from Central Aceh. The city of Lhokseumawe was separated from the regency of North Aceh.

14. "Tsunami Relieve: Why Acehnese Still Wait for Houses", 8 December 2006, <http://www.indonesia-relief.org/mod.php?mod=publisher&op=viewarticle&cid=18&artid=1719>.

15. In the 1990s, the debate over the lowest fertility rate in any province in Indonesia would not have gone lower than 1.8.

16. More detailed discussions on people movement in Indonesia are referred to others such as Hugo (1987), Tirtosudarmo (2009), and Ananta and Arifin (2008). Forced migration is rarely discussed. Hugo (2006) has comprehensively discussed the issues on forced migration in Indonesia from a historical perspective.

17. Transmigration is formerly the colonialization programme under the Dutch Government, to bring people from the Island of Java to the Outer Islands, particularly Sumatera, to work. Under the Government of Indonesia, transmigration continues to be government-sponsored migration.

18. Internally displaced persons (IDPs) are people who are forced to flee their home, but who remain within their country's borders.

19. Our calculation on the number of out-migrants from North Maluku in the period 1995–2000 was 48,480, consisting of 13,046 persons migrating to North Sulawesi (Badan Pusat Statistik 2001).

20. In the period 2000–05, we found that 16,529 persons migrated out from North Maluku. There were 3,842 moving out to North Sulawesi and 5,153 to East Java (Badan Pusat Statistik 2006*b*).

21. Among the 33,448 out-migrants from Gorontalo, 38 per cent (12,712 persons) moved to North Sulawesi in the period 1995–2000 (Badan Pusat Statistik 2001). In the following period, 2000–05, the share of out-migrants to North Sulawesi increased to 47.7 per cent. Yet, the number of out-migrants declined from the previous period. The total number of out-migrants from Gorontalo in 2000–05 was 15,616 persons, and those out-migrating to North Sulawesi totalled 7,443 persons (Badan Pusat Statistik 2006*b*).

22. As presented in Table 5 (Leow 2001*b*), the Javanese in Singapore consisted of more men (40,584) than women (39,755) in 2000. Meanwhile, apart from the Javanese, the number of Boyanese, the people coming from Bawean Island in East Java, is also significant. There were 51,046 Boyanese consisting of 26,399 men and 25,647 women.

23. Some of them marry "indigenous people" and this creates a confused generation with problems in defining their own identity. But, this is a common phenomenon in mixed marriages. In a lot of literature on the ethnic Chinese, there were two groups: the *peranakan* Chinese and the *totok* Chinese. Many ethnic Chinese who were born and growing up during Indonesia New Order are Indonesian citizens having "Indonesian" names and speaking Bahasa Indonesia and even local languages. However, as argued by Chua (2004), it becomes irrelevant for most Chinese Indonesians to classify themselves as either *peranakan* or *totok*. Many of them cannot define themselves in one of these categories as there is no strong basis for them to be either one of these.

24. Detailed discussions on the development of Confucianism in Indonesia are referred to by studies such as Suryadinata 1974; Suryadinata 1998; Suryadinata 2005; and Coppel 2002.

25. The statistics on Total Fertility Rates by religion were estimated by Ananta, Arifin, and Bakhtiar (2004).

26. North Sumatera's TFR was 2.78 for the period 1996–99, East Nusa Tenggara's TFR was 3.09 for the same period; Papua's TFR was 3.0; and West Kalimantan's TFR was 2.75 (Badan Pusat Statistik 2001).

27. West Java's TFR was 2.34; East Java's, 1.71; and Central Java, 2.29. The statistics on Total Fertility Rates by province were estimated by BPS, Bappenas, and UNFPA (2005).

28. Article 7 of Law no. 22/1999 mandates local governments to cover all fields of governance that are not mandated to the central government. Those mandated to the central government are international affairs, defence and security, judicature, monetary and fiscal matters, religion and authorities in other fields covering national planning and macronational development control, financial balance fund, state administration and state economic institutional systems, human resources development, natural resources utilization, as well as strategic high technology, conservation, and national standardization. The local governments, as stipulated in Article 11 (2), must perform the duties in fields of public works, health, education and culture, agriculture, communication, industry and trade, capital investment, environment, land, cooperative and manpower affairs.

29. The statistics for the year 2000 refer to the results of the 2000 Indonesian Population Census.

REFERENCES

Adeney-Risakotta, Bernard. "Christians and Politics in the Twenty-first Century Indonesia". In *21ˢᵗ Century Indonesia: Challenges Ahead*, edited by Evi Nurvidya Arifin and Bernhard Platzdasch. Singapore: Institute of Southeast Asian Studies, forthcoming.

Ananta, Aris. "Commentary. Demand for Democracy in Indonesia: A Demographic Perspective". *Asian Population Studies* 2, no. 1, 2006.

————. "The Population and Conflicts". In *Aceh: A New Dawn*, edited by Aris Ananta and Lee Poh Onn. Singapore: Institute of Southeast Asian Studies, 2007.

Ananta, Aris and Evi Nurvidya Arifin. "Changing Faces of Indonesia's Population". In *21ˢᵗ Century Indonesia: Challenges Ahead*, edited by Evi Nurvidya Arifin and Bernhard Platzdasch. Singapore: Institute of Southeast Asian Studies, fortcoming.

————. "Demography and Population Mobility Transition in Indonesia". Paper presented at PECC-ABAC Conference on "Demographic Change and International Labor Mobility in the Asia Pacific Region: Implications for Business and Cooperation", Seoul, Korea, 25–26 March 2008.

Ananta, Aris, Evi Nurvidya Arifin and Bakhtiar. "Chinese Indonesians in Indonesia and the Province of Riau Archipelago: A Demographic Analysis". In *Ethnic Chinese in Contemporary Indonesia*, edited by Leo Suryadinata. Singapore: Institute of Southeast Asian Studies, 2008.

————. "Ethnicity and Ageing in Indonesia, 2000–2050". *Asia Population Studies Journal* 1, no. 2 (2005): 227–43.

Arifin, Evi Nurvidya. "Muslims in Indonesia: Socio-economic and Demographic Profile". Paper presented at the XXVI International Population Conference of the International Union for the Scientific Study of Population (IUSSP), Marrakech, Morocco, 27 September–2 October 2009.

Arifin, Evi Nurvidya and Aris Ananta. "Employment of Older Persons: Diversity across Nations and Sub-nations in Southeast Asia". In *Older Persons in Southeast Asia: An Emerging Asset*, edited by Evi Nurvidya Arifin and Aris Ananta. Singapore: Institute of Southeast Asian Studies, 2009.

————. "Older Persons in Southeast Asia: From Liability to Asset". In *Older Persons in Southeast Asia: An Emerging Asset*, edited by Evi Nurvidya Arifin and Aris Ananta. Singapore: Institute of Southeast Asian Studies, 2009.

Arifin, Evi Nurvidya, Aris Ananta, and Tiodora Hanumaon Siagian. "Demography and Politics in the New Aceh". *Masyarakat Indonesia Majalah Ilmu-ilmu Sosial Indonesia* XXXIII, no. 1 (2007): 9–40.

Badan Pusat Statistik. *Estimasi Parameter Demografi Fertilitas, Mortalitas dan Migrasi: Hasil Survei Penduduk Antar Sensus 2005* (*Demographic Estimations: Fertility, Mortality and Migration, Results of the 2005 Intercensal Population Census*). Jakarta: Badan Pusat Statistik, 2006a.

————. *Hasil Sensus Penduduk 2010 Data Agregat per Propinsi*. Jakarta: Badan Pusat Statistik, 2010.

————. *Penduduk dan Kependudukan Aceh Pasca Gempa & Tsunami: Hasil Sensus Penduduk Nanggroe Aceh Darussalam 2005* (Post-Earthquake and Tsunami Population of Aceh: Results of the 2005 Population Census of Nanggroe Aceh Darussalam). Jakarta: Badan Pusat Statistik, 2005a.

————. *Population of Indonesia. Results of the 2000 Population Census. Series L2.2.* Jakarta: Badan Pusat Statistik, 2001.

————. *Population of Indonesia: Results of the Intercensal Population Census 2005.* Jakarta: Badan Pusat Statistik, 2006*b*.

————. *Proyeksi Penduduk Per Provinsi menurut Kelompok Umur dan Jenis Kelamin: 2005–2015* (Age-Sex Population Projection by Province: 2005–2015). Jakarta: Badan Pusat Statistisk, 2007.

————. *Statistik 60 Tahun Indonesia Merdeka.* Jakarta: Badan Pusat Statistik, 2005*b*.

————. *The Trends of Socio-Economic Indicators 2008.* Jakarta: Badan Pusat Statistisk, 2008.

Bakker, Laurens. "Land, ethnicity and politics". *Inside Indonesia*, October–December 2009, <http://insideindonesia.org/content/view/1250/176/>.

BPS, Bappenas, and UNFPA. *Indonesia Population Projection: 2000–2025.* Jakarta: Badan Perencanaan Pembangunan Nasional, Badan Pusat Statistik, United Nations Population Fund, 2005.

Brojonegoro, Bambang. "Three Years of Fiscal Decentralization in Indonesia: Its Impacts on Regional Economic Development and Fiscal Sustainability". Paper presented at the International Symposium on "Fiscal Decentralisation in Asia Revisited", organized by Center of Excellence, Research on Economic Systems, Graduate School of Economics, Institute of Economic Research, and Asian Public Policy Program, Hitotsubashi University, Tokyo, 20–21 February 2004, <http://www.econ.hit-u.ac.jp/~kokyo/APPPsympo04/Indonesia(Bambang).pdf>.

Chua, Christian. "Defining Indonesian Chineseness under the New Order". *Journal of Contemporary Asia* 34, 2004.

Coppel, Charles A. *Studying Ethnic Chinese in Indonesia.* Singapore: Singapore Society of Asian Studies, 2002.

Cutura, Josefina and Makiko Watanabe. "Decentralization and Violent Conflicts: The Case of North Maluku, Indonesia". Prepared for Dr Scott Guggenheim and World Bank Serp Team. World Bank Office, Indonesia.

Fitriani, Fitria, Bert Hofman, and Kai Kaiser. "Unity in Diversity? The Creation of New Local Governments in a Decentralising Indonesia". *Bulletin of Indonesian Economics Studies* 41, no. 1 (2005): 57–79.

Hamid, Ahmad Farhan. *Jalan Damai Nanggroe Aceh Darussalam: Catatan Seorang Wakil Rakyat Aceh.* Jakarta: Penerbit Suara Bebas, 2006.

Hartanto, Wendy and Terence H. Hull. *Provincial Fertility Adjusted for Under-recording of Women in the SDKI 2002–3 and 2007.* Directorate Population and Labour Force Statistics, BPS-Statisics Indonesia and The Australian Demographic and Social Research Institute, the Australian National University, September 2009.

Hugo, Graeme. "Changing Pattern and Processes in Population Mobility". In *Indonesia Assessment: Population and Human Resources*, edited by Gavin W. Jones and Terence H. Hull. Singapore: Institute of Southeast Asian Studies, 1997.

Jones, Gavin. "Sub-national Population Policy: The Case of North Sulawesi". *Bulletin of Indonesian Economic Studies* 25, no. 1 (1989): 77–104.

———. The "Flight from Marriage". In *South East and East Asia: Journal of Comparative Family Studies* XXXVI, no. 1 (2003): 93–120.

Jones, Gavin W. and Bina Gubhaju. "Trends in Age at Marriage in the Provinces of Indonesia". Asia Research Institute Working Paper Series No. 105, June 2008.

Koning, Juliette. "On Being 'Chinese Overseas': The Case of Chinese Indonesian Entrepreneurs". Asia Research Centre, Copenhagen Discussion Papers 2006–05. <http://chinaworld.cbs.dk/cdp/paper/juliette.pdf>, 2006.

Kurniawan, Kemas Ridawan. "The Post-Crisis Indonesian Tin Town: With Reference to Mentok — Bangka". *International Journal of Environmental, Cultural, Economic and Social Sustainability* 1, 2005.

Leow, Bee Geok. *Census of Population 2000: Advance Data Release*. Singapore: Singapore Department of Statistics, 2001*a*.

———. *Census of Population 2000 Statistical Release 1: Demographic Characteristics*. Singapore: Department of Statistics, Ministry of Trade and Industry, Republic of Singapore, 2001*b*.

Mackie, Jackie. "How Many Chinese Indonesians". *Bulletin of Indonesian Economics Studies* 41, no. 1 (2005): 97–101.

Mayer, Judith. "Land and Social Justice". *Inside Indonesia*, October–December 2009, <http://insideindonesia.org/content/view/1248/47/>.

Resosudarmo, Budy P., Chris Manning, and Lydia Napitupulu. "Papua II: Challenges for Public Administration and Economic Policy under Special Autonomy". In *Working with Nature against Poverty: Development, Resources and the Environment in Eastern Indonesia*, ibid.

Resosudarmo, Budy P., Lydia Napitupulu, Chris Manning, and Velix Wanggai. "Papua I: Challenges of Economic Development in an Era of Political and Economic Change". In *Working with Nature against Poverty: Development, Resources and the Environment in Eastern Indonesia*, edited by Budy P. Resosudarmo and Frank Jotzo. Singapore: Institute of Southeast Asian Studies, 2009.

Sekimoto, Teruo. "Pioneer Settlers and State Control: A Javanese Migrant Community in Selangor, Malaysia". *Southeast Asian Studies* 32, no. 2 (1994): 173–96.

Siagian, Tiodora Hadumaon and Goranga L. Dasvarma. "The Masculinisation of the Sex Ratio in Indonesia". Paper presented at the conference "Female Deficit in Asia: Trends and Perspectives", Singapore, 5–7 December 2005.

Sulistiyanto, Priyambudi. "Local Elections and Local Politics in Indonesia: Emerging Trends". In *21ˢᵗ Century Indonesia: Challenges Ahead*, edited by Evi Nurvidya Arifin and Bernhard Platzdasch. Singapore: Institute of Southeast Asian Studies, forthcoming.

Suryadinata, Leo. "Buddhism and Confucianism in Contemporary Indonesia: Recent Developments". In *Chinese Indonesians: Remembering, Distorting, Forgetting*, edited by Tim Lindsey and Helen Pausacker. Singapore: Institute of Southeast Asian Studies, 2005.

————. "Confucianism in Indonesia: Past and Present". *Southeast Asia* (Southern Illinois University) 3, no. 3 (Spring 1974): 881–903. Republished in Leo Suryadinata, *The Chinese Minority in Indonesia: 7 Papers*, pp. 33–62. Singapore: Chopmen Enterprises, 1978.

————. "Konghucuisme dan Agama Konghucu di Indonesia: Sebuah Kajian Awal". In Leo Suryadinata, *Negara dan Etnis Tionghoa: Kasus Indonesia*, pp. 157–93. Jakarta LP3ES and Centre for Political Studies, November 2002. Revision of article published in *Pergulatan Mencari Diri: Konfusiaisme di Indonesia*. Yogyakarta: Interfidel, 1995.

————. "State and Minority Religion in Contemporary Indonesia: Recent Governemt Policy towards Confucianism, Tridharma and Buddhism". In *Nation-State, Identity and Religion in Southeast Asia*, edited by Tsuneo Ayabe, pp. 5–24. Singapore: Singapore Society of Asian Studies, 1998,

Suryadinata, Leo, Evi Nurvidya Arifin, and Aris Ananta. *Indonesia's Population: Ethnicity and Religion in a Changing Political Landscape*. Singapore: Institute of Southeast Asian Studies, 2003.

Tirtosudarmo, Riwanto. "Mobilitas Penduduk dan Konflik: Analisis dan Prospek Menjelang Abad ke-21" (Population Mobility and Conflict: Analysis and Prospect toward the 21st century). In *Mobilitas Penduduk di Indonesia* (Population Mobility in Indonesia), edited by Aris Ananta and Chotib. Jakarta: Lembaga Demografi Fakultas Ekonomi Universitas Indonesia and Kantor Menteri Negara Kependudukan/BKKBN, 1996.

————. "Mobility and Human Development in Indonesia". *Human Development Research Paper 2009/19*. United Nations Development Programme, June 2009.

Turner, Mark. "Implementing Laws 22 and 25: The Challenge of Decentralization in Indonesia". *Asian Review of Public Administration* XIII, no. 1 (January–June 2001): 69–82.

Turner, Sarah and Pamela Allen. "Chinese Indonesians in a Rapidly Changing Nation: Pressures of Ethnicity and Identity". *Asia Pacific Viewpoint* 48, no. 1 (2007): 112–27.

Widjojo, Muridan S. "Papua Road Map". *Inside Indonesia*, October–December 2008, <http://insideindonesia.org/content/view/1137/47/>.

8

Industrial Relations in the Democratizing Era

Indrasari Tjandraningsih

With the process of democratization, industrial relations in Indonesia today have a new image that has continuously been seeking its form since the downfall of Soeharto on 21 May 1998. The toppling of the symbol, and primary player of Indonesia's authoritarian New Order government, brought forth a new era towards a democratic society. The democratization process became the context for industrial relations dynamics in Indonesia, with the opening up of opportunities for freedom of association, stoking hopes of bringing the position of trade unions on a par with employers and the government. In brief, with the new system of industrial relations in place, the role of trade unions has been enhanced and increasingly taken into account by the other two players (the government and employers). The enhanced role is, among other signs, indicated by the participation of trade unions in the formation of labour laws, their active role in wage councils to determine minimum wages, the labour masses' show of force every first of May, and their success in rejecting the revision of the ministerial regulation on wages, as well as the revision of Law 13/2003. The revision of the Law 13/2003 would have paved the way for more flexibility in the labour market. Enhancing the role of trade unions is assumed to bring improvement in working conditions and employees' welfare as the bargaining position of the trade unions will be much greater.

In-depth observations suggest that equality in the positions of the three players (trade unions, the government, and employers) in industrial relations must be understood far more carefully, as there are three situations (decentralized government, freedom of association, and labour market flexibility) that frame the characteristics of industrial relations in Indonesia within this *Reformasi* era. These three situations evolve and develop together to create a condition that quite objectively makes it difficult to create equal relations among the three players. The three situations also point to the fact that ideologically, industrial relations in the post-New Order era of Indonesia have featured neo-liberalism through the means of democracy.

This chapter shows how the characteristics and dynamics of industrial relations in the *Reformasi* era occur in the framework of the three situations, implying the existence of a push-and-pull of power and interests among the involved parties, and their implications on investment practices and employees' welfare in Indonesia. It must be emphasized that the system of industrial relations in Indonesia, with its various revisions, occurred out of the interaction among the economic policies and capital at the global level, the development of domestic political situations, and the structural characteristics of the labour market, which is still marked by an excess of supply of labour.

This chapter, starting with the first section, briefly outlines industrial relations in New Order times (prior to *Reformasi*), which were marked by repressive labour policies for the sake of economic growth, through industrialization and integration into the global economy. The second section describes the transition phase from an authoritarian climate to a stage of democracy amidst an economic crisis that swept through Asia causing a multihued industrial relationship, but also leading to the emergence of new local players as an outcome of regional autonomy policies. Section 3 deals with the industrial relation situation during the *Reformasi* period, and finally, Section 4 discusses the implications of existing industrial relations for investment practices and workers' welfare.

PRIOR TO *REFORMASI* (1968–98)

As has been written by numerous scholars and observers of industrial relations in Indonesia, the system of industrial relations, almost throughout the New Order era, was marked by stringent, harsh, and thus effective labour regulations. These regulations were used to control trade unions through various policies ranging from the formation of a single trade union that was under the control of the government, to the development of repressive labour policies following a "security approach" model. The FBSI (Federasi Buruh Seluruh Indonesia, All Indonesia Workers Federation) was founded in 1973 as the single trade union, and afterwards changed into the SPSI (Serikat Pekerja Seluruh Indonesia, All Indonesia Workers Union) in 1985. The repressive labour policies were reflected in the development of the HPP (Pancasila Labour Relations) in 1974, which later became HIP (Pancasila Industrial Relations)[1] in 1984. These policies followed a no-nonsense style from legalizing military intervention in labour disputes in 1986, to the killing of labour activists in 1993 and 1994, and the jailing of trade union activists in 1996 (Manning 1993 and 1998, Bourchier 1994, Saptari 1995, Cox Edwards 1996, Masduki 1996, Kammen 1997, Hadiz 1997, Ford 1999, Sutanto and Elliot 2000, Aspinall 2001, Tornquist 2003, Caraway 2004, Soeprobo 2004, Silaban 2009, Solidarity Centre 2009). Strict policies towards the labour movement were imposed in support of the industrialization policy that was based on the development of export-oriented industries, and as an incentive for foreign investments in order to encourage economic growth. This economic industralization policy and strategy was also adopted as Indonesia's response to the trend of global economic integration and the direction of capital movements to seek out low-wage production locations in all corners of the world. Furthermore, this period was marked by low-wage politics, as Indonesian workers' wages were the lowest, at US$0.23 per hour, compared with Malaysia's at US$0.82, Philippines, US$0.64, Thailand, US$0.68, and South Korea, US$1.97 per hour (quoted from Masduki 1996).

In this period, more precisely towards the end of the 1980s, export oriented, medium- and large-scale labour-intensive industries started to grow, filling orders for consumer goods from global consumers, especially for garments, shoes, electronics, automotive products, and children's toys. In Tangerang, starting from the 1970s, industrial centres grew along with those in Bandung, Bogor (see also Mather 1983, White 1993, Hadiz 1997) in West Java. The same also occured in Semarang and Solo in Central Java in the subsequent years, followed by Surabaya, Sidoarjo, Pasuruan in East Java, Medan (North Sumatera) as well as in Makassar, South Sulawesi. These regions were the primary industrial areas that grew rapidly and became the heartbeat and dynamic centres of Indonesia's industrial relations. The factories constructed in these areas were foreign owned (especially by Japan, South Korea, and Taiwan) as well as locally owned and operated by work orders from international brand names in line with international subcontracted production linkages.

These regions were strictly monitored by the government as activism, labour strifes, and work stoppages (strikes) had occured in them (Manning 1993, Kammen 1997, Nugroho 2003). In order to guarantee that industrial activity functioned smoothly and to anticipate workers' actions, it was common to find military retirees or active military officers holding positions as corporate executives, especially in the role of personnel managers. It was also common to find workers' conflicts being settled by the security apparatus or at the local military authority's headquarters (see also Manning 1998, Hadiz 2000). This practice was legitimized by the decree of the minister for manpower of 1986 no. 342, concerning military intervention in industrial conflict.

At the beginning of the 1990s and in the midst of repression towards workers, there was a phenomenal struggle by activists against the regime in power, especially with the setting up of two trade unions, independent from the government controlled SPSI, namely SBM-SK (Serikat Buruh Merdeka Setia Kawan, Freedom and Friendship Trade Union) and SBSI (Serikat Buruh Sejahtera Indonesia, Indonesian Prosperous Trade Union). Whereas SBM-SK had a short lifespan due to internal problems, SBSI politically grew stronger and became the symbol of collective struggle. This was mainly done through organizing mass work stoppages in Medan, North Sumatera, in 1994 and demanding that the minimum wage be increased to more than Rp. 7,000, at the time when the average minimum wage was only Rp. 3,500 (see also Manning 1998). Nonetheless, this effort resulted in the detention of labour leader Muchtar Pakpahan.

An interesting fact is that in the middle of this repressive labour regime, the New Order government decreed a regional minimum wage, with periodic increases, so that wages could keep pace with the minimum physical needs level. This minimum wage policy, as inferred by Manning (1998, pp. 223–24), indicated the goverment's attempt to raise workers' income directly and remove one of the motives for the workers' strikes. The government had four arguments for its minimum wage policy. They were that an increase in wages would increase productivity; that labour costs were just a minor fraction (no more than 10 per cent) of total production costs; that paying a minimum wage will replace paying illegal levies that had contributed to a sharp hike in production costs; and finally, that an increase in minimum wage would have multiplier effects on work opportunities (Manning 1998). Another study (Suryahadi et al. 2002) stated that the minimum wage policy was undertaken as a government response towards domestic and international pressures from those concerned about the poor working conditions and low wages endured by workers at a time when the Indonesian economy was becoming increasingly industrialized.

This was a government policy that was pro-labour and was implemented seriously. It brought violating employers to court, and involved participation by the military in collaboration with labour offices (Depnaker — Ministry of Manpower) in the regions to ensure that the policy was complied with (Manning 1998). However, this labour policy had instead resulted in the higher frequency of workers' strikes — a feature of industrial relations in the early 1990s. Low wages and non-compliance with the minimum wage regulation had been the main cause of the rising trend of industrial strife.

By the end of its leadership and in the same year as the economic crisis, the New Order government issued a Law on Manpower no. 25/1997 that replaced the two previous laws and various labour regulations that had been strongly rejected, especially due to their restrictions on strikes, imposition of trade union registration, promotion of low wages, and finally, defiance of international labour standards (Suwarto and Elliot 2000, Habibi 2009). One item that was overlooked in the massive rejection of this new law was the legalization of a work contract system, which represented an initial form of flexible industrial relations. It appears that at the point when the law was first executed, workers and NGOs who supported labour rights were so excessively focused on the right to organize that they did not pay attention to the incorporation of the provision for a flexible labour market into the Manpower Law. This was a system that later, in the *Reformasi* period, became the primary characteristic of industrial relations and the main problem faced by workers as it created more flexible working conditions without any job security.

It can be summarized that in general, during the New Order era, employers practically enjoyed the full support of the government and benefited from exclusive rights in running their businesses, while workers had to abide by government regulations in order to keep their jobs, and at the same time avoid pressure from the military. These conditions characterized the difference with the situation during the *Reformasi* times, when workers were appeased by the seemingly pro-labour, flexible labour market policies. The government needs these policies to ensure that employers could continue to work while avoiding societal pressures as a result of the decentralization policy, which is elaborated further in Section 3 of this chapter.

TRANSITION PERIOD (1999–2001)

July 1997 was a significant point in time for Indonesia as it was marked by a change in the nation's political and economic order. The Asian crisis swept through Indonesia and the value of the rupiah plummeted, while companies suffered financial chaos due to the steep rise in the cost of imported raw materials, as well as a debt burden denominated in U.S. dollars. Workers were laid off immediately on a large scale, especially in labour-intensive sectors, including manufacturing industry, banking, and the construction sector (Manalu 1999, Tjandraningsih 1999, Manning 1999, Lont and White 2003, Breman and Wiradi 2004), which in turn resulted in an increase in the number of unemployed to 13.7 million (<http://www.twnside.org.sg/title/mass-cn.htm>).

Work layoffs without any predetermined procedures by companies were justified by the crisis conditions. There was no revolt by the trade unions as the workers understood the situation — that the layoffs were necessary and inevitable.

The crisis also provided the momentum for adjusting the production strategy from a centralized to a decentralized one through the implemention of the subcontracting system, the putting-out system[2] and a flexible work relationship (Tjandraningsih 1999, Habibi 2009).

The severe economic crisis promptly changed into a multidimensional crisis, a term used by many observers. This forced President Soeharto to receive a package of aid and economic reform programmes from the International Monetary Fund (IMF) in May 1998, a year after the crisis began in Indonesia, by signing Letter of Intent, drawn up by the IMF for Indonesia, and watched over by the IMF director. One of the economic recovery programme items that Indonesia had to agree on was to reform its rigid labour market (read: very protective of workers) in order to become more flexible (read: pro-capital). In essence, the flexible labour market policy was introduced to convert the rigid labour market into a more flexible one. The policy was meant to adjust the labour market to the competitive climate of the increasingly more liberal global economy through removing various government regulations in the labour market that were burdensome to businesses and hindering investment, labour absorption and economic growth (Nugroho 2004, Tjandraningsih and Nugroho 2009, Habibi 2009). In other words, because the rigid Indonesian labour market had become quite problematic for foreign investors, a new policy had to be introduced to improve the "investment climate", that is, to make foreign investors comfortable putting their money in Indonesia to reverse the drop in foreign direct investment as a result of the Asian crisis. The guidance for labour policies towards a more flexible direction was clearly inserted in the 21st Letter of Intent. It stipulated that constructing a strong industrial relations framework was central to the creation of work opportunities, welfare improvement, and worker skills, as well as creating a stable business climate. The instrument to achieve that condition was the existence of labour regulations that guaranteed a balance between efforts to protect the rights of workers and those to preserve a flexible labour market (Habibi 2009, Juliawan 2010).

The restructuring of the labour market to make it more flexible was conducted by the IMF in collaboration with the ILO (International Labour Organization), which was based on ILO's spirit and principles (Habibi 2009). The principles stated that in order to realize flexible labour relations, rules concerning apprentice work, part-time labour, and outsourcing, had to be addressed. The Letter of Intent and ILO principles became the reference base for drawing up a liberal package of labour laws, that is, Law no. 21/2000 on Trade Unions, Law no. 13/2003 on Employment, and Law no. 2/2004 on Dispute Resolution.[3]

The economic crisis forced Soeharto to step down as international and national support for his leadership had been withdrawn. He was replaced by Vice-President Habibie, who immediately carried out a range of important policy changes to show a different administrative path from his predecessor. Within the realm of industrial relations, in a time frame of less than a month after taking power, the new administration ratified ILO Convention no. 87 on freedom of association. In the period between June 1998 and May 2000, five of ILO's basic conventions were ratified (Caraway 2004, Tjandra 2007, Suryomenggolo 2009, Ford 2009), regulations were issued to open up opportunities for trade union registration, and, in a phenomenal move, there was a ruling on severance pay (KepMen 150/2000) that determined severance payments in large amounts, and even for workers guilty of misconduct. This last regulation triggered off some resistance from an employer's association that put pressure on the government to revise the regulation (SMERU 2002, Caraway 2004, <www.indosiar.com> 2002, Kompas 2002). The government was then forced to issue a revised regulation (KepMen 78/2001). This then sparked off a countermovement from workers who felt that their rights had been revoked, resulting in waves of workers' demonstrations in various parts of the country.[4]

The emergence of democracy took place with the birth of independent trade unions and the acknowledgement of their political position. Freedom of association had paved the way for dozens of labour federations and unions at the national level, along with thousands of factory-level trade unions. Trade union organizations spread out not only among manufacturing industry workers (who were comprised of blue-collar workers), but also among white-collar workers in the financial and hotel service sectors, as well as among journalists and workers in the public sector and state-owned enterprises (SOEs) (Mizuno et al. 2007, Tjandraningsih 2007, Tjandra 2007, Suryomenggolo 2009, Ford 2009). These unions, according to their backgrounds, can be divided into five groupings, namely the SPSI; unions that broke away from SPSI; older unions from the 1960s that resurrected themselves; independent unions; and finally, unions facilitated by labour NGOs (Tjandraningsih 2007). SMERU (2002) reported that at the end of 2001, the Depnaker (Ministry of Manpower) had registered sixty-one trade union federations, one confederation, 144 national-level trade unions, and 11,000 trade unions at the factory level (2002). Overall, these unions had organized more than eight million workers (Tjandra 2007).

The freedom of association, besides taking shape in the form of numerous trade unions, was also manifested in the involvement of unions in drawing up three manpower laws (UU). They were Law of Trade Unions which concerned the freedom of association, the Manpower Law, and the Dispute Resolution (Suryomenggolo 2009). Unlike the process of drawing up the Trade Union Law prior to *Reformasi*, when the government only included the SBSI, the government and parliament in the transition period invited the involvement of ten trade unions to set up a "Small Team" or *Tim Kecil* to produce the Law on Manpower. However, the involvement of the ten trade unions had drawn protests from other, uninvited trade unions (Suryomenggolo 2009, Habibi 2009).

It was also during this transition period that the government's decentralization policy, a political reform package for Indonesia as formulated by the IMF, was implemented. The decentralization policy had a very speedy and rushed process. As monitored by Perdana and Friawan (2007), this policy was to be implemented in a very short period, despite the fact that it carried extremely radical changes. Discussions were carried out only among its supporters and there were almost no representatives from the regions that would be enormously responsible for its implementation. In a span of two years, the regional government had to bear responsibility for six important livelihood aspects, namely, education, health, environment, labour, public services, and natural resources management (Aspinall and Fealy 2003). All these six aspects were previously the responsibility of the central government.

In line with the system of industrial relations, these policies brought with them a wider implication, including jurisdiction over planning, managing, and controlling manpower issues, which along with five other important aspects (as mentioned above) were handed over to the regional governments. Regional autonomy in the field of employment had already created problems and excesses that had been brought about by changes in the administrative structure and bureaucracy, which meant a lower competency and professional standard in the management of manpower issues (AKATIGA-TURC-LabSosio 2006). Besides that, industrial relations were also disrupted by the emergence of local and informal authorities, along with an increase in legal or illegal levies from regional governments to gain regional income (AKATIGA 2007, Juliawan 2008).

It should be noted that all observations concerning the situation during this transitional phase reflect the dynamics of industrial relations at the national level, and illustrate a struggle of interests and attitudes of industrial relations elites who represented their own respective institutions. There were almost no observations or analyses on what had occurred at the local grass roots level, especially concerning union members specifically, and the labour force generally, which was also directly affected by the national policy. With the economic crisis and employers' strategies to overcome it, there had been a change in the character of the formal industrial workforce sector. There was then a preference among employers for single and young (eighteen to twenty-five years of age) female workers who had just graduated from high school, with a definite employment or contract period (Tjandraningsih 1999). Furthermore, the layoffs during the crisis also caused the migration of the productive labour force from the formal to the informal sectors.

REFORMASI ERA (2002–TODAY)

Some of the characteristics of industrial relations in the *Reformasi* era are that they are liberal, flexible, and decentralized. Other features are a de-industrialization tendency (which has been causing much concern to economists[5]) and a low quality labour market, indicated by the low educational background of the workers, high levels of unemployment and underemployment (8 per cent and 30 per cent respectively), as well as the oversupply of labour. Furthermore, de-industrialization and labour oursourcing practices have resulted in a rising percentage and number of workers in informal sectors.

Within the context of the labour market, the number of trade unions kept rising, and by 2008, based on verification by the Ministry of Manpower, registration lists showed that there were three confederations (KSPSI, KSBSI, and KSPI), ninety federations, and tens of thousands of company-level trade unions. However, according to the same sources, total membership in these numerous unions came up to only 3.4 million workers. This meant that in comparison to membership figures at the beginning of the freedom of association period (8.2 million workers), there was a drop in the number of organized workers by more than 50 per cent within five or six years. This situation occurred in conjunction with the implementation of a flexible labour market policy to create a friendly and pro-business environment that became the primary jargon for economic development in Indonesia. Since the creation of UU 13/2003 that legalized contract work and put labour outsourcing practices into effect, employers have converted their labour force structure to one based on a labour relations status. Nowadays it is quite normal within companies to have three groups of workers according to their status, namely permanent workers, contract workers, and outsourced workers.[6] There is a rising tendency for companies to try to reduce the number of permanent workers and increase the size of the contract and outsourced workers. Several sources indicate that the typical composition of a workforce in a company is as follows: 20 per cent permanent workers, 30 per cent contract workers, and 50 per cent outsourced workers. One new company that produces, among other things, elementary school uniforms for students in the United States, has a factory in Sukabumi, West Java, which employs a total of 2,300 workers, all of whom work with a one-year contract status.[7] A study based on contract workers and outsourcing practices conducted in the metals sector in the Riau Islands, West Java, and East Java provinces, shows a similar tendency: fewer permanent workers and increasing numbers of contracted and outsourced workers.[8]

The same study also confirms that the change in status from permanent worker to non-permanent worker has cut down the membership in trade unions and has thus weakened union's influence. Traditionally, members of trade unions have been workers with permanent status; therefore, a reduction in the number of permanent workers in essence reduces the number of union members. Contract and outsourced workers are not interested in becoming union members, nor do they dare to join unions for fear of losing their current employment opportunities (AKATIGA-TURC-LabSosio 2006, FPBN 2005, Juliawan 2010, Tjandraningsih, Herawati and Suhadmadi 2010). In fact, weakening trade unions is one of the reasons for, as well as objectives of, flexible labour market policies. From the viewpoint of the proponents of a flexible labour market, labour unions are one of the obstacles to the running of smooth business as they have the power to demand workers' rights. Therefore, they argue that the power of trade unions needed to be restricted (Tjandraningsih and Nugroho 2009, Habibi 2009). Amid this situation, various multinational organizations continue to urge the Indonesian Government to speed up the improvement of the investment climate by publishing many surveys about the cost of doing business, and obstacles in making investments in Indonesia. These numerous surveys show that the list of barriers to investment include poor infrastructure, the high frequency of legal and illegal levies, weak law enforcement, energy shortfalls, high bank interest rates, as well as labour issues.[9] The above list of barrier to investment was confirmed by a survey at the microlevel that contains employers' opinion that the main investment blocks are illegal and legal levies in the form of taxes and fees, the poor performance of government apparatuses, and bad infrastructure (AKATIGA 2007).

It is interesting and important to note that survey results from multi-national organizations — often published in the mass media — become the basis for foreign and domestic businessmen to urge the government to make the orderly revision of labour and manpower regulations its top priority. The Law (UU) on Manpower, which accommodates and legalizes flexible work practices through its provisions on contract workers and outsourcing, is still deemed as too rigid. The protection of workers' rights, especially the right to receive severance payments, add to that rigidity.[10] In 2005, the government responded to these requests by issuing a Presidential Decision in which revisions would be made towards UU 13/2003, based on a proposal by APINDO and several foreign investor groups (Juliawan 2010).

Sections to be revised are the articles on contract workers, outsourcing, and right to severance payment. It was proposed that a worker may be contracted for up to five years (up from the two years then); outsourcing can be done in all work sectors from every stage of the production process, and not be limited to supporting fields; and the right to severance pay would be revised from nine months to seven months. The entire planned revision would shift the labour market in a more flexible direction, which would allow employers to recruit and dismiss employees at a low cost (Juliawan 2010).

This planned revision received strong objections from workers, resulting in numerous protests through mass workers' demonstrations held by trade unions throughout the nation. During the celebration of May Day (1 May 2006) in Jakarta, the trade unions collectively showed their strength by assembling more than 100,000 workers to reject the revisions. The waves of continual demonstrations forced the government to postpone the planned revisions and to make a request to the five state universities to conduct an academic study on UU 13/2003. The results of the study have not been widely publicized to either employers or the trade unions even up to now.[11]

Celebrations for first of May Labour Day have also coloured industrial relations in Indonesia. Since 2002, the first of May has been an annual ritual for workers to display their existence as well as the problems they face to the public. The celebrations are conducted by gathering the masses at government power centres in the capital city and provincial capitals. At the beginning of the *Reformasi* era, employers and the government were still awkward about how to handle these May Day celebrations. However, after a couple of years of these celebrations, and being accustomed to them, employers now grant permission, and even provide facilities, for workers to celebrate that day. Accommodation and acknowledgement from the government concerning May Day was symbolically demonstrated by President Susilo Bambang Yudhoyono who celebrated it together with workers in the industrial regions.[12]

Another important issue that has characterized industrial relations in Indonesia up to the present is the decline in performance and competency of government apparatus in handling labour matters in the regions. The classical problem, and, simultaneously, the source of problems in industrial relations, is weak supervision. This has been acknowledged by high-ranking officials at manpower/labour offices in various regions, and even by the minister for manpower and labour (*Kompas*, 23 March 2010).

One of the consequences of weak control is poor law enforcement. In the regional autonomy era, supervision practices have worsened and labour office apparatuses seem to have become increasingly powerless in the face of many violations of their own regulations. Besides being the result of insufficient numbers of labour inspectors, poor supervision is also related to the low competence of the inspectors. In many industrial areas, the ratio of labour inspectors to number of companies to be overseen is worrisome. In Tangerang, for the 2,300 companies to be overseen, there are only seven inspectors; in Batam, for 4,000 companies, there are only three; in Bekasi, for 3,000 entities, only five; in Karawang, for 1,400 companies, only seven; and finally, for the hundreds of companies in Pasuruan, there are only five inspectors.[13] At the national level there are 2,089 labour inspectors while the estimated need is 3,463 persons (*Kompas*, 23 March 2010). Moreover, ever since regional autonomy was put into effect and labour/manpower matters became the responsibility of regional

governments, the placement of officials is based more on availability and
rotation schedules of civil servants, rather than on competence to do the
job. In various regions, staff members at the local labour offices originally
came from the department of landscapes and cemeteries, or were former
traditional market supervisors (*mantri pasar*), animal husbandry inspectors,
members of the local government's civil police (*satpol PP*), and so forth.
There is a tendency among regional governments to be reluctant to allocate
funds for the type of labour inspector training that would give labour
inspectors certificates.

The weak control of labour inspectors contributed to the industrial
riot in Batam in April 2010.[14] It is only recently that this weak control
became a national issue because it has been mentioned by both trade unions
and employers. This was also acknoweledged by the highest authority in
the labour office in Batam.

Limitations in supervision also result in the common practice of factories
closing down without giving severance pay to the workers as stipulated
by the law. This also leaves thousands of workers unemployed. The notes
and experiences of trade union activists in West Java show that factories,
especially those producing shoes and garments, which employed thousands
of workers, suddenly halted their production without any announcement.
Moreoever, the managers of some of these companies, who originated
from South Korea and Taiwan, fled and returned to their countries. The
production infrastructure (factory and machinery) left behind become
difficult to confiscate as all of it have been leased.[15] Companies of this
type tend to operate in Indonesia for three to five years, and afterwards
close down. Furthermore, some big enterprises went bankrupt due to the
hike in electricity and fuel costs in 2005, or they lost out due to business
competition, or suffered from the strong flow of smuggled goods from
China from 2005 onward. Some of the entrepreneurs left their workers to
fend for themselves, and to struggle for their rights to claim severance pay
by auctioning off the remaining company assets from their capital goods
(assets). To handle the problem of supervision, the government has taken
three actions. The first is to make supervision a priority, that is, to inspect
the companies that are potential problems, that is, those with more than
500 workers or those with high risks in the production process or newly
operated companies. The second is to base supervision on reports from the
workers. The third is to involve trade unions in the supervision.

Regional autonomy has not turned out to make the provinces capable
of managing and supervising workers. In many regions, the same excuse was
heard. The proposed regional regulations much demanded by the labour

unions often contradicted with the Law (UU), which represents the highest ruling and could not be overturned by any regulations, including regional regulations, below them. In connection with outsourcing, for example, the call for sanctions on companies that are violating a regional regulation cannot be imposed because the Law (UU) itself does not mention sanctions against violators, except for administrative sanctions, such as the issue of a note of warning (*nota peringatan*). In other words, regional authorities cannot execute heavier punishments than the sanctions determined within the Law (UU). The imposition of administrative sanctions is also rare because of worries on the part of local labour officials who are afraid that if most of the companies had administrative sanctions imposed on them, and if too many companies were affected, there would be a mass pull-out by companies from that region.[16]

On the other hand, the responsibility of the regions to generate their own revenue has sparked off the creativeness from the regional governments to issue regional regulations to collect taxes and fees, thus forcing companies to become sources of regional revenue.[17] Various levies and fees on companies are laid on their business related activities, such as street lighting, downloading of goods, installation of fire equipment, garbage disposal, and more. These levies are very burdensome to the companies, but hard for them to avoid. Furthermore, the companies counter the numerous fees and levies from the regional administrations by clamping down on labour costs through reducing non-wage payments and/or using outsourced workers.

Regional autonomy has brought with it a rise in the number of local informal leaders such as religious leaders as well as ruffians (known as *preman*) who step into industrial matters and offer their services to factories as their security agents, labour suppliers, and worker controllers. The local ruffians force companies to take their offers, or companies ask them to protect factory operations from any trouble made by local people or workers. There are practices where strikes have been countered by local ruffians, and conflicts occur between unions and locals concerning matters in labour recruitment and outsourcing practices (Nugroho and Arif 2009).

While the number of unions has increased, the total number of their members has continued to decline, the bargaining position of workers has grown weaker, and their welfare has gone downhill. In general, the implementation of the minimum wage is no longer a problem as compliance with paying the minimum wage has increased, compared with the transition period. However, the minimum wage is often regarded as the maximum wage, and companies are not willing to offer wages higher than the minimum ones. When regulations state that the minimum wage is only applicable to workers who have work experience of less than one year, the practice is that all workers, regardless their experience, are paid the minimum wage. In other words, the minimum wage regulation has been used by some companies not to pay wages higher than the minimum one. For example, Tjandraningsih and Herawati (2009) found that the minimum wage is also given to workers with two years, eight years, and even twelve years of experience. They also revealed that a study on decent wage in three provinces, namely, Banten, West and Central Java, showed that the average minimum wage could only cover 62.4 per cent of the workers' real living expenses.

The implementation of labour force flexibility has erased the certainty of work for workers, since a short-term contract (one year on average) can only be extended to a maximum of two years. Workers' welfare has decreased as they only have the right to earn a basic salary, which is lower than the one paid to permanent workers, and their additional benefits have become limited. Relative to the international standard, current Indonesian workers' wages can be said to have declined compared with those in 2000.

Ironically, this low wage has been used to attract foreign investment. For example, the investment coordinating board (BKPM) cited data from the Economic Intelligence Unit (2009) to show how cheap Indonesian workers are in their investment promotion: Indonesian workers' wages were only US$0.6 per hour, or the lowest compared with India ($1.03), the Philippines ($1.04), Thailand ($1.63), China ($2.11) and Malaysia ($2.88).

BKPM's efforts to attract foreign investment by promoting low workers' wages in Indonesia is a reminder of the New Order's low-wage policy, which means a step backwards in policy direction. The low-wage strategy shows the gap in the government's understanding of the changing demands from companies facing global competition, and the work quality/qualification of the Indonesian labour force. Concerned with global competition, investors demand on-time delivery and high work quality, as well as an efficient bureaucratic service. At the same time, Indonesian textile and garment entrepreneurs who have witnessed industrial development in Vietnam and China, say that in terms of skills and quality, the output of Indonesian workers is far higher than workers in the two countries. They also state that in reality, if bureaucratic fees and various levies could be removed, the companies could even afford to double the minimum wage.

Furthermore, one important development that has become a phenomenon in industrial relations is the age limit on employing workers in factories because of employers' preference for outsourcing and contract work. In recruiting labour, companies now require women to be between the ages of eighteen and twenty-four and men to be between the ages of eighteen and twenty-seven years. The workers must also be single. Female workers above twenty-four years old are no longer able to apply for work in companies. This fact may mean that work opportunities in the formal sector are becoming increasingly limited for persons of certain ages. An important question to bring up which must be immediately answered is what will be the condition of Indonesia's labour market when the majority of those in their productive years cannot enter the formal sector?

Labour disputes, demonstration, and strikes have also remained characteristics of industrial relations in Indonesia during the *Reformasi* era. Reasons for disputes are still about normative rights, that is, basic workers' rights guaranteed by the law, rejection of outsourcing practices, and promotion to permanent workers status.

Layoffs are also a feature of industrial relations in the *Reformasi* era. The increase in electricity and fuel prices in 2005, along with the financial crisis in the United States, has had a great impact on the massive number of layoffs. AJI (*Aliansi Jurnalis Indenden*) Indonesia, basing its report on the records of the Ministry of Manpower and Transmigration, stated that there had been 51,000 workers laid-off. Nonetheless, APINDO records show a much higher number of 237,000 workers who were laid off from October 2008–March 2009, with most of them from the textile and garments, footwear, automotive, oil palm plantation, and construction sectors (*AJI* 2009).

Although compliance with the minimum wage has increased relatively speaking, this fact cannot be taken as an indicator of a rise in workers' welfare. Indeed, there are indications that the welfare of workers is declining with the widening spread of outsourcing practices. In East Java, wages of outsourced workers at a multinational company's food segment are only 40 per cent of permanent workers' wages (AKATIGA-TURC-LabSosio 2006), while in the centres of the metal industry (Batam, West Java and East Java), the average difference in total wages between a permanent and outsourced worker has almost reached 30 per cent (initial finding of Tjandraningsih, Herawati and Suhadmadi 2010). The practice of outsourcing has also forced job seekers to pay for entry into the labour market. Since UU 13/2003 was enacted, almost no company has recruited its labour force by itself, but they have all used the services of labour agencies. Job seekers now have to use these agencies to obtain work, and have to pay a number of fees to get a work placement.[18] Mandatory payments by job seekers to placement agencies vary from revenue stamp costs for contract signing, health examination costs, worker's uniform costs, registration fees, to placement fees, ranging from Rp. 10,000 to Rp. 1,800,000 (Tjandraningsih, Herawati and Suhadmadi 2010). Fee payments by job seekers, recorded by labour union management and labour NGOs)in industrial centres of Batam, Jabotabek, Bandung, Semarang, Pasuruan, and Medan, have become widespread and varied. The records also show that the total amount of expenditure influences the wages received. According to union activists in Bekasi-West Java, the length of the contract period is determined by the amounts paid.[19]

The excesses of the labour market flexibility policy have become the reason for labour unions to protest against that policy. They show that labour market conditions and policies have not brought about the assumed trickle down effect — that economic growth would create a better distribution of employment opportunities which would result in an improved distribution of income (Tjandraningsih and Nugroho 2009). One result of the policy is the weakening of trade union power, as a result of the decline in their membership and the loss of motivation for workers to join trade unions. Also, social security, a requirement for the flexibility policy, has never been realized. Worse, the Law on a National Social Security System (no. 40/2004) has yet to be implemented even now.

The entire situation shows the complexity of industrial relations in Indonesia, in effect, making it difficult to view things in a black or white manner. The government's policy within the corridors of liberalization and democratization is in line with global capitalism's tendency to move ever more freely, amid stiff economic competition. This policy has been implemented through the labour law (UU) package and the policy of governmental decentralization that has created a system of industrial relations which has changed in a direction that has not benefited workers.

TOWARDS INDUSTRIAL RELATIONS THAT LEAD TO PROSPERITY

The character of industrial relations in Indonesia today shows the government's compliance with global capitalistic pressures and its implementation of conditions to improve the investment climate. The government has been put under pressure by global forces to liberalize labour regulations, flexibilize the labour market, and decentralize labour affairs. The policies and laws of labour indicate a shift of the pendulum in the government's stand and in protection for workers. The pendulum is moving farther away from workers' interests, with employers gaining support and facilities in the labour market directly or indirectly. Moreover, basic problems with regard to the regulation and management of the labour market have not been touched upon, such as a labour market information system for unskilled workers, supporting facilities for skill enhancement, and a social security system (Nugroho and Tjandraningsih 2007).

In addition, the main problems not directly related to industrial relation matters, but are part of employers' grievances, are corruption, poor infrastructure, unsteady energy availability, smuggling, inefficient bureaucracy, and regional autonomy. Regional autonomy has brought about high costs, and the issue has not been effectively managed. Various problems in industrial relations, including labour strife, are, in fact, a chain reaction to the major problems stated above.

The tendency of the government and employers to deal with the labour market's lack of flexibility and the emphasis on labour as the reason for a non-favourable investment climate in Indonesia show the inadequate will of the the government and employers to tackle the main structural aspects that lead to the high costs of doing business in Indonesia. The situation is aptly captured in a statement from employers in Bandung who once said, "It is easier to face the workers than the bureaucracy and government apparatus, as the demands of the authorities in this era of regional autonomy, if unfulfilled, will create more problems for the businesses".[20]

The policy framework for a liberal, flexible, and decentralized government, with its freedom of association, has not immediately raised workers' bargaining position, but instead shows a tendency towards the reverse. The struggle of trade unions in demanding workers' welfare still entails a long journey to achieving success, especially because of the lack of government support, which leaves the unions to struggle single-handedly.

The flexibility policy, which is the tone in Indonesia's industrial relations today, shows a gradual decline in workers' welfare and their certainty of work. The practice of flexibility has also brought limitations to work by making it extremely short, narrowing employment opportunities in the formal sector for the productive labour force, and making the supervision function complicated within industrial relations.

The entire situation, if not immediately overcome, will, in the not-too-distant future, bring about a backlash to the government efforts to improve Indonesia's investment climate and eradicate poverty. Poor working conditions and a massive lack of employment opportunities will cause more workers' actions and protests that will certainly create an uncomfortable environment for businesses. Eventually this will only discourage businesses from being carried out in Indonesia. Government decisiveness and support are needed to face various problems that crop up in industrial relations, and to make Indonesia an investor-friendly nation, bringing prosperity to its citizens. This road map is also being taken by China, Thailand, and various developed countries, including Japan and the United States. The ever-stringent and fierce global competition can only be won by those nations that have strong and consistent governments that rule with a spirit of justice.

NOTES

1. The philosophy of HIP was harmony and equality in relations between employers and workers.
2. In the putting-out system, a central agent contracts out work to subcontractors who complete the work in their own facility, often their own home.
3. For a detailed process of the formulation of the three laws, see Suryomenggolo (2009).
4. *Kompas*, 15 June 2001, <http://berita.liputan6.com/sosbud/200105/13043/>.
5. In some regions, firms were said to be closed down when, in fact, they just relocated their industries to other regions with lower wages. Textile and garment factories in North Jakarta and Tangerang, for example, closed down factories and moved them to Semarang and Solo in Central Java. Manufacturing plants in Jabotabek (Jakarta-Bogor-Tangerang-Bekasi) shut down factories and shifted to Sukabumi and Subang in West Java. Therefore, during the two years, industrialization occurred in those two West Java regencies, as foreign investors from Malaysia, South Korea, and China moved in to establish garment and shoe factories. Therefore, the phenomenon of de-industralization should be studied more thoroughly; <http://www.indotextiles.com/index.php?option=com_content&task=view&id=540&Itemid=72>; <http://cetak.kompas.com/read/xml/2009/09/28/16001332/Investor.Asing.Antusias.Berinvestasi.di.Sukabumi>; <http://www.kontan.co.id/index.php/bisnis/news/34147/Relokasi-Pabrik-Garmen-China-Itu-Isu-Lama), and <http://www.kbn.co.id/web2009/id/news-detail/195> (accessed 23 June 2010).
6. Permanent workers are those directly recruited by the company and working for an undetermined period until retirement; contract workers are those directly recruited by the company and working for a certain time period; outsourced workers are recruited with the assistance of a labour services agency (popularly called "an outsourcing company"), and work for a six-month up to a one- or two-year period. Some outsourced workers may also work for a three-month period.
7. Findings of a survey on decent wages by AKATIGA-SPN-Garteks-FES 2009.
8. The study was conducted in collaboration with FSPMI (Federation of Indonesian Metalworkers Union), AKATIGA, and FES, a German NGO.

9. <http://www.kontan.co.id/index.php/nasional/news/29432/Enam-Hambatan-Investasi-di-Indonesia>; <http://indonesiafile.com/content/view/857/47/>.
10. Multinational institutions such as the ADB (Asian Development Bank), in one of their labour market surveys on Indonesia in 2003, stated that in the preceeding two to three years, labour market policies became too populist, thus causing a negative impact on the investment climate (Juliawan 2010).
11. The recommendation of the study includes, among other things, the enhancement of the government role in facilitating just industrial relations, in protecting outsourced workers, and in the review of layoff and severance payments.
12. <http://hariansib.com/?p=2432>; <http://www1.surya.co.id/v2/?p=8162>.
13. Interviews with various regional labour office heads.
14. <http://www.thejakartapost.com/news/2010/04/23/%E2%80%98racist-remark%E2%80%99-sparks-batam-riot.html>, <*metrotvnews.com/itm-beta/hot.../shipyard-workers-riot-in-batam*>, <http://www.thejakartaglobe.com/home/riot-sweeps-batam-dry-dock/371040> (accessed 23 June 2010).
15. Companies such as these were called "bodong" (bogus) as they operated without capital. Some of the *modus operandi* used by companies to shut down factories was to suggest weekend vacations for workers, and at the start of the following week, the returning workers were met by locked gates and an announcement that the factory had stopped operations. That method was also used after Idul Fitri holidays.
16. Interviews with local labour office authorities, May 2010.
17. Nugroho and Arif (2009).
18. Findings of several trade unions; *Kompas*, 23 March 2010, FPBN (2004), Nugroho and Arif (2009), Juliawan (2010), Tjandraningsih, Herawati and Suhadmadi (2010).
19. Interviews with trade union activists in Bekasi.
20. Interviews with West Java textile producers, March 2007. See also Nugroho and Arif (2009).

REFERENCES

AJI-Solidarity Center-FES-ILO. *Hujan Batu Buruh Kita:Kumpula Liputan Perburuhan — Living under Stone Rain: Stories about Indonesian Labors.* Jakarta: AJI Indonesia, 2009.

AKATIGA. *The Impact of the ATC Phasing Out in Indonesia: Where Do We Stand?* Bandung: AKATIGA, 2007.

AKATIGA-TURC-LabSosio. *Promoting Fair Labour Regulations in Indonesia: A Study and Advocacy in Improving Local Level Investment Environment in Tangerang and Pasuruan.* Bandung: AKATIGA, 2006.

Aspinall, Ed. "Democratisation, the Working Class and the Indonesian Transition". *Review of Indonesian and Malaysian Affairs* 33, no. 2 (1999): 1–32.

Aspinall, Ed. and Greg Fealy. "Introduction: Decentralisation, Democratisation and the Rise of the Local". In *Local Power and Politics in Indonesia: Decentralisation and Democratisation*, edited by Ed. Aspinall and Greg Fealy. Singapore: Institute of Southeast Asian Studies, 2003.

Bourchier, David, ed. "Indonesia's Emerging Proletariat: Workers and Their Struggles". Annual Indonesia Winter Lecture Series no. 17. Melbourne: Monash University, 1994.

Breman, Jan and Gunawan Wiradi. *Masa Cerah dan Masa Suram di Pedesaan Jawa*. Jakarta: LP3ES-KITLV, 2004.

Caraway, Teri L. "Protective Repression, International Pressure and Institutional Design: Explaining Labor Reform in Indonesia". *Studies in Comparative International Development* 39, no. 3 (2004): 28–49.

Edwards, Alejandra Cox. "Labor Regulations and Industrial Relations in Indonesia". Paper presented at a joint Ministry of Manpower-World Bank workshop entitled, "Indonesian Workers in the 21st Century: Workshop for Economic Reforms and Labor Market Restructuring for Indonesia". Jakarta: Ministry of Manpower and World Bank, 2–4 April 1996.

Ford, Michele. *Workers and Intellectuals: NGOs, Trade Unions and the Indonesian Labour Movement*. Singapore: National University of Singapore Press, 2009.

Habibi, Muhtar. *Gemuruh Buruh di Tengah Pusaran Neoliberalisme: Pengadopsian Kebijakan Perburuhan Neoliberal Pasca Orde Baru*. Yogyakarta: Penerbit Gava Media & Jurusan administrasi Negara FISIPOL UGM, 2009.

Hadiz, Vedi. *Workers and the State in New Order Indonesia*. London and New York: Routledge, 1997.

Juliawan, Benny Hari. "Extracting Labour from its Owner". *Critical Asian Studies* 42, no. 1 (2010): 25–52.

Kammen, Douglas. "A Time to Strike: Industrial Strikes and Changing Class Relations in the New Order Indonesia". Ph.D. thesis. Ithaca: Cornell University, 1997.

Lont, Hotze and Benjamin White. "Critical Review of Crisis Studies, 1998–2002: Debates on Poverty, Employment and Solidarity in Indonesia". In *Indonesia in Transition: Work in Progress*, edited by Henk Schulte Nordholt and Gusti Asnan. Yogyakarta: Pustaka Pelajar, 2003.

Manalu, Saut. "Kebijakan Perburuhan di Masa Krisis". *Jurnal Analisis Sosial* 4, no. 2 (1999): 1–23.

Manning, Chris. *Indonesian Labour in Transition: An East Asian Success Story?* Cambridge University Press, 1998.

―――. "Structural Change and Industrial Relations during the Soeharto Period: An Approaching Crisis?". *Bulletin of Indonesian Economic Studies* 29, no. 2 (1993): 59–95.

Masduki, Teten. "Labour Conditions in Indonesia: Workers Rights in Indonesia in the Era of Export Oriented Industry: A Background Briefing", 1996. <http://

www.asia-pacific-action.org/southeastasia/indonesa/publications/doss1/teten. htm> (accessed 7 March 2008).

Mather, Celia. "Rather than Make Trouble, It's Better Just to Leave: Behind the Lack of Industrial Strife in Tangerang region of West Java". In *Women, Work and Ideology in the Third World*, edited by Haleh Ashfar. London: Tavistock, 1983.

Mizuno, Kosuke, Indrasari Tjandraningsih, and Rina Herawati. *Direktori SerikatPekerja/Serikat Buruh Indonesia.* Bandung: AKATIGA, 2007.

Nugroho, Hari. "Masalah Upah dan Gelombang Pemogokan Buruh". *Masyarakat, Jurnal Sosiologi* 12 (1993): 27–40.

Nugroho, Wisnu and Ahmad Arif. "Yang Terjepit Jatah Preman dan Jawara". In ILO *Hujan Batu Buruh Kita: Kumpulan Liputan Perburuhan*, edited by AJI-Solidarity Center-FES. Jakarta: AJI Indonesia, 2009.

Nugroho, Yanuar. "Menyoal Kebijakan Fleksibilitas Pasar Tenaga Kerja". Paper presented at the seminar "Fleksibilitas Pasar Tenaga Kerja terhadap Prospek Dunia Kerjadi Kawasan Asia". Jakarta: Pusat Kajian Asia Timur, Universitas Katolik Atmajaya, 9 March 2004.

Perdana, Ari and Deni Friawan. "Economic Crisis, Institutional Changes and the Effectiveness of Government: The Case of Indonesia", 2007. <www.csis.or.id/ working_paper_file/76/wpe102.pdf> (accessed 13 June 2010).

Saptari, Ratna. "Rural Women to the Factories: Continuity and Change in East Java's Kretek Industry". Ph.D. thesis. Amsterdam: Universiteit van Amsterdam, 1995.

Silaban, Rekson. *Reposisi Gerakan Buruh: Peta Jalan Gerakan Buruh Indonesia Pasca Reformasi.* Jakarta: Sinar Harapan, 2009.

SMERU. *Industrial Relations in Jabotabek, Bandung and Surabaya during the Fredom to Organize Era.* Jakarta: SMERU, 2002.

Soeprobo, Tara. "Indonesian Industrial Relations: A Continuing Learning Process". Paper presented at the International Industrial Relations 5th Asian Regional Congress. Seoul, 23–26 June 2004.

Suryahadi, Asep et al. "Upah dan Kesempatan Kerja: Dampak Kebijakan Upah Minimum terhadap Penyerapan Tenaga Kerja di Sektor Formal Perkotaan". *Jurnal Analisis Sosial* 7, no. 1 (2002): 17–36.

Suryomenggolo, Jafar. "Labour, Politics and the Law: A Legal-Political Analysis of Indonesia's Labour Law Reform Program". In *Labour, Management and Development Journal*, 9–2008 Special Edition — "Indonesian Labour since Suharto: Perspectives from the Region", 2009. <http://www.nla.gov.au/ openpublish/index.php/lmd> (accessed 8 June 2010).

Suwarno, Sutanto and Jan Elliott. "Changing Approaches to Employment Relations in Indonesia". In *Employment Relations in the Asia Pacific: Changing Approaches*, edited by Greg Bamber et al. NSW: Allen & Unwin, 2000.

Tjandra, Surya. "Dua Level Gerakan Buruh Pasca Reformasi". Paper presented in the workshop, "Refleksi Tujuh Tahun Kebebasan Berserikat di Indonesia" kerjasama AKATIGA-di. Jakarta: AKATIGA-Center for Southeast Asian Studies, Kyoto

University, 7 August 2007.

Tjandraningsih, Indrasari. "Krisis Ekonomi dan PHK: Maknanya bagi Perempuan". *Jurnal Analisis Sosial* 4, no. 2 (1999): 61–74.

————. "Potret Serikat Pekerja/Serikat Buruh di Indonesia Pasca Reformasi". In *Direktori Serikat Pekerja/Serikat Buruh di indonesia*, edited by Kosuke Mizuno et al. Bandung: AKATIGA-CSEAS, 2007.

Tjandraningsih, Indrasari and Hari Nugroho. "The Flexibility Regime and Organised Labour in Indonesia". *Labour, Management and Development Journal, 9–2008 Special Edition — "Indonesian Labour since Suharto: Perspectives from the Region"*, 2009. <http://www.nla.gov.au/openpublish/index.php/lmd> (accessed 18 August 2009).

Tjandraningsih, Indrasari and Rina Herawati. *Menuju Upah Layak: Survey Upah Buruh tekstil & Garmen di Indonesia*. Bandung: SPN-Garteks SBSI-AKATIGA-FES-Twaro, 2009.

Tjandraningsih, Indrasari, Hari Nugroho, and Surya Tjandra. *Buruh versus Investasi? Mendorong Peraturan Perburuhan yang Adil di Indonesia*. Bandung: AKATIGA, 2008.

Tjandraningsih, Indrasari, Rina Herwawati and Suhadmadi. *Diskriminatif & Eksploitatif: Praktek Kerja Kontrak dan Outsourcing Buruh di Sektor Metal di Indonesia* [*Discriminatory and Exploitative: Contract Work and Labour Outsourcing in Metal Industry in Indonesia*]. Bandung: AKATIGA-FSPMI-FES, December 2010.

Tornquist, Olle. "Buruh dan Demokrasi? Refleksi tentang Kebuntuan Politik di Indonesia". In *Gerakan Demokrasi di Indonesia pasca-Soeharto*, edited by A.E. Priyono et al. Jakarta: DEMOS, 2003.

White, Benjamin. "Industrial Workers on West Java's Urban Fringe". In *Indonesia Assessment, Labour: Sharing in the Benefits of Growth?*, edited by Chris Manning and Joan Hardjono. Canberra: Department of Political and Social Change Research School of Pacific Studies, Australian National University, 1993.

9
Decentralization and Domestic Trade Interdependence

Siti Astiyah, Salomo P. Matondang, and Guruh Suryani Rokhimah[1]

INTRODUCTION

Regional economic development is influenced by many factors and primarily by interaction among regions through the exchange of goods, services and labour, as well as policy interactions at the regional, national and international levels. Shaffer (1993) argues that regional economic development is affected by interaction with other regions or countries due to limited resources, potential product availability, and the potential for leakage in each region. Meanwhile Blakely (1989) states four factors influencing regional economic development: employment opportunities in the region, with emphasis on the quality of labour; base of regional development, including the availability of sound economic institutions; location as an asset, based on the environmental quality; and finally, knowledge as a resource in the context of knowledge-based development. Therefore, the regional economic development process requires elements such as formation of new institutions that support regional economies, the development of potential and/or new alternative industries, increase in labour capacity to enhance product quality, search for avenues for market expansion, technology transfer, and an opening of new investment opportunities for businesspeople. Furthermore, amidst the globalization era, different regions may react differently towards mounting competition, which comes not only from other regions within Indonesia, but also from foreign markets. This situation persuades every region in Indonesia to improve its economic longevity.

In the era of regional autonomy and fiscal decentralization, the regional economy plays an important role in achieving and accelerating national economic development. Fiscal decentralization is a natural consequence of the policies that enhance greater autonomy in the local district. The basic principle which undergirds this mechanism is the idea that "money follows actions". The delegation of government authority carries with it budgetary consequences in the form of increasing the central government fund that must be allocated to the regions, where the actions take place. Correspondingly, fiscal decentralization has increased regional governments' authority in determining the pace and level of their regional economic development. At the same time, one of the best ways to increase regional economic development has been the entwinement of trade cooperation among various regions. This is expected to become a strong base for improving Indonesia's economy, as well as a healthy foundation for Indonesia to join the ASEAN Economic Community in 2015.

This chapter, consisting of four sections, discusses regional domestic trade in particular during the regional autonomy and fiscal decentralization era. Section 2 examines regional autonomy and selected economic indicators. Following that, Section 3 discusses regional domestic trade interdependence. It includes a discussion on, and the impact of, weakening demand for export on regional output. Finally, the last section concludes the issues outlined above with closing remarks and key recommendations.

DECENTRALIZATION AND SELECTED ECONOMIC INDICATORS

Concepts and Roles of Decentralization

Conventionally, there are three types of decentralization (United Nations Development Programme 2009). The first is deconcentration or administrative decentralization. This refers to decentralization of the national government authority to subnational governments or regional branches of national ministries and agencies. In Indonesia, deconcentration has been achieved through provincial governments and branches of national ministries.

The second type of decentralization is delegation. Delegation is a decentralized arrangement in which some governmental functions are transferred to subnational governments. All subnational governments in

Indonesia are responsible for delivering certain services delegated by the national government.

The third type is devolution, also known as political decentralization. This refers to the transfer of powers or functions from the national government to subnational governments. Devolution provides subnational governments with certain key powers. This is the strongest form of decentralization and entails transferring some authority with regard to decision making, finance, and management. Devolution is the main element of Indonesia's decentralization.

Moreover, decentralization is expected to have some positive implications. The central government's role has moved from a controlled policy framework, through direct administration of the economy, to macroeconomic management (Goodman and Segal 1994). The impact of the relaxation of the central government's control should be followed by greater responsibilities of local governments in accelerating the economic welfare of local society.

In 2001, Indonesia started implementing its regional autonomy policy and fiscal decentralization. This resulted in the opening of an additional number of new autonomous regions. By 2008, the number of recorded provinces had increased to thirty-three; and the number of municipalities to 477.

From an economic perspective, Indonesia's regional autonomy and fiscal decentralization have enhanced each region's roles in managing its regional economy. This was shown in the central government's budget allocation to the regions in the form of a fiscal-balance fund. Thus, the increase in regional governments' roles in economic development is expected to be followed by an improvement in the region's economic welfare.

The decentralization policy is also purported to be one of the regional approaches for reducing the disparity in intraregional development and increasing the pace of growth in regional economies. The legal framework of decentralization in Indonesia was initially based on Regional Government Act no. 22/1999 and Fiscal Equalization Act no. 25/1999, which were further amended to Regional Government Act no. 32/2004 and Fiscal Equalization Act no. 33/2000. In Regional Government Act no. 22/1999, the fundamental theme included encouraging community empowerment, fostering initiative and creativity, and enhancing the community's role. But with the changes in the state structure and demands of regional autonomy, the law was amended and thus became Regional Government Act no. 32/2004. Differences between both laws can be seen in Table 9.1.

TABLE 9.1
Differences between Act No. 22/1999 and Act No. 32/2004

Act No. 22/1999		Act No. 32/2004	
Central Government (Article 7 paras. 1 and 2)	Forms of authority: 1. Foreign politics; 2. Defence and security; 3. Justice; 4. Monetary and fiscal; 5. Religion; 6. National planning at the macro level; 7. Fiscal balance fund; 8. National administrative system and national economic institution; 9. Development and empowerment of human resources; 10. Efficient use of national resources and strategic high technology; 11. Conservation; national standardization.	Central Government (Article 7 paras. 1 and 2)	Forms of authority: 1. Foreign politics; 2. Defence; 3. Security; 4. Justice; 5. National monetary and fiscal; 6. Religion.

Provinces	As an autonomous region:
	1. Governmental sectors across district and city, including public works, transportation, forestry, and plantation.
	2. Specific sectors:
	  a. Planning and control of regional development at the macro level;
	  b. Training on certain fields, allocation of potential human resources and research which covers provincial areas;
	  c. Managing regional port;
		Provinces (Article 13 paras. 1 and 2)	Compulsory affairs:
			1. Planning and control of development;
			2. Planning, utilization, and control of layout;
			3. Organization of public order and society reassurance;
			4. Provision of public facilities and infrastructure;
			5. Handling of the health sector;

TABLE 9.1 *(Cont'd)*

Act No. 22/1999	Act No. 32/2004
d. Environmental control; e. Promotion of trade and cultural/tourism; f. Handling of endemic diseases and plant bugs; g. Planning of provincial layout; h. Authority which is not or has not been implemented by the city or district.	6. Provision of education and allocation of potential human resources; 7. Handling of societal problems across districts/cities; 8. Services in the employment sector across districts/cities; 9. Facilitating the development of cooperatives, small and medium enterprises, across districts/cities; 10. Environmental control; 11. Land services across districts/cities; 12. Population services, and civil records; 13. General administration of government services; 14. Investment administration services across districts/cities; 15. Other basic services which cannot be implemented by the districts/cities; 16. Other mandatory matters mandated by legislation. Optional affairs: Governmental affairs which realistically exist and have the potential to improve public welfare in accordance with the condition, uniqueness, and potential of the concerned regions.

TABLE 9.1 *(Cont'd)*

Act No. 22/1999	Act No. 32/2004
Districts/Cities	Districts/Cities (Article 14 paras .1 and 2)
Includes all government authority other than those stipulated in Articles 7 and 9. Governmental areas which must include: Health; Education; Culture; Agriculture; Transportation; Industry; Trade; Investment; Environment; Land.	Compulsory affairs: 1. Planning and control of development; 2. Planning, utilization, and control of layout; 3. Organization of public order and society reassurance; 4. Provision of public facilities and infrastructure; 5. Handling of the health sector; 6. Provision of education; 7. Handling of societal problems; 8. Services in the employment sector; 9. Facilitating the development of cooperatives, small and medium enterprises; 10. Environmental control; 11. Land services; 12. Population services, and civil records; 13. General administration of government services; 14. Investment administration services; 15. Other basic services; 16. Other mandatory matters mandated by legislation. Optional affairs: Governmental affairs which realistically exist and have the potential to improve public welfare in accordance with the condition, uniqueness, and potential of the concerned regions.

Source: Lapera (2001).

In the basic logic of decentralization, as shown in Figure 9.1, decentralization is embodied in the form of regional autonomy, that is, granting the right, authority, and obligation to the region to organize and manage local government, and to ensure that community interests (public policies) are autonomous (independent). Decentralization is also interpreted as an effort to maximize the role of the government (through the local government) in services and regulations to empower local communities since local governments are considered to be closer to the people and better at knowing their needs. Therefore, the response from local governments to community needs will be quicker and more accurate, ultimately making government policy more effective, efficient, and economical.

Before getting into a discussion on domestic economic integration during the political decentralization era, this section will start by discussing a selected number of economic indicators to analyse whether decentralization has improved regional economic welfare or not. Though decentralization's main objective is to give the district (*kabupaten*) and city (*kota*) more authority, the following section uses authority from the provincial level due to the limited availability of data at the district/city level.

FIGURE 9.1
Basic Logic of Decentralization

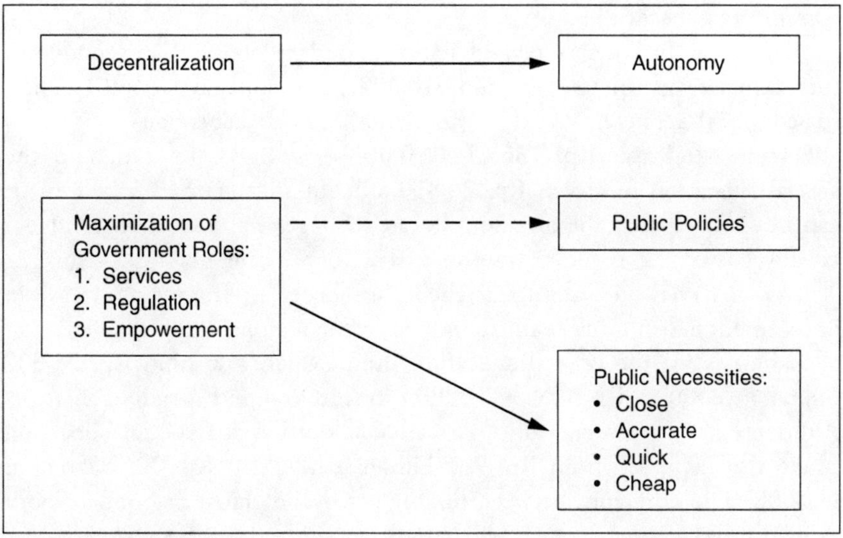

Source: Kartasasmita (2007).

Regional Budget

Regional autonomy and fiscal decentralization allow local governments to have authority in setting their own regional budgets with approval from the local legislative bodies. Their power is allocated at both the provincial and lower, district/city levels. Although the major sources of income for local governments still come from the central government's budget, in the form of *Dana Alokasi Umum* (general allocation fund) and *Dana Alokasi Khusus* (special allocation fund), the decision on the allocation itself, such as funding for local government programmes, has been delegated to the local level.

The source of general and special allocation funding mentioned above comes from the central government budget. At least 25.0 per cent of the central government's domestic revenue must be allocated to the general allocation fund. Among the regions, the allocation itself is based on each region's weighting ("role") among all the regions, and the weightings are based on regional economic necessities, which are the actual fiscal needs of the region, and their regional economic potential, which refer to the potential economic development levels that could be achieved by the regions. Unlike the general allocation fund, the amount for special allocation fund is not predetermined. The allocation at the regional level is used to finance the region's special necessities, especially the necessities that cannot be estimated using the general allocation fund calculation, and/or national priorities or commitment necessities.

Based on Indonesia's revised national budget of 2009, the budgeted total expense was Rp. 691,535,743,610,000, approximately US$69.1 billion (based on the rate of US$1 = Rp. 10.000). The allocation for general allocation fund was Rp. 186,414,100,000 (±US$18.6 billion); and the special allocation fund was Rp. 24,819,588,800,000 (±US$2.5 billion). It can be inferred that the amount allocated for general allocation fund has already passed the required threshold of 25.0 per cent.

As observed in Table 9.2, there has been an increasing trend in government expenditures being allocated to the regional budget. The largest allocation is for the general allocation fund, which rose from Rp. 28.807 billion in 2000 to Rp. 179.507 billion in 2009, almost a sixfold increase. Although not as dramatically, the actual allocation for special allocation funds also increased from Rp. 701 billion in 2001 to Rp. 20,787 billion in 2008. The difference between the budgeted and actual amount for both expenditures was relatively small compared with the difference in other types of expenditures.

TABLE 9.2
National Budget, 2000–08
(in rupiah billion)

Pengeluaran	2000	2001	2002	2003	2004	2005	2006	2007	2008
Budget									
Government Expenditures	223,907	340,705	345,605	377,248	430,041	565,070	699,099	752,370	989,494
Regional Budget Expenditures	33,894	81,055	97,808	119,314	130,004	153,402	220,850	254,201	292,423
Balance Budget	33,894	81,055	94,038	109,927	123,149	146,160	216,798	244,608	278,436
Revenue Sharing Funds	3,542	20,008	24,266	29,925	37,368	52,567	59,564	62,726	77,727
General Allocation Funds	30,352	60,346	69,114	76,978	82,131	88,766	145,664	164,787	179,507
Special Allocation Funds	–	701	658	3,024	3,650	4,828	11,570	17,094	21,202
Special Autonomy	–	–	3,770	9,387	6,855	7,243	4,052	9,593	13,987
Actual									
Government Expenditures	221,467	341,565	322,180	376,505	427,187	511,619	666,212	757,650	985,731
Regional Budget Expenditures	33,075	81,055	98,204	120,314	129,723	150,464	226,180	253,263	292,433
Balance Budget	33,075	81,055	94,656	111,070	122,868	143,221	222,131	243,967	278,715
Revenue Sharing Funds	4,268	20,008	24,884	31,369	36,700	49,692	64,900	62,942	78,420
General Allocation Funds	28,807	60,346	69,159	76,978	82,131	88,765	145,664	164,787	179,507
Special Allocation Funds	–	701	613	2,723	4,037	4,764	11,566	16,238	20,787
Special Autonomy	–	–	3,548	9,244	6,855	7,243	4,049	9,296	13,719

Source: Ministry of Finance (2010).

The fiscal balance fund is funded from the domestic revenue budget, which is allocated to all regions to finance their local needs in the context of decentralization. According to Act no. 33/2004 Article 10, the Fiscal Balance Fund consists of Revenue Sharing from property tax, transfer duty on acquisition of land and buildings, individual income tax, and natural resources revenue; the General Allocation Fund (DAU) and finally, the Special Allocation Fund (DAK). Act no. 33/2004 made changes to the flow of funds from the central government to the regions. In this Act, components of the Fiscal Balance Fund remained unchanged. The only change was in the the flow of fund's proportion.

With fiscal decentralization, each region has three rights on financial sources, which can be used to implement their local authority. The first is the right to levy taxes based on Act no. 34/2000 on Regional Taxes and Levies. The second is the right to obtain the fiscal balance fund. And the third is the right to borrow money, including from other countries, although in reality the regions still need permission from the minister for finance to borrow money from abroad. Simultaneously, each region has three obligations. The first is that regions should be able to manage their funds consistently with (not contradictory to) the central government policies. Second, regions are required to manage their funds efficiently, effectively, accountably, and transparently. And third, regions must take responsibility for and report the usage of their funds.

Figure 9.2 summarizes government revenue flows to the fiscal balance fund. Out of the total net domestic revenues, 26.0 per cent is allocated as general allocation fund to the regions. Revenue from the national budget consists of domestic tax revenue and non-tax revenues. The domestic tax revenue consists of only domestic tax. Tax on international trade does not go to domestic tax revenue, but to the national treasury.

The domestic tax, allocated to the regions, comprises of 20.0 per cent income tax, 90.0 per cent property tax, and 80.0 per cent transfer duty on acquisition of land and building. Non-tax revenues received by the regions comprise revenue from natural resources, meaning oil and gas, geothermal resources, mining, forestry, and fisheries.

Inequalities Among Regions

Decentralization is expected to reduce inequalities among regions. With the increasing role of local governments, local leaders are expected to be more aggressive in reducing the income gap between regions. In this section, regional inequality is seen by examining the role of Gross Regional

FIGURE 9.2
Structure of the National Budget

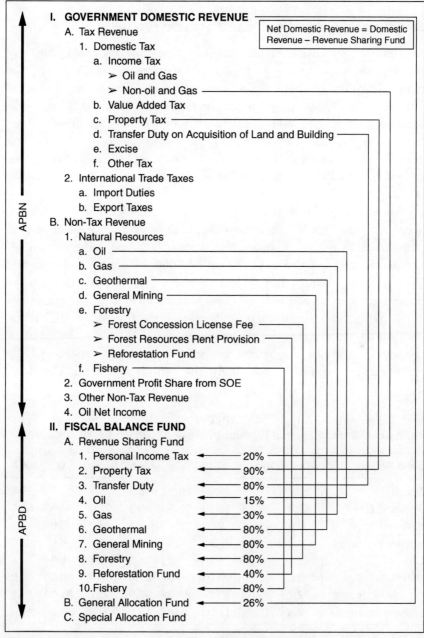

Domestic Product (GRDP) in each region, using the Williamson index in the eight-year period before and after the start of decentralization.

Structure of Gross Regional Domestic Product

As measured by GRDP in each region, there still exists a big disparity between the eastern and western regions of Indonesia. Although the economic contribution from the western regions[2] has slightly decreased after six years following the implementation of decentralization, they still continue to dominate Indonesia's economy by contributing almost 80 per cent of the national economy during the period, 2000 to 2007. On the other hand, although relatively small, the contribution from the eastern regions increased slightly to about 18.8 per cent of total economic activity in 2007 (see Table 9.3).

Moreover, as shown in Figure 9.3, three provinces in Java (Jakarta, West Java, and East Java) contribute approximately 46.0 per cent of total economic activity. This finding indicates that Java remained the centre of national economic activities in the period 2000–07. East Kalimantan and Riau are two provinces outside Java that together, primarily through the oil and gas sector, contribute 12.0 per cent to total economic activities.

Looking from the sectoral economic perspective, we find that the dominant sectors in the western regions of Indonesia are the financial and business service, "electricity, gas and water supply", trade, and the manufacturing industry. Interestingly, the contribution from "electricity,

TABLE 9.3
Share of Gross Regional Product by Region (constant price), 2000–07

Region	2000	2001	2002	2003	2004	2005	2006	2007
Sumatera	22.8	21.8	22.0	20.3	19.9	19.6	19.5	19.4
Java and Bali	59.9	60.2	60.1	60.3	60.9	61.2	61.5	61.8
Kalimantan	9.6	9.7	9.6	9.4	9.3	9.2	9.0	8.8
Sulawesi	4.2	4.2	4.3	4.3	4.3	4.4	4.5	4.5
Others	3.4	4.0	4.1	5.8	5.5	5.7	5.5	5.5
National	100.0	100.0	100.0	100.0	100.0	100.0	100.0	100.0
Western Indonesia	82.7	82.0	82.1	80.6	80.9	80.7	81.0	81.2
Eastern Indonesia	17.3	18.0	17.9	19.4	19.1	19.3	19.0	18.8

Source: Calculated from Badan Pusat Statistik (2010).

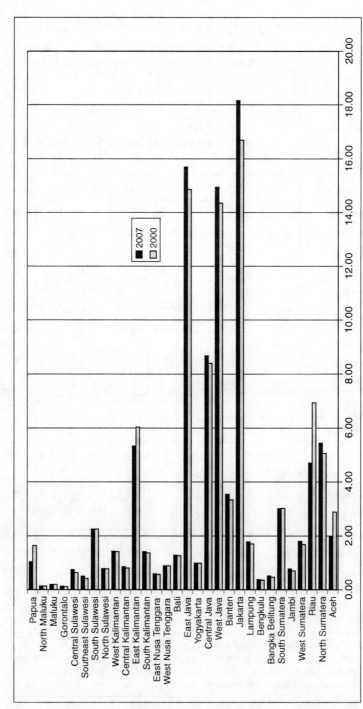

FIGURE 9.3
Share of GDRP by Province: 2000 and 2007
(in per cent)

Source: Badan Pusat Statistik (2010).

gas, and water supply" in Java and Bali increased from 2002–07.[3] At the same time, sectors that primarily contributed to the eastern regions of Indonesia are mining and quarrying as well as agriculture, livestock, forestry, and fishery (see Table 9.4).

TABLE 9.4
Share of GDRP by Economic Sectors, 2002 and 2007

2002

Region	1	2	3	4	5	6	7	8	9
Sumatera	29.9	50.8	17.1	24.7	19.2	17.3	20.4	8.6	20.2
Java and Bali	46.7	9.7	69.3	69.4	64.3	71.7	61.6	85.1	63.2
Kalimantan	8.7	24.3	11.3	2.5	7.3	5.6	8.9	3.0	5.2
Sulawesi	9.1	2.6	1.8	2.7	5.8	3.3	5.8	2.3	7.0
Others	5.5	12.6	0.5	0.8	3.5	2.0	3.3	0.9	4.4
National	100.0	100.0	100.0	100.0	100.0	100.0	100.0	100.0	100.0
Western Indonesia	76.7	60.5	86.4	94.1	83.5	89.1	82.1	93.8	83.4
Eastern Indonesia	23.3	39.5	13.6	5.9	16.5	10.9	17.9	6.2	16.6

2007

Region	1	2	3	4	5	6	7	8	9
Sumatera	31.6	47.4	16.5	10.2	20.5	16.7	20.8	10.6	20.7
Java and Bali	44.9	9.9	72.3	82.8	62.7	72.5	62.0	81.5	63.0
Kalimantan	8.7	29.0	8.7	2.9	7.3	5.5	8.3	3.6	5.4
Sulawesi	9.4	3.8	1.9	3.2	6.0	3.3	5.5	3.1	6.7
Others	5.4	9.9	0.6	0.9	3.5	2.0	3.4	1.3	4.2
National	100.0	100.0	100.0	100.0	100.0	100.0	100.0	100.0	100.0
Western Indonesia	76.5	57.3	88.8	92.9	83.2	89.2	82.8	92.1	83.7
Eastern Indonesia	23.5	42.7	11.2	7.1	16.8	10.8	17.2	7.9	16.3

Note: 1 = Agriculture, livestock, forestry, and fishery, 2 = mining and quarrying, 3 = manufacturing industry, 4 = electricity, gas and water supply, 5 = construction, 6 = trade, hotel, and restaurant, 7 = transportation and communication, 8 = financial, ownership, and business services, 9 = services

Source: Calculated from Badan Pusat Statistik (2010).

Regional Disparities: Williamson Index

Besides the GRDP share, an analysis of disparities among regions is also conducted using the Williamson Index. This is a tool used to calculate the degree of income inequality among regions. It is calculated from GDP per capita and population per region. A smaller index, the closer the index to zero, indicates a smaller gap. A larger index, further from zero, shows a widening inequality. The index can be greater than one.

Figure 9.4, using the non-oil and non-gas per capita income, shows that the disparity index among regions in total (national) has seen a significant decline from 1.05 in 2000 to 0.90 in 2007. This is mainly related to the decline in disparity among regions within Sumatera. However, if the oil and gas sector is taken into account, it will show that interregional disparities during the implementation of decentralization did not experience any decline. It even slightly increased, as indicated by the rising disparity index from 0.81 in 2000 to 0.83 in 2007. This increase could be associated with the increased disparity among the regions (provinces) in Java-Bali, which indicates that the improvement in interregional disparity is most likely associated with the reduced role of the oil and gas sector.

FIGURE 9.4
Williamson Index: Indonesia, Total, 2000–07

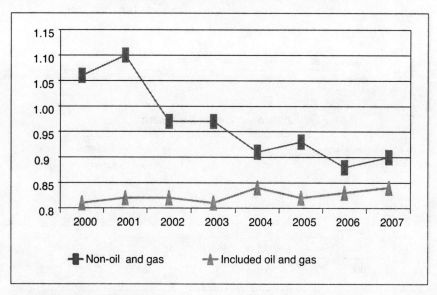

Source: Calculated by the authors.

If the disparity is calculated on the basis of the grouping of the islands, which means Sumatera, Java-Bali, Kalimantan, Sulawesi, and the Others (of the islands) as shown in Figure 9.5, then the discrepancy among the

FIGURE 9.5
Williamson Index: Indonesia, by Region, 2000–07

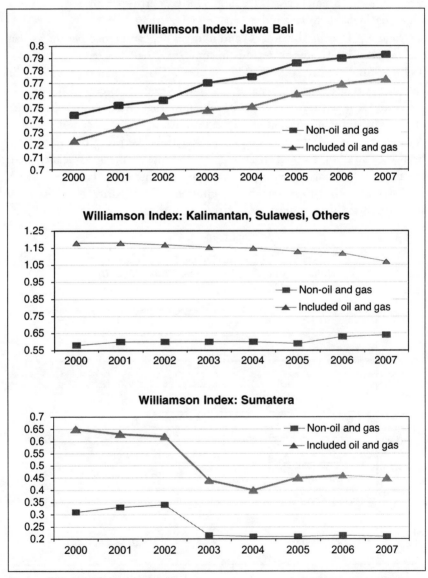

Source: Calculated by the authors.

provinces on each island would be different. In this case, the highest disparity occurred in Kalimantan, Sulawesi, and the Others, while the lowest disparity occurred in Sumatera.

The level of disparity among regions in Kalimantan, Sulawesi and the Others depends on whether the index includes the oil and gas sector or not, as the East Kalimantan province has the biggest oil and gas resources in Indonesia. With the exclusion of the oil and gas sector, the imbalance of per capita income among the regions in Kalimantan, Sulawesi, and the Others is not high, relatively speaking, and even lower than that in Java-Bali. Nevertheless, during the implementation of the decentralization policies, excluding oil and gas sector, disparities among regions within Kalimantan, Sumatera, and the Others, even excluding the oil and gas sector, did not show any decrease.

Meanwhile, taking the oil and gas sector into account, the disparities among regions in Kalimantan, Sulawesi, and the Others showed a relatively high disparity, when compared with the other islands in Indonesia. This is related to the natural resources that are primarily located in Kalimantan. But, with the decreasing role of the oil and gas sector, the growth of per capita income in areas with rich natural resources has been relatively slower. Conversely, the per capita GDP of provinces that are not rich in natural resources has risen faster, thus resulting in a declining regional disparity. With the oil and gas sector taken into account, the disparity index fell from 1.189 in 2000 to 1.064 in 2007. On the other hand, the disparity index without the oil and gas sector increased slightly. In other words, by excluding the contribution of oil and gas, the disparity among regions in Kalimantan, Sulawesi, and others has not shown a significant improvement, or even worsened during the implementation of decentralization from 2001 to 2007 (latest data).

Regionally, the interregional disparity among the provinces in Java-Bali have shown a slight increase during the decentralization era. The disparities may be associated with the relatively high per capita income in Jakarta and low per capita income in other provinces. Jakarta is the capital of Indonesia, as well as the centre of trade and services. Some provinces outside Jakarta (such as East Java, Banten, and West Java) also have a relatively high per capita income. In contrast, Yogyakarta and Central Java have relatively low per capita income compared with other provinces on the island of Java.

Although Riau and Nanggroe Aceh Darussalam (NAD) have relatively large oil and gas natural resources, Sumatera has the smallest disparity index compared with the other islands. As in Kalimantan, the declining role of oil and gas sector in the economy has caused a corresponding decline in the growth of per capita income in oil and gas rich regions. Simultaneously, provinces that do not depend on oil and gas natural resources have sustained rapid progress. Hence, the disparity among regions in Sumatera has significantly decreased in both oil and gas producing regions and non-oil and gas producing regions.

Generally, it can be inferred that during the implementation of decentralization policies, interregional disparities, in terms of per capita income, did not experience a significant decrease. However, based on the grouping of islands, the disparity among regions in Sumatera has decreased significantly. Sumatera is also the island with the lowest interregional disparity.

Classification (Types) of Regions

Two approaches of classification

Decentralization is expected to enhance regional economic development, meaning that regional leaders are expected to better understand the needs of their communities in the development process. Therefore, to observe whether decentralization can improve the regions' "status", we need to compare their status before decentralization (1993–96) and after decentralization (2004–07).

The latest data used are from 2007 due to the lack of other data at the time of writing. The data from 1993 to 1996 are used to represent the period before decentralization as the severe economic crisis period from 1997–98 caused a very large contraction in economic growth. Average values are calculated to evaluate the status of each region relative to other regions. Using the average value as the boundary means that there will always be a case in which some regions are below average (less advanced), which could be a reflection of the underdevelopment of certain regions compared with other regions.

There are several approaches in determining the classification of areas (areas typology). The simplest approach is to utilize the level of welfare and development capacity of the regions. The level of welfare is measured using per capita income and the development capacity is indicated by economic growth.

Hence, regions are classified into four groups. First we have the stagnant and not growing low per capita income group, which consists of regions with below average income per capita and below average economic growth. The second is the stagnant and not growing high per capita income, consisting of regions with above average income per capita, but below average economic growth. Third is the growing low per capita income, consisting of regions with below average income per capita, but above average economic growth. And the fourth classification is for the growing high per capita income consisting of regions with above average income per capita and above average economic growth.

The classification of areas can also be determined using the level of human development. This follows the argument that although economic growth is important, the ultimate goal of economic development is not solely growth itself, but improving the quality of human resources. Therefore, the classification of the regions is made with respect to the combination of income per capita and the human development index (HDI), rather than economic growth.

In line with this, the United Nations Support Facility for Indonesian Recovery (2000) stated the importance of improving human development and democracy in economic development. It discussed three models of development, shown in Figure 9.6, which represents the relationship between human development (education and health), economic growth, and democracy. The first is "Cruel Choice plus Trickle Down". Here, economic growth is the driving engine and prerequisite for both democracy and human development. The second model is "Virtuous Triangle". In contrast to the first model, this model presents human development (education and health) as the main driver for high economic growth and democracy, while showing that economic growth and democracy reinforce one another. The third model is "Endogenous Growth and Democracy". Like in the second model, human development is the main driver of economic growth. However, it only affects democracy indirectly through its effect on economic growth.

Therefore, regions can also be classified by inserting human development as the decisive variable in classifying regions (Kuncoro 2004). Using HDI and average per capita income (excluding the oil and gas sector) for classifying regional typology can produce four regional groups: above average regional per capita income with above average human development; above average regional per capita income with below average human development; below average regional per capita income and low level of human development; and below average regional per capita income with above average human development.

Figure 9.7 shows the area typology of provinces according to the two approaches. Using the first approach (per capita income and economic

FIGURE 9.6
Relationship among Human Development, Economic Growth, and Democracy

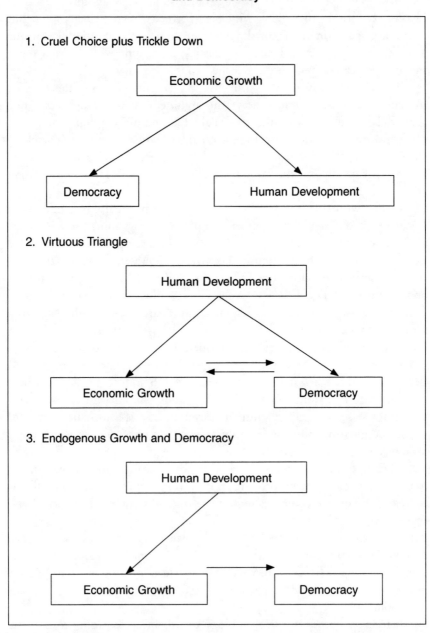

Source: UNSFIRS (2000).

FIGURE 9.7
(a + b) Regional Typology

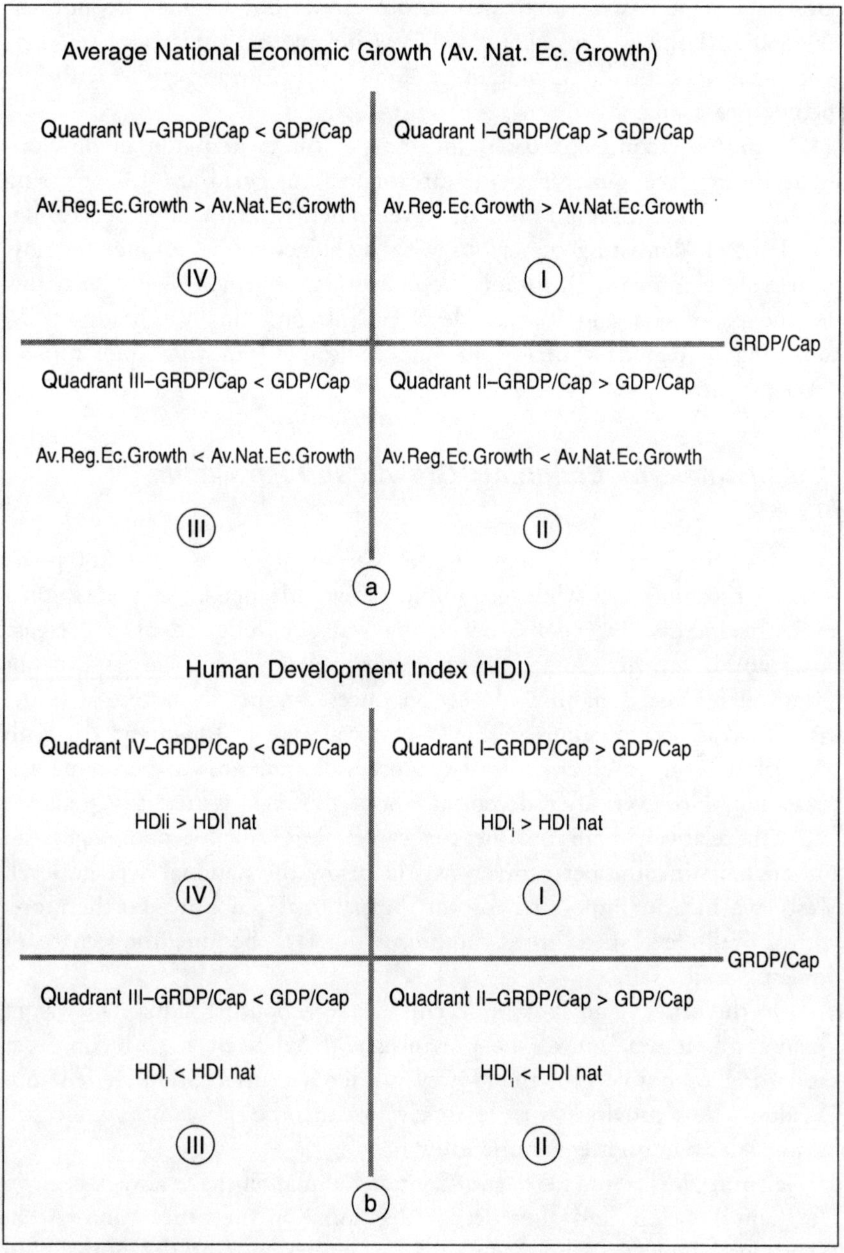

Average National Economic Growth (Av. Nat. Ec. Growth)

Quadrant IV–GRDP/Cap < GDP/Cap	Quadrant I–GRDP/Cap > GDP/Cap
Av.Reg.Ec.Growth > Av.Nat.Ec.Growth	Av.Reg.Ec.Growth > Av.Nat.Ec.Growth
(IV)	(I)
	GRDP/Cap
Quadrant III–GRDP/Cap < GDP/Cap	Quadrant II–GRDP/Cap > GDP/Cap
Av.Reg.Ec.Growth < Av.Nat.Ec.Growth	Av.Reg.Ec.Growth < Av.Nat.Ec.Growth
(III)	(II)

(a)

Human Development Index (HDI)

Quadrant IV–GRDP/Cap < GDP/Cap	Quadrant I–GRDP/Cap > GDP/Cap
HDIi > HDI nat	HDI_i > HDI nat
(IV)	(I)
	GRDP/Cap
Quadrant III–GRDP/Cap < GDP/Cap	Quadrant II–GRDP/Cap > GDP/Cap
HDI_i < HDI nat	HDI_i < HDI nat
(III)	(II)

(b)

Source: Prepared by the authors.

growth), there are four quadrants to represent each category. Quadrant I covers the growing regions with high income per capita. Quadrant II covers the regions with high income per capita, but stagnant economies. Quadrant III shows the regions with low income per capita and stagnant economies. And finally, Quadrant IV shows the growing regions with low income per capita.

With the second approach (income per capita and human development index), the quadrants are categorized as: Quadrant I, consisting of the regions with high human development and income per capita; Quadrant II, consisting of regions with high income per capita, but low human development; Quadrant III, consisting of regions with both low income per capita and human development; and finally, Quadrant IV, consisting of regions with low income per capita, but with high human development.

Classification by Economic Growth and Per Capita Income

As shown in Table 9.5, between the periods 1993–96 and 2004–07, GDP per capita rose while economic growth declined. At the regional level, the increase in income per capita was also followed by a decrease in economic growth. Some provinces grew quickly while others did not grow much. The dynamics of the provinces can be illustrated with the case of West Java. Regions within West Java were in Quadrant III, with relatively low income per capita and slow economic growth before decentralization. However, after decentralization, the regions rose to Quadrant IV, with relatively high income per capita, but slow economic growth. Although its income per capita was still below the national average level, West Java had an important role in the national economy. Furthermore, with a well developed infrastructure, West Java became the centre of domestic trade.

On the other hand, before decentralization, South Kalimantan was in Quadrant I. It was one of the provinces with relatively high income per capita and economic growth. However, after decentralization, it fell into Quadrant II, a province with relatively low income per capita, while still having relatively high economic growth..

Jakarta, North Sumatera, and Central Kalimantan have always been in Quadrant I, before and after decentralization. On the other hand, Aceh, West Nusa Tenggara, and Maluku have always been at the bottom, in Quadrant III.

TABLE 9.5
Classification of Regions based on Income Per Capita
and Economic Growth: 1993–96 and 2004–07

Years 1993–96

		Income per capita	
		Low (<Rp. 1,763,060)	High (>Rp. 1,763,060)
GDP Growth (2000 constant)	High (>6.35)	West Sumatera, South Sumatera, Lampung, Central Java, Yogyakarta, East Jawa, West Kalimantan, North Sulawesi Utara, South Sulawesi, East Nusatenggara (Quadrant IV)	North Sumatera, Jakarta, Bali, Central Kalimantan, South Kalimantan, Papua (Quadrant I)
	Low (<6.35)	Aceh, Jambi, Bengkulu, West Java, Central Sulawesi Tengah, Southeast Sulawesi, Maluku, West Nusa Tenggara (Quadrant III)	Riau, East Kalimantan (Quadrant II)

Years 2004–07

		Income per capita	
		Low (<Rp. 7,367,761)	High (>Rp. 7,367,761)
GDP Growth (2000 constant price)	High (>5.69)	West Sumatera, Riau, Jambi, South Sumatera, West Jawa, East Jawa, East Kalimantan, Central Sulawesi, Southeast Sulawesi (Quadrant IV)	North Sumatera, Bengkulu, Jakarta, Central Kalimantan (Quadrant I)
	Low (<5.69)	NAD, Lampung, Central Jawa, Yogyakarta, Bali, West Nusa Tenggara, East Nusa Tenggara, South Sulawesi, Maluku (Quadrant III)	West Kalimantan, South Kalimantan, North Sulawesi, Papua* (Quadrant II)

Note: * The average GDP per capita of Papua was slightly below the national average in 2004, but its GDP per capita in 2007 was slightly above the national average. Thus although the average was below the national average it is mainly due to the fact that its GDP in previous years was relatively low. It can therefore be classified in Quadrant 2.

Source: Prepared by the authors.

Classification by Economic Growth and Human Development

In general, as indicated by the thresholds of the human development index (HDI) in Table 9.6, there was an increase in the human development index

TABLE 9.6
Classification of Regions based on Income Per Capita and HDI:
1999 and 2005

Year 1999

		Income per capita	
		Low (<Rp. 1,914,490)	High (>Rp. 1,914,490)
HDI (national, 1999)	High (>64.4)	Aceh, West Sumatera, Jambi, Bengkulu, West Java, Central Java, Yogyakarta, North Sulawesi, Maluku (Quadrant IV)	North Sumatera, Riau, DKI Jakarta, Bali, Kalimantan Tengah, East Kalimantan (Quadrant I)
	Low (<64.4)	South Sumatera, Lampung, East Java, West Nusa Tenggara, East Nusa Tenggara, South Sulawesi, Southeast Sulawesi, Papua (Quadrant III)	West Kalimantan, South Kalimantan (Quadrant II)

Year 2005

		Income per capita	
		Low (<Rp. 6,588,970)	High (>Rp. 6,588,970)
HDI (national, 2005)	High (>69.28)	North Sumatera, West Sumatera, Jambi, South Sumatera, Bangka Belitung, West Java, Central Java, Yogyakarta, Bali, Central Kalimantan (Quadrant IV)	Riau, DKI Jakarta, East Kalimantan (Quadrant I)
	Low (<69.28)	Aceh, Lampung, East Java, West Nusa Tenggara, East Nusa Tenggara, South Kalimantan, West Kalimantan, South Sulawesi, Southeast Sulawesi, Central Sulawesi, Gorontalo, Maluku, North Maluku (Quadrant III)	Papua (Quadrant II)

Source: Prepared by the authors.

after decentralization. The figure also shows that provinces with relatively higher income per capita are not necessarily those with a higher human development index. Before decentralization, West Kalimantan and South Kalimantan were in Quadrant II, with high economic growth, but low human development. However, after decentralization, they fell to the bottom, Quadrant III, with relatively low income per capita and human development. On the other hand, Lampung, East Java, West Nusa Tenggara, East Nusa Tenggara, South Sulawesi, Southeast Sulawesi, and Central Sulawesi have always been in Quadrant III.

After decentralization, Papua was the only province with relatively high income per capita and low human development. Moreover, Riau, Jakarta, and East Kalimantan were always at the top in Quadrant I, with high income per capita and high human development.

Table 9.7 shows that high economic growth is not necessarily accompanied by high human development. Provinces in Quadrant II are those with relatively high economic growth, but relatively low human development. The provinces that show both high economic growth and human development can be seen in Quadrant I. These are the four provinces in Sumatera (West Sumatera, Jambi, South Sumatera, and Bengkulu), three provinces in Java (Jakarta, West Java, and Central Java), and two provinces in Kalimantan (East Kalimantan and Central Kalimantan).

TABLE 9.7
Classification of Regions based on 2001–05 GDP Growth and 2005 HDI

		GDP Growth	
		Low (<3.14)	High (>3.14)
Human Development Index (2005	High (>69.29)	Riau, Bangka Belitung, D.I. Yogyakarta, Bali, Maluku (Quadrant IV)	West Sumatera, Jambi, South Sumatera, Bengkulu, DKI Jakarta, West Java, Central Java, East Kalimantan, Central Kalimantan (Quadrant I)
	Low (<69.29)	Aceh, Banten, East Nusa Tenggara, South Kalimantan, North Maluku, Papua (Quadrant III)	North Sumatera, Lampung, East Java, West Nusa Tenggara, West Kalimantan, South Sulawesi, Southeast Sulawesi, Cental Sulawesi, Gorontalo (Quadrant II)

Source: Calculated by the authors.

DOMESTIC REGIONAL ECONOMIC INTERDEPENDENCE

Regional Trade Interdependence

The regional trade interdependence analysis in this section uses data on interregional input-output (IRIO) 2005, which describes the relationship among sectors and regions in the economy. A region cannot run its economy without the support of other regions. Other than its limited input resources (natural resources, human resources, and finance/capital), a region is also dependent on other regions as it uses them to market its regional products.

IRIO data show how big the relationship between one region (in this case the province) is with another. In other words, a region can be identified according to whether it has a strong relationship with other regions through intersectoral transactions in the economy. An IRIO report is compiled every five years, on the assumption that new economic structure changes only once in five years. The analysis in this section uses IRIO 2005, the latest available data.

Due to limited resources faced by each region, it is expected that a region's economic conditions will correlate highly with its neighbours. Nonetheless, using IRIO 2000 and IRIO 2005, Bank Indonesia and University of Indonesia (2007) showed that the economic interconnection among regions had changed during 2000–05. A region's economic performance was not highly correlated with that of its neighbours.

Table 9.8 shows a summary of IRIO 2000 in which almost all provinces had a close trade[4] relationship with their adjacent provinces, as well as provinces in Java (mostly East Java and Jakarta). The province of East Java is the centre of the interprovince network in Indonesia, followed by DKI Jakarta, East Kalimantan, and South Sulawesi. Nevertheless, the regional trade interconnection in these provinces has changed.

Based on the IRIO 2005, a large number of provinces in Indonesia have a close relationship with West Java and Jakarta. Table 9.9 shows that in 2005 all provinces (except Aceh) had the strongest trade relationships with either West Java or Jakarta. This is different from year 2000, shown in Table 9.8, when there were nine provinces outside Java which had close trade relationships with other provinces. The change in number indicates a strengthening of relationship between most of the provinces in Indonesia with Jakarta, and especially, West Java.

Furthermore, the centre of regional trade[5] interconnection has also changed because the centre of trade relations between provinces has moved

TABLE 9.8
Trade Relations between Provinces for 2000 based on IRIO 2000

		IRIO 2000		
No.	Province	I	II	III
1	Aceh	**North Sumatera**	East Java	**Riau**
2	North Sumatera	Jakarta	**Aceh**	East Java
3	West Sumatera	Riau	**South Sumatera**	East Java
4	Riau	**South Sumatera**	Jakarta	East Java
5	Jambi	**South Sumatera**	Jakarta	**Riau**
6	South Sumatera	**Riau**	East Java	Jakarta
7	Bangka Belitung	Jakarta	**South Sumatera**	East Java
8	Bengkulu	**South Sumatera**	Lampung	Jakarta
9	Lampung	Jakarta	East Java	Central Java
10	Jakarta	West Java	Banten	East Java
11	West Java	Jakarta	Central Java	East Java
12	Banten	Jakarta	West Java	East Java
13	Central Java	East Java	West Java	Jakarta
14	Yogyakarta	Central Java	East Java	West Java
15	East Java	Central Java	Jakarta	West Java
16	West Kalimantan	East Java	**East Kalimantan**	Jakarta
17	Central Kalimantan	**East Kalimantan**	East Java	Central Java
18	South Kalimantan	**East Kalimantan**	East Java	Central Java
19	East Kalimantan	Jakarta	East Java	Central Java
20	North Sulawesi	East Java	East Kalimantan	**South Sulawesi**
21	Gorontalo	East Kalimantan	East Java	**South Sulawesi**
22	Central Sulawesi	East Java	East Kalimantan	**South Sulawesi**
23	South Sulawesi	East Java	East Kalimantan	Jakarta
24	Southeast Sulawesi	**South Sulawesi**	East Java	East Kalimantan
25	Bali	East Java	Central Java	Jakarta
26	West Nusa Tenggara	East Java	Central Java	Jakarta
27	East Nusa Tenggara	East Java	West Java	Central Java
28	Maluku	South Sulawesi	Papua	East Java
29	North Maluku	South Sulawesi	East Java	Papua
30	Papua	Jakarta	East Java	East Kalimantan

Note: Column I indicates the strongest relationship, column II indicates the second strongest, and column III the third strongest.

Source: Bank Indonesia and University of Indonesia (2007).

TABLE 9.9
Trade Relations between Provinces for 2005 based on IRIO 2005

		IRIO 2000		
No.	Province	I	II	III
1	Aceh	Riau	Jakarta	West Java
2	North Sumatera	**West Java**	Jakarta	Central Java
3	West Sumatera	Jakarta	West Java	Riau
4	Riau	**West Java**	Central Java	Jakarta
5	Jambi	**West Java**	Jakarta	Banten
6	South Sumatera	**West Java**	Jakarta	East Java
7	Bangka Belitung	**West Java**	Jakarta	East Java
8	Bengkulu	**West Java**	Jakarta	North Sumatera
9	Lampung	**West Java**	Jakarta	East Java
10	Jakarta	East Java	West Java	North Sumatera
11	West Java	East Java	Jakarta	Central Java
12	Banten	**West Java**	Jakarta	East Java
13	Central Java	**West Java**	Jakarta	North Sumatera
14	Yogyakarta	**West Java**	East Java	Jakarta
15	East Java	**West Java**	Jakarta	North Sumatera
16	West Kalimantan	**West Java**	East Java	Jakarta
17	Central Kalimantan	**West Java**	Central Java	Jakarta
18	South Kalimantan	Jakarta	Central Java	West Java
19	East Kalimantan	Jakarta	West Java	East Java
20	North Sulawesi	**West Java**	Jakarta	West Java
21	Gorontalo	**West Java**	East Java	Jakarta
22	Central Sulawesi	Jakarta	West Java	Central Java
23	South Sulawesi	Jakarta	Central Java	West Java
24	Southeast Sulawesi	Jakarta	East Java	West Java
25	Bali	Jakarta	West Java	Central Java
26	West Nusa Tenggara	**West Java**	Jakarta	Central Java
27	East Nusa Tenggarar	East Java	Central Java	Jakarta
28	Maluku	Jakarta	East Java	West Java
29	North Maluku	Jakarta	West Java	South Sulawesi
30	Papua	**West Java**	Jakarta	Banten

Note: Column I indicates the strongest relationship, column II indicates the second strongest, and column III the third strongest.

Source: Bank Indonesia and University of Indonesia (2007).

from East Java to West Java. Almost all the provinces in Indonesia, except East Nusa Tenggara province, had close relations with West Java in 2005. In other words, it can be concluded that West Java has become the centre of domestic trade.

In relation to the development of the interconnection among provinces (via trade), there has been a general indication that there was a strengthening of connection among provinces in Java from 2000 to 2005 (as shown in the increasing number of provinces outside Java which have strong relationships with provinces in Java). Nevertheless, this should not be seen as significant as it only occurs relative to their relationships with other provinces. Meanwhile, in absolute terms (viewed from the nominal value of trading), trade among provinces themselves is still increasing and the market mechanism seems to have functioned well. People sell to a region where the price is higher and buy from a region where the price is lower. Thus, people from outside Java may find that they get higher prices when they sell their commodities in Java, and obtain lower prices when they buy commodities in Java.

Table 9.10 illustrates the inputs for each province from their three biggest supplying provinces (excluding the province itself), with West Java province being the most dominant. This indicates that apart from the region itself, West Java has a very significant role as an input provider to almost all provinces in Indonesia. The cells in bold show that West Java has become an input supplier for nineteen of the thirty provinces. In order to meet their input requirements, apart from West Java, most of the provinces also depend on DKI Jakarta and East Java. The three largest inputs needed by most provinces are indicated by their sector number shown in parentheses in Table 9.10 (see Appendix for a list of sectors and their numbers).

One example is NAD (Nanggroe Aceh Darussalam). To produce output in its province, NAD needs input from other provinces, particularly from West Java, Jakarta and East Java. Sector 26 (construction), sector 27 (trade), and sector 29 (land transportation) are the three largest inputs supplied by West Java to NAD. However, not all NAD's inputs are supplied by West Java. Some of the inputs for sectors 29 and 27 come from DKI Jakarta, while some of sector 26 inputs come from East Java.

Another example is DKI Jakarta. DKI Jakarta, in addition to supplying itself with inputs, needs input from West Java, East Java and Central Java. The three largest of its inputs supplied by West Java are sectors 26, 13 (textile and textile products), and 24 (other industries). Although almost all provinces in Indonesia are associated with West Java to meet their needs, it does not mean that West Java is able to supply all of its own

TABLE 9.10
Purchase of Inputs from the Three Biggest External Provinces

		I	II	III
1.	Aceh	West Java (26,31,27)	Jakarta (29,31,27)	East Java (10,12,26)
2.	North Sumatera	West Java (26,27,24)	Jakarta (27,31,29)	Central Java (29,31,27)
3.	West Sumatera	West Java (12,29,13)	Jakarta (31,35,30)	East Java (12,21,19)
4.	Riau	West Java (22,12,11)	Central Java (29,12,26)	Jakarta (27,16,22)
5.	Jambi	West Java (29,27,30)	Jakarta (29,30,31)	Banten (3,15,24)
6.	South Sumatera	West Java (26,17,35)	Jakarta (27,29,10)	East Java (10,4,12)
7.	Bangka Belitung	West Java (26,31,35)	East Java (26,27,28)	Jakarta (20,27,35)
8.	Bengkulu	Jakarta (30,29,27)	West Java (30,3,26)	Banten (12,1,35)
9.	Lampung	West Java (29,26,35)	East Java (4,12,26)	Banten (26,35,24)
10.	Jakarta	West Java (26,13,24)	East Java (26,28,35)	Central Java (28,25,26)
11.	West Java	Banten (21,22,18)	East Java (12,28,21)	Central Java (29,25,12)
12.	Banten	Jakarta (31,27,29)	West Java (31,27,29)	Riau (25,28,30)
13.	Central Java	West Java (26,35,11)	East Java (26,9,21)	Jakarta (35,29,27)
14.	Yogyakarta	West Java (26,24,35)	Jakarta (29,35,31)	East Java (26,12,28)
15.	East Java	West Java (12,27,26)	Jakarta (27,26,24)	North Sumatera (27,10,26)
16.	West Kalimantan	West Java (27,30,3)	Jakarta (30,27,35)	Banten (26,3,24)
17.	Central Kalimantan	Central Java (30,29,12)	West Java (26,30,35)	Jakarta (30,35,29)
18.	South Kalimantan	Central Java (27,30,31)	Jakarta (26,30,12)	West Java (30,29,31)
19.	East Kalimantan	Jakarta (30,31,27)	East Java (12,26,18)	West Java (7,31,8)
20.	North Sulawesi	West Java (26,35,27)	East Java (26,12,28)	Jakarta (30,29,31)
21.	Gorontalo	West Java (29,26,27)	East Java (26,27,35)	Jakarta (29,35,31)
22.	Central Sulawesi	West Java (29,35,30)	Central Java (29,8,31)	Jakarta (29,35,30)
23.	South Sulawesi	Central Java (31,29,26)	West Java (3,26,27)	Jakarta (31,29,27)
24.	Southeast Sulawesi	West Java (26,3,6)	Jakarta (29,30,6)	Central Java (26,35,31)
25.	Bali	Jakarta (31,35,27)	West Java (25,13,31)	Central Java (31,28,35)
26.	West Nusa Tenggara	South Sumatera (8,29,27)	Central Java (29,8,31)	West Java (8,29,12)
27.	East Nusa Tenggara	Central Java (29,27,30)	East Java (12,26,4)	West Java (26,29,27)
28.	Maluku	East Java (26,15,31)	West Java (27,31,30)	Jakarta (31,30,29)
29.	North Maluku	West Java (27,3,31)	Jakarta (30,31,27)	East Java (26,27,12)
30.	Papua	West Java (8,31,27)	East Java (26,8,12)	Jakarta (8,27,31)

Note: Details of economic sectors are referred to in the Appendix of the chapter.

Source: Calculated from IRIO (2005).

needed inputs. Banten, East Java and Central Java are three provinces (not including the province of West Java itself) providing the largest inputs to West Java.

On the other hand, outputs produced in each province are not only used for the region itself, but are also sold to other regions as well. Table 9.11 shows that in addition to providing outputs to meet the needs of their own provinces, most of the provinces in Indonesia also sell their output to DKI Jakarta. This can be seen from the cells in bold, which show that eighteen of the thirty provinces are selling their generated outputs to DKI Jakarta. In other words, most of the provinces have trade relations with DKI Jakarta, which is the main market area outside their own province. Furthermore, in addition to DKI Jakarta, the other main markets include East Java and West Java. The largest outputs which are sold to most provinces are shown in parentheses in Table 9.11.

As an example, outputs generated by the NAD are not only used to fulfil NAD's needs, but also other provinces' needs as well. The three provinces that use the largest number of output from NAD are Riau, Jakarta, and Banten. Furthermore, the three largest outputs from NAD that were sold to Riau were from sectors 27 (trade), 4 (livestock), and 2 (other food crops).

Another example is the outputs generated by Yogyakarta, which are not only used domestically, but are also used by East Java, DKI Jakarta, and Banten. The three largest outputs from DI Yogyakarta sold to East Java were from sectors 13 (textile and textile products), 35 (other services), and 2 (other food crops).

The existence of interregional trade is likely to affect the relationship in regional price levels. In other words, it may create the possibility of correlations between the inflation rate in one region and inflation rates in other regions. If there is a strong and significant correlation, it will have implications for inflation control policies, especially regional inflation. Although the possibility is open for interregional correlation of inflation because of the interregional trade linkages, "the law of one price" may not come into existence due to the difference in transportation costs and regional economic policies. For example, because the cost of transportation from Bandung (West Java) to Palembang (South Sumatera) is not the same as that from Bandung to Banjarmasin (South Kalimantan), the prices of the products from Bandung sold in Palembang are also different from those sold in Banjarmasin. Furthermore, decentralization has opened up room for the local leadership to conduct regional economic policies, resulting in differences between those in Palembang and those in Banjarmasin.

TABLE 9.11
Sale of Outputs to the Three Biggest External Provinces

No.	Province	I	II	III
1.	Aceh	Riau (27,4,2)	Jakarta (3,4,8)	Banten (7,8,29)
2.	North Sumatera	**Jakarta (17,10,19)**	East Java (10,17,28)	West Java (10,20,8)
3.	West Sumatera	**Jakarta (19,13,12)**	West Java (12,8,10)	Riau (6,19,13)
4.	Riau	**Jakarta (3,11,12)**	West Java (3,5,7)	Banten (7,11,10)
5.	Jambi	**Jakarta (15,10,27)**	Banten (7,10,29)	East Java (10,15,29)
6.	South Sumatera	**Jakarta (17,9,10)**	West Java (9,10,7)	Banten (7,10,9)
7.	Bangka Belitung	**Jakarta (3,10,5)**	West Java (3,10,20)	East Java (10,3,6)
8.	Bengkulu	North Sumatera (3,6,2)	West Java (5,12,10)	Jakarta (12,10,2)
9.	Lampung	**Jakarta (3,4,15)**	Riau (4,3,11)	East Java (3,7,11)
10.	Jakarta	East Java (33,23,35)	Banten (23,35,33)	North Sumatera (33,23,28)
11.	West Java	East Java (22,13,17)	Jakarta (13,17,19)	North Sumatera (21,22,13)
12.	Banten	West Java (18,20,12)	Jakarta (20,13,17)	East Java (13,20,17)
13.	Central Java	West Java (9,12,3)	Jakarta (9,12,13)	Riau (9,2,27)
14.	Yogyakarta	West Java (13,35,2)	Jakarta (13,15,35)	Banten (27,35,29)
15.	East Java	**Jakarta (12,19,8)**	West Java (12,20,1)	Central Java (20,1,19)
16.	West Kalimantant	East Java (15,11,6)	West Java (10,5,15)	Central Java (10,15,27)
17.	Central Kalimantan	West Java (3,5,12)	Jakarta (15,5,10)	East Java (4,10,3)
18.	South Kalimantan	**Jakarta (15,17,13)**	West Java (12,3,5)	East Java (17,10,15)
19.	East Kalimantan	**Jakarta (5,9,16)**	West Java (10,5,15)	South Kalimantan (9,18,16)
20.	North Sulawesi	**Jakarta (15,8,10)**	East Java (10,15,6)	West Java (8,30,29)
21.	Gorontalo	**Jakarta (3,4,10)**	East Java (10,3,35)	South Sulawesi (10,4,3)
22.	Central Sulawesi	**Jakarta (3,12,15)**	East Java (15,3,5)	North Sulawesi (5,12,27)
23.	South Sulawesi	**Jakarta (19,3,6)**	Central Java (19,11,27)	East Java (6,2,3)
24.	Southeast Sulawesi	**Jakarta (3,6,11)**	East Java (6,12,8)	East Kalimantan (12,29,27)
25.	Bali	**Jakarta (31,13,15)**	East Java (13,35,2)	North Sumatera (28,2,33)
26.	West Nusa Tenggara	West Java (8,12,2)	Jakarta (8,12,4)	Banten (8,27,2)
27.	East Nusa Tenggara	East Java (4,2,6)	Jakarta (2,31,27)	Riau (27,29,30)
28.	Maluku	**Jakarta (15,11,31)**	Banten (27,7)	East Java (15,30,3)
29.	North Maluku	**Jakarta (3,6,27)**	West Nusa Tenggara (5,27)	East Java (3,27,29)
30.	Papua	West Java (8,27,11)	Jakarta (8,27,11)	Banten (8,27,6)

Notes: Column I refers to the strongest relationship; column II indicates the second strongest; and column III the third. Numbers within parentheses refer to various sectors.

Source: Calculated from IRIO (2005).

Meanwhile, due to the existence of trade relations among regions, the economic growth of various regions will also likely affect other areas. The results of GRDP (Gross Regional Domestic Product) growth cross-correlation indicate that there is a medium-level correlation between the economic growth of provinces,[6] indicated by the correlation coefficients, which are between 0.50–0.74. The complete results of GRDP growth cross-correlation are summarized in Table 9.12.

The table also indicates that the growth of GDRP in most provinces has had a positive correlation with the growth in other provinces. For example, West Java, the centre of domestic trade, has a positive correlation with ten other provinces. Nevertheless, several provinces do show a weak correlation with other provinces, with correlation coefficients of less than 0.5. This does not necessarily mean that the provinces do not have any relationship with other provinces. Rather, although a relationship may exist, it may not be significant.

From the above explanation, it appears that there are trade relations among regions. In addition, there is also a correlation among GDP growths

TABLE 9.12
Cross-Region Correlation Coefficient Matrices

No.	Province	Correlation Coefficient > 0.5
1	Aceh	–
2	North Sumatera	–
3	West Sumatera	Riau, Bengkulu, Banten, Gorontalo, Maluku, North Maluku, Papua
4	Riau	West Sumatera, South Sumatera, Jakarta, West Java, Banten, North Sulawesi, Gorontalo, Maluku, North Maluku
5	Jambi	Papua
6	South Sumatera	Riau, Jakarta, West Java, East Java, Banten, South Kalimantan, North Sulawesi, West Sulawesi, Maluku, North Maluku
7	Bangka Belitung	West Sumatera, Banten, Gorontalo.
8	Bengkulu	–
9	Lampung	–
10	Riau Archipelago	–
11	Jakarta	Riau, South Sumatera, West Java, Banten, North Sulawesi, West Sulawesi, North Maluku

TABLE 9.12   *(Cont'd)*

No.	Province	Correlation Coefficient>0.5
12	West Java	North Sumatera, Riau, South Sumatera, Jakarta, East Java, Banten, South Kalimantan, North Sulawesi, West Sulawesi, North Maluku
13	Central Java	East Java, Central Sulawesi, South Sulawesi, Maluku
14	Yogyakarta	South Sulawesi
15	East Java	South Sumatera, West Java, Central Java, South Sulawesi
16	Banten	North Sumatera, West Sumatera, Riau, South Sumatera, Bengkulu, Jakarta, West Java, Gorontalo, North Maluku, Papua
17	Bali	North Sumatera, Papua
18	West Nusa Tenggara	–
19	East Nusa Tenggara	North Sumatera
20	West Kalimantan	–
21	Central Kalimantan	South Sulawesi
22	South Kalimantan	North Sumatera, South Sumatera, West Java, North Maluku
23	East Kalimantan	–
24	North Sulawesi	Riau, South Sumatera, Jakarta, West Java, Gorontalo, West Sulawesi, North Maluku
25	Central Sulawesi	Central Java, East Java, Maluku
26	South Sulawesi	Central Java, Yogyakarta, Central Kalimantan
27	Southeast Sulawesi	–
28	Gorontalo	West Sumatera, Riau, Bengkulu, Banten, North Sulawesi, North Maluku
29	West Sulawesi	South Sumatera, Jakarta, West Java, North Sulawesi, North Maluku
30	Maluku	West Sumatera, Riau, South Sumatera, Riau Archipelago, Central Java, East Java, Central Sulawesi, North Maluku
31	North Maluku	South Sumatera, West Sumatera, Riau, South Sumatera , Jakarta, West Java, East Java, Banten, South Kalimantan, North Sulawesi, Gorontalo, West Sulawesi, Maluku
32	West Papua	West Sumatera, Banten, North Maluku
33	Papua	Jambi, Bali

Source: Calculated by the authors.

in some areas (see Table 9.13). As a result, this provides the opportunity to increase the level of domestic economic integration. The existence of regional economic interdependency should be linked to the efforts to improve the economic competitiveness[7] of each region, which will in turn improve the economic competitiveness of Indonesia. Competitiveness associated with economic relations among regions may be raised by identifying areas of economic sectors which have good competitiveness at the national and global levels. Meanwhile economic relations through interregional trade have implications for regional economic conditions such that if there is a sudden and large change in an area that has close trade relations with other regions, then the other regions will also be affected.

Simulated Impact of Declining Exports

IRIO 2005 is used to simulate the impact of the recent global recession on the provincial economic performance through the interregional linkages. The simulation shows how changes in output in one region affect output in other regions. The use of IRIO 2005 assumes that the economic structure remained unchanged from 2005 until the occurrence of the global recession. Therefore, the results presented here show what would have happened in the region during the declining export period (because of the global recession), if the pattern of interregional linkages in Indonesia during the global crisis was the same as that in 2005.

To calculate the impact of weakening demand for export on regional output, we make several additional assumptions. The first is that the decline in exports only occurred in the selected five provinces: Jakarta, Banten, South Sulawesi, East Kalimantan, and North Sumatera. Second, exports in each province are assumed to decline by 10.0 per cent in the following sectors: textile and textile products in DKI Jakarta; footwear in Banten; plantation in South Sulawesi; wood, rattan, and bamboo products in East Kalimantan; and finally, palm oil in North Sumatera.

The simulation of the impact of the global recession on regional outputs presents the impact of the decline of each export commodity on the output of all provinces. The decrease of export commodities in a province will affect the output not only in the related provinces, but also in other provinces due to trade integration among them. Provinces with high interconnectedness, especially as suppliers of raw materials, will be more significantly affected, compared with other provinces with relatively low interconnectedness. This study, however, does not present the direct impact of the decline of each export on its regional output, but more on

TABLE 9.13
Cross-Region Correlation Coefficients (annual growth rate of GRDP)

NO.	Province	Aceh	North Sumatera	West Sumatera	Riau	Jambi	South Sumatera	Bengkulu	Lampung	Bangka Belitung	Riau Archipelago	Jakarta	West Java	Central Java	Yogyakarta
1	Aceh	1.000													
2	North Sumatera	-0.013	1.000												
3	West Sumatera	0.161	0.364	1.000											
4	Riau	0.035	0.425	0.600	1.000										
5	Jambi	-0.117	0.393	0.193	-0.026	1.000									
6	South Sumatera	-0.188	0.400	0.465	0.670	-0.054	1.000								
7	Bengkulu	0.093	0.145	0.635	0.433	0.154	0.400	1.000							
8	Lampung	0.189	-0.063	0.072	-0.045	-0.356	0.101	-0.081	1.000						
9	Bangka Belitung	0.400	-0.370	-0.214	-0.361	-0.477	-0.329	-0.126	0.304	1.000					
10	Riau Archipelago	-0.099	-0.119	0.262	0.096		0.027	0.063	0.367	0.109	1.000				
11	Jakarta	-0.267	0.488	0.418	0.634	0.235	0.795	0.301	-0.080	-0.586	-0.185	1.000			
12	West Java	-0.061	0.631	0.372	0.672	0.032	0.799	0.217	-0.015	-0.229	-0.155	0.696	1.000		
13	Central Java	-0.158	0.030	0.175	0.217	-0.365	0.385	0.005	0.407	0.100	0.414	0.184	0.300	1.000	
14	Yogyakarta	-0.128	-0.351	-0.345	-0.147	-0.540	0.040	-0.104	0.342	0.298	0.367	-0.226	-0.085	0.310	1.000
15	East Java	-0.199	0.321	0.436	0.463	-0.257	0.582	0.168	0.242	-0.175	0.378	0.492	0.551	0.654	0.189
16	Banten	-0.122	0.583	0.852	0.653	0.255	0.535	0.604	-0.121	-0.293	0.051	0.569	0.567	0.136	-0.366
17	Bali	0.043	0.575	0.400	0.224	0.496	0.044	0.074	-0.451	-0.352	-0.224	0.222	0.311	-0.225	-0.748
18	West Nusa Tenggara	0.020	-0.111	0.252	-0.434	0.268	-0.190	0.090	-0.076	0.101	0.113	-0.339	-0.267	-0.112	-0.261
19	East Nusa Tenggara	0.002	0.512	-0.153	-0.016	0.452	0.011	-0.078	-0.328	-0.240	-0.742	0.211	0.241	-0.188	-0.405
20	West Kalimantan	0.464	0.151	0.495	0.086	0.304	-0.135	0.416	-0.045	0.019	-0.033	-0.090	-0.064	-0.102	-0.524
21	Central Kalimantan	-0.061	-0.132	0.083	0.187	0.015	0.250	0.341	0.184	0.035	0.322	0.129	-0.093	0.361	0.286
22	South Kalimantan	-0.182	0.574	0.311	0.279	0.154	0.512	0.318	-0.116	-0.329	0.101	0.426	0.613	0.232	0.036
23	East Kalimantan	-0.336	-0.109	-0.315	-0.111	0.034	-0.180	-0.122	-0.038	-0.193	-0.234	0.040	-0.039	-0.432	0.004
24	North Sulawesi	-0.169	0.416	0.380	0.719	0.076	0.847	0.315	0.059	-0.440	-0.014	0.777	0.748	0.307	0.142
25	Central Sulawesi	0.018	0.283	0.360	0.350	-0.408	0.468	0.234	0.429	-0.002	0.444	0.181	0.463	0.669	0.366
26	South Sulawesi	-0.232	-0.436	-0.054	0.033	-0.374	0.316	0.144	0.436	0.210	0.425	-0.042	0.006	0.504	0.663
27	Southeast Sulawesi	0.092	-0.178	-0.040	0.083	-0.307	0.388	0.239	0.362	0.120	0.052	0.123	0.083	0.210	0.136
28	Gorontalo	0.015	0.411	0.660	0.596	0.261	0.321	0.526	0.038	-0.169	0.059	0.382	0.429	0.138	0.007
29	West Sulawesi	0.012	0.365	0.429	0.382	0.256	0.626	0.271	0.141	-0.220	-0.034	0.521	0.520	0.267	-0.041
30	Maluku	0.045	0.242	0.526	0.500	-0.227	0.555	0.284	0.387	-0.007	0.556	0.322	0.291	0.500	0.183
31	North Maluku	-0.170	0.555	0.595	0.719	-0.008	0.695	0.356	-0.029	-0.315	0.068	0.660	0.766	0.270	-0.045
32	West Papua	0.089	0.246	0.571	0.338	0.049	0.196	0.417	-0.100	0.028	-0.121	0.289	0.317	0.046	-0.462
33	Papua	-0.168	0.231	0.060	0.133	0.524	-0.107	0.124	-0.360	-0.350	-0.181	0.197	-0.043	-0.478	-0.516

Source: Calculated by the authors.

East Java	Banteni	Bali	West Nusa Tenggara	East Nusa Tenggara	West Kalimantan	Central Kalimantan	South Kalimantan	East Kalimantan	North Sulawesi	Central Sulawesi	South Sulawesi	Southeast Sulawesi	Gorontalo	West Sulawesi	Maluku	North Maluku	West Papua	Papua
1.000																		
0.490	1.000																	
-0.049	0.464	1.000																
-0.190	0.075	0.329	1.000															
-0.263	0.131	0.360	-0.086	1.000														
-0.091	0.410	0.420	0.449	0.082	1.000													
0.169	0.004	-0.543	-0.146	-0.161	-0.059	1.000												
0.466	0.414	0.358	-0.052	0.055	-0.051	-0.085	1.000											
-0.127	-0.114	-0.098	-0.267	0.030	-0.158	-0.357	-0.102	1.000										
0.499	0.454	-0.002	-0.454	0.106	-0.244	0.258	0.491	-0.044	1.000									
0.740	0.321	-0.126	-0.043	-0.274	-0.014	0.122	0.431	-0.283	0.377	1.000								
0.269	-0.178	-0.724	-0.137	-0.515	-0.366	**0.551**	-0.026	-0.028	0.287	0.320	1.000							
0.118	-0.191	-0.265	-0.033	-0.298	-0.205	0.236	-0.010	-0.217	0.118	0.238	0.392	1.000						
0.388	**0.731**	0.157	-0.195	0.120	0.169	0.186	0.369	-0.090	**0.530**	0.267	0.003	-0.277	1.000					
0.362	0.356	0.052	-0.062	0.164	-0.066	0.187	0.275	-0.165	**0.733**	0.324	0.216	0.158	0.377	1.000				
0.514	0.328	-0.019	-0.042	-0.374	-0.062	0.396	0.341	-0.539	0.479	**0.568**	0.254	0.333	0.318	0.422	1.000			
0.538	**0.713**	0.315	-0.198	0.126	-0.062	-0.004	0.551	-0.144	**0.768**	0.495	-0.073	-0.113	**0.646**	**0.546**	**0.536**	1.000		
0.165	**0.690**	0.404	0.101	0.200	0.476	-0.097	0.217	-0.127	0.094	0.049	-0.373	-0.264	0.484	-0.058	0.095	**0.501**	1.000	
-0.404	0.170	**0.521**	-0.027	0.216	0.113	-0.200	0.068	0.169	-0.094	-0.477	-0.530	-0.098	0.053	-0.168	-0.114	0.036	0.215	1.000

the total impact, taking into account interregional trade linkage. Based on the above scenario, the weakening demand for exports between regions will affect regional output at different levels. This negative impact on regional output is not only seen in the five selected provinces, but also in many other provinces which have trade relations with them. Nonetheless, the impact on each region differs depending on their trade relationships. Some provinces may not be significantly affected as they might not have a significant trade relationship with the five provinces.

The results of this simulation shows that the total impact of the decline in exports in the five provinces mainly affect the regional output in the five provinces themselves (DKI Jakarta, Banten, South Sulawesi, East Kalimantan, and North Sumatera). The highest impact is on the output in Banten, while the least impact is on the output in DKI Jakarta. The high impact in Banten might be attributed to the second-round effect from Jakarta, its neighbour. The declining output in Jakarta, because of the global recession, may have aggravated the decline in demand for output in Banten.

The impact of a decline in export in one sector is also seen in other sectors in the same province. An example of this is seen in Banten. As mentioned earlier, the assumption is that export in footwear declined by 10.0 per cent. This decline, through interregional linkages, also influenced other sectors in Banten, mainly textile and textile products, estate crops, trade, transportation, the financial sector, and services. The negative impact of textile and textile products on output was relatively high. This decline in output may have been because of the weakening demand for exports of textile and textile products in Jakarta. Furthermore, the impact of change in output demand in DKI Jakarta to Banten was not only felt in the textile and textile products sector, but also in the food and beverage processing sector.

South Sulawesi is assumed to suffer a 10.0 per cent decline of exports from its plantation, but this has affected other sectors in South Sulawesi, including rubber and rubber products, as well as petrochemical products. For East Kalimantan, the impact has not only been on wood, rattan, and bamboo products, but also on forestry as well.

Finally, during the era of decentralization, regional government has a very important role to improve its own economy, including creating and implementing policies to reduce the impact of CAFTA (China–ASEAN Free Trade Agreement) on interregional trade in Indonesia. Here are some examples of the recommended policies. The first is to eliminate high economic costs and raise regional economic competitiveness. The second is to improve governance in local government as a means to achieve economic development with justice. The third is to provide facilities and incentives for innovation or to develop their regional champion products that have high competitiveness in the national and global markets. The fourth is to improve the implementation of public policies, such as improved health services and schools, which enhance the quality of human resources.

In addition, with the implementation of CAFTA since the beginning of January 2010, a tariff exemption of up to 0 per cent between China and ASEAN means that Indonesian products would now be competing with relatively cheaper products from China. Furthermore, the existence of interregional linkages means that the impact of CAFTA on one province may spread to other provinces as well, and in turn will affect the social welfare of the affected regions.

CONCLUDING REMARKS

Although decentralization has benefited in some ways, it has yet to become optimal. Decentralization, implemented at the district level, has increased public participation in the democratic process through direct election of regional leaders by their own local communities. This way, the regional development can contribute positive growth in improving each region's economy. However, generally, decentralization does not seem to be able to reduce the economic gap between regions significantly.

Seven to eight years after the start of the implementation of the decentralization policy, economic disparities between the western and eastern regions of Indonesia still remain at a very high level. This is shown by their contribution to economic activity. Western Indonesia still contributed to almost 80 per cent of the national economy from 2001 to 2007. Moreover, the contribution from the eastern part of Indonesia mainly comes from the oil and gas producing provinces, such as East Kalimantan.

The finding on the still high regional economic disparities is also supported by results of the Williamson Index calculations, which show that the relative imbalance among the provinces has not changed much during the implementation of decentralization. In some provinces, decentralization may have contributed to the rise in the provinces' status according to provincial classifications. However some provinces have suffered a decline in status, and some others have the same status.

Data from IRIO 2000 and 2005 indicate that the domestic trading centre has moved from East Java to West Java. In addition, there are also indications that trade relations among the regions outside Java are directed more to the island of Java, than at other provinces on the same islands. For example, the province of North Sumatera (located on the island of Sumatera) has more trade relations with the provinces in the island of Java, than those on the island of Sumatera itself.

The existence of trade relations among the regions also contributes to economic interdependence among the regions. The implication is that a sudden and large economic change in one area can also affect other areas to varying degrees. Therefore, each region also needs to strengthen its own economy in order to suppress any sudden and large external negative impacts.

The simulation exercise illustrates how the decline in one sector in a province can have wide ramifications, not only on other sectors within its own province, but also on other sectors in other provinces. Furthermore, the second-round effect due to the existence of interregional linkage is also important.

Finally, decentralization has been expected to increase regional economic development because of the larger role of local governments. For example, regional leaders can further accelerate economic growth by developing regional industries that have good competitiveness on the national and global levels.

However, there are also indications that high economic growth is not always accompanied by an increased human development index. Therefore, decentralization should also provide a great opportunity for local leaders to improve public policies in human development, in order to increase their regions' and nation's competitiveness.

NOTES

1. We thank Naila (research assistant from the University of Indonesia) for some data analysing, especially in input-output analysis.
2. Western Indonesia includes all provinces in Sumatera, Java, and Bali; while Eastern Indonesia consists of the remaining provinces.
3. Year 2002 is chosen because it is one year after the implementation of regional autonomy in Indonesia. The year 2007 is chosen based on data availability at the time of writing.
4. Close trade is defined as trade relations (tight) that are reflected through the interregional trade in input and output among the regions.
5. Centre regional trade is defined as areas that became the centres of trade relations (either as input sellers or output buyers).
6. Growth cross correlation is a correlation of economic growth rates in two provinces, examining whether the growth rates in the two provinces go together

or not, and measuring the magnitude of the correlation. In this research, a correlation of at least 0.5 is assumed to be significant.

7. The competitiveness of a region can be seen from several variables, such as the regional economy, financial systems, infrastructure and natural resources, science and technology, human resources, institutions and good governance, and management and microeconomics. A study explaining a region's competitiveness is found in Suseno et al. (2008).

REFERENCES

Badan Pusat Statistik. "Gross Regional Product by Region 2000–2007". <www.bps. go.id> (accessed 23 June 2010).

Bank Indonesia and University of Indonesia. "Identification of Regional Economic Zone in Indonesia during the Decentralization Era — Identifikasi Wilayah Perekonomian di Indonesia dalam Era Desentralisasi". Unpublished. Jakarta, 2007.

Blakely, Edward J. *Planning Local Economic Development: Theory and Practice.* Thousand Oaks, California, United States: Sage Publications, 1989.

Djaja, Komara. "Impact of the Global Financial and Economic Crisis on Indonesia: A Rapid Assessment". Notes prepared for the International Labour Organization. Unpublished paper. Jakarta: ILO 2009.

Goodman, David S. and Gerald Segal. *China Deconstruct: Politics, Trade, and Regionalism.* New York: Routledge in Asia Series, 1994.

Kartasasmita, Ginandjar. "Penyelenggaraan Otonomi Daerah Guna Mewujudkan Nyata Good Governance" [Implementation of Decentralization to Develop Real Good Governance]. Paper presented at PERSADI national seminar, Pekanbaru, 16 June 2007.

Kuncoro, Mudrajad. *Otonomi & Pembangunan Daerah: Reformasi, Perencanaan, Strategi, dan Peluang* [Decentralization and Regional Development: Reform, Planning, Strategy, and Opportunity]. Jakarta: Erlangga, 2004.

Lapera, Team. *Otonomi Versi Negara* [Decentralization in Government Version]. Yogyakarta: Lapera Pustaka, 2001.

Ministry of Finance, Republic of Indonesia. "National Budget 2000–2008". <www. depkeu.go.id> (accessed 23 June 2010).

Resosudarmo, Budy P. and Ditya A.Nurdianto. "Fundamentals of Input-Output Analysis with an Application to the 2005 Indonesian Inter-Regional Input-Output Table". CSIRO, 2007. <www.csiro.au>.

Shaffer, Ron. *Community Economics: Economic Structure and Change Smaller Communities.* Ames, Iowa: Iowa State University Press and Blackwell Publishing Company, 1989.

Soesastro, Hadi and M. Chatib Basri. "The Political Economy of Trade Policy in Indonesia". Center for Strategic and International Studies Working Paper Series, WPE092. Jakarta: CSIS, March 2005.

Suseno, Siti Astiyah, Armida S.A, Nurry Effendi, Bagdja Muljarijadi, and Viktor Pirmana. *Profil dan Pemetaan Daya Saing Ekonomi Daerah Kabupaten/Kota di Indonesia* [Regional Profile and Economic Competitiveness in Indonesia]. Jakarta: Rajawali Pers, 2008.

United Nations Development Programme. "Putting People First: A Compact for Regional Decentralization". In *Indonesia Human Development Report 2001*. New York: Oxford University Press, 2001.

————. "Risalah Desentralisasi" [Note of Decentralization]. Unpublished meeting report. Jakarta, 2009.

United Nations Support Facility for Indonesian Recovery. "Indonesia: The National Human Development Report, 2000". Jakarta: UNSFIRS and UNDP, 2000.

Appendix

Sectors in the Indonesian Interregional Input-Output Data

Sector
1 Rice
2 Other Food Crops
3 Estate Crops/Plantation
4 Livestock
5 Forestry
6 Fishery
7 Oil, Gas and Geothermal Mining
8 Coal and Other Mining
9 Oil Refinery
10 Palm Oil Processing
11 Marine Captured Processing
12 Food and Beverage Processing
13 Textile and Textile products
14 Footwares
15 Wood, Rattan and Bamboo products
16 Pulp and Papers
17 Rubber and Rubber products
18 Petrochemical products
19 Cement
20 Basic Metal
21 Metal Products
22 Electricity Equipments and Machineries
23 Vehicle
24 Other Industries
25 Electric, Gas and Clean Water
26 Construction
27 Trade
28 Hotel and Restaurant
29 Land Transportation
30 Water Transportation
31 Air Transportation
32 Communication
33 Financial Sector
34 Government and Military
35 Other Services

Source: Bandan Pusat Statistik (2010).

PART IV
Search for New Paradigms

10

EMBRACING ASEAN ECONOMIC INTEGRATION 2015: A Quest for an ASEAN Business Cycle from Indonesia's Point of View

Yati Kurniati and Aida S. Budiman

INTRODUCTION

Indonesia, as part of ASEAN, having proclaimed its end goal of regional cooperation to achieving regional economic integration (ASEAN Economic Community or AEC) in 2015, has inevitably embrace this commitment through the fullest preparation in its domestic economy. However, while the commitment brings benefits and the opportunity for it to compete in globalized markets, it also exposes Indonesia's economy to external shocks.

As the biggest economy in ASEAN, Indonesia needs to equip its domestic players fully with sufficient knowledge on the targets, benefits, and opportunities, as well as the challenges of the regional economic integration. Therefore, it is important to understand the potential benefits to be gained and the challenges to face from AEC 2015. Currently, the trade volume and financial linkages of the ASEAN region have increased rapidly, both intraregionally and with the rest of the world. However, one main challenge for the economies in the region, including Indonesia, is to reap the benefits from the deepening economic and financial integration, while minimizing the possible costs from such an integration. This condition inevitably means embarking on a new paradigm to manage the economy amid the regional integration process.

The path to regional economic integration is pursued through the liberalization of goods and services, investment, skilled labour, and freer capital flows, following the ASEAN blueprint for national preparedness. A reporting and monitoring system has also been developed to ensure implementation while allowing assessment on a better way to achieve economic integration. Regionally, the monitoring system is established at various levels and by related agencies,[1] coordinated at the ASEAN Leaders' Summit — the summit attended by leaders of ASEAN. At the national level, each country works on its agenda through working committees which address subsequent issues and follow liberalization schedules. In Indonesia, all the work (economic and financial areas) at the national level is coordinated by the coordinating Ministry of Economy, while the economic area is particularly monitored by the Ministry of Trade.

At the macro level, the process of dynamic transformation to accelerate economic and financial integration into the global market has raised an important question on the characteristics of Indonesian business cycle. A higher degree of integration in trade and the financial sector is expected to support the synchronization of business cycles, which would greatly influence policy coordination and possibly lead to monetary union. Nonetheless, theoretical models have produced ambiguous results regarding the relationship between trade and financial linkages on the one hand, and business cycle synchronization on the other (Garcia-Herrero and Ruiz 2008). Empirical studies in advanced countries find a positive linkage; but, the empirical findings for emerging and developing countries show mixed results. For the latter countries, the relationship depends on several conditions, including the patterns of trade, that is, intra- versus inter-industry trade (Choe 2001; Rana 2007; Shin and Shon 2006; Shin and Wang 2003 and 2004), production structure (Kumakura 2006; Imbs 2004; Herrero 2008), and an industry's special shock (Frankel and Rose 1998).

More synchronized business cycles would presumably mean stronger and faster transmission of shocks across countries, hence providing the ground for regional policy coordination. Therefore, a knowledge of the characteristics of Indonesian business cycle synchronization within ASEAN, would provide profound insights not only on the feasibility of monetary policy coordination in the region, but also for a better understanding of the trade intensity and financial linkages within ASEAN, as well as Indonesia's bilateral relations with Malaysia, the Philippines, Singapore, and Thailand respectively. The knowledge will help shed light on future policies that are to be pursued.

The main objectives of this chapter are to explore efforts needed to increase the synchronicity of Indonesian business cycle with the rest of ASEAN-5 (Malaysia, Philippines, Singapore, and Thailand)[2] and to highlight related policy implications. As business cycle synchronization would be best promoted through economic integration, it is important to fulfil the five pillars or elements of the liberalization schedule of ASEAN economic integration. Inevitably, the findings will establish a new paradigm for Indonesia in tackling the issues of regional economic integration. Moving forward, Indonesia has to put its regional commitment onto its national agenda as well as its future policies. Furthermore, sufficient safeguard measures must be taken to ensure that Indonesia obtains benefits for its real sector and macroeconomic stability from the AEC.

This chapter comprehensively investigates the effect of trade and financial linkages, and the similarities of production structure to explain business cycle synchronization between Indonesia and the ASEAN-4 (with each member individually, and all members simultaneously). While most of the studies estimate a cross-sectional data set by computing time-average bilateral data over the period of study, this chapter focuses on finding the bilateral business cycle synchronization between Indonesia and each of the other four major ASEAN countries. Moreover, it also analyses the average of ASEAN-4, using a system of equations to capture the indirect effects of trade and financial linkages on business cycle synchronization, with quarterly data from the period January 1983–April 2008.

The chapter is organized into five sections. The next section discusses the impact of the latest arrangement of the ASEAN economic community on Indonesian economy and the relationship with business cycle synchronization. Section 3 provides a theoretical background for our study that includes literature reviews, as well as the model and data used in the chapter. Section 4 presents both the descriptive and analytical analyses on the data. And finally, Section 5 provides some concluding remarks.

ASEAN ECONOMIC COMMUNITY

AEC: Definition and Targets

The ASEAN Economic Community[3] or AEC is the realization of the end goal of economic integration: creating a stable, prosperous, and highly competitive ASEAN economic region in which there is a free flow of goods, services, investment and capital, as well as equitable economic development, and reduced poverty and socio-economic disparities (Bali Concord II, October 2003). This end goal, referred to as ASEAN Vision 2020, was first declared at the ASEAN Leaders Summit in December 1997. The establishment of the ASEAN Economic Community was expedited from 2020 to 2015 by the Cebu Declaration during the 12th ASEAN Summit in the Philippines on 13 January 2007. There were two main reasons for accelerating the integration. The first reason is to respond to the emergence of China and India as the new economic powers, and the second is to address the need for ASEAN to build a resilient and sustainable economic region. The economic integration is expected to deliver competitiveness,[4] better regional standards based on international best practices, and an acknowledgment of intellectual property rights. Moreover, the considerable size of integration, with a population of over 580 million and total GDP of US$1.5 trillion in 2008, also offers substantial economic benefits.

In order to ensure a smooth integration path, as well as to incorporate consistent and coherent interrelated and mutually reinforcing elements in the AEC, a blueprint has been made, containing the commitment of each member of ASEAN to implement the agreed strategic schedule to establish the AEC. The commitment to achieve the AEC was further sealed by the declaration of the ASEAN Charter during the 13th ASEAN Summit in 2007. This was a landmark for a new type of regional cooperation after forty years of exercising regional cooperation in ASEAN ways.[5]

To monitor the implementation progress of the blueprint and strategic schedule, the ASEAN Baseline Report will be compiled as a scorecard for the accomplishment of each element. The performance of each member country on its pre-agreed flexibilities will be shown on this scorecard which will be accessible to the stakeholders.

One important characteristic of the AEC is the establishment of ASEAN as a single market and production base, a framework for achieving the ASEAN Vision 2020 as conveyed in the Bali Concord II. This single market and production base ought to comprise five core elements or pillars, namely: free flow of goods; free flow of services; free flow of investment; free flow of capital, and finally, free flow of skilled labour. Although some debates emerged during the initiation of ASEAN Vision 2020, the issuance of the ASEAN Blueprint helped shed light on the end form of ASEAN integration. Using Balassa's integration stage, it was concluded that the end stage of ASEAN integration is economic integration without a customs union (see Table 10.1). Nevertheless, contrary to the sequential suggestion from Balassa's

TABLE 10.1
Bela Balassa Integration Stage vs. ASEAN's Integration Plan

Stage	ASEAN's Elements and Development
Preferential Trading Area (PTA)	A preferential trading area within ASEAN began in 1977. At this stage, certain goods within ASEAN were given privilege through reductions in tariff.
Free Trade Area (FTA)	In 1992, ASEAN launched the AFTA (ASEAN Free Trade Area). Tariff was to be reduced to 0 per cent among ASEAN-6 in 2010, but for Cambodia, Laos, Myanmar, and Vietnam only in 2018. At this stage, individual country is free to determine applied tariff to non-ASEAN countries.
Customs Union (CU)	No barrier for movement in products among members, which must apply common external tariff (CET) for non-member countries. This stage is not applied to ASEAN (CET).
Common Market (CM)	Next stage of customs union with no barrier in movement of production factors. The formation of AFTA was followed by ASEAN Frameworks Agreement on Services (AFAS) in 1995 and ASEAN Investment Area (AIA) in 1998, which was then modified into ACIA (ASEAN Comprehensive Investment Agreement) in 2008.
Economic Union	Common market with significant harmonization for national economic policies, including structural policy. To achieve a single market and production base, ASEAN has begun the policy of harmonization process, among others, through the ASEAN Single Window (ASW) initiative to facilitate trade flows, Mutual Recognition Agreement (MRA) to facilitate flows in services and skilled labour, as well as in capital market regulation. Currently, priority has been set to mitigate the non-tariff barriers within ASEAN.
Total Economic Integration	Integration in monetary, fiscal, and social policies, followed by the establishment of supranational bodies. Substantial national sovereignty will be relinquished at this stage.

Source: Bank Indonesia (2008).

integration process, the accomplishment of the economic integration stage in 2015 is simultaneously done with customs union (without CET: Common External Tariff) and a common market stage. This type of integration is different to the one pursued by the European Union, the CFA Franc Zone, the Gulf Cooperation Council Monetary Union, which contain a monetary union. Currently understanding the importance of attaining the converging criteria across member countries to establishing the credibility of the pact, ASEAN is not pursuing a monetary union yet. It is hoped that the economic integration will bring member countries to a common stage in the economic development. More importantly, one specific characteristic of ASEAN integration is to ensure the creation of a region with equitable economic development, despite the existing development disparities, as well as the proliferation of bilateral trade agreements between individual member countries in ASEAN and other countries. This characteristic has made the ASEAN economic integration quite unique compared with others.

AEC and the Indonesian Economy[6]

In theory, the regional economic integration will produce benefits including efficient allocation of resources, better economics of scale, larger source of capital (including human capital), as well as the establishment of economic specialization for each member country. Empirical studies on the impact of ASEAN economic integration have pointed to positive effects on production costs of the electronic sector and regional GDP (Bank Indonesia 2008, p. 284). The impact on lowering production costs ranges from 10.0 to 20.0 per cent, whilst GDP is estimated to increase by 10.0 per cent. However, the positive impacts are based on the assumption that all the preconditions for the regional integration are satisfied. An example of this is the precondition of free movement of goods and factors of production to bring about economic efficiency.

It is expected that the AEC will eventually turn ASEAN into a single market and production base, offering, as mentioned earlier, a market with GDP of more than US$1.5 trillion and a population of about 580 million. About 80.0 per cent of the population is the productive age group (younger than 44 years old), thus promising a rosy market and a substantial labour force.

Furthermore, the AEC will offer the region a lucrative investment opportunity, owing to its stable, resilient, and promising economic growth, amid maintained macroeconomic and financial stability. The experience of enduring the last global economic crisis of 2008/09 has proved the resilience of ASEAN in maintaining its economic growth as it was able to weather the global economic and financial turmoil because of its better economic fundamentals and financial conditions.

With the attainment of the conditions stated above, Indonesia may gain sizeable benefits from the integration. In terms of the labour markets, almost 40.0 per cent of the ASEAN labour force resides in Indonesia, offering abundant human capital, a sizeable market, a choice of centres for industry and investment destinations. Facilitating the standardization of skilled labour through the use of Mutual Recognition Arrangements (MRAs) will support the Indonesian labour movement in the region as it can potentially provide more remittance revenue.

In terms of export destination, the average share of Indonesian trade with ASEAN (2000–08) only reaches some 21.0 per cent of its total trade, implying an opportunity for market diversification. Indonesia has also taken on the role as coordinator in developing the priority sector of wood-based products and automotives. Moreover, Indonesia could also leverage the regional initiative on infrastructure, standardize business practices, and harmonize regulations to support domestic economic development. An example of these is the initiative on an information and processing centre of custom release and cargo clearance, or the so-called ASEAN Single Window in 2008 for ASEAN-5 and Brunei. The ASEAN Single Window requires the implementation of a National Single Window (NSW) system and Indonesia has complied by operating its NSW since November 2007.

To reap the gains from the ASEAN economic integration Indonesia should prepare a blueprint and strategic plan well. It is important for Indonesia to play a significant role in the regional integration and to minimize the negative impacts on its domestic economy. Domestic business players should have the same playing field as regional players to ensure an equal competitive level. In this respect, there are several areas that need to be taken into consideration. These areas include: improvement of its competitive advantage in export products and human capital, improvement of its investment climate, an alignment between regional commitments and the national agenda, and the achievement of macroeconomic and financial stability.

An assessment of goods in the priority sectors, as pilot projects for the ASEAN integration, shows that ASEAN's comparative advantage lies mostly in resource-based products. Furthermore, using the Revealed Comparative Advantage (RCA) indicator to measure these products' comparative advantage, there are at least five ASEAN countries that have comparative advantage in the priority sectors of agro-based, rubber-based and wood-based products, as well as fisheries. This may partly explain that the level of intra-ASEAN trade, despite the trade liberalization initiative in the region, amounted to only 20.0–25.0 per cent of total ASEAN trade. The RCA indicator also shows that Thailand has a comparative advantage on seven priority sectors compared with five in Indonesia, and four in Malaysia and the Philippines. Furthermore, the recorded top ten Indonesian export commodities, except for crude palm oil, do not show good RCAs. Therefore, Indonesia needs to improve its strategic export development by increasing the intra-ASEAN share of its total trade, as well as export competitiveness.

Indonesia should also pay serious attention to the free flow of skilled labour pillar by ensuring its labour competencies. It is envisaged that the skilled labour movement within ASEAN will be facilitated through the issuance of visa and employment passes as a regional working permit. As a guideline, the formulation of the Mutual Recognition Arrangements (MRAs) and core competencies in the services sector will be established gradually for priority sectors. In 2006, Indonesia supplied 23.0 per cent of intra-ASEAN labour, the second highest after Myanmar (27.0 per cent). However, using 2004–05 data, only 5.3 per cent of the Indonesian labour force were university graduates, compared with some 13.0 per cent in the Philippines and Thailand, and 18.0 per cent in Malaysia. Hence, it is important for Indonesia to improve the quality of its human resources in order to meet the criteria of the MRAs and core competencies.

In terms of investment flows, the assessment of current regulations for direct portfolio and other investments reveals an insignificant limitation on capital movement between residents and non-residents. An increasing and sizeable amount of capital flow has also occurred in Indonesia, in particular, from the portfolio investment. The challenge is to acquire a more sustainable foreign capital flow, preferably in the form of direct investments. It is important for Indonesia to improve its investment climate to gain such flows, though various indicators on its competitiveness have shown that several areas have improved, including improvement of infrastructure, ease of doing business, and macroeconomic stability.

All in all, these improved areas should be included on the national agenda of its development plan. Moreover, its regional commitments to the AEC should be translated into the national implementation plan, equipped with a proper monitoring scheme. Indonesia needs to move towards greater economic convergence in the region in order to support its own economic efficiency. The relevant statistics include its inflation rate, GDP per capita, and external debt ratio.

The AEC and Business Cycle Synchronization

The correlation of business cycles among countries in the world has been a great concern of decision-makers, because of the rapid development in technological information and financial flows that make economic policies in one country contagious to another. Business cycle here refers to the fluctuations in economic activity over a period of several years involving shifts between periods of expansion or boom, and periods of contraction or recession. The synchronization of business cycles shows the strength of the correlation of the cycles between or among countries. The higher the correlation, the more synchronized are the business cycles of the countries.

There are at least two important reasons for synchronizing business cycles (Garcia-Herrero and Ruiz 2008). The first is that the more business cycles are synchronized, the stronger and faster the transmission of shocks across countries will be. This stronger and faster transmission can in turn provide, and become an important reason, for international policy coordination. The second is that the synchronization of business cycles has profound implications for the design and functioning of common currency areas.

Due to the possibility of greater monetary cooperation in operating a full-fledged monetary union with a common currency, the importance of business cycle synchronization was further underscored by Moneta and Rüffer (2009). Business cycle synchronization is also a crucial criterion for the creation of an optimal currency area (Mundell 1961). This criterion is particularly important due to the loss of direct control over national monetary policy. Alesina, Barro and Tenreyco (2002, in Mongelly 2002) have argued that countries exhibiting large co-movements of outputs and prices have the lowest costs resulting from abandoning monetary independence *vis-á-vis* their partners. If the business cycle is mostly driven by external factors, the domestic policy aimed at economic stabilization will probably have been less influenced by the creation of an optimal currency area.

Meanwhile, the development of intra-ASEAN activities, through the continuing increase of intratrade share and financial links in the region, has shown some positive signs. The continuing increase in inter and intra-regional integration is likely to have a positive effect on regional growth dynamics and on the extent of business cycle synchronization. At this point regional integration is only aimed at economic union, and does not have the business cycle synchronization that will greatly influence the ability for policy coordination and the possibility to establish a monetary union in the future.

THEORETICAL BACKGROUND

Theoretical models do not give a clear prediction on the relationship between trade, financial linkages, and business cycle synchronization (Garcia-Herrero and Ruiz 2008). Moreoever, the empirical evidence on these issues have also shown mixed results. Kose and Yi (2001) suggested that the impact of higher trade integration on synchronization cycles depends on the nature of trade and type of shocks affecting economies. Integration could increase or decrease the synchronization cycles. The standard theory predicts that the opening of trade may lead to increased specialization in production and a change in the inter-industry patterns of international trade. If business cycles are dominated by industry-specific shocks, then trade induced specialization will lead to a decrease in business cycle correlations. However, if trade is dominated by intra-industry trade, then industry specific shocks may lead to more symmetric business cycles (Frankel and Rose 1998; Rana 2007). Furthermore, in the case of intensive trade relations, wide economic shocks in one country will generally have an effect on the demand for goods from other countries. The nature of intra-industry trade can be measured by using the Grubel-Llyod Index (1975), also known as Intra Industry Index (IIT), used by Inklaar et al. (2008). The economic structure similarity is measured using the Imbs' approach (2004), which is in the form of a similarity index of production structure. Empirical findings on these indicators have concluded that similarity in production structure, rather than bilateral trade linkage, has been more dominant in explaining output synchronization (Kumakura 2006).

As for financial linkages, some studies have pointed out a positive relationship between financial integration and business cycle co-movements, both in output and consumption, in the case of advanced economies (Imbs 2004 and 2006). Rose and Spiegel (2004) have placed an emphasis on the occurrence of indirect effects of trade on output synchronization. Stronger trade links might increase financial linkages because they promote FDI in export-oriented sectors, or because they foster international loans. Heathcote and Perry (2004) and Garcia-Herrero and Ruiz (2008) found a reversed indirect effect in which stronger financial links may allow for the relocation of capital among countries through comparative advantage, thus increasing opportunities for trade, and resulting in a decoupled business cycle. Other studies on the impact of integration on output synchronization have been conducted by Kalemli-Ozcan et al. (2003), Helpman and Razin (1978), who showed that stronger financial links may lead to greater specialization in the separation of production and consumption, thus making it less costly to achieve greater specialization in production and differentiation in economic structures of the region.

Previous studies have generally used an estimation from a single equation to test the relevance of trade and financial channels (Frankel and Rose 1998; Kose, Prasad and Terrones 2003). The fact that there may be an indirect effect that may have a correlation opposite to the direct effect might account for the generally small impact found in the studies that used single-equation regressions. To address the possibility of conflicting indirect effects, Imbs (2004 and 2006) and Herrero (2008) estimated a system of simultaneous equations to incorporate the direct and indirect effects on the synchronization of output.

Model and Data

In order to understand the potential existence of multidirectional channels of influence among trade and financial linkages that affect business cycles, this chapter, following the study by Imbs (2006) and Garcia-Herrero and Ruiz (2008), uses a system of equations to capture the indirect effects of trade and financial linkages on business cycle synchronization. The system of equations consists of:

$$\log(\rho_{IND,i,t}) = \alpha_0 + \alpha_1 \log(T_{IND,i,t}) + \alpha_2 \log(F_{IND,t}) + \alpha_3 \log(S_{IND,i,t}) + Z_{\rho,t} + \varepsilon_\rho \quad (1)$$

$$\log(T_{IND,i,t}) = \beta_0 + \beta_1 \log(S_{IND,i,t}) + \beta_2 \log(F_{IND,t}) + Z_{T,t} + \varepsilon_T \quad (2)$$

$$\log(F_{IND,t}) = \delta_0 + \delta_2 \log(T_{IND,i,t}) + Z_{F,t} + \varepsilon_F \quad (3)$$

$$\log(S_{IND,i,t}) = \delta_0 + \delta_1 \log(T_{IND,i,t}) + Z_{S,t} + \varepsilon_S \quad (4)$$

where:

$\rho_{IND,i,t}$ is the business cycle synchronization between Indonesia's output growth and country i's at time t

$T_{IND,i,t}$ is the bilateral trade linkage between Indonesia and country i at time t

$S_{IND,i,t}$ is the index of similarity of economic structure between Indonesia and country i

$F_{IND,t}$ is the financial linkage of Indonesia with the rest of the world

$Z_{\rho,t}$, $Z_{T,t}$, $Z_{F,t}$, and $Z_{S,t}$ are the vectors of exogenous determinants of business cycle correlation, bilateral trade intensity, financial openness, and the index of similarity, respectively.

This chapter uses the Hausman specification error test (Hausman 1976) to examine whether there is any simultaneity problem in the equation system. Should there be any simultaneity problem, then the system of equation is solved by using the Two Stage Least Squares, developed by Theil (1953), to get consistent and efficient estimators.

The business cycle synchronization $(\rho_{i,t})$ of the two countries is measured as the bilateral correlation of de-trended real economic activities. Real GDP growth rate is de-trended by using Baxter and King's band pass filter (1999). A higher correlation of (de-trended) GDP growth signifies a higher synchronization of business cycle between the two countries, or more precisely, between Indonesia and the ASEAN region.

A measurement of trade linkage[7] $(T_{i,t})$ is carried out using the most common form of measurement, which is taking the sum of bilateral exports and imports between Indonesia and each ASEAN partner country, and dividing it by the sum of their GDPs (IMF 2002; Frankel and Rose 1998; Imbs 2004; Herrero and Rüiz 2008). The higher T indicates a tighter trade linkage between the two countries.

$$T_{IND,i,t} = \frac{X_{IND,i,t} + M_{IND,i,t}}{GDP_{IND,t} + GDP_{i,t}}$$

The sources of bilateral trade data used for calculating trade linkages or trade intensity (total export and import) come from the IMF's *Direction of Trade Statistics*.

In the case of trade linkages, a number of studies, such as Portes and Rey (2005), have suggested that gravity variables play an important role in explaining trade linkages between two countries. The gravity model states that bilateral trade flows are positively related to the product of two countries' economic sizes and negatively related to the distance between them. Following the simple version of this gravity model by Deardorff (1998), this chapter constructs the gravity variable as:

$$\frac{per\ cap\ GDP_{IND} \times per\ cap\ GDP_i}{Distance_{IND\ to\ i}}$$

To understand the pattern of specialization in international trade, this chapter uses an indicator of intra-industry trade, IIT, to measure the share of bilateral trade that can be attributed to intra-industry trade. IIT index is measured using the Grubel-Lloyd index (1974):

$$IIT^k_{ij} = 1 - \frac{|X^k_{ij} - M^k_{ij}|}{(X^k_{ij} + M^k_{ij})}$$

The share of intra-industry trade (IIT) is calculated as one minus the absolute difference between exports (X) of industry k, from country i to country j, and imports (M) of industry k from country j to country i, divided by the total bilateral trade for industry k. The share per industry is then aggregated using the share of trade in k industry to the total trade between the two countries. For calculating intra-industry trade, this chapter utilizes data from UN Comtrade, Standard International Trade Classification (SITC) 2 digit. The higher the IIT, the higher is the intra-trade industry within the two countries.

To measure financial linkages, this chapter uses a global financial integration measurement, rather than a bilateral financial linkage measurement due to limitations in obtaining data on the long series of bilateral financial flows between Indonesia and other ASEAN countries. This chapter applies the aggregate quantity measure constructed by Lane and Milesi-Ferretti (2001), which is the sum of stocks of external assets and liabilities from foreign direct investments, portfolio investments, and other investments:[8]

$F_{IND,t} = \dfrac{FA_t + FL_t}{GDP_{IND,t}}$. As an alternative, this chapter utilizes a flow concept instead

of Milesi-Ferretti's stock concept. The financial flows data are constructed from the Indonesian Balance of Payments. The higher sum of Financial Asset (FA) and Financial Liabilities (FL) over GDP indicates a higher financial linkage between Indonesia and the global financial market.

Nevertheless, we argue that the financial linkage of a country depends on the degree of its financial account liberalization. To measure the extent of openness in capital account transactions, this chapter employs a financial openness index calculated by Chinn-Ito (2007),[9] called the KAOPEN index, in order to show the relative degree of financial openness among ASEAN countries. The higher the values this index takes on, the more open the country is to cross-border capital transactions. This indicator is computed from Chinn's website.

Furthermore, the index of economic structure similarity is measured by using the absolute distance shares of production between Indonesia and each of the other ASEAN countries, showing the discrepancy in the economic structure between Indonesia and other ASEAN countries. This measurement of economic similarity (Imbs 2004) can be expressed as[10]

$$S_{IND,i,t} = \Sigma_{n=1}^{N} |S_{n,IND,t} - S_{n,i,t}|$$

where N is the number of sectors. Note that $S_{IND,i,t}$ represents the absolute discrepancies in the economic structures, as in Imbs (2004). $S_{n,i,t}$ is the share of industry n in country i at time t. $S_{IND,i,t}$ might take values between 0, for identical structures, and 2, for disjointed production structure. A higher value implies less similarity between the structure of Indonesia's production and that of country i. This chapter also uses several control variables in its regression analyses, such as inflation differential and oil price, as potential sources of global shocks that could influence business cycle synchronization.

Finally, the expected signs of the parameters in the equations are summarized in Figure 10.1. Using the quarterly data of five ASEAN countries, the period of estimation in this chapter is from 1983 to 2008.

FIGURE 10.1
Expected Relationship across Variables in the System of Equations

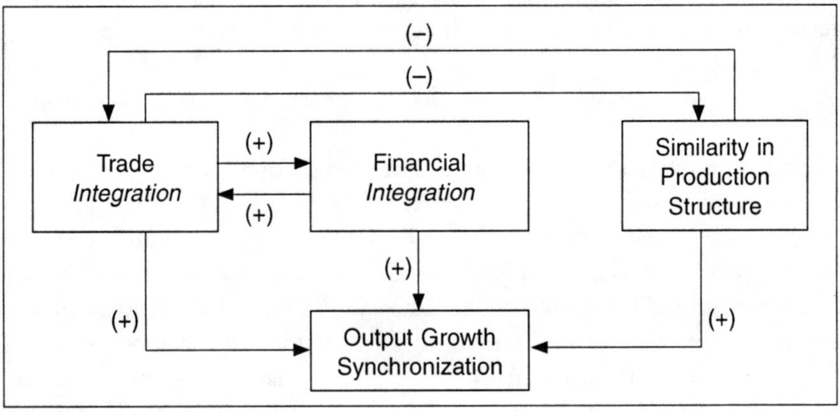

Source: Created by the authors.

STYLIZED FACTS AND EMPIRICAL RESULTS

Stylized Facts

Intra-ASEAN trade has shown progress as seen from the continuing increase of its intra-trade share in the region, from 17.0 per cent in 1990 to 26.5 per cent in 2008 (see Figure 10.2). With regard to financial links, the degree of financial openness among ASEAN countries is quite varied (see Figure 10.3). Among these countries, Singapore, followed by Indonesia,

FIGURE 10.2
Intra-ASEAN Trade
(percentage to total exports)

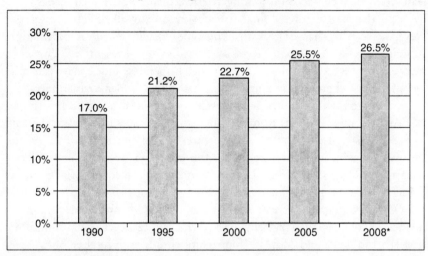

Note: * Up to September 2008
Source: Calculated from International Monetary Fund (2009).

FIGURE 10.3
Financial Openness of ASEAN Countries, as of 2007
(Chin-Ito normalized index)

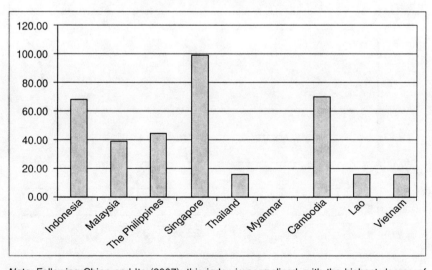

Note: Following Chinn and Ito (2007), this index is normalized, with the highest degree of financial openness captured by the value of 100, and the lowest by zero.
Source: Chinn, Menzie D., and Hiro Ito (2007).

has adopted the most liberal financial system, with the highest financial openness (Chinn-Ito, normalized index being at 100). Thailand has the least open financial account among the five major ASEAN countries, and Laos has the most regulated financial account among all ASEAN countries. Nevertheless, this chapter finds that this index heavily relied on information submitted in IMF's *Annual Report on Exchange Arrangements and Exchange Restrictions* (AREAER). Hence, the financial openness index may lead to a biased view if there is no explanation on the area under evaluation.

Compared with the other less developed financial market countries in ASEAN, Cambodia seems to have a high financial openness index. Yet this is due to its non-clarification on the measures in financial sector. As for Indonesia, having adopted a regime for free exchange, its total financial flows have risen substantially from 2002–08, indicating an increase in financial linkages with the global financial system (see Figure 10.4).

With the gradual increase in ASEAN intra-trade and some degree of financial openness, a few patterns of bilateral business cycle synchronization between Indonesia and ASEAN (four major countries in total or ASEAN-4) as well as bilaterally with Singapore, Thailand, the Philippines and Malaysia, have been noticed. In general, the degree of business cycle synchronization

FIGURE 10.4
Financial Flows of Indonesia
(Foreign Assets + Foreign Liabilities)

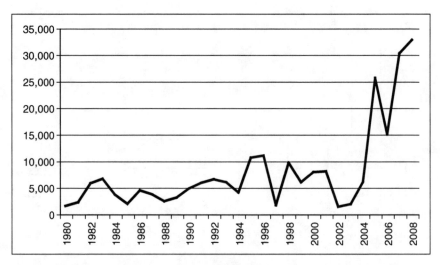

Source: Calculated from raw data of Capital and Financial Account of Balance of Payment, provided by Bank Indonesia (2009).

has increased substantially, particularly from 1990 to 2000, and moved variedly afterwards (see Figure 10.5). As opposed to the increase or flattening pattern of all ASEAN-4 and other countries since 2000, the business cycle co-movement between Indonesia and Singapore has tended not to move together. The closest synchronization shown is the high correlation between Indonesia, Malaysia, and Thailand, mostly from 2006–08.

FIGURE 10.5
GDP Synchronization
(Ten-Year Rolling Correlation of Detrended GDP Growth)

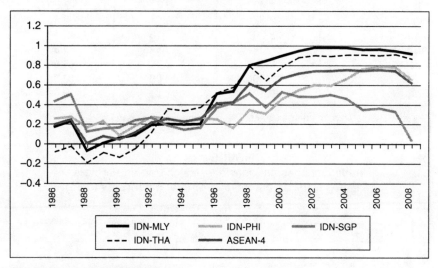

Source: Calculated from CEIC Data.

Within ASEAN, more interesting facts are found for Indonesia's trade pattern. As shown from different indicators in trade linkages,[11] trade linkage between Indonesia and all ASEAN countries, including with ASEAN-4, have strengthened over the observation period. The share of Indonesian's trade with ASEAN has increased from 12.8 per cent of total Indonesian trade in the 1980s, to 21.2 per cent in 2000, thus surpassing Indonesia's trade share with major trading partners including Japan, the United States, and European countries (see Table 10.2).

Figure 10.6 shows that this share, in particular post-1990, has increased overtime. As reflected in the well traced trade linkages between the share of Indonesia's trade to ASEAN and ASEAN-4, more than 92.0 per cent of the Indonesia-ASEAN's trade was with four major ASEAN countries.

TABLE 10.2
The Average Share of Indonesian Trade with Its Major Trading Partners
(percentage to total Indonesian trade)

	1980–89	1990–99	2000–08
Malaysia	0.65	2.15	4.21
The Philippines	0.84	0.70	1.11
Singapore	10.56	8.42	11.04
Thailand	0.67	1.54	3.31
ASEAN-4	**12.72**	**12.81**	**19.66**
ASEAN Total	**12.84**	**13.58**	**21.20**
China	1.43	3.71	7.56
Korea	2.62	6.11	6.36
Japan	38.20	25.13	18.18
ASEAN+3	**55.09**	**48.52**	**53.30**
Australia	2.35	3.70	3.56
U.S.	17.00	13.06	10.35
Euro	9.16	13.33	9.69

Source: Calculated from International Monetary Fund (various years).

FIGURE 10.6
Trade Linkages: Indonesia — Major Trading Partners
(bilateral trade as percentage of total Indonesian trade)

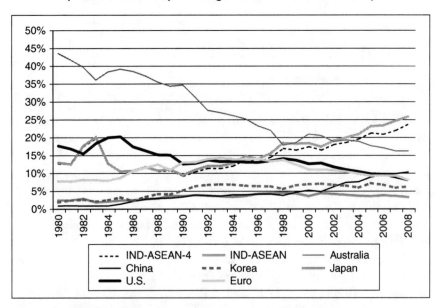

Source: Calculated from International Monetary Fund (various years).

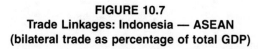

FIGURE 10.7
Trade Linkages: Indonesia — ASEAN
(bilateral trade as percentage of total GDP)

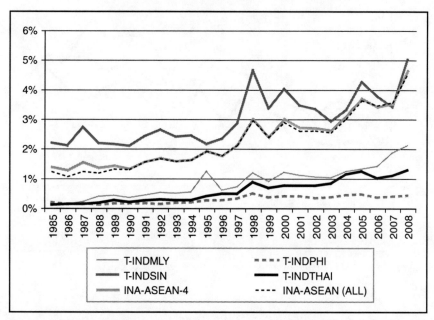

Source: Calculated from International Monetary Fund (various years).

The bilateral trade linkages with the four major ASEAN countries have also shown a similar trend, yet to varying degrees (see Figure 10.7). The highest trade linkage has occurred between Indonesia and Singapore, followed subsequently by Malaysia, and Thailand, with the lowest being with the Philippines.

Looking further into the structure of industries, this chapter observes that Indonesia has an increasing trend of intra-industry trade mostly with Thailand and Malaysia (see Figure 10.8). The least significant upward trend is seen with the Philippines, while the trend with Singapore has picked up since 2005. These facts explain that despite the strong trade linkage between Indonesia and Singapore, the degree of business synchronization between the two countries is a loose one. Concurrently, Singapore shows the highest, and increasing index of difference with Indonesia's production structure (see Figure 10.9). The next highest difference in production structure is that with Malaysia[12] while the index of differences with Thailand and the Philippines are relatively small.

FIGURE 10.8
Intra-Industry Trade

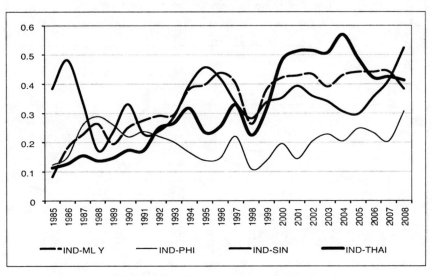

Source: Calculated from International Monetary Fund (various years).

FIGURE 10.9.
Structural Production Differences
between Indonesia and ASEAN-4

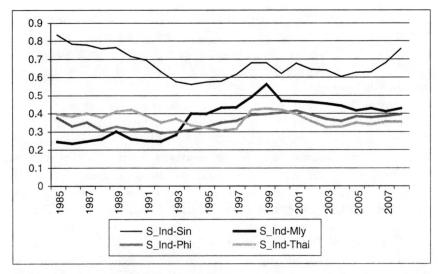

Source: Calculated from CEIC Data.

Empirical Findings

Employing the four equations mentioned earlier, this section explores the factors behind the business cycle synchronization between Indonesia and ASEAN-4, and other individual major ASEAN countries.

The estimated results (Appendices A to E) point out the strong impact of trade linkages in promoting the synchronization of business cycle between Indonesia and ASEAN-4, as well as bilaterally with individual major ASEAN countries. Meanwhile, Indonesia's financial integration with the global market has a negligible role in influencing the business cycle co-movements of the ASEAN region. The exception is its relations with Malaysia, where financial links are inversely related to the co-movement of output between Indonesia and Malaysia. As expected, we also find that the differences in the structures of production are statistically significant and have a negative effect on the co-movement of the business cycles between Indonesia and ASEAN-4 (and bilaterally with Thailand). This means that similarity in production structure will directly foster business cycle synchronization. In other words, any common sectoral shocks would result in business cycle synchronization. Such a significant effect of trade linkages on business cycle correlation has been supported by the increasing trend of intra-trade industry between Indonesia and ASEAN-4 countries (see Figure 10.8).

However, financial linkages have no significant impact on business cycle synchronization. The result is related to the high mobility of capital where the transfer of financial resources across countries is easier with stronger financial integration, thus dampening the correlation with GDP growth. Investors may diversify their resources to countries that are less correlated with one another. Currently, Indonesia's financial transactions are more active, in terms of both frequency and value, with developed countries.

As for the control variables, our system of equations (for bilateral relations) signify that the development of oil prices has been an important factor in driving economic fluctuations and significantly fostering the business cycle correlation between Indonesia and Malaysia, as well as with the Philippines and Thailand.

The second and the third columns of Appendix A show the two-way causal relationship of trade and financial linkage. The relationships between trade and financial links are observed in Indonesia's relations with Singapore and ASEAN as a whole. In other words, the promotion of trade linkages and enhancement of financial links are expected to strengthen each other. For example, a stronger trade linkage may result in a greater financial link through the FDI trade link and financing, which in turn also strengthen the trade linkage. Such a causal relationship provides an incentive towards greater integration in trade and financial flows. Higher trade will then support closer business cycle correlations.

Furthermore, in line with the result of Aizenman and Noy (2004), the financial linkages (column 3 in the appendix table) are mostly determined by the gravity variable and the degree of financial openness of the country (in the case with ASEAN-4, Singapore, and the Philippines), as well as trade linkages (with ASEAN-4 and Singapore).

CONCLUSION AND RECOMMENDATIONS

Only a few years remain until we arrive at year 2015, the year that ASEAN has committed to establishing the ASEAN Economic Community. Indonesia cannot withdraw from its commitment, but it can become well prepared in facing it. Therefore, Indonesia needs a new paradigm in managing its economy in order to gain the full benefits of the ASEAN Economic Community 2015. Along with other preparations for the AEC, understanding the nature of business cycle synchronization is one important effort that would help Indonesia benefit from AEC.

Having synchronized business cycle is also preferable for regional economic integration that seeks to move towards monetary union. Although the end stage of AEC 2015 is economic integration, it may be good for Indonesia to increase the degree of business cycle synchronization with ASEAN to ensure compatibility with any possible policy coordination and future agenda of the AEC. This chapter's assessment shows that the correlation between the business cycle of Indonesia with the average of ASEAN-4 and bilaterally with Malaysia, Thailand, and the Philippines have shown some degree of synchronization. However, promoting further business synchronization is important for Indonesia to enhance its trade linkages within ASEAN. At this stage, the impact of the differences in the structure of production on co-movement of business cycles in ASEAN-4 has been found to be significant, particularly between Indonesia and Thailand.

Although the contribution of financial linkage to the business cycle synchronization is less pronounced, there is still evidence of a two-way relationship of trade and financial linkage between Indonesia and the average of ASEAN-4, as well as with Singapore. Hence, it is also important for Indonesia to look for ways to boost its financial linkages. Boosting financial linkages may support higher trade linkages, particularly those in the form of FDI trade links and trade financing. Two important factors for enhancing financial links found in this result are the financial openness and gravity index. Nonetheless, when allowing greater capital mobility, safeguards must be put in place against potential macroeconomic instability and systemic risk that may arise from the liberalization process, including the right to adopt the necessary measures to ensure macroeconomic and financial stability.

All in all, it is found that business cycle synchronization would be promoted through economic integration. These results have at least three policy implications for Indonesia. First, to boost the economic integration, it is important for Indonesia to ensure the implementation of the AEC's five pillars in its strategic schedule. The elements are pillars for achieving regional economic integration, which should have positive effects in increasing the trade linkage of Indonesia with the region. To this end, strong political will, as well as a change in the mindset of all domestic players, including policy-makers, businessmen, and households, are needed to shape Indonesia into becoming an efficient, innovative and competitive economy, able to compete with other ASEAN countries. Furthermore, in enhancing trade linkages, more microeconomic studies on the real sector would be advisable in determining development strategies.

The second policy implication is promoting financial linkages within ASEAN. This condition has not only led towards higher trade linkages, but also towards diversifying the source of financing. The diversification of capital sources will somewhat compensate for the vulnerability from sudden reversals of capital flows. And finally, the third policy implication is to put Indonesia's macroeconomics and financial stability as its first lines of defence.

Since there are a few years before 2015, Indonesia needs to equip its domestic players immediately and fully with sufficient knowledge on the target of regional economic integration, benefits, and opportunities, as well as challenges. Therefore, it is important to understand what benefits are potentially to be gained from the AEC in 2015 and what challenges have to be dealt with. Thus, adding the variable of the regional economic integration commitment to the equation, a new paradigm in managing the economy needs to be established.

As a first step in reaping potential gains from such an economic integration, a well prepared blueprint and strategic plan initiated and coordinated by the Government of Indonesia should be seriously prepared. It is important for Indonesia to play a significant role in the regional integration and minimize the negative impact on its domestic economy.

Domestic business players and market participants should have a level playing field with regional players to ensure an equal competitive level. In this respect, there are several areas that need to be taken into consideration, namely: improvement in competitive advantage in the export of particular products and human capital, improvement in the investment climate, alignment between its regional commitment and national agenda, and finally, the achievement of macroeconomic and financial stability.

Moving forward, Indonesia should put these areas of improvement on the national agenda of its development plan. A well prepared national blueprint and strategic implementation plan should be developed in an integrated manner. Furthermore, its regional commitment should be translated into the national development plan, equipped with a proper monitoring scheme. And, on a final note, these efforts should be taken cautiously through introducing sufficient safeguard measures to ensure benefits for the real sector, as well as macrostability for the sustainability of the process and the competitiveness of the economy.

NOTES

1. To create the monitoring system at the national level, different related agencies have their own benchmarks to achieve. For example, for the freer flow of capital, there are two agencies, namely Bank Indonesia and Securities Exchange Commission.
2. In the rest of the chapter, this term is replaceable with ASEAN-4.
3. AEC, together with the ASEAN Security Community and the ASEAN Socio-Cultural Community, has envisaged the ASEAN Community.
4. McKinsey & Company (2003) estimated that ASEAN would see 10.0–20.0 per cent lower production costs for consumption goods.
5. The ASEAN way means a voluntary approach. There is no enforcement, and everybody is expected to be polite enough to understand the reasons. The issuance of the blueprint and strategic schedule has changed the approach towards one that is more rule based.
6. This part is an excerpt from Bank Indonesia (2008).
7. Note that for comparison purpose in Section 4.1, another indicator for trade linkage, which is the sum of bilateral exports and imports between Indonesia and the ASEAN countries, over Indonesia's total trade, is also introduced.
8. The FA and FL described in Lane and Milesi-Ferreti's paper are available at <http://www.imf.org/external/pubs/ft wp/2006/ data/wp0669.zip>. We update the data using financial flows data from Balance of Payments, adjusted with the International Investment Position data.
9. Chinn-Ito financial openness index is publicly available at Ito's website <http://web.pdx.edu/~ito/> or Chinn's <http://www.ssc.wisc.edu/~mchinn/research.

html>. *KAOPEN* is based on the binary dummy variables that codify the tabulation of restrictions on cross-border financial transactions reported in the IMF's *Annual Report on Exchange Arrangements and Exchange Restrictions (AREAER).*

10. Note that due to practical reasons, the negative sign in front of the equation as suggested by Imbs (2004) has been deleted so that the logs form can be done to calculate the empirical result. Therefore, the expected sign of this variable in the empirical result will be different to that suggested in Figures 10.1 and 10.2.

11. Two trade linkage indicators are used, namely: Indonesia's trade with country *i* as a percentage of total trade, as reflected in Table 10.2, Figures 10.5 and 10.6; and Indonesia's trade with country *i* as a percentage of GDP, as reflected in Figure 10.7.

12. Similarly, a previous study that measured the concentration index (Herfindahl-Hirschman Index) of export commodities in some Asian countries (Kurniati et al. 2008) showed that Indonesia's HHI was the lowest (0.17), while Thailand, Malaysia and Singapore were 0.25, 0.27 and 0.34 respectively, meaning that the export commodities of Indonesia were more diversified, and exports commodities of Singapore were more concentrated on certain products. The higher the product concentration, the higher the impact of a specific industry shock transmitted.

REFERENCES

Aizenman, J. and I. Noy. "Endogenous Financial and Trade Openness". NBER Working Paper 10496, 2004.

Bank Indonesia. *Masyarakat Ekonomi ASEAN 2015: Memperkuat Sinergi ASEAN ditengah Kompetisi Global.* Jakarta, 2008.

Baxter, M. and R. King. "Measuring Business Cycle: Approximate Band Pass Filters for Economic Time Series". *Review of Economics and Statistics* 81 (1999): 575–93.

Cheung, et al. "Measuring Economic Integration: The Case of Asian Economies". BIS Paper No. 42, 2008.

Chinn, Menzie D. and Hiro Ito. "A New Measure of Financial Openness". *Journal of Comparative Policy Analysis,* May 2007.

Choe, J.I.. "An Impact of Economic Integration through Trade: On Business Cycles for 10 East Asian Countries". *Journal of Asian Economics* 12 (2001): 569–86.

Deardorff, V. Alan. "Determinant of Bilateral Trade: Does Gravity Work in a Neoclassic World?". In *Regionalization of the World Economy*, edited by Jeffrey A. Frankel. Chicago: University of Chicago Press, 1998.

Frankel, J. and A. Rose. "The Endogeneity of the Optimum Currency Area Criteria". *Economic Journal* 108 (1998): 1009–25.

Garcia-Herrero, A. and J.M. Ruiz. "Do Trade and Financial Linkages Foster Business Cycle Synchronization in a Small Economy?". Banco de Espana, Documentos de Trabajo 0810, 2008.

Grubel, H.G. and Lloyd, P.J. "The Empirical Measurement of Intra-Industry Trade". *Economic Record* 47, no. 120 (1971): 494–517.

Heathcote, J. and F. Perri. "Financial Globalization and Real Regionalization". *Journal of Economic Theory* 119, no. 1 (2004): 207–43.

Helpman, E. and A. Razin. *A Theory of International Trade and Uncertainty*. New York: Academic Press, 1978.

Imbs, J. "The Real Effects of Financial Integration". *Journal of International Economics* 68, no. 2 (2006): 296–324.

———. "Trade, Finance, Specialization and Synchronization". *Review of Economic and Statistics* 86, no. 3 (2004): 723–34.

Inklaar, Robert, Richard Jong-A-Pin, and Jakob de Haan. "Trade and Business Cycle Synchronization in OECD Countries: A Re-examination". *European Economic Review* 52, 2008.

International Monetary Fund. *Direction of Trade Statistics*. Washington, D.C.: IMF, 2009.

———. *Direction of Trade Statistics*. Washington, D.C.: IMF, various years.

Kalemli-Ozcan, S., B. Sorensen, and O. Yosha. "Risk Sharing and Industrial Specialization: Regional and International Evidence". *American Economic Review* 93 (2003): 903–18.

Kose, A., E. Prasad and M. Terrones. "How Does Globalization Affect the Synchronization of Business Cycle?". *American Economic Review Papers and Proceedings* 93, no. 2 (2003): 57–62.

Kose, A. and K. Yi. "International Trade and Business Cycles: Is Vertical Specialization A Missing Link?". *American Economic Review Papers and Proceedings* 91 (2001): 57–62.

Kumakura, M. "Trade and Business Cycle Co-movements in Asia-Pacific". *Journal of Asian Economics* 17 (2006): 622–45.

Lane P. and G.M. Milesi-Ferretti. "The External Wealth of Nations Mark II: Revised and Extended Estimates of Foreign Assets and Liabilities, 1970–2004". IMF Working Paper WP/06/69, 2006.

Moneta, Fabio and Rasmus Ruffer. "Business Cycle Synchronization in East Asia". *Journal of Asian Economics* 20 (2009): 1–12.

Mongelli, Francesco Paolo. "New Views on the Optimum Currency Area Theory: What is EMU Telling Us?". ECB Working Paper No. 138, 2002.

Mundell, Robert A. "A Theory of Optimum Currency Areas". *American Economic Review* 51 (1961): 657–65.

Portes, R. and H. Rey. "The Determinant of Cross Border Equity Flows". *Journal of International Economics* 65, no. 2 (2005): 269–96.

Pradumna B. Rana. "Trade Intensity and Business Cycle Synchronization: The Case of East Asia". ADB Working Paper Series on Regional Economic Integration No. 10, 2007.

Rose, A. and M. Spiegel. "A Gravity Model of Sovereign Lending: Trade, Default, and Credit". IMF Staff Papers 51, 2004.

Shin, K. and C.H. Sohn. "Trade and Financial Integration in East Asia: Effects on Co-movements". *World Economy* 29, no. 12 (2006): 1649–69.

Shin, K. and Wang Y. "Trade Integration and Business Cycle Co-movements: The Case of Korea with Other Asian Countries". *Japan and the World Economy* 16 (2004): 213–30.

———. "Trade Integration and Business Cycle Synchronization in East Asia". *Asian Economic Papers* 2 (2003): 1–20.

Appendix A

INDONESIA — ASEAN-4

Dependent Variables	Business Cycle Correlation (TSLS)	Trade Links (TSLS)	Financial Links (OLS)	Differences in Production Structure (OLS)
Constant	14.848** (2.819)	−2.285** (−2.041)	−0.939 (−0.216)	0.060 (0.725)
Trade Link	4.872*** (3.135)		1.053 (1.940)*	0.089*** (3.060)
Financial Link	1.819 (1.229)	0.164* (1.657)		
Differences in Production Structure	(−4.693)** (−2.538)	0.7193 (0.812)		
Inflation Differential	−0.621 (−1.028)			
Oil Price	−3.432 (−1.649)			
Dummy Crisis (1998 = 1, 2008 = 1)	−2.543** (−2.251)	0.145 (0.776)	0.801 (1.576)	
Gravity			0.537 (2.981)***	
Financial Openness			2.107 (2.093)**	
Lag Dependent Variable		0.613*** (2.669)		0.668 (6.688)***
R squared	0.56	0.79	0.54	0.79
DW stat	2.43	1.65	1.83	1.74

Notes: (1) ASEAN-4 consists of Singapore, Malaysia, the Philippines, and Thailand.
(2) Based on Hausman specification error test results, there are no simultaneity problems in financial links and production structure equations, hence those equations are solved using OLS.
(3) t-statistics in parentheses.
(4) * significant at 10 per cent; ** significant at 5 per cent; *** significant at 1 per cent
(5) All variables measured in logs except dummy variables.

Source: Authors' calculation.

Appendix B

INDONESIA — SINGAPORE

Dependent Variables	Business Cycle Correlation (TSLS)	Trade Links (TSLS)	Financial Links (OLS)	Differences in Production Structure (OLS)
Constant	13.946** (2.635)	−2.350*** (−3.527)	−1.529 (−0.415)	0.268* (1.737)
Trade Link	3.145** (2.414)		1.117 (3.935)***	0.096** (2.361)
Financial Link	−0.045 (−0.106)	0.069** (2.259)		
Differences in Production Structure	2.047 (1.383)	−0.548* (−1.841)		
Inflation Differential	0.108 (0.278)			
Oil Price	−0.885 (−1.025)			
Dummy Crisis (1998 = 1, 2008 = 1)	−2.403*** (−2.960)	0.446*** (3.547)	0.611* 1.946	
Gravity			0.612*** (4.644)	
Financial Openness			1.836** (2.387)	
Lag Dependent Variable		0.577*** (5.024)		0.840*** (11.251)
R squared	0.59	0.76	0.55	0.85
DW stat	1.62	1.87	1.86	1.72

Notes: (1) Based on Hausman specification error test results, there are no simultaneity problems in financial links and production structure equations, hence those equations are solved using OLS.
(2) t-statistics in parentheses
(3) *significant at 10 per cent; ** significant at 5 per cent; *** significant at 1 per cent
(4) All variables measured in logs except dummy variables.

Source: Authors' calculation.

Appendix C

INDONESIA — MALAYSIA

Dependent Variables	Business Cycle Correlation (TSLS)	Trade Links (TSLS)	Financial Links (OLS)	Differences in Production Structure (OLS)
Constant	7.074*** (3.513)	−1.305 (−0.873)	1.914 (0.323)	0.202 (1.522)
Trade Link	0.617** (2.352)		−0.338 (−0.754)	0.099** (2.709)
Financial Link	−0.931*** (−3.262)	0.049* (1.934)		
Differences in Production Structure	1.504 (1.570)	0.486 (1.207)		
Inflation Differential	0.326* (1.934)			
Oil Price	1.244*** (4.546)			
Dummy Crisis (1998 = 1, 2008 = 1)	0.243 (1.135)	0.248 (1.416)	1.006** (2.333)	
Gravity			0.800*** (3.053)	
Financial Openness			−0.298 (−0.197)	
Lag Dependent Variable		0.714*** (4.545)		0.701*** (6.316)
R squared	0.89	0.88	0.45	0.87
DW stat	1.62	2.40	1.77	1.85

Notes: (1) Based on Hausman specification error test results, there are no simultaneity problems in financial links and production structure equations, hence those equations are solved using OLS.
(2) t-statistics in parentheses
(3) * significant at 10 per cent; ** significant at 5 per cent; *** significant at 1 per cent
(4) All variables measured in logs except dummy variables.

Source: Authors' calculation.

Appendix D

INDONESIA — THE PHILIPPINES

Dependent Variables	Business Cycle Correlation (TSLS)	Trade Links (TSLS)	Financial Links (OLS)	Differences in Production Structure (OLS)
Constant	3.305 (1.113)	−1.325 (−1.273)	−3.048 (−0.645)	−0.643*** (−2.909)
Trade Link	1.185*** (3.927)		0.423 (0.963)	0.155*** (5.450)
Financial Link	−0.216 −1.627	0.012* (2.012)		
Differences in Production Structure	−2.321 (−1.044)	−1.554 (−0.922)		
Inflation Differential	0.035 (0.278)			
Oil Price	0.648** (2.633)			
Dummy Crisis (1998 = 1, 2008 = 1)	−0.141 (−1.021)	0.378* (1.929)	1.017* (1.969)	
Gravity			0.560** (2.189)	
Financial Openness			2.613* (1.860)	
Lag Dependent Variable		1.069*** (3.627)		0.669*** (6.986)
R squared	0.73	0.76	0.53	0.64
DW stat	1.50	2.07	1.76	1.84

Notes: (1) Based on Hausman specification error test results, there are no simultaneity problems in financial links and production structure equations, hence those equations are solved using OLS.
(2) t-statistics in parentheses
(3) * significant at 10 per cent; ** significant at 5 per cent; *** significant at 1 per cent
(4) All variables measured in logs except dummy variables.
Source: Authors' calculation.

Appendix E

INDONESIA — THAILAND

Dependent Variables	Business Cycle Correlation (TSLS)	Trade Links (TSLS)	Financial Links (TSLS)	Differences in Production Structure (OLS)
Constant	3.224 (0.958)	0.160 (0.147)	12.783 (1.606)	−0.351 (−1.686)
Trade Link	0.895*** (2.906)		−1.618 (−1.578)	0.000 (0.010)
Financial Link	−0.363 (−0.724)	−0.186 (−1.463)		
Differences in Production Structure	−1.520* (−1.978)	−1.991*** (−2.212)		
Inflation Differential	0.298 (0.957)			
Oil Price	0.517 (0.728)			
Dummy Crisis (1998 = 1, 2008 = 1)	0.092 (0.214)	0.642*** (3.164)	1.007* (1.962)	
Gravity			1.246*** (2.926)	
Financial Openness			−4.803 (−1.432)	
Lag Dependent Variable		0.973*** −15.596		0.658*** (3.887)
R squared	0.72	0.94	0.52	0.50
DW stat	1.56	2.30	1.91	1.60

Notes: (1) Based on Hausman specification error test results, there is no simultaneity problems in production structure equations, hence that equation is solved using OLS.
(2) t-statistics in parentheses
(3) * significant at 10 per cent; ** significant at 5 per cent; *** significant at 1 per cent
(4) All variables measured in logs except dummy variables.

Source: Authors' calculation.

11
Governance and Economic Performance

Muljana Soekarni and Sjamsul Arifin

INTRODUCTION

With the ending of the Cold War, governance has received increasing attention, which has in turn changed the global geopolitical game. Since then, official donor countries and creditors have started to impose sound macroeconomic policies, a healthy regulatory environment, more transparent and accountable public institutions, and the protection of property and investors' rights. These factors have become essential prerequisites for attracting foreign direct investment and accessing financial markets on reasonable terms. Another factor underlying the rising importance of governance is the spread of democratic practices in the late 1980s all the way through the decade of 1990s. On the other hand, the absence of the rule of law and accountable system of governance led to rent seeking and corruption (Abed and Gupta 2002).

The term "governance" has numerous definitions as well as interpretations. Peters (2008) suggested that governance refers to the provision of some means of collective steering for the economy and society. He also recognized that there are various interpretations as to what governance really refers to. To reflect the different characteristics, various adjectives have been added to the basic concept of governance, such as: network governance, focusing on the capacity of networks to deliver governance; new governance network, meaning ability to cope with complexity and respond to social changes; good governance, denoting the reduction of corruption and the creation of greater accountability, commonly used by international donors; and finally, quality of governance, mainly used by scholars to explain the characteristics of a political system in its efforts to promote good living standards.

The World Bank (1992) defined governance as the exercise of economic, political, and administrative authority in managing a country's affairs at all levels incorporating the aspects of economic governance (decision-making processes that affect a country's economic activities), political governance (the process of decision-making to formulate policies), and administrative governance (the system of policy implementation). Moreover, it considers participation, rule of law, transparency, responsiveness (to stakeholders), equity, effectiveness, and efficiency as major components of governance.

Kaufmann, Kraay, and Mastrussi (2009) defined governance as the traditions and institutions by which the authority in a country is exercised. This includes how governments are elected, supervised, and replaced; the government's capacity to formulate and implement sound policies; and the observance of civil rights as well as the quality of the institutions in managing the economy and social interactions. The World Bank also conducts a regular survey on World Governance Indicators, measuring governance in the following six dimensions: voice and accountability; political stability and absence of violence; government effectiveness; regulatory quality; rule of law; and control of corruption.

Shimomura (2003) summarized the key indicators of governance as following: accountability, transparency, openness in exercising power of government; rule of law, competent and credible judiciary; predictable public conduct; institutionalized capacity; corruption control; and finally control of military expenditure.

In view of the complexity, broadness, and often vagueness of the definition, researches have been widely conducted to establish the relation of governance to economic growth and per capita income, hence to improved welfare. The quality of governance is supposed to have a significant bearing on economic growth. However, most of these studies are qualitative in nature and only a few are based on empirical evidence. This chapter attempts to examine empirically the impact of governance on economic growth, per capita income, and foreign direct investment (FDI) using data from thirty countries.

A new feature of the statistical analysis is the use of unobservable (latent) variables. Most economic analyses assume that the variables are observed, though there are many unobservable variables. Or, they limit their analysis by using only the observed determinants, assuming that those observables are determinants of the unobservable variables. Nevertheless, the observable variables may not function as determinants, but as indicators of the unobservable variables. Indicators are variables that are influenced by unobservable variables, rather than being the ones determining unobservable variables.

This chapter also reviews the governance activities in Indonesia which were officially introduced by the establishment of the National Committee on Corporate Governance after the crisis of 1997. The analysis of governance itself is another feature of this chapter, contributing to a new perspective in examining Indonesia's economic performance. In other words, this chapter focuses on governance, which is the process of producing the output, rather than the output itself.

This chapter is organized into five sections. The next section reviews the role of governance in economic theories, particularly from institutional economics. Then, in Section 3 it discusses Indonesia's experiences in conducting good governance, as well as examines its position relative to other ASEAN countries. Subsequently, in Section 4, it performs a statistical analysis on the impact of governance on economic performance, controlled by the competitiveness in twelve countries. And finally, the chapter closes with a conclusion, including policy recommendations and suggestions for further research.

GOVERNANCE IN ECONOMIC THEORIES

In economic literature, the origin of governance can be traced back to institutional economics which deals with transaction costs, revealing the shortcomings of neoclassical assumptions. Particularly, as described in North (1992), neoclassical theory was not designed to account for the process of economic change as a complete theory of economic change needs the integration of other disciplines such as demographics, stock of knowledge, and institutions. Furthermore, economic performance is largely determined by the kind and quality of institutions that support markets.

Pioneered by the work of Coase (1937), there has been growing interest within the social sciences, especially economics and politics that integrate theoretical and empirical research investigating the role of institutions in promoting or hampering economic growth. It includes works in transaction costs, political economy, property rights, hierarchy and organization, and public choice.

Dethier (1999) conducted a survey to examine the transmission channel through which governance influences economic performance. He took the view that governance is the science of government behaviour dealing with historical, cultural, social, and political determinants. In his argument, economic theory emphasizes efficiency, while political and sociological theories emphasize the role of authority, beliefs, and ideology. Welfare distribution needs the combination of both disciplines in order to provide a valuable explanation to political economic questions. Dethier further argued that political and market failures are rooted in the same problems, namely informational and transactional problems. As a result, the analysis of governance needs an interdisciplinary approach.

Khan (2007) mentioned that governance may be used to gauge the divergence in economic performance across developing countries. He stated a difference between market enhancing governance and growth enhancing governance. The former, he argued, deals with the role of governance in minimizing transaction costs to deliver an efficient market. The main objectives of this kind of governance include: achieving and maintaining stable property rights; maintaining good rule of law and efficient contract enforcement; minimizing expropriation risks; and minimizing rent seeking and corruption. Growth enhancing governance, on the other hand, deals mainly with government role in developing countries to minimize high transaction costs. It pays special attention to the effectiveness of institutions in speeding up the transfer of assets and resources to productive sectors, and acceleration of the absorption and learning of technologies. The main objectives of growth enhancing governance are: transferring assets and resources to productive sectors; providing incentives for achieving technology acquisition and productivity enhancement; and maintaining political stability in social transformation.

Sachs (2005) argued that there are eight major factors hampering economic growth, with bad governance being one of them.[1] Economic development requires a government-oriented approach towards development, including financing infrastructure projects, providing social services, creating an environment conducive to investment, and enforcing law and order. When a government does not perform these tasks well, the economy will deteriorate and in an extreme case, a "state failure" may arise, which may lead to a destructive spiral of instability.

Meanwhile, Prasad et al. (2003) initially intended to prove whether there is a relationship between financial integration and economic growth. He found that while it is difficult to find a strong and robust effect of financial integration on economic growth, there is some evidence of a "threshold effect". The threshold effect determines a country's "absorptive capacity", identified in terms of human capital, depth of domestic financial market, quality of governance, and macroeconomic policies. In this regard, some studies (Aitken and Harrison 1999; Bailliu 2000; and Arteta, Eichengreen, and Wyplosz, 2001) showed that foreign capital flows do not seem to generate positive productivity spillovers to countries with relatively low absorptive capacity. Instead, positive spillovers are more likely detected in countries with relatively high levels of absorptive capacity. Furthermore, Reisen and De Soto (2010) concluded that the quality of governance affects a country's ability to benefit from international capital flows — that FDI inclined to go to countries with good governance.

With the spread of democratization all over the world, Rivera-Batiz (2002) examined how democracy affects long-run economic growth through its impact on the quality of governance of the country, and sought to establish the link between democracy and quality of governance. The result showed that the quality of governance is substantially higher in the more democratic countries. In addition, democracy is a key determinant of growth, provided that it is associated with improved governance. His findings also show that stronger democratic institutions affect governance by constraining the actions of corrupt officials.

Shimomura (2003) found that since the turn of the 1990s, aid donors have become more demanding with respect to good governance, democracy, and the protection of basic human rights. He stated that these factors are considered pivotal for sustained economic development. Shimomura's view in earlier researches provides evidence that most empirical studies on the relationship between governance and development use regression analysis with mixed findings. He argued that the mainstream approach has three basic shortcomings, namely: a mismatch between the problem structure and analytical tools, inadequate attention to stages of development, and an overly simplistic approach to development. Therefore, Shimomura sought to address these shortcomings through focusing on ASEAN countries and attempted to supplement the mainstream approach through case studies.

With regard to the relationship between governance and the financial crisis in Asia, the implementation of governance, especially corporate governance, has been partly an important requirement of economic changes in solving the financial crisis. As mentioned in Sato (2010), a study conducted by the Asian Development Bank (ADB) on five Asian countries suggested that the absence of good corporate governance could bring about a serious impact on a country's economy and even spread to its neighbouring countries. This report shows how weakness in corporate governance had been one of the main factors causing the 1997–98 Asian financial crisis. In other words, countries that had good governance could survive the economic crisis. Moreover, the lack of transparency in economic governance was also partially responsible for the crisis.

INDONESIA'S EXPERIENCES

Transition in Governance

According to Syakhroza (2007), from 1997 to 2007 Indonesia was said to have been in the stage of governance awareness. The term "aware" in the stage of awareness refers to understanding the existence of several aspects of corporate governance. These aspects are achieved through socialization and communication with all the stakeholders in various organizations on the need to adopt principles of good governance. Indonesia had taken a number of concrete actions involving various parties in this period and had therefore passed the stage and entered the stage of conformity, which was predicted to last until 2016.

The stage of conformity involves deep understanding of issues and the implementation of corporate governance so that communication becomes more important. Here, all shareholders should have the willingness to adopt changes, mindsets beyond compliance, and the commitment to implement good corporate governance.

In discussing governance in Indonesia, following McCawley's framework (2005), we distinguish between issues of governance at the macro and micro levels. Issues at the macro level include constitutional reforms and the overall role of the government itself. Governance of micro issues, on the other hand, involves institutions, especially state owned enterprises (SOEs) and commercial firms, including banks, and is defined as good corporate governance (GCG).

Corruption and Good Governance

As far as governance and corruption are concerned, the International Monetary Fund (2008) found that the relationship between the two is closely linked since an environment characterized by poor governance offers greater incentive and scope for corruption. Researches on the impact of anti-corruption reforms in Indonesia have shown that so far there has been no effect on actual reduction of corruption. For example, the study by Hamilton-Hart (2001), pointed out that there are two bodies dedicated to monitoring and fighting corruption — the Indonesian Ombudsman Commission (KON) and the State Official's Assets Auditing Commission (KPKPN). These two bodies are not given adequate funding or effective power by the government to conduct thorough investigations to prosecute corrupt officials.

The study conducted by The Partnership for Governance Reforms in Indonesia (PGRI), found that 75.0 per cent of the public regarded public sector corruption to be very common, and 65.0 per cent of the respondents reported that they had experienced corruption involving public officials. It was also found that corruption exacts a high cost from society as up to 5.0 per cent of household incomes was used to pay bribes to public officials. Moreover, 35.0 per cent of business enterprises reported that they had not made new investments due to the high costs caused by corruption (Sumarto et al. 2004).

Meanwhile, the Institute for Economic and Social Research (2004) found that regional autonomy increased business uncertainty and the cost of doing business at the local level. It also found that unofficial payments (bribes) made to government officials do not necessarily reduce economic efficiency. Rather, it increases efficiency, since businesses can cut time and paperwork when they need to deal with government officials.

The Regional Autonomy Implementation Monitoring Committee (KPPOD) in 2002 selected ninety regions to examine their business climate by measuring each region's security, economic potential, human resources, local bureaucratic culture, quality of infrastructure, local government regulations, and regional finances. It found that regions that attract more businesses are more likely to show better security, a better local bureaucracy culture and government regulations, and better human resources, confirming the assertion that good governance is a necessary condition for businesses to invest in a region (Sumarto et al. 2004).

One of the important measures to eradicate corruption in Indonesia was the establishment of the Corruption Eradication Commission (KPK). The legal basis for the formation of this commission was Law no. 30/ 2002, on the Corruption Eradication Commission. KPK has been given a mandate to conduct corruption eradication professionally, intensively, and continuously in order to create a just, prosperous, and peaceful society as corruption tends to have a negative impact on the state's budget and economy, obstructing the national development. To make this commission more effective, it receives reports from the public as well (Komisi Pemberantasan Korupsi 2009).

KPK's duties, authority, and obligations are as follow: to coordinate with institutions authorized to combat acts of corruption; to supervise institutions authorized to combat acts of corruption; to conduct preliminary investigations as well as investigations and prosecutions against acts of corruption; to conduct corruption prevention activities; and finally, to conduct the monitoring of state governance. From these duties we see that KPK is not only supposed to monitor the state of governance, but also conduct corruption prevention, among other things by recording and cross-checking the Wealth Reports of State Officials (LHKPN). Out of 51,803 mandatory reports, 47,204 were reported and 41,640 were announced to the public in 2008.

In 2008, preliminary investigation activities were conducted in seventy cases. Investigations were conducted in fifty-three cases, including seven cases carried over from 2007 and forty-six new cases in 2008. As for sentences, twenty-three cases were prosecuted in 2008. Furthermore, the number of investigations, in 2008, in particular, was almost double compared with that of 2007 which had only twenty-nine cases.

With the existence of KPK, some of the activities that were formerly considered normal business practices have changed. For example, gifts received by government or state enterprise officials in excess of a certain amount in value have to be reported, and approval has to be sought from KPK. Otherwise, they may be considered a kind of gratification which is against the law. Some internal operating procedures which are prone to corruption, such as those relating to procurements and business travel, have been revised and improved to make the procedures more prudent and transparent.

The Financial Crisis and Good Corporate Governance

The experience from the 1997–98 crisis showed that the absence of one of the governance principles, namely transparency, had led to an unfavourable perception of the country's economy. In 1997 many countries in Asia failed to publish complete economic data such as foreign exchange reserves, short-term foreign debts, and in particular, private debts. Even if they published the data, they did not do it frequently. For example, the real sector data was only available on a yearly basis, not on a quarterly basis. Accordingly, economic analyses were not based on the most complete and recent data; thereby, prompting investors' herd behaviour which finally brought about a contagion effect.

In Indonesia, the concept of good corporate governance (GCG) was also introduced by the Indonesian Government and the International Monetary Fund in an effort to recover the Indonesian economy from the 1997–98 crisis. This effort was put in a Letter of Intent, signed by both parties.

During the most recent global crisis, the importance of governance became more marked. The financial crisis was triggered by speculative derivatives that originated from U.S. subprime mortgages as there was inadequate governance regulations for new financial products. Today, all countries realize the importance of governance for sophisticated financial products. Even, Budiono, the then governor of Bank Indonesia and currently vice-president of the Republic of Indonesia, mentioned that the financial sector, especially banks, should return to its basic functions and role as a financial intermediary, rather than an intermediary for speculative activities (Boediono 2009). In addition, we view that risk management is also another form of governance that should prudently be implemented by commercial banks and other financial institutions whereby central banks and other financial regulators can ensure its effective enforcement.

In order to create a stronger banking structure, in early 2004, Bank Indonesia launched the Indonesian Banking Architecture (IBA), a programme to be introduced over the following ten years. The IBA consists of six pillars, namely: a sound structure for banks, an effective regulation system, independent and effective bank supervision, a strong/sound banking industry, adequate supporting infrastructure, and consumer protection (see Figure 11.1).

FIGURE 11.1
The Architecture's Six Pillars

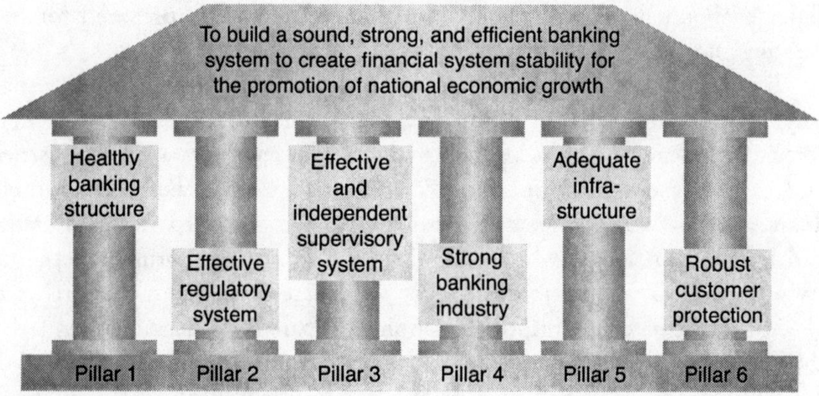

Source: Bank Indonesia (2003).

The vision of this programme is to create a strong, sound, and efficient banking system with the expectation of creating a stable financial system in order to support national economic growth. Moreover, to reduce asymmetric information between banks and their customers, Bank Indonesia also established the Information Credit Bureau in order to enable banks to get better information regarding their customers.

There are three documents that may be used as references in implementing the GCG by commercial banks in Indonesia. The first is "Enhancing Corporate Governance for Banking Organization", published for the first time in 1999 by the Basel Committee on Banking Supervision and Bank for International Settlements (BIS), and further revised in February 2006. The second is "Guidelines for Good Corporate Governance of Indonesian Banks", published by the National Committee on Corporate Governance Policy in January 2004. And the third is Bank Indonesia Regulation no. 8/4/PBI/2006, in conjunction with no. 8/14/PBI/2006 concerning the Implementation of Good Corporate Governance for Commercial Banks, respectively enacted on 30 January and 5 October 2006.

Out of the aforementioned documents, the one issued by Bank Indonesia, as the regulator for supervising banks in Indonesia, is the only document that is legally binding. The guidelines published by the Basel Committee are morally imperative since members of the BIS are from central banks. Meanwhile, the guidelines published by the National Committee are not voluntarily binding or imperative for commercial banks and are instead merely used as references.

In addition to these three documents, there is also a fourth document as a complement entitled "Policy Brief on Corporate Governance of Banks in Asia", published in June 2006 by the Organization for Economic Cooperation and Development (OECD). This document is especially prepared for the banking industry in Asia.

From the operational point of view, banks have two specific features that may not be found in other industries (Levine 2003 and 2005). The first is that banks are relatively less transparent compared with other industries due to asymmetric information. For example, as will be seen in their financial reports, a large percentage of their assets are in the form of credit and longer-term loans, while their liabilities are in the form of deposits, savings accounts, and current accounts, which are in the main of short-term maturity. Mismatched, imprudent, non-transparent management and the abuse of power have brought about bankruptcy to a number of banks.

The second is that regulator intervention has been relatively high both at the macro and micro level. The Basel Chairman, Jaime Caruana

(2005), stated that corporate governance's coverage was broader than the Basel II Framework. He further elaborated that Basel II contributed to the implementation of effective corporate governance through the three Cs, namely, Control, Culture, and Clarity.

With the implementation of GCG, the performance of bank lending is expected to be more favourable as banks will be better managed and credit expansion will be more robust and reach a wider customer basis.

Therefore, it is necessary to implement improvements in the banking sector immediately. In this case, Bank Indonesia has continued to make efforts to improve the implementation of GCG in banks through self-assessment or internal evaluation, in accordance with Bank Indonesia Regulation of 2006, subject to annual review.

Complying with article 65 of Bank Indonesia Regulation no. 8/4/PBI/2006 concerning Implementation of Good Corporate Governance (GCG) for Commercial Banks, banks conducted self-assessments on their implementation of GCG in 2007. The assessment undertaken by either banks or supervisors on 110 out of 130 commercial banks at the time resulted in a composite value lower than 2.5. This shows that, in general, the implementation of GCG by banks was classified as "good". A comparison of the assessments by banks and supervisors shows that whether in composite value or each factor's value, the assessment conducted by banks is better than the assessment conducted by supervisors.

Assessed by the banks, foreign banks had the best performance in terms of the implementation of GCB (1.515). The worst (2.174) were banks classified as joint banks. On the other hand, assessed by supervisors, Shariah banks performed best (1.6735), and local development banks were the weakest (2.652).

One of the criteria of governance — fairness and asymmetric information between banks and their customers — has not been fully met in Indonesia. Currently, Bank Indonesia is establishing a Credit Bureau Information to improve bank information about their customers.

For the implementation of GCG in state owned enterprises (SOEs), a state minister/head of Capital Investment and State Owned Enterprise Development Board has issued a decree, no. KEP-23/M-PM.PBUMN/2000, concerning the development of GCG practices in limited liability companies. This decree describes GCG as a sound corporate principle that is applied in corporate management and merely implemented to maintain corporate interest in the efforts of achieving corporate goals and objectives (Khairandy and Malik 2007).

Indonesia's agenda for putting GCG into practice is presently divided into three activities, namely, adopting the national policy, improving the regulation framework, and developing initiatives in the private sector. In implementing GCG in Indonesia, the National Committee had issued some guidelines for GCG in 2001. These guidelines were then followed by the issuance of the Guidelines by Sector, Guidelines for Audit Committee, and Guidelines for Independent Commissioners in 2004. The corporate management reform under GCG principles in SOEs was confirmed by the enactment of a SOE ministerial decree concerning the establishment of an Audit Committee for State Owned Enterprises on 4 June 2002.

Another relevant ministerial decree was no. Kep-117/M-MBU/2002, which, among other things, stipulated three issues. The first is that corporate governance is a process and structure to be employed by SOE organ in order to enhance corporate success and accountability in realizing the long-term value of shareholders. Under the relevant laws and ethics, corporations must persistently take other shareholders into consideration. The second is that SOEs are required to apply GCG and/or use GCG consistently as the operational basis. And the third is that GCG principles shall include transparency, self-reliance, accountability, responsibility, and fairness.

It is worth noting however, that as concluded in Khairandy and Malik (2007), GCG in Indonesia has not been well implemented yet. There are some problems hampering the application of GCG in Indonesia. Four of these are corporate practices, domination of shareholder, ineffectiveness of the performance of regulators and financial institutions, and weak protection of creditors and investors.

To this end, since banks and other financial companies are concerned, problems in non-bank and non-financial companies are also problems for regulators that monitor the implementation and imposition of sanctions of GCG.

Indonesia in ASEAN

Indonesia's relative position among the five ASEAN countries with respect to the overall competitiveness index and governance can be seen in Figures 11.2 and 11.3 respectively. Figure 11.2 shows that out of 134 countries, Indonesia was in the 55th position in the overall competitiveness index.[2] Among the five Southeast Asian countries, Singapore was the best, scoring top ranking, and Indonesia was fourth. Similarly, in terms of governance, as seen in Figure 11.3, Indonesia was also ranked fourth, and Singapore, first.[3]

FIGURE 11.2
Overall Index

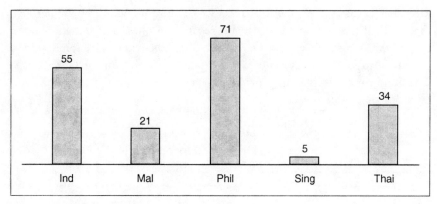

Source: World Economic Forum (2008).

FIGURE 11.3
Governance

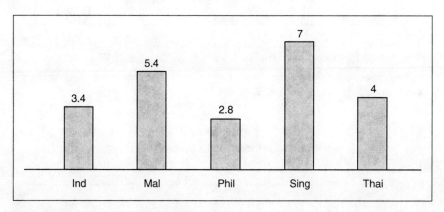

Source: World Economic Forum (2008).

Figure 11.4 indicates that the overall competitiveness index is associated with per capita GDP in the sense that the more competitive the country, the higher is its income per capita. In this regard, the overall competitiveness index of Indonesia (inverted scale) was associated with a lower income level, whereas Singapore, with its higest overall index, also has the highest income level. Furthermore, the lowest overall index was seen in the Philippines, which also has the lowest per capita income.

A further observation on the relation between governance and per capita GDP also suggests that among the ASEAN countries, the ones that carried a better score in governance were the ones with the higher per capita GDP (see Figure 11.5). In this regard, Indonesia's governance index of 3.4 was associated with a GDP of US$1,925, while the highest index (7) in Singapore was associated with a per capita income of US$35,163. The implication is that improving governance and promoting economic growth can reinforce each other.

FIGURE 11.4
Overall Index and Income

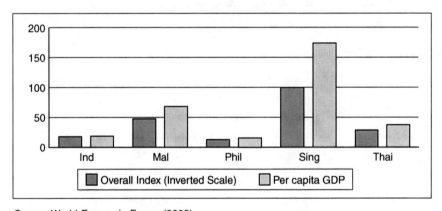

Source: World Economic Forum (2008).

FIGURE 11.5
Governance and Income

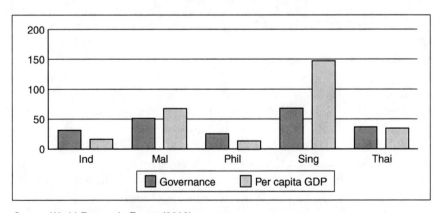

Source: World Economic Forum (2008).

As mentioned earlier, the concept of governance covers various aspects, definitions, and elements. Nevertheless, all definitions have certain elements in common. In this chapter, the elements of governance specifically refer to those of the World Economic Forum (2008), which mentioned eighteen elements of governance. However, for simplification, this chapter reduces the number to twelve: Property Rights, Intellectual Property Rights, Investor Protection, Public Trust of Politicians, Judicial Independence, Reliability of Police Service, Wastefulness in Government Spending, Burden of Government Regulation, Legal Framework Efficiency, Favouritism in Decisions Made by Government Officials, Strength of Auditing and Reporting Standard, and Firms Ethical Behaviour. As shown in Figure 11.6, we group the twelve elements into four variables. The first is the variable on "legal certainty", indicated by property rights, intellectual property rights, and investor protection. The second is the one on "public trustworthiness", indicated by public trust of politicians, judicial independence, and the reliability of the police service. The third is "government efficiency", measured by wastefulness in government spending, burden of government regulation, and legal framework efficiency. Finally, the fourth is "transparency", measured by favouritism in decisions made by government officials, strength of auditing and reporting standard, and the ethical behaviour of firms.

With these twelve elements, Singapore had the highest score among the five ASEAN countries, as it had the highest score for all twelve elements observed. As with other indicators, Indonesia ranks fourth and the Philippines ranks the lowest. Indonesia's relative strength mainly rests on the "government efficiency" and "transparency" variables, with each having a score of 3.8. The score of "government efficiency" is 3.8, the average of the scores on Spending Waste (4.4), Regulatory Burden (3.5), and Legal Framework (3.6); while the score of "transparency" is the average of the scores of Policy-making (3.2), Auditing and Reporting Standard (4.6), and Ethical Behaviour (3.7). However, it should be noted that the score of "3.8" out of "8.0" indicates that Indonesia's performance on governance, including on those two variables, is less than satisfactory.

STATISTICAL ANALYSIS

Variables and Hypotheses

In most research in economics, governance is treated as a dummy variable when, in fact, it is an unobservable and abstract concept (Shimomura 2003). In addition, researchers frequently use proxies that may not be

FIGURE 11.6
Impact of Governance on Economic Performance

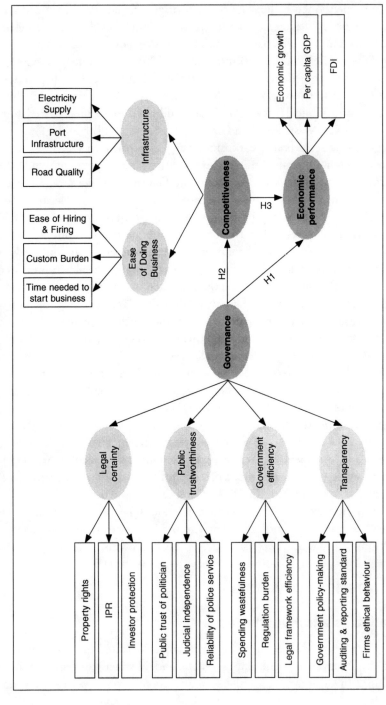

Source: Created by the authors.

directly linked to governance. For example, Rivera-Batiz (2002) used the extent to which a country is open to international trade as a proxy for the quality of governance, though governance is much more than simply free trade. The use of the degree of capital account liberalization also only indirectly measures governance. In fact, Prasad et al. (2003) showed that the composition of capital flows to a country depends on its absorptive capacity, which is in turn affected by governance.

To overcome these shortcomings, Shimomura sought to address this limitation by conducting a case study. Although the method he used has the advantage of in-depth analysis concerning a particular topic, some limitations still exist. For example, this method cannot claim external validity, so the findings cannot be generalized (Trochim 1999; Zikmund 2003).

The statistical model employed here examines the impact of good governance on economic performance, controlled by competitiveness. It uses data from thirty countries — fifteen industrial countries and fifteen emerging markets — taking into account their geographical representation and covering the period 2008–09. The industrial countries selected include the United States, Switzerland, Denmark, Sweden, Singapore, Germany, the Netherlands, Japan, Canada, Hongkong, the United Kingdom, Korea, France, Taiwan, and Australia. The developing countries include: Brunei, Cambodia, Indonesia, Malaysia, the Philippines, Thailand, Vietnam, China, India, Pakistan, Egypt, Argentina, Brazil, Mexico, and Colombia.

As governance comprises an institutional environment within which individuals, firms, and governments interact to generate income and wealth in the economy, good governance in this chapter is hypothesized to affect economic performance positively, directly and/or indirectly through competitiveness. For example, a government's attitude toward markets, freedoms, and efficiency of operations may be a very important determinant of economic growth; excessive bureaucracy and red tape, over-regulation, corruption, dishonesty in dealing with public contracts, lack of transparency and trustworthiness, and/or political dependence on the judicial system, may impose significant economic costs to businesses; private institutions may constitute an important element in the process of creating wealth; private sector transparency can be essential for businesses as it ensures access to information in a timely manner; and an economy is likely to do well if its businesses are run honestly and abide by strong ethical practices.

Competitiveness, defined as a set of institutions, policies, and factors that determine the level of productivity of a country (World Economic Forum 2008), is one of the key factors explaining an economy's growth potential. The best possible environment for the exchange of goods requires minimum impediments to business activities such as distortionary or burdensome taxes, and restrictive and discriminatory rules on FDI. Efficiency and flexibility of labour markets are also critical for ensuring that workers are allocated to their most efficient use for the economy, and that the labour market has the flexibility to rapidly mobilize workers, including hiring and dismissing workers at a low cost. A well developed infrastructure reduces the effect of distance between regions. Furthermore, effective modes of transportation for goods, people, and services, enable entrepreneurs to get their goods to the market in a secure and timely manner. Economies also depend on electricity supplies that are free of interruptions and shortages so that businesses and factories can work unimpeded.

Governance and competitiveness are expected to contribute to sustained high economic growth. Sustained high growth over an extended period of time will result in high income per capita for a country. Therefore, it is expected that the outcome from having governance is associated with high economic growth and per capita GDP. The rate of economic growth, however, is expected to be different between industrial and developing countries. In industrial countries, because the income base is well above that of developing countries, the rate of economic growth is lower than that in developing countries. In other words, the rate of economic growth in developing countries is expected to be higher, because of their low income base. Good governance and competitiveness imply a favourable business environment that does not discriminate between domestic and foreign investors. Therefore, FDI can also be used as another indicator of economic performance. The hypotheses for these are presented in Table 11.1.

The statistical model used in this chapter comprises three important variables: governance, competitiveness, and economic performance. Governance is an unobservable, exogenous variable hypothesized to affect the competitiveness and economic performance of a country. Competitiveness is an unobservable endogenous variable hypothesized to be affected by governance, and, in turn, affects a country's economic performance. And lastly, economic performance is an unobservable endogenous variable hypothesized to be affected by both governance and competitiveness.

Governance is measured by four other unobservable variables, namely: legal certainty, public trustworthiness, government efficiency, and transparency. Each of these variables is indicated by three observable indicators. Legal certainty is measured by property rights, intellectual property rights, and investor protection; public trustworthiness, by public trust of politicians, judicial independence, and reliability of the police

TABLE 11.1
Hypotheses

H1	Governance has a positive and significant impact on economic performance.	
	H1a	The impact of governance on economic growth is smaller than that on per capita GDP in industrial countries.
	H1b	The impact of governance on economic growth is bigger than that on per capita GDP in developing countries.
H2	Governance has a positive and significant impact on competitiveness.	
H3	Governance has a positive and significant impact on economic performance through competitiveness.	

Source: Created by the authors.

service; government efficiency, by degree of spending wastefulness, regulation burden, and the legal framework's efficiency; and finally, transparency, by government policy-making, auditing and reporting standard, and firms' ethical behaviour.

Competitiveness is measured by two unobservable variables: ease of doing business and infrastructure. Each variable has three observable variables. Ease of doing business is indicated by ease of hiring and firing, the custom burden, and time needed to start a business; and infrastructure, by electricity supply, port infrastructure, and road quality.

And lastly, economic performance is indicated by three observable indicators: economic growth, per capita GDP, and FDI (see Figure 11.6).

Structural Equation Modelling (SEM)

Structural Equation Modelling (SEM) is a multivariate technique which combines aspects of multiple regression (for examining causal relationships) and factor analysis (for measuring unobservable variables) to estimate simultaneously a series of interrelated and dependent relationships (Hair et al. 1998). There are four reasons for considering SEM an appropriate model for this research. The first is that it consists of a set of causal relationships whereby the exogenous variables also become the endogenous variables so that they need to be solved simultaneously. Second, some variables consist of latent variables which are explained by other latent variables, with each of these being represented by a number of observed variables. Third, the data contain a combination of metric and non-metric data. Fourth, the model has more than one dependent variable.

SEM is considered to be a powerful model, increasingly used in research of behavioural sciences for the causal modelling of complex, multivariate data sets in which the researcher gathers multiple measures of proposed constructs (Geven, Straub, and Boudeau 2000). Similarly, the multivariate technique has also been applied by Yi (2003) to estimate the relationship between political institutions (consisting of political uncertainty, political stability, and political freedom) and economic performances. Contrary to the first generation statistical tools such as regression (for example the OLS, logit, anova, and manova), SEM enables researches to answer a set of interrelated research questions in a single, systematic, and comprehensive analysis, through simultaneously modelling the relationships among multiple independent and dependent constructs.

There are eight advantages to SEM (North Carolina State University 2005). First, compared with multiple regression, SEM has more flexible assumptions (particularly allowing interpretation even in the face of multicollinearity). Second, a confirmatory factor analysis is used to reduce measurement error by having observable indicators, rather than assuming observable variables to be determinants of unobservable variables. Third, SEM utilizes a graphical modelling interface. Fourth, SEM has the ability to test the overall models, rather than the coefficients individually. Fifth, SEM has the ability to test models with multiple dependent variables. Sixth, SEM is able to model mediating variables, rather than being restricted to an additive model such as in the OLS regression. Seventh, SEM has the ability to model error terms. Eighth, SEM is able to test coefficients across multiple variables between subject groups.

Source of Data

With the exception of economic growth, all data are collected from the Global Competitiveness Report of 2008–09, published by the World Economic Forum (2008). This report provides comparable data for 134 countries, covering twelve pillars of competitiveness, classified under three main categories: basic requirements, efficiency enhancers, and innovation and sophistication factors. All the data, with the exception of economic growth and per capita GDP, serve as observable indicators to measure unobservable variables, as shown in Table 11.2. They are non-metric data in the form of a Likert scale ranging from 1 to 8. The data on economic

TABLE 11.2
Variables, Constructs and Indicators

VARIABLE	CONSTRUCT	INDICATORS
Governance	Legal certainty	property rights intellectual property rights investor protection
	Public trustworthiness	public trust of politician judicial independence reliability of police service
	Government efficiency	spending wastefulness regulation burden legal framework efficiency
	Transparency	government policy-making auditing and reporting standard firms ethical behaviour
Competitiveness	Ease of doing business	time needed to start business custom burden ease of hiring and firing
	Infrastructure	road quality port infrastructure electricity supply
Economic performance		economic growth per capita GDP FDI

Source: Constructed by the authors.

growth is obtained from *International Financial Statistics*, an International Monetary Fund's publication.

Data Processing

The data collected are processed based on the Structural Equation Modelling (SEM), with the support of software LISREL, version 8.8. The processing of data using SEM is conducted in two steps, commonly referred to as the "two step approach" (Wijanto 2008). The first step is the Measurement Model using Confirmatory Factor Analysis (CFA). This analysis is intended to ensure that the various indicators or observed variables that have been determined theoretically really fit in each group of those latent variables.

The analysis on measurement model includes the overall Goodness of Fit Index (GOFI), which measures the correspondence of the actual or observed input matrix with the predicted one from the proposed model. Furthermore, it is intended to assess the overall model fit with one or more goodness of fit measures. GOFI, reflected in six indicators, is shown in Table 11.3. To assess the validity of the measurement model, the standard loading factor (SLF) must be ≥ 0.50; the construct reliability, ≥ 0.70; and the variance extract reliability, ≥ 0.50.

The second step is the Structural Model, as a set of one or more dependent relationships linking the hypothesized model's construct. The structural model is most useful in representing the interrelationships of variables in dependent relationships. The structural model which shows the causal relation between variables must meet the significant level of the t-value ≥ 1.96.

TABLE 11.3
Goodness of Fit

No.	Indicators	Value
1.	NFI (*Normed Fit Index*)	≥ 0.90
2.	NNFI (*Non-Normed Fit Index*)	≥ 0.90
3.	CFI (*Comparative Fit Index*)	≥ 0.90
4.	IFI (*Incremental Fit Index*)	≥ 0.90
5.	RFI (*Relative Fit Index*)	≥ 0.90
6.	GFI (*Goodness of Fit Index*) as the outcome of valitdity and reliability analysis	≥ 0.90

Source: Hair et al. (1998).

Hypothesis Testing and Interpretation

As shown in Figure 11.7, data processing produces an outcome as a path diagram, reflecting the impact of the independent variables on the dependent variables. The analysis of this hypothesis testing is conducted by assessing the significance of the causal relationship between two variables on the basis of its t-value. The causal relationship is considered significant when it meets

FIGURE 11.7
Path Diagram and Outcome

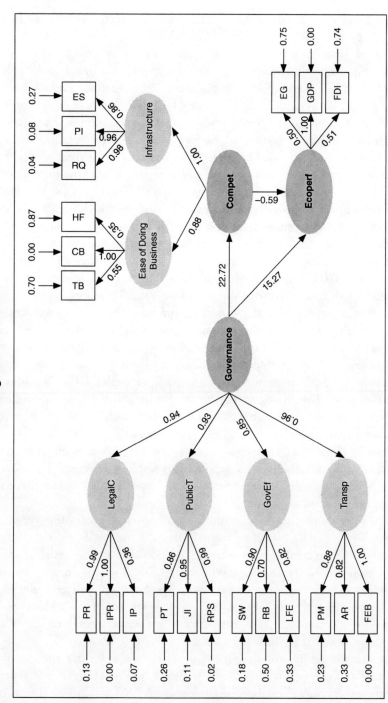

the t-value ≥ 1.96. The impact of the t-value between variables can be seen in the path diagram of the Structural Model, shown in Figure 11.7.

Our first hypothesis is that governance has a direct, positive, and significant impact on economic performance, measured by economic growth, per capita GDP, and FDI. We find that our statistical examination does not reject the hypothesis at a t-value of 15.27. This finding is consistent with the theory and empirical research that governance has a positive and significant impact on economic performance. The most significant impact is found on per capita GDP. It is considered reasonable since a good track record of governance can only be established over an extended period of time, and as governance improves, per capita GDP also rises. The finding on the impact of governance on FDI is consistent with earlier studies in which good governance is associated with a more stable type of capital inflow in the form of FDI, rather than with the volatile type of capital inflow. The impact on economic growth only barely meets the significant level of ≤ 0.05. One possible explanation is that this research combines selected industrial countries with the developing countries.

To further examine the almost insignificant impact of governance on economic growth, we make two subhypotheses, by separating the sample of industrial countries from that of developing countries. The first sub-hypothesis is that in industrial countries the impact of governance on economic growth is smaller than that on per capita GDP. We find out that this sub-hypothesis is not rejected.[4] In other words, in industrial countries, governance matters more for higher levels of per capita income than for economic growth. The second sub-hypothesis is that in developing countries the impact of governance on economic growth is bigger than that on per capita GDP. This sub-hypothesis is also not rejected.[5] Therefore, in developing countries, governance is more important for economic growth than for per capita income.

As the theory suggests, in the case of developing countries, economic growth is generally higher compared with that in the developed countries because of their smaller income base. On the other hand, although economic growth is higher, the income level is lower than that in industrial countries. Industrial countries with good economic performance will generally record economic growth of between 3.0 to 4.0 per cent. Meanwhile, within developing countries, the higher performing countries exhibit a growth rate ranging from 7.0 to 10.0 per cent.

Our second hypothesis is that governance has a positive and significant impact on competitiveness. Our statistical examination shows that the hypothesis is not rejected at the t-value of 22.72. This finding is consistent with earlier theory and empirical research. The elements of governance in this study support a country's competitiveness. For example, as mentioned at the beginning of this chapter, the absorptive capacity of a country to a large extent depends on governance.

Our third hypothesis is that governance has an indirect, positive, and significant impact on economic performance through competitiveness. The finding shows that governance has no significant impact on economic performance through competitiveness (the t-value of –0.58 as displayed in Table 11.4). Hence, this hypothesis is rejected. There are some possibilities as to why this hypothesis is rejected. First, the model only includes two contructs explaining variable competitiveness, namely "ease of doing business" and "infrastructure". In fact, other constructs can be included, such as higher education and training; goods market efficiency; and financial market sophistication. However, those constructs should be explored in future studies as this study mainly focuses on governance. Second, more countries can be included in the sample.

TABLE 11.4
Direct and Indirect Effects

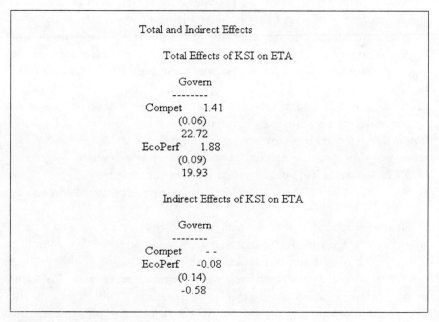

Total and Indirect Effects	
Total Effects of KSI on ETA	
	Govern
Compet	1.41
	(0.06)
	22.72
EcoPerf	1.88
	(0.09)
	19.93
Indirect Effects of KSI on ETA	
	Govern
Compet	- -
EcoPerf	-0.08
	(0.14)
	-0.58

Source: Calculated by the authors.

CONCLUDING REMARKS

From the statistical examination based on thirty countries, we conclude that governance has a significant impact on per capita income. The impact of governance on per capita income is more pronounced when it is complemented by other variables, namely ease of doing business and infrastructure. However, the impact of governance on per capita income of emerging markets is less pronounced. This may be explained by the fact that given the same quality of governance, the complementary impact of other variables (ease of doing business and infrastructure) is stronger in industrial countries than in emerging markets.

We also find that governance has a significant impact on economic growth. However, this is more evident in developing countries than in developed countries. Furthermore, governance has a positive and significant impact on FDI. As is the case with its impact on per capita income, the impact of governance on FDI is stronger in industrial countries than in emerging markets. This may be explained by their absorptive capacity, in that this type of capital inflow, to a large extent, depends on the recipient countries' absorptive capacity. Countries with higher absorptive capacity tend to receive more FDI rather than other inflow types.

Based on our observation on governance activities, both at the macro and micro levels, we found that Indonesia is now more aware of the need for good governance, following the financial crisis of 1997. The establishment of the National Committee on Corporate Governance Policy marked the first important step in establishing governance in Indonesia. This endeavour was further strengthened by the incorporation of good governance in the Letter of Intent signed by the IMF and the Government of Indonesia. Furthermore, in the banking area, a regulation has been issued by Bank Indonesia concerning governance. In the same vein, a Ministerial Decree, relating to state owned enterprises, has also been put into effect. By the end of 2007, Indonesia had already passed the stage of awareness of governance and was thus starting the stage of conformity to be continued through to year 2016.

It was recognized that at the regional level, Indonesia has yet to achieve an optimal stage of governance as currently, among the five founding ASEAN countries, Indonesia ranks fourth. This is partly due to the fact that governance has not been well implemented. Nevertheless, in terms of corruption eradication movement, following the establishment of the Eradication Corruption Commission (KPK), some significant quantitative progress has been achieved. This was reflected by an increasing number of investigations, which rose from twenty-nine cases in 2007, to fifty-three cases in 2008.

It should be born in mind, however, that the research on governance is still preliminary in nature and not very exhaustive. In addition, the variables are also limited to a few pertinent variables. Thus, more variables can be added and a more rigorous analysis can be conducted in order to arrive at a stronger conclusion. More dependent variables may also be included on the composition of capital flows. For example, it is worth exploring if stronger governance will have a significant impact on achieving more stable capital flows and vice versa.

Data from other sources that provide a better proxy for FDI may yield a better statistical estimate. More rigorous research on the different magnitudes of impact of governance on economic growth, per capita income and FDI in industrial countries and emerging markets may be worth further exploration.

Finally, we recommend that the Government of Indonesia should continue to implement its policies on improving governance in order to induce higher economic growth. However, to maximize the impact on economic growth, the government should also improve the ease of doing business and infrastructure. As part of having good governance, the government should shy away from speculative behaviour. For example, banks should return to their basic function, which is to operate purely as an intermediary institution.

NOTES

1. The eight major problems identified by Sachs include: poverty trap, physical geography, fiscal trap, governance failure, cultural barriers, geopolitics, lack of innovation, and demographics trap.
2. The lower the index, the better the performance.
3. The higher the index, the better the governance.
4. The standard loading factor of governance is 0.66, lower than the 0.99 for per capita GDP.
5. The standard loading factor for governance is 1.00, larger than the 0.53 for that of per capita GDP.

REFERENCES

Abed, George T. and Sanjeev Gupta, eds. *Governance, Corruption and Economic Performance*. Washington, D.C.: International Monetary Fund, 2002.

Aitken, Brian and Ann Harrison. "Do Domestic Firms Benefit from Direct Investment?" *American Economic Review* 89 (June 1999): 605–18. Cited in Kenneth Rogoff Eswar, Shang-Jin Wei, and M. Ayhan Kose. "Effects of Financial Globalization on Developing Countries: Some Empirical Evidence". Occasional Paper No. 220. Washington, D.C.: IMF, 2003.

Arteta, Carlos, Barry Eichengreen, and Charles Wyplosz. "On the Growth Effects of Capital Account Liberalization". Unpublished paper. University of California, Berkeley, 2001. Cited in Kenneth Rogoff Eswar, Shang-Jin Wei, and M. Ayhan Kose. "Effects of Financial Globalization on Developing Countries: Some Empirical Evidence".

Bailliu, Jeannin. "Private Capital Flows, Financial Developments, and Economic Growth in Developing Countries". Bank of Canada W.P. No. 2000–15. Ontario, Canada, 2000. Cited in Kenneth Rogoff Eswar, Shang-Jin Wei, and M. Ayhan Kose. "Effects of Financial Globalization on Developing Countries: Some Empirical Evidence".

Bank Indonesia. *Annual Report on Indonesia*. Jakarta: Bank Indonesia, 2003.

Boediono. "Hidup di Tengah Krisis Dunia" [Living amidst World Crisis]. Speech delivered at the Annual Banking Meeting. Bank Indonesia, Jakarta, 30 January 2009.

Caruna, Jaime. "Basel II and Corporate Governance Issues". Speech at the 2nd Islamic Financial Service Board (IFSB) Summit 2005: The Rise and Effectiveness of Corporate Governance in the Islamic Financial Service Industry. Doha, 24 May 2005. <http://bis.org/review/r05025a.pdf,Doha> (assessed 6 July 2010).

Coase, R.H. "The Nature of the Firm". *Economica*. New Series 4 no. 16 (November 1973): 386–405.

Dethier, Jean-Jacques. "Governance and Economic Performance: A Survey". ZEF Discussion Paper No. 5. Centre for Development Research (ZEF), University of Bonn, 1999. <http://www.zef.de>.

Gefen, David, Delmar W. Straub, and Maine-Claude Boudoeau. "Structural Equation Modeling and Regresion: Guideline for Research Practice". *Communication of the Association for Information Systems* 4, Article 7, 2000.

Hair, Joseph F., Jr., Rolph E. Anderson, Ronald L. Tatham, and William Black. *Multivariate Data Analysis*. New Jersey 5th ed. New Jersey: Prentice-Hall International, Inc., 1998.

Hamilton-Hart, Natasha. "Anti Corruption Startegies in Indonesia". *Bulletin of Indonesian Economics Studies* 37, no. 1 (2001): 65–82.

Huidobro, F. Maria. *Governance, Politics and the Environment: A Singapore Study*. Singapore: Institute of Southeast Asian Studies, 2008.

Institute for Social and Economic Research. "Construction of Regional Index of Doing Business". Laporan akhir tahun [Final Report], December 2001. In "Governance and Poverty Reduction: Evidence from Newly Decentralized Indonesia", by Sudarno Sumarto et al. SMERU Working Paper. Jakarta: SMERU, 2004.

International Monetary Fund. "The IMF and Good Governance". A Factsheet, September 2008. <http://www.imf.org/external/np/exr/facts/gov.htm> (accessed 17 April 2009).

Kaufmann, Daniel, Aart Kraay, and Massimo Mastrussi. "Governance Matters VIII: Aggregate and Individual Governance Indicators 1996--2008". WPS4978. World Bank, Washington, D.C., 2009.

Khairandy, Ridwan and Camelia Malik. "Good Corporate Governance, Perkembangan Pemikiran dan Impelementasinya di Indonesia dalam Perspektif Hukum" [Good Corporate Governance, the development of ideas and its implementation in Indonesia in Law Perspective]. Yogyakarta: Kreasi Total Media, 2007.

Khan, H. Mushtaq. "Governance,Economic Growth and Development since 1960s". DESA Working Paper No. 54. New York: United Nations Department of Economics and Social Affairs, August 2007.

Komisi Pemberantasan Korupsi. *Laporan Tahunan 2009* [*Annual Report* 2009]. Jakarta: Komisi Pemberantasan Korupsi, December 2009.

KPPOD. "Pemeringkatan Daya Tarik Investasi Kabupaten/Kota:Studi Kasus di 90 Kabupaten/kota di Indonesia" [The Ranking of Investment Attractiveness Across Districts/Cities: A Case Study of 90 Districts/Cities in Indonesia]. Komite Pemantauan Pelaksanaan Otonomi Daerah, Jakarta, 2002. In "Governance and Poverty Reduction: Evidence from Newly Decentralized Indonesia", by Sudarno Sumarto et al. SMERU Working Paper. Jakarta: SMERU, 2004.

Maher, Maria and Thomas Anderson. "Corporate Governance: Effects on Firms Performance and Economic Growth". OECD, 1999. <http://www.ecgi.org/research/accession/cgeu.pdf> (accessed 4 July 2010).

McCawley, Peter. "Governance in Indonesia: Some Comments". Tokyo: Asian Development Institute, 2005. <http://www.adbi.org/files/2005.09.dp38.governance> (accessed 6 July 2010).

North Carolina State University. *Structural Equation Modeling*, 2005. <http://faculty.chass.ncsu.edu/garson/PA765/structur.htm> (accessed 6 July 2010).

North, Douglass C. *Institutions and Performance of Economics over Time*. In *Handbook of New Institutional Economics*, edited by Claude Ménard and Mary M. Shirley. Berlin Heidelberg: Springer-Verlag, 2008.

Peters, B. Guy. "Governance Through the Political System: Making and Implementing Policy". Department of Political Science, University of Pittsburgh, available at <www.montreal2008.info/site/images/PAPER/section1/Peters%20-1.4pdf>, 2008.

Prasad, Eswar, Kenneth Rogoff, Shang-Jin Wei, and M. Ayhan Kose. "Effects of Financial Globalization on Developing Countries: Some Empirical Evidence". Occasional Paper No. 220. Washington, D.C.: IMF, 2003.

Prasetyantoko, A. *Corporate Governance, Pendekatan Institutional (Institutional Approach)*. Jakarta: PT Gramedia Pustaka Utama, 2008.

Reisen, Helmut and Marcelo Soto. "Which Types of Capital Inflows Foster Developing-Country Growth". *International Finance* 4, no. 1 (Spring): 1–14,

200. Cited in "Effects of Financial Globalization on Developing Countries: Some Empirical Evidence", by Eswar Prasad, Kenneth Rogoff, Shang-Jin Wei, and M. Ayhan Kose.

Rivera-Batiz, Fransisca L. "Democracy, Governance, and Economc Growth: Theory and Evidence". Review of Development Economics 6, no. 2 (2002): 225–47.

Sachs, Jeffrey. *The End of Poverty: How We Can Make It Happen in Our Lifetime.* London: Penguin Books, 2005.

Sato, Yoichiro. "Growth and Governancein Asia: Framework of Analysis". <http://www.apcss.org/.../Pub_Growth Governance/Pub_Growth/Governancech1.pdf> (accessed 6 July 2010).

Shimomura, Yasutami, ed. *The Role of Governance in Asia.* Singapore: Institute of Southeast Asian Studies, 2003.

Sumarto, Sudarno et al. "Governance and Poverty Reduction: Evidence from Newly Decentralized Indonesia". SMERU Working Paper. Jakarta: SMERU, 2004.

Sutojo, Siwanto and John E. Aldridge. *Good Corporate Governance — Tata Kelola Perusahaan yang sehat* [Good Corporate Governance as healthy corporate governance]. Jakarta: PT Damar Mulia Pustaka, 2005.

Syakhroza, Akhmad. "Pemberdayaan Sektor Riel untuk Mempercepat Pertumbuhan Ekonomi Melalui Peningkatan Good Corporate Governance". In "Pemberdayaan Sektor Riil untuk Mempercepat Pertumbuhan Ekonomi Melalui Peningkatan Good Corporate Governance" [Empowering Real Sector to Enhance Economic Growth by Increasing Good Corporate Governance]. Bank Indonesia, Proceedings of Roundtable Discussion, compiled by Ferry Syafruddin, Guruh Suryani Rokhimah. Jakarta, 12 December 2007.

Trochim, William M.K. *The Research Methods Knowledge Base.* 2nd ed. Ithaca: Cornell University Custom Publishing, 1999.

Wijanto, Setyo H. *Structural Equation Modelling.* 1st ed. Jakarta: Graha Ilmu, 2008.

World Bank. *Governance and Development.* Washington, D.C.: The World Bank, 1992.

World Economic Forum. *The Global Competitiveness Report, 2008–2009.* Geneva: WEF, 2008.

Zikmund, William L. *Business Research Methods.* 7th ed. Ohio, U.S.: Thomson Learning, 2003.

12

A SEARCH FOR A WORLD DEVELOPMENT PARADIGM: With Specific Recommendations for Indonesia[1]

Aris Ananta

IN NEED OF REVOLUTIONARY IDEAS

The rising default on subprime mortgages in the United States 2007 was just a trigger for the recent global financial and economic crises. In the past, many worldwide financial crises have occurred, particularly in the emerging markets. Each of these crises, including the recent 2008–09 global crisis, has been preceded by a large inflow of foreign capital, very strong credit growth, excessive leverage,[2] as well as asset (mostly property) price bubbles. Subsequently, asset prices collapsed and a financial crisis came about. The difference between the global 2008–09 crisis and 1997–98 Asian one, however, is that the global crisis started in the United States rather than in the emerging markets as in the 1997–98 crisis. Furthermore, the global crisis was the first crisis that had transpired in the United States since the 1930s Great Depression. Unlike its predecessors, the recent crisis was not just a regional crisis, but rather a global one.

Nobody can hide from the current global meltdown as it hit both the rich and the poor. Nonetheless, the poor has suffered and will continue to suffer the most. This has been the case not only for the recent crisis, but the ones before as well.

The current financial crisis initially hit a selected group of employees, particularly those working in financial sectors, which were mostly comprised of middle and upper income groups. It then spread to real sectors, embracing a wider group of employees, and thus affecting both lower income groups and the poor. In addition, a new group of transitory poor has been created as a result of the crisis. Another important feature of the impact of a crisis on the poor is the role of food expenditure among the poor. Food is usually the biggest component of spending among the poor. Whatever happens to food significantly affects the welfare of the poor, badly or well.

Indeed, Sen (2009a) described 2008 as a year with three crises: food, fuel, and finance. He had even anticipated full-scale depression for 2009, one even larger than the 1930s Great Depression. Fortunately, however, the year 2009 ended differently. Even, Kassel and Jones (2009) concluded that the decade of 2000–09 had ended on a hopeful note, that the world economy had recovered, and growth could continue.

Nevertheless, has it been a real recovery? Is it only a recovery of conventional economic growth? And has there been any fundamental change in economic management between the current time (June 2010) and the one before the global crisis in the middle of 2007? If there has not been any fundamental change in the way the world manages the economy, then other deeper crises may emerge more frequently. The Dubai crisis in November 2009, the debt crisis in the euro zone countries that emerged since early 2010, the new speculative bubbles in emerging economies (including China), and the threat of inflation, may set off a warning for the repetition of the crisis. Furthermore, global climate change and population ageing may aggravate the crises.

Currently, there is no consensus on the recipe of how to come out of the crisis fully and on how to live post-crisis. No event like this recent crisis has ever happened before. Some economists may have their own theories to these questions, but they still do not have any idea on how to implement them, thus giving away to the complex intertwine of economic, business, political, and social issues. It is very natural, as reported in Jeska (2009), that the economic elite in the 2009 World Economic Forum at Davos admitted that they did not have the answer to the question on the way out of the crisis. The most they said was that this crisis was an opportunity. As reported in the *Straits Times* (2009*a*), in an interview with the *BBC* on 19 March 2009, even Lee Hsien Loong, the prime minister of Singapore, acknowledged that Singapore would recover only after the global economy healed. He further said that what the government could do was to buffer the impact of the crisis and wait for the storm to pass. On his part, Dominique Strauss-Kahn, the managing director of IMF, at a meeting at the International Labour organization (ILO) on 22 March 2009, warned that for many countries the recent global crisis could represent the root of social unrest and threats to democracy. In some, it could lead to war (Walker 2009).

Keynes, an economist in the 1930s, revolutionized economic theory and reformed world economic policies in 1930s. Before the Great Depression of 1930s, economic policies were mostly free from government intervention. Market mechanism alone was believed to correct any disequilibrium in the economy. Nevertheless, the market mechanism policies did not work well. Thus, J.M. Keynes made a radical change by suggesting government intervention in the economy through increased government spending in order to increase aggregate demand and consequently to give a bankrupt economy an uplift. Accordingly, Keynes' radical idea also created "macroeconomics", a subject in economics taught worldwide currently.

However, it was not easy for Keynes to implement his idea as he had to counter mainstream policy-makers, including the U.S. Government. Hence, his idea was realized only after President Roosevelt gave full political support for the suggested economic reform.

In Indonesia, Widjojo Nitisastro, who later became the architect of the New Order economic development, and his colleagues at the Faculty of Economics, University of Indonesia, had also proposed a radical change to the development paradigm in 1963. The proposal, which may seem ordinary and simple seen at the current time, was to use an economic analysis in making development policies, and to utilize the strength of market mechanism in development planning. Nitisastro did not recommend complete reliance on the market mechanism, but rather he proposed the wide use of market mechanism and government intervention in many areas where the market has failed.[3] In particular, he recommended that the government plan for long-term development.

His proposal was made in August 1963, at the inauguration of his professorship at the Faculty of Economics, University of Indonesia, in a speech entitled, "Analisa Ekonomi dan Perencanaan Pembangunan" [Economic Analysis and Development Planning]. However, Sukarno, the

Indonesian president at the time, failed to recognize the importance of economic analysis in development policies. In fact, as described by Seda (2005), he was reported to have proudly said, "Van de economie ken ik geen bal van" [I am illiterate on economy] to his fellow Dutch visitor. Politics was his primary agenda.

Starting in 1959, Sukarno implemented the "Ekonomi Terpimpin" [Controlled Economy], where the government had the most important role in industry, plantation, and trade. To implement his plan, Sukarno created the DEPERNAS [Dewan Perancang Nasional] for National Development Planning, without involving any economist in it at all (Budiman and Soesastro 2005).

Nonetheless, Nitisastro's radical proposal was finally implemented after the big political change from Sukarno to Soeharto in 1966. With strong political support from Soeharto, the new leader of Indonesia at the time, Nitisastro's economic paradigm became fully implemented. Since then, the Indonesian economy has changed drastically.

During the recent 2008–09 global crisis, Jopseph Stiglitz, a noble prize winner in economics, also took a radical path. As described in Stiglitz (2010*a*), he even blamed economists for the recent global crisis saying that they assumed the existence of rational behaviour of market participants and competitive and efficient financial markets.[4] Like J.M. Keynes and Widjojo Nitisastro, Stiglitz also needed strong and full political support from the world elite (including economists) in order to find and implement a new development paradigm.

Therefore, now is the time to re-examine conventional ideas and to recreate revolutionary ideas, as Keynes did in 1930s and Nitisastro did in 1960s. Furthermore, this time, the economic issues do not deal with economics alone, but rather take political, social, and business aspects into consideration as well. Thus, interdisciplinary groups of scholars need to work towards a new development paradigm. Reforms should also be done to the contents for the teaching of economics worldwide. We need more than economists, because of the interdisciplinary nature of the current issues and challenges. We need a group of people from various disciplines to come up with a revolutionary development paradigm.

This chapter proposes a fundamental change to the development paradigm, so as to produce a lasting and fair development paradigm with minimal boom and bust. It aims to trigger a modest contribution towards a deeper understanding of current world issues and the search for a new paradigm, which will ensure sustainable economic and political development. A revolutionary interdisciplinary solution is needed to prevent the repetition of the financial crisis and to promise a more sustainable and peaceful development in both developing and developed countries.

Ideally, the examination of a development paradigm should cover a very broad range of issues, covering, for example, political, social, and economic issues. However, due to limited time and space, this chapter only deals with economic issues — more particularly, the financial and real sectors of the economy. It also suggests specific recommendations for the new Government of Indonesia, starting in October 2009.

This chapter consists of seven sections. The next section examines the importance of political support in introducing new development paradigms. It is followed by the third section which discusses the debate on stimulus package versus the creation of confidence in the short run as a remedy for the recent crisis. The fourth section shows the importance of understanding the speculation economy, the main source of the recent crisis. Section 5 then focuses on the three objectives of the development proposed as a replacement for the growth-oriented development paradigm, as a way to avoid repeating the crisis. Section 6 presents policy recommendations which consist of general ones, for the world as a whole, and some specific ones aimed at Indonesia (though they may also be applicable for other countries). This chapter then ends with concluding remarks.

POLITICAL ELITES AND DEVELOPMENT PARADIGMS

The recent global crisis had some social and political implications. Even Simon Johnson, a former chief economist of the International Monetary Fund (2007–08), in Johnson (2009) argued that the political weight in the crisis was great. The interest of the elite in the financial market had contributed significantly to the crisis — even with the backing of governments.

At the "New World, New Capitalism" symposium hosted in Paris by French President Nicolas Sarkozy and former British Prime Minister Tony Blair in January 2009, financial-based capitalism had been attacked as "an immoral system". Sarkozy argued that this kind of system has been diametrical to the basic ideas of capitalism itself. Therefore, he argued, capitalism needs different values and has to accept a stronger role of government. Moreover, Blair recommended a search for a new financial architecture that is not based on maximum short-term profits. German Chancellor Angela Merkel also proposed looking at the old German idea of "social market economy" and using it as a new international order.[5]

The financial sector was even more seriously blamed at the 22 March 2009 meeting of International Labour Organization, where Dominique

Strauss-Kahn, the IMF managing director, stressed that: "You can put in as much stimulus as you want. It will just melt in the sun as snow if at the same time you are not able to have a generally smaller financial sector than before but a healthy financial sector at work." (Walker 2009).

The food crisis has also triggered alarmed warnings from some of the world's leading politicians. A report from the ministers of the G-8 (Group of Eight Nations), prepared in April 2009, mentioned a possible, permanent global food crisis. At that time, the prices of agricultural products in many developing countries remained very high, not far from their 2008 peak. Furthermore, the rising number in the world population will necessitate a fast increase in world food production, especially in developing countries. If this condition is not met, the world will face a structural food crisis, which will bring with it insecurity and instability in world politics (Blas 2009).

During the first half of 2009, people wondered whether the world would really face a prolonged depression, worsened by a food crisis, and resulting in global insecurity and instability. Would the world be able to find an "exit" from the current crisis? If yes, would the recovery and, with some luck, the boom, be sustainable, and would it prevent other, or even more severe crises from taking place in the future?

What really happened has been better than what people had feared. Worldwide government policies aimed at avoiding the worst case scenario from happening might have borne fruit. In June 2009, some "green shoots" were observed as people started talking about recovery and post-crisis economic policies. By August 2009, the world recession might possibly have been over, with positive second quarter growth rates reported in Hong Kong, Singapore, Japan, Frence, and Germany.

Nevertheless, the "recovery" may simply be a harbinger for a deeper, wider, and longer financial, economic, and even social and political crises. Indeed, in August 2009, Asian markets fell again. Financial market investors may not have been confident about the sustainability of the rising global stock market. This was similar to what happened after the crash in 1929: stock market initially rose before another, and longer, collapse of the stock market. Therefore, either more fundamental issues underlying this business cycle should be looked into or, we surrender to the "fact" that this cycle is normal and we cannot do anything about it.

Despite the "promising" signs, however, the need for financial sector reform remains strong. Ben Bernanke, chairman of the U.S. Federal Reserved, on 21 August 2009, urged that the financial system needs a structural reform, particularly in its regulatory framework. Otherwise, the crisis of 2007–09 would occur again.[6]

The feeling that the recession was over was also reported in the *Asia Pacific Times* (2009*a*), that business as usual had been seen again in Wall Street with "no regret" on the part of the business sector, which did not feel guilty about what had caused the crisis. Speculation through structured bonds, huge executive salaries, and extraordinarily large bonuses were back on Wall Street. Barack Obama, the president of the United States, was irked by this absence of regret among businesses in Wall Street. He stated that, "You do not get the impression that the culture of behaviour has changed as a result of what has happened." The important question therefore is whether we have solved the fundamental issues that have caused the more frequent, wider, and deeper crises in recent years. If not, then the usual pattern of recovery, boom, large inflow of foreign capital, rising credit growth, and so on — in other words, the boom-bust asset price cycle — will be repeated before we face another, and deeper, crisis again.

Then, on 21 January 2010, Barack Obama announced a radical reform for the U.S. financial architecture. He banned deposit-taking banks from doing propriety trading that is unrelated to serving customers. The main purpose of the overhaul was to reduce the number of dangerous risk-taking activities of the banks, and to allow banks to fail without collapsing the whole banking sector and society and thus, to eliminate systemic risk. This has been the most far-reaching overhaul of Wall Street, the icon of the U.S. financial market, since the Great Depression of 1930s (Hui 2010, Braithwaite 2010, and *Financial Times* 2010*a*).

To get approval from the Congress for the bill on financial reform, Obama strongly attacked Wall Street for resisting the reform. On 22 April 2010, Obama told the audience in Wall Street not to fear the bill and that, "Unless your business model depends on bilking people, there is little fear from these new rules" (*Financial Times* 2010*b*).

The spirit of Obama's overhaul has actually been recommended by Boediono, then governor of Bank Indonesia (Indonesian central bank), during a speech at the Indonesian annual banking meeting on 30 January 2009. He stressed that financial institutions, especially banks, had to "return to the basics". Banks should fully concentrate on providing funding for real activities, rather than dealing with speculative ones (Boediono 2009).

On a wider issue, on 14 September 2009, Nicolas Sarkozy launched a report on "Measurement of Economic Performance and Social Progress", published by a commission created by Sarkozy in February 2008. This commission consists of world renowned economists, with Joseph Stiglitz, a Nobel Prize winner from Columbia University, as the chair of the commission; Amartya Sen, a Nobel Prize winner from Harvard University, as the chair adviser; and Jean-Paul Fitoussi, from l'Institute d'Etudes Politiques (IEP) as the coordinator of the commission. The report urged the world to overhaul the standard measures of economic performance. Wrong statistics such as GDP may have presented wrong pictures of society. An increase in GDP could be a misleading index for the quality of life. For example, a traffic jam, accompanied by rising pollution, may reflect a rise in sales of cars, an indication that there is a growing economy. Angel Guria, secretary general of the Organization for Economic Co-operation and Development (OECD), welcomed this report and affirmed that OECD was ready to help create new indices.[7]

The commission recommended three things: adjustment of the measurement of GDP, creation of new statistical indicators of well-being and happiness, and the enhancement of environment and financial sustainability. Emphasis must also be given to the distribution of income and wealth, as well as education and health. Furthermore, it aims to achieve the following: identify the limitations of GDP as an indicator of economic performance and social development; seek other information needed to produce more relevant indicators of social development; examine the feasibility of alternative means of measurement; and also, to find ways to present statistical information with an appropriate tool.[8]

Amartya Sen, a Nobel Prize winner in economics, in Sen (2009*a*), separated short-run from long-run issues, the immediate current crisis from the fundamental long-run issue. Moreover, he posed two fundamental and one short-run questions to be answered. The first is whether we really need "new capitalism" or a "new world". The second is what kind of economics are needed to solve the world issues today? In addition, what kind of institutions and priorities do we need? The third question is, in fact, based on the immediate issue of how we can get out of the recent crisis with the least damage. Nonetheless, he also argued that a crisis provides an opportunity to re-examine long-term issues, and, in particular, to address long neglected issues such as the environment, health care, and public transport.

Sen (1999) argued that development should not be measured with narrow indicators such as rising gross national product, industrialization, technological progress, and social modernization. Although all of these are important, they are simply means of achieving broader and more important goals of development. Sen saw development as a process of expanding real freedom to be enjoyed by all people. With Sen's approach, conventional macroeconomic variables are simply means of development. In other words, most textbooks on macroeconomics do not actually talk about development, but rather only deal with some important means of development.

STIMULUS PACKAGES VERSUS CONFIDENCE

Economic paradigms have constantly been changing after world crises. One famous example is the revolutionary idea J.M. Keynes brought to the teachings of economics during the Great Depression in the 1930s. Mainstream economics until the 1930s believed that there was no need for government intervention. Government intervention was taboo. Yet, the Great Depression had shown that government had to intervene in order to boost aggregate demand through increased government spending. This is what is now widely referred to as a "stimulus package". The main message in his book, *General Theory of Employment, Interest, and Money*, published in 1936, was that governments must intervene to bring an economy out of depression. Since then, there have been an increasing number of Keynesian economists.

Since the 1980s, however, mainstream economists have again been dominated by those who view government intervention as taboo. The spirit of pre-Great Depression, with minimal government intervention, had overwhelmed everybody everywhere in the world. Nevertheless, Keynes, along with his many disciples and new converts, seem to have emerged from the grave in the recent global recession. Almost all countries are now engaged in economic stimulus packages. In fact, some countries have even felt the pressure to increase their stimulus package, as they may otherwise be seen as odd or strange countries.

Yet, as mentioned in the *Asia Pacific Times* (2009*b*), stimulus packages may have been designed, taking both economic and political aspects into account. Keynes had mentioned that money could be spent on anything to boost aggregate demand. Therefore, the choice of where to spend then depends on the perceived economic and political benefits for the policy-makers. For example, it may be easy to agree with the plan to increase spending on schools and roads, but it will be controversial to agree with spending the same amount of money to help car producers. Furthermore, it is difficult to distinguish between businesses having difficulties because of their own greed and mistakes, and those that are innocent victims of the global recession. Nonetheless, the best stimulus package may still be good old spending on public services and facilities such as infrastructure, education, and environment.

By August 2009, world economies may have shown the positive impact of stimulus packages and indicated that the world recession could be over. Thus, Keynesian economists seem to have been able to reduce the pain from the global recession and help avoid a catastrophe such as the 1930s Great Depression. However, it is still not clear whether the world has really hit the bottom and is in the process of recovering. Should governments continue with their stimulus packages? How will governments finance their budget deficits if the recession persists for a long time? How about the possible inflationary effect once recovery is underway? Thus, a large question remains as to whether governments have really solved the underlying crisis, or if the "good news" is simply just a respite before the occurrence of another deeper crisis.

Sen (2009*a*) argued that we should take a relook at the theory of Arthur Cecil Pigou, a great economist from Keynes' times, who was also from Cambridge. Pigou paid much more attention to the psychology of the economy and the way it influences business cycles. Sen observed that the huge stimulus package injected in the American and European economies by governments, banks, and other financial institutions, have not yet resulted in rising confidence in the financial market. In actuality, the lack of confidence in financial market has created a "multiplier effect" to maintain and even sharpen the general gloom, thus resulting in a psychological collapse. This is what has been referred to as the "Pigovian process of infectious pessimism".

It should be noted that confidence in this context refers to the small group of world and/or regional elites who control the financial markets. This confidence is also strongly related to speculation. When the financial sector strongly dominates the economy, the whole economy becomes a speculation economy, producing more "virtual" rather than "real" goods and services. This speculation economy is very sensitive to changes in perception among the elites in the financial sectors. This perception can be very dynamic, but also very fragile as confidence can change very quickly.

In the last two decades, the fluctuations of the real sector in the economy have relied much on the boom and gloom of the financial sector, particularly the speculative behaviour of the elites in the financial market. The elites' perception on the world economy and politics is the most important determinant of the performance of financial markets. Should we continue living in a world, determined by the perception of elites in the financial markets? With their wealth, they may even influence the economies and politics of certain countries and the world itself.

SPECULATION ECONOMY

Types of Financial Institutions

Each player in the financial market tries to anticipate what the other players will do. Their perception on the reaction of the "market" (other players in market) will determine what each player will do. If a player thinks that everybody will buy a stock, then he/she will also buy the stock before its price rises. In reality, however, this type of "herd" behaviour will only further raise the price. Then, with prices rising, the players will believe that another increase will occur and thus more players will buy the stock which, in effect, will keep strengthening the spiralling rise of the stock. This rising trend will only end after a "significant" number of players feel that the prices will be no longer rising. With that feeling, they will withhold buying or even start selling. The prices will then stop rising and bring more people to think that they will not rise again and may actually start to decline soon. With this sentiment, people will sell their stocks and prices will actually decline. This further induces people to think that the prices will continue to go down even further, and thus, they will sell even more — triggering a fast downward spiral. If this trend does not stop, the financial market will crash.

Consequently, the capital market is clearly not an inherently stable and "convergent" market. It will not "naturally" reach equilibrium. In other words, an increase in price will not result in a decline in quantity demanded, but instead increase the demand and further raise the price. In other words, the price does not converge to an equilibrium. This is a disequilibrium, in which the nature of the capital market is the underlying source of capital market instability.

Nevertheless, the financial market is not necessarily bad and should not be completely eliminated. The creation of money, along with the resulting financial system, has helped economies grow very fast. Cox (2006) called finance, central banks, and the global market the arteries of capitalism, with Wall Street in New York and the City of London as the two most well-known landmarks of capitalism. The financial sector is the "blood" of the real production economy as too little money in circulation stalls production and too much money makes the money worthless. Financial institutions coordinate those who want to save and those who want to invest. They also match people who are more risk averse with those who are greater risk lovers. Moreover, financial sectors link the present with the future.

There are three broad types of financial institutions. The first are banking institutions, which function as intermediaries between those who want to save and those who want to borrow. They receive money from those who want to save and put that money in many forms, including the ones that cannot be liquidated quickly, as long as they are ready to return the money when the depositors ask for their money back. The institutions receive a "fee" for this service. This type of banks is often referred to as commercial banks.

The second type is the investment bank. Here, savers put in their money by buying financial products in capital markets that are to be used by firms or governments. This capital market includes the stock market, bond market, commercial papers, foreign exchanges, and various "derivatives", including futures, swaps, and options.

And the third type is the universal bank. Universal bank mixes the features of both banks mentioned above.

We also watch another kind of financial institution that is hidden under commodity markets. The small groups of elites who work in the financial market can also switch their speculative activities to commodity markets such as property, fuel, and food. Even retailers can function as banking institutions when they encourage customers to buy on credit, discouraging the customers from paying cash.

Vulnerability of Financial Systems

Cox showed that there is a positive correlation between financial development and economic growth. Countries with well developed banking systems and capital markets are more likely to have higher growth rates. In emerging economies, it is relatively easy to develop the banking system, but it is quite difficult for them to build a strong capital market as they need a strong financial infrastructure that will provide, for example, a sufficient accounting standard, a legal system, and bankruptcy provisions. Agenor and Montiel (1996) even mentioned that the availability of a capital market is the key economic feature that distinguishes developed economies from developing economies.

The financial systems in the United States, according to Cox, work very well. When the United States suffered from a banking crisis in 1990, the capital market provided an alternative source of financing. On the other hand, when the capital market was suffering in 1998, the banking system filled the gap. Cox believed that it was the lack of an adequate alternative, namely a capital market, that made Japan experience such a deep recession.

Cox further went on to quote Alan Greenspan on what he said about Japan not having a spare tyre when the one in use got flat.

However, because of the important role of banks in an economy, a failure in the banking system can have a much worse impact on the economy then any other failures in other industries. Therefore, governments have paid close attention to regulating the banking system, but have left the non-banking financial institutions less regulated.

Worse, there has been a rising tendency for the formation of non-banking institutions which also function like banks. Cox mentioned that even General Motors (GM), a non-banking institution, provides credit.[9] Furthermore, many American companies prefer to raise money through the capital market, rather than borrowing from the banks. This is what is called the process of disintermediation.

Because of the unregulated nature of non-banking institutions, the United States introduced the Glass-Steagall Act in 1933, which prohibited commercial banks from acting as an investment bank and underwriting insurance. In the United States, commercial banks have easy access to the the U.S. Federal Reserve and accept deposits which are insured by tax payers. On the other hand, investment banks do not accept deposits and are not insured by tax payers. Therefore, commercial banks have lower risks. However, when the Act was repealed in 1999, it resulted in worries about conflicts of interests. For example, a bank that lends to clients and gives advice for mergers and acquisitions, can also, at the same time, speculate with its own money in the capital market (Krugman 2009).

In the United States, although a Community Reinvestment Act was passed in 1997, it only applied to depository banks, the traditional banks. During the 2000s, there has been a spectacular growth in the sharing of assets outside the traditional banking system, particularly in money and funding markets. This has made the system very vulnerable to a classic type of bank run because when people lose confidence in institutions, they will withdraw their short-term capital. Worse, unlike the commercial banks, these institutions are not insured.

International Capital Flows and Financial Crises

Krugman (2009) further showed how rapid international capital flows have been the underlying factor for the 1930s Great Depression, the 1997–98 Asian crisis, and the recent global recession. At the beginning of the 1930s

Great Depression, Keynes had already indicated that the economic engine was strong, but that the world financial system on the other hand did not work well. The world then regulated its financial systems which created a strong safety net. As a result, international flows of capital were curtailed. Although it had lost its dynamics, the world financial system was then more secure. Subsequently, starting in 1990s, international flows of capital have once again risen rapidly and financial globalization has been transformed into a very dangerous phenomenon.

Boomgaard and Brown (2000) concluded that the trigger of the 1930s depression in Southeast Asia was external to the region, but that there was also an underlying internal factor: an oversupply of primary commodities and a rising scarcity of new agricultural land, resulting in higher rents and lower wages, more debts and more landlessness.

The recent global crisis in Southeast Asia is similar to the 1930s depression as it was also preceded by high growth and triggered by an external factor. However, unlike the 1930s depression, an important internal factor in the recent global recession has been the dramatic rise in the financial sector's contribution to the region's GDP.

A study by the Asian Development Bank (ADB) had mentioned that Asia was hit harder than other developing regions because of its past success in expanding its financial sector internationally. The contribution of financial assets to gross domestic product increased from 250.0 per cent in 2003 to 370.0 per cent in 2007. In Latin America, on the other hand, the contribution had only increased by 30.0 per cent. As a result, Latin America suffered less than Asia. Haruhiko Kuroda, the president of ADB, mentioned four related consequences of the global crisis on Asian economies. The first is the decline in exports, including those in the entire production chain. The second is the flight of capital from Asia's financial and capital markets. The third is the restrained credit availability, particularly for those in labour intensive and small- and medium-sized enterprises. The fourth is the drop of remittances from overseas migrant workers. Kuroda had predicted that the twelve to eighteen months from March 2009 would be a very difficult period for Asian economies. However, he remained optimistic about the future of Asia and believed that it would be one of the first regions to recover from the current crisis and would, in fact, be stronger than before the crisis (*Asia Times Online* 2009).

In January 2010, the world economy seemed to have returned to "normal" again. As reported by Reuters (2010), the Institute of International Finance (IIF) predicted that private capital inflows to emerging markets would rapidly rise by two thirds in 2010, particularly because of the rapid growth in countries such as Brazil and China.[10] These are recognized as short-term capital. Moreover, they moved into emerging markets because these markets promise a much better place to invest compared with the weak advanced economies. The IIF further observed a significant danger in the renewed excess of capital in emerging economies: it may create new bubbles and trigger new financial instability in the global financial market.

THREE MAIN OBJECTIVES OF DEVELOPMENT

Ananta (2008) suggested an alternative interdisciplinary model. He mentioned three main objectives of development, namely: people centred development, environmentally friendly development, and good governance. Therefore, new statistical indicators must be developed to measure this type of developments. This is an example of what Sen (2009*b*) argued as being a direct measurement of the quality of life, well-being, and freedom that may be created by development, in contrast to the inanimate GDP or GNP, which is an indirect measurement of development. The focus on the use of GDP or GNP assumes that growth is the goal of development, when it is actually only a means of development. Income and opulence can be considered important only as long as they can help people achieve a good and worthwhile quality of life.

Sen also posited that this kind of argument was used by Mahbub Ul Hag who pioneered the use of the human development approach which resulted in the now famous Human Development Index (HDI), popularized by the UNDP since 1990. It is a shift from means-based methods of the GDP or GNP towards direct measurements of human lives itself, within the limited availability of statistics.

It should be noted that the variables mentioned as the goals of development can simultaneously be inputs for strengthening the conventional macroeconomic variables (such as income), which in turn can raise the likelihood of achieving the mentioned goals of development. In other words, as Sen (1999) had stated, the variables mentioned as the goals of development are, at the same time, also the principal means of development.

Monetary policies should also be geared towards these three objectives, rather than merely supporting the achievement of conventional macroeconomic variables. They can support the achievement of macroeconomic variables as long as the macroeconomic variables support the achievement of the three important goals of development.

People-centred Development

There are four important elements in people-centred development: health, education, freedom to move, and freedom from fear. Health does not only entail a long life, but also means a healthy life. Because health, rather than economic growth, is an objective of development, we may, for example, raise the question as to whether we should spend more on medicine and support the growth of the pharmaceutical industry, or should we instead save our spending and concentrate on preventive behaviour and promoting healthy lifestyles? The first choice clearly encourages people to take more medicine, creating a boom in the pharmaceutical industry, which will in turn contribute to higher economic growth. However, taking the perspective of the people-centred development model, the health of people is much more important than an economic growth that takes place through the boom of pharmaceutical industry. Encouraging the pharmaceutical industry is only important if this business promotes the quality of life, in particular, health of the people, rather than economic growth. In other words, health is one of the main objectives, while economic growth is only one of the means to create a healthy population.

The growth-oriented model also attempts to increase the health of the people, but this model sees a healthy population only as a means to promote economic growth. Healthy population is simply seen as a productive factor of production. The people-centred development model, on the other hand, does not see healthy population as only and simply an important input of production, but, more importantly, views the health of the people itself is an important objective of development, regardless of whether it contributes to economic growth. Although it can be an important input towards economic growth, the more important issue is that having a healthy population is in itself an important goal of development.

Education is also seen as an important element of economic development by the growth-oriented model. An educated population, it argues, is very important as it is seen as a productive factor of production. An educated population can significantly contribute to economic growth. On the other hand, in the people-centred development model, an educated population itself is an objective of development, regardless of their contribution towards economic growth. Having an educated population does not necessarily mean having people with formal degrees, but rather having people with an awareness of, and information and knowledge about their surroundings and society, and who are able to express their opinions as well. Educated people are also an important feature of "good governance", discussed later in this chapter.

In the growth-oriented model, the ability to move factors of production is expected to increase the ability to find the best economic opportunity through the widening of the geographic market. People should also have the ability to move around. Free movement of factors of production (through free trade, free capital movement, and free movement of labour) is viewed as increasing the overall efficiency. In contrast, the people-centred development model views the freedom to move itself is an objective of development. It is seen as one of the basic human rights, and not simply a factor of production. Sen (1999) emphasized that one of the crucial challenges faced by many developing countries is freeing the labour market from explicit or implicit bonds. People should have access to an open labour market, regardless of their skills, and without any restrictions since goods, services, and capital can also move freely.

Finally, people should enjoy freedom from fear. In the growth-oriented model, freedom from fear implies that it will create a conducive environment where the people can work more productively. In the people-centred model, however, freedom from fear is one of the objectives of development, whether or not it contributes to economic growth.

Environmentally Friendly Development

An environmentally friendly development emphasizes the need to consider environmental issues explicitly in any economic model, particularly in the alternative models. Mainstream economics has actually incorporated environmental issues by treating destruction of the environment as one of the significant costs of development. With this approach, the cost towards the environment is deducted in measuring economic development. Indeed, macroeconomic theory has the concept of Net National Income or Net Domestic Product, rather than only Gross National Income or Gross Domestic Product. The change from "gross" to "net" reflects the depreciation of the economy, including the destruction of the environment. Moreover, the concept of "Green GDP" attempts to incorporate the destruction of the environment in the measurement of national income or domestic product. At the same time, in mainstream economics, environmental improvement can be seen as an important input in raising the productivity of the workers.

However, there are many aspects of development that cannot be reflected in monetary terms. The calculation of green GDP is still trapped in a growth-oriented model in which economic growth is seen as the most important goal of development.

In the alternative development model, with environmentally friendly development, improving the environment (and preventing the destruction of the environment) is, on its own, one of the goals of development and not simply just a cost or input of development. It is right to say that the destruction of the environment should lead to a reduction in the calculation of national income or domestic product, and that the improvement of the environment should raise income or domestic product. However, that is not the main reason for improving the environment. The main reason for improving the environment is that an improved environment is itself one of the important objectives of development, regardless of whether it promotes economic growth or not.

In the environmentally friendly development model, there is no discussion on the trade-off between economic growth and an improved environment as economic growth in this model is seen as only one of the inputs in improving the environment.

Statistics on the environment should, for example, include quality of the environment, renewable and non-renewable natural resources, natural and man-made disaster, and global issues such as climate change.

For example, should Indonesia continue selling its forest and coal for the sake of economic growth, regardless of the effects on its environment? Should Indonesia continue to keep environment issues outside economic policies? The time has come to regard economic growth as a means to promote environment, in stark contrast to the view that taking care of the environment can slow down economic development.

This change in paradigm is particularly important in tackling current global issues such as climate change. Nevertheless, during the United Nations Climate Change Conference in Copenhagen in December 2009, political leaders from many countries were still confused and stalled when negotiating their right to economic growth while ignoring the negative impacts on the environment. It is unfortunate that there has been no shift of paradigm from the economic growth-oriented model towards an environmentally friendly development during this conference.

Therefore, the effort of the United Nations (UN) is promoting the concept of a "Global Green New Deal (GGND)" should be supported by world political leaders. The world political elites should be brave enough to abandon the conventional growth-oriented economic models, and moving towards environmentally friendly economic development. Otherwise, the world economy will only recover following the "business as usual" economic model, without learning anything from previous, and particularly, the most recent global crisis; and the world economy will continue destroying its environment, endangering the welfare of the future world population. A further discussion on the concept of GGND can be found in Barbier (2010).

Good Governance

As in people-centred development and environmentally friendly development, good governance is also not simply a means to promote economic growth. Good governance is in itself one of the important objectives of development. We need to achieve good governance regardless of whether or not it promotes economic growth, although economic growth can be used as a means to create good governance. Therefore, with this concept of development, we never ask whether the creation of good governance "sacrifices" economic growth or not. Rather, we should question if the effort in trying to achieve high economic growth has slowed down governance or if it has, in fact, created bad governance.

Placing good governance as one of the important objectives of development in Indonesia became more urgent during the Reform period after 1998, with the fall of the authoritarian government of Soeharto. The fall of Soeharto and the democratization of Indonesia, as argued by Bakti (2000), has resulted in the demand from the Indonesian population for "good governance" and a fair distribution of the fruit of development. Furthermore, as posited by Ananta (2006), the "below replacement fertility" level in some big provinces and the "almost below replacement fertility" level in other provinces of Indonesia, may have further raised the demand for a democratic society and, therefore, the demand for good governance.

Unfortunately, because the subject of governance is relatively new, it is still difficult to measure governance. Different institutions propose different ways to define and measure good governance. As early as 1992, the World Bank (World Bank 1992), concerned with the sound development management of economies, defined governance as "the manner in which power is exercised in the management of a country's economic and social resources for development". The World Bank argued that good governance was necessary in public and private business, as well as to promote accountability for economic and financial performances.

The Partnership (*Kemitraan*) in Indonesia, for example, defined governance as a process to formulate and implement policies through the interaction among four arenas of governance, namely, the government, bureaucracy, economic society, and civil society. In the arena of government, it looked at three functions: regulatory framework, budget allocation, and coordination of development. In the arena of bureaucracy, it also looked at three functions: revenue collection, public services, and regulating the economy. As for the arena of economic society, it looked at only one function — government tender and project implementation. While in the arena of civil society, it also looked at one function, namely, advocacy. The Partnership used six principles to evaluate each arena: participation, fairness, accountability, transparency, efficiency, and effectiveness.[11]

Finally, in this chapter, good governance is seen as more than just a simple means to development. Moreover, good governance is a process, but this very process is in itself an objective of development. Bad governance is seen as creating a feeling of social injustice and, therefore, resulting in a lowering of the welfare of society. A comprehensive discussion on justice in economic development can be found in Sen (2009*b*).

POLICY RECOMMENDATIONS

This chapter recommends a drastic change from a growth-oriented model to a development model with three equally important objectives: people-centred development, environmentally friendly development, and good governance. Income growth is seen as only one important means of development. Thus, it is recommended that both real and monetary sector policies be geared towards the achievement of these three objectives.

However, a drastic reform on teaching economics and policies can only be implemented with strong political support. Keynes had the chance to revolutionize the teaching of economics because he had strong political support from Roosevelt, the president of the United States at the time, which was during the depression in the 1930s. Similarly, today, in order to change the world development paradigm, strong support from the world political elites is just as equally important as it was during the time of Keynes.

In the following section, two groups of recommendations are provided. One is for the world in general, and the other is specifically for Indonesia, although it may also be applicable to other countries.

General Recommendations

Reform on World Financial Architecture

Is there any way of reforming the financial sector such that we can reduce, if not eliminate, the role of speculation economy, in particular the role of financial markets? Should we let the financial market return to its function as the lubricant of the real economy, rather than let it have a separate "life" in itself, producing "paper assets" only? How much resources (including human resources) should be allocated to the financial sector vs. the real sector?

Perhaps, we need to regulate the inherently unstable shadow banking, and the resulting credit creation. And rather than focusing only on inflation of consumer goods, central banks should concentrate on targeting asset price stability, so as to help manage credit creation and, therefore, avoid financial instability.

Furthermore, a central bank and any other institution should provide better information on financial products to enhance the financial literacy of the general public. Consumers tend to be much more illiterate in financial markets than in other markets. Perhaps, all risky financial products should have labels such as, "The Central Bank has found that this financial product can be harmful to your financial health."

A financial policy should be geared towards meeting the needs of the real economy and not on growth itself. The possibility of too much growth in the financial sector relative to the real economy should be of concern as it indicates an unsustainable economic growth.

Most importantly, monetary policy should focus on avoiding or curtailing speculation economy, by managing credit creation and by not allowing non-banking institutions to provide credit, and commercial banks to engage in speculative activities.

One main function of a central bank is to avoid financial tsunamis. As argued by Krugman (2009), banking should include all activities which allow all those who put their money into the institution to have ready cash. It is, however, acceptable for the institutions to put the money somewhere else, including in assets that cannot be liquidated quickly. Any non-bank institution may carry out this function like a bank and still be called a bank. The shadow banking system is the "non-bank bank" or parallel banking system. Non-bank financial institutions are not banks from the regulatory perspective, but they are actually banks because they perform the functions of banks.

Krugman argued that the much less regulated shadow banking system has been the most important underlying factor in the current global financial crisis. The crisis in subprime mortgage undermined confidence in the shadow banking system. As a result, people withdrew their funds from the market and, thus, the system became vulnerable. He concluded that "a relatively small quantity of risky assets was able to undermine the confidence of investors and other market participants cross a much broader range of assets and markets". On the other hand, traditional banks have also ventured onto the capital market, an inherently unstable system.

Because the root cause of instability has been the absence of strong regulations in the shadow banking system, the government should intervene in order to stabilize the unstable shadow banking system. One way to do this is through regulating the capital market. Cooper (2008) posited that a central bank should therefore stabilize the financial sector through regulating credit creation, a foundation of the wealth generation process. A central bank should also move from inflation targeting to managing credit. As the market for goods and services is relatively stable, there is not much need for intervention.

On the other hand, the capital market, particularly those involved in credit creation, is inherently unstable. It can be noted here, that one way to get the highest yield from the money (debt) market is to create credit for the longest possible term, of the lowest quality, and with the least reliable investors. This is a very high-risk lending strategy and entails a highly unstable money market. Ironically, this system has also been praised as the most important indicator of a rich economy. Because of this, developing countries have been racing to create a capital market, hoping to follow the wealth creation of developed economies soon.

Therefore, a central bank should intervene in credit creation. Krugman argued that inflation will be taken care of as soon as the economy is able to avoid excess credit and monetization. A central bank should prevent asset price bubbles before the resultant debt stock turns so huge that it will then demand monetization. In general, a central bank should intervene before the boom busts. The main function of a central bank is to prevent the economy from accumulating excessive unmanageable debt stock. Then, financial stability will also become price stability. Financial stability means avoiding financial tsunamis, through allowing smaller boom-bust cycles. Short-term cyclicality should be fine.

A Re-Examination of the Growth-Oriented Model

The trickle-down effect model assumes that growth will be distributed amongst the people. Therefore, economic growth is seen as the most important indicator of economic development. Textbooks on macroeconomics tend to focus on determinants of rising income and economic growth. The market mechanism has been hailed as the best instrument in raising people's welfare, where welfare is simply measured by income, or, at most, wealth.

On the other hand, economic theories have already recognized many limitations in the measurement of national income and have examined the failure of the market in providing welfare for people. Even, economic theories mention that not all outputs of the market mechanism are efficient. For example, oligopolistic markets do not produce efficient outputs. Furthermore, economics also questions, "What is efficient?" and, "Is efficiency always desirable?"

It is time to relearn economics theory. Welfare economics should be taught at an undergraduate or even introductory level. Textbooks on macroeconomics should be rewritten to reflect non-income aspects of development. Perhaps, there can be a blend of development economics and macroeconomics.

One of the popular growth-oriented models is the export-driven model. Literature on economic development in the 1950s and 1960s was full of import-substitution or "infant industry" models, where a country was best thought to reduce or stop imports, and, rather, protect domestic "infant" industries. Nevertheless, by late 1970s, economists were amazed by the economic success of the four dragons (the four relatively small economies of Hong Kong, South Korea, Taiwan, and Singapore), which did not follow the import-substitution strategies. Instead, they followed the export-driven models, inspired by the success of Japan, where they promoted export and import. They encouraged foreign direct investment and did not protect domestic "infant" industries.

Since then, export driven models have been the mantra of many countries, particularly, developing countries. However, the recent global crisis has shown that these models have not worked well. The more a country depends on export, the more the country suffers during the crisis. Is there an alternative to this model? For a big country such as Indonesia, an economic model focusing on integrating its large domestic economy may be more relevant. It does not mean that it shuts down international trade and capital flow. Rather, it simply means that priority is given to integrating the large domestic economy, tapping the richness of its own large economy. One problem with the export driven model is that its focus on the international market can mislead policy-makers into paying less attention to their domestic economic potentials.

Moreover, during the recent crisis, issues on free trade and capital flow may not have been relevant because other economies were also suffering. Every country suffered and therefore international free trade and capital movement did not help much. It is different from the 1997–98 Asian crisis where countries such as Indonesia, South Korea, and Thailand were the hardest hit while most of the rich countries still maintained their purchasing power. In the 1997–98 crisis, the countries suffering from the crisis were helped by other countries through free trade and capital movement.

Therefore, one lesson from the recent crisis is the realization of the importance of the domestic potential, and the need to reduce the dependence on foreign markets. This is particularly true for large countries such as China, India, and Indonesia. It is also true for countries such as Vietnam and the Philippines. These countries need to spend more time integrating their own large domestic economies. Moreover, policies paying more attention to the domestic economy, including integrating the domestic economy, are not against policies to have regional or international economic integration. Their economies should continue to stay open for international markets, but more effort should be spent on creating free and easy trade, capital flow, as well as low skill- and high skill-labour flow within their own large and diverse countries.

At the same time, internally integrated national economies will bring larger benefits for regional and international economic integration. Thus, by paying more attention to their domestic economies, developing countries will become more prosperous, and their prosperity will be beneficial for both regional and international economies.

Specific Recommendations for Indonesia

The theme of the National Medium-term Development Plan (RPJMN) for the period 2010–14 is people's welfare, maturing democracy, and justice.[12] The theme does not include achieving high economic growth rate — though all (three) presidential candidates in their campaigns for the presidential election in 2009 debated economic growth rates, with one trying to outdo the others. Those with lower targets of economic growth mentioned the existing constraints to justify why they had such a low growth rate target. It is also very interesting to note that when President Susilo Bambang Yudhoyono made a speech in the plenary session of the Regional Representative Council (DPD) on 19 August 2009, before his second term inauguration in October 2009, he described the vision of Indonesian development as "development for all", and introduced six strategies. One of the strategies was raising the quality of life of the people in Indonesian development. He mentioned education, health, and environment as the components of quality of life. He defined environment not only as a physical environment, but also as a social and political environment. He also noted the relevance of good governance in running the development. Nevertheless, despite his awareness of the fallacy of the assumption of "trickle down effect", where economic growth is assumed to increase automatically the welfare of all people, he still considered economic growth a priority. He further mentioned that development should follow the "growth with equity" model.[13]

The currently famous "Asian Tigers" had started a new development paradigm, an export promoting growth model, during the 1960s. Nevertheless, times have changed. Now, Indonesia should be brave and start a new development paradigm. This time, the paradigm must be away from the GDP growth model. Consequently, the Indonesian Government has correctly chosen "people's welfare, maturing democracy, and justice" as the theme of its medium-term development plan. Therefore, economic growth should be only seen as a means of development, rather than an objective of development. To implement this theme, the government needs to prepare more specific policies and statistics to measure the development.

In a three-day workshop (the so-called "retreat") at Tampak Siring, Bali, Indonesia, from 19–21 April 2010, President Yudhoyono mentioned that the government has followed a "pro-growth, pro-jobs, and pro-poor" strategy. Although the president still mentioned "growth" as an important target of development, this new vision promises change to its development paradigm. It is hoped the Government of Indonesia will be sufficiently brave to initiate a more fundamental change of paradigm, one that moves away from the growth-oriented model, towards a paradigm that recognizes that economic growth is not a target, but simply one of the many means to achieve three development objectives: people-centred development, environmentally friendly development, and good governance. Then, its membership in the G-20 can be used as an opportunity to share the Indonesian experience in the fundamental change that has taken place in its development paradigm. Hopefully, one day, with the fundamental change, the Indonesian experience in development will be mentioned in many textbooks on economic development and macroeconomics as an important turning point for new development paradigms.

The following are some recommendations for the Government of Indonesia. Some of the recommendations may have already been implemented by the government and, thus, they can be seen as supporting the existing policies.

Real Sector

1. Indonesia should give more priority to reducing poverty, rather than raising economic growth. A lower growth rate is fine as long as poverty rate declines.
2. Indonesia should continue its export, but more attention should be spent on its large domestic market. Other countries are interested in Indonesia's large market, and, therefore, Indonesia should not forget its own wealth.
3. Indonesia should continue inviting foreign investment. However, foreign investment should not be seen as the most important means for Indonesian development. Indonesia should pay more attention to creating a healthy business climate for domestic investment, particularly for small and medium enterprises.
4. Indonesia should continue integrating itself with its neighbouring countries and the world, but Indonesia should not forget to integrate its own domestic economy too. Paying attention to the integration of the Indonesian domestic economy is not a kind of protectionism. A well integrated Indonesian economy is also beneficial to its neighbouring countries, as well as the world economy.
5. To achieve the three objectives of development (people-centred development, environmentally friendly development, and good governance), Indonesia needs to utilize new statistics, in addition to the existing ones. This is a suggestion taking into account the current capability of Indonesia Statistics (BPS) to produce the statistics. More detailed statistics can be developed later on.

Every three months
Statistics on poverty and income inequality
Statistics on health status
Statistics on population mobility
Statistics on the people's sense of security

Every six months
Statistics on quality of the environment
Statistics on renewable and non-renewable natural resources
Statistics on natural and man-made disasters
Statistics on production of emission of CO_2
Statistics on consumption of goods and services which are produced by high emissions of CO_2
Statistics on good governance

Every year
Statistics on poverty by occupation, working status, and sector
Statistics on poverty by education and health status

Monetary Sector

Policies in the monetary sector should be geared toward the achievement of the three objectives of development, instead of economic growth. In tandem with the real sector, monetary policies should also be pro-poor. With regard to the world financial crisis and the global effort to restructure the world financial architecture, this chapter recommends that the Government of Indonesia prioritize minimizing, if not eliminating, speculative behaviour in the Indonesian economy.

1. Banks should return to their function as intermediary of savings and investments. In this regard, the promotion of *shariah* finance, which is against speculative activities (*gharar*) and activities resulting in speculative products (*masyir*), is very important.
2. Indonesia should minimize its dependence on credit-led growth, where credit expansion is seen as very important for development. Expansion of credit is not necessarily a good thing.
3. Indonesia should supervise the speculation economy and inform customers on the risks of financial products. One way to go about this is for Indonesia to put a label to risky products, such as "This product may be harmful to your financial health."
4. In addition to the existing inflation, Indonesia should stabilize asset (particularly property) inflation, as it is an indication of speculative behaviour in the economy. Moreover, the statistics on this should be released every month.
5. Indonesia should regulate its financial market.
6. Indonesia should lower and stabilize the inflation rate for lower-income groups as lower-income people usually face a higher inflation rate.
7. Indonesia should have higher interest rates for small savers in order to give the lower-income groups more incentive to save and invest for themselves.

CONCLUDING REMARKS

Ananta (2003) showed how there had been a very gloomy prediction on the Indonesian social, economic, and political conditions during the

1997–98 crisis in Indonesia. This so-called doomsday or alarmist scenario was painted by national and international elites, including the World Bank and IMF. The reality, however, was much better than expected by this scenario. Thus, it is either that the alarmist scenario had been exaggerated, or policy-makers had responded well to the doomsday warning.

Whatever the explanation may be, Southeast Asian countries recovered from the 1997–98 crisis and soon afterwards, they forgot to search for the causes and remedies of the crisis. Another crisis, one that is more severe and globalized, came in 2008. People, particularly scholars, had again been debating and searching for new development paradigms. Then, in January 2010, we seem to have been able to cure the "pain" from the global crisis, to exit from the crisis with the least damage. Furthermore, during the recent crisis, as in all crises, the rich seem to have recovered much sooner than the poor. Unfortunately, the apparent global recovery may have reduced the effort to search for a new development paradigm. People, in particular those in the financial sectors, may have returned to the usual way of doing business, as they did before the recent global crisis. Yet, the debt crisis in Greece and its surroundings, as well as the overheated economy in China and some other countries, are still a possible trigger for another deeper worldwide crisis. Climate change and ageing population may aggravate the threat of another crisis as well.

During the 2008–09 crisis, the world was debating on two ways to rescue itself from the recession. One is the "U.S." way, which emphasizes increasing aggregate demand through fiscal stimulus. The other is the "European" way, which prioritizes the regulation of the world financial system. As reported in the *Straits Times* (2009*b*), the summit of the world leaders in the G-20 (Group of 20 policy-makers) on 2 April 2009 produced a communiqué supporting the two approaches. It pledged to provide emergency aid to cushion the economic meltdown and increase resources to International Monetary Fund (IMF), and cash to revive trade to help governments cope with their economic and social difficulties. It also strongly dealt with regulation of the world financial system by putting a strong limit on hedge funds, executive pay, credit rating companies, and risk taking by banks. During the summit, British Prime Minister Gordon Brown said the G-20 had committed to a transatlantic compromise and attempted to reform the rules of capitalism. He asserted that the globalized economy had surpassed the ability of individual governments to monitor and control it.

What scholars and research institutions should do is to gather people from all disciplines to work closely together in coming up with proposals for a new world development paradigm. The proposals for this cannot depend on economists only, but must also involve non-economists, such as those in the fields of sociology, political science, business, public policy, law, and international relations.

At the same time, we have to come up with a long-term resolution, to find the cure to the disease, rather than simply eliminate the pain. This will ensure that a similar, or even worse, crisis will not happen again. The conventional, existing growth models have been proven wrong. Thus, we need revolutionary ideas on both the short run and long run fronts. One of them is the fundamental shift away from growth oriented model. Monetary policies should also move away from the growth orientation.

This chapter proposes the use of three objectives of development to replace mainstream economic growth models. The three objectives are people-centred development, environmentally friendly development, and good governance. All policies, including monetary policies, must be geared towards the achievement of these three objectives. In particular, this chapter also recommends the drastic reduction, if not elimination, of dangerous speculative behaviour in the economy, particularly in the financial sectors.

This chapter is just a very small contribution to the creation of a new world development paradigm. Therefore, using both quantitative and qualitative approaches, as well as both economic and non-economic theories, more effort should be done to further elaborate on the proposed development paradigm. It is hoped that many scholars are and will be interested in this endeavour and will then work together towards creating a new paradigm. Furthermore, mathematically inclined economists may contribute to quantifying the new development paradigm. Finally, working together with non-economists is a must as well.

NOTES

1. This is a preliminary output of the author's ongoing contemplation on a "world development paradigm". It began as a short note presented by the author at the public seminar on "Poverty, Food, and Global Recession in Southeast Asia", conducted in Singapore by the Institute of Southeast Asian Studies, on 27 March 2009. The earlier drafts have also been presented in seminars conducted by the Faculty of Economics, Lambung Mangkurat University (Banjarmasin, South Kalimantan); Faculty of Economics, Airlangga University (Surabaya, East Java); Faculty of Economics, Sebelas Maret University (Solo, Central Java); Bakrie School of Management (Jakarta); the Graduate Study Program, Sriwijaya University (Palembang, South Sumatera); as well as Bank

Indonesia (Jakarta). The author would like to acknowledge valuable inputs from the participants and discussants on these occasions.

2. In simple language, leverage is about money borrowed for speculative activities.

3. His speech can be read in *Pengalaman Pembangunan Indonesia. Kumpulan Tulisan dan Uraian Widjojo Nitisastro* [Experiences of Indonesian Development: A Collection of Writing and Notes of Widjojo Nitisastro]. No name of the author-editor provided. Jakarta: Penerbit Buku Kompas, 2010.

4. Readers may also be interested in reading Stiglitz (2010*b*), particularly the chapter on "Reforming Economics", where he discussed four themes in the war on economic ideas: macroeconomics, monetary policy, finance, and economics of innovation.

5. Source: "Capitalism's New Clothes", *South China Morning Post*, 21 February 2009, A13 and "Speech by Chancellor Angela Merkel at the Paris conference; "New World, New Capitalism", available at <www.germany.info/Vertretung/ usa/en/_PR/P_Wash/2009/01/09_Merkel_Paris_SP-PR,archiveCtx=2028290. html> (accessed 17 March 2009).

6. The statement was mentioned at the Federal Reserve Bank of Kansas City's Annual Economic Symposium in Jackson Hole, Wyoming, 21 August 2009. See "Full text: Bernankes Jackson Hole Speech", *Financial Times Online*, 21 August 2009.

7. Based on Ben Hall, "GDP Branded a Poor Gauge of Progress", *Financial Times*, 14 September 2009, and "France Eyes Happiness as Economic Indicators", Associated Press, Agence-Presse, as published in the *Straits Times*, 15 September 2009.

8. See the complete report from the commission at <www.stiglitz-sen-fitoussi. fr/documents/rapport_anglais.pdf> (accessed 23 September 2009).

9. We know now that General Motors has collapsed.

10. IIF is an association of financial services firms, with 380 members in all over the world.

11. The Partnership applied its study using the province as the unit of analysis and made a ranking of provinces according to the created index of governance, which showed that Jakarta has the best governance, and North Sumatera, the worst. More information about the index is available at <www.kemitraan. or.id/govindex/metodology.php> (accessed 4 January 2010).

12. Bappenas, "Laporan Penyelenggaraan Musrenbangnas RPJMN 2010–2014" (Jakarta: Kementerian Negara Perencanaan Pembangunan Nasional/Badan Perencanaan Pembangunan Nasional, December 2009).

13. Susilo Bambang Yudhoyono, "Pidato Pembangunan Nasional dan Perspektif Daerah di Depan Sidang Paripurna Khusus DPD", Jakarta, 19 August 2009, available at <http://www.dpd.go.id/dpd.go.id/documents/rka/rka_naskah_ pidato_20090819_154016.doc> (accessed 28 January 2010).

REFERENCES

Agenor, Pierre-Richard and Peter J. Montiel. *Development Macroeconomics*. Princeton, United States: Princeton University Press, 1996.

Ananta, Aris. "Commentary. Demand for Democracy in Indonesia: A Demographic Perspective". *Asian Population Studies* 2, no. 1, March 2006.

————. "Suatu Wacana Paradigma Pembangunan di Indonesia" [A View on Indonesian Development Paradigm]. *Radar Banjarmasin*, 12 March 2008.

Ananta, Aris, ed. *The Indonesian Crisis: A Human Development Approach*. Singapore: Institute of Southeast Asian Studies, 2003.

Asia Times Online. "AT: Doom, Gloom, and Hope for Asia". *Asia Times Online*, 12 March 2009.

Bakti, Andi Faisal. "Good Governance and Conflict Resolution in Indonesia: From Authoritarian Government to Civil Society". In *Good Governance and Conflict Resolution in Indonesia: From Authoritarian Government to Civil Society*, edited by Andi Faisal Sakti. Jakarta: IAIN Press and Logos Publishing Co., 2000.

Barbier, Edward B. *A Global Green New Deal*. Cambridge: Cambridge University Press, 2010.

Blas, Javier. "World Faces Lasting Food Crisis and Instability, Warns G8 Report". *Financial Times*, 7 April 2009, p. 1

Boediono. "Hidup di Tengah Krisis Dunia" [Living amidst World Crisis]. Speech presented at the Annual Banking Meeting, Bank Indonesia, Jakarta, 30 January 2009.

Boomgaard, Peter and Ian Brown. "The Economies of Southeast Asia in the 1930s Depression. An Introduction". In *Weathering the Storm: The Economies of Southeast Asia in the 1930s Depression*, edited by Peter Boomgaard and Ian Brown. Singapore: Institute of Southeast Asian Studies, 2000.

Braithwaite, Tom. "Obama Hammers Wall Street Banks". *Financial Times*, 21 January, 2010.

Budiman, Aida and Hadi Soesastro. "Pendahuluan" [Introduction]. In *Pemikiran dan Permasalahan Ekonomi di Indonesia dalam Setengah Abad Terakhir. 1959–66* [Economic Ideas and Issues in the Last Half Century. 1959–66], edited by Hadi Soesastro et al. Yogyakarta: Penerbit Kanisius, 2005.

"Business as Usual". *Asia Pacific Times*, August 2009*a*.

Cooper, George. *The Origin of Financial Crisis: Central Banks, Credit Bubbles and the Efficient Market Fallacy*. New York: Vintage Books, 2008.

Cox, Simon, ed. *Economics: Making Sense of the Modern Economy*. London: Profile Books Ltd., 2006.

"How to Avoid Depression: Whether Stimulus Packages Succeed or Fail Depends on How the Money is Spent". *Asia Pacific Times*, Section B, p. 9, February 2009*b*.

Hui, Polly. "Obama Bank Plan Unlikely to Concern Asia: Analysts". Agence France-Press, 24 January 2010.

Jeska, Andrea. "A Message We Already Know: Looking Back at the 2009 World Economic Forum in Davos". *The Asia Business Forum*, March 2009, p. 10.

Johnson, Simon. "The Quiet Coup". *The Atlantic Outline*, May 2009.

Kassel, Johanna and Cleve Jones. "The Decade in Markets". *Financial Times*, 21 December 2009.

Krugman, Paul. *The Return of Depression Economics and the Crisis of 2008*. New York: W.W. Norton & Company Inc., 2009.

"New Jobless Flood Food Pantries: From a Crutch for the Neediest to a Lifetime in Upscale Suburbs". *International Herald Tribune*, 21–22 February 2009, p. 2.

"Obama Calls on Banks to Support Reforms". *Financial Times*, 22 April 2010*b*.

"Obama in Declaration of War on Wall Street". *Financial Times*, editorial, 21 January 2010*a*.

Reuters. "Davos-Capital Inflows to Emerging Markets Rebound- IIF", 26 January 2010. <ww.reuters.com/article/idUSLAG00606320100126> (accessed 28 January 2010.

Seda, Frans. "Sistem Ekonomi Nasiobnal di Bawah Soekarno". In *Pemikiran dan Permasalahan Ekonomi di Indonesia dalam Setengah Abad Terakhir. 1959–1966* [Economic Ideas and Issues in the Last Half Century. 1959–1966], edited by Hadi Soesastro et al. Yogyakarta: Penerbit Kanisius, 2005. The original article was "Bung Karno dan Sistim Ekonomi Nasional" [Bung Karno and National Economic System], written on 1 August 1991. The article was republished in *Frans Seda-Simfoni Tanpa Henti — Ekonomi Politik Masyarakat Baru Indonesia* [Frans Seda — a Never Ending Simphony — the Political Economy of New Indonesian Society], edited by Daniel Dhakidae et al. Jakarta: Grasindo, 1992.

Sen, Amartya. *Development as Freedom*. New York: Anchor Books, 1999.

———. "Capitalism Beyond the Crisis". *New York Review of Books* 56, no. 5, 26 March 2009*a*.

———. *The Idea of Justice*. London: Penguin Books Ltd., 2009*b*.

"Singapore Can't Spend Its Way Out of Recession". *Straits Times*, 20 March 2009*a*, p. A3.

Stiglitz, Joseph. "Crisis Exposed 'Major Flaws' in Economics Ideas". Slide presentation for a speech in the Allied Social Science Association Meeting. Atlanta, 2 January 2010, as cited in the *Business Times*, 4 January 2010*a*.

———. *Freefall: America, Free Markets, and the Sinking of the World Economy*. New York: W.W. Norton & Company Inc., 2010*b*.

"Trillion-dollar Cushion for Economies". *Straits Times*, 3 April 2009*b*. p. 1.

Walker, Kristy. "Finance Crisis 'Could Lead to War', IMF Warns". *MailOnline*, 23 March 2009. <www.dailymail.co.uk/news/worldnews/article-1164273/Finance-crisis-lead-war-IMF-warns.html?ITO=1490#> (accessed 23 March 2009).

World Bank. *Governance and Development*. Washington, D.C.: World Bank, 1992.

Index

CPSIA information can be obtained at www.ICGtesting.com
Printed in the USA
LVOW111737240412

278949LV00010B/62/P